DIRTY COMEDIAN

A MEMOIR OF STAND-UP'S DARK UNDERBELLY

J.C. Scales

This book is for Frank Chu, Virginia the Tamale Lady, anyone who hates Pauly Shore, the corner of 16th and Mission in San Francisco, and all the ADHD kids who got crammed in the screw-up trailer instead of diagnosed.

ISBN: 978-0-578-32286-5

Contents

Foreword

Most famous comedians love *cancel culture* because they chose the soft, network-friendly way to get famous in the first place, many years ago, at the beginning of their careers, because they are pussies—also because their uncle is probably a producer, or the owner of the Comedy Store, which is…surprise!—why they were chosen to be spokespeople for the more profitable and vanilla end of pop culture. Talent was never a requirement.

Cancel culture, wokeness, PC culture, Customer Service Voice—these are just methods to forbid *wildness, childlike exhuberance*, or whatever the dinosaurs that never relinquish power are calling it this year. Just new names for old ways to criminalize youthful expression. These fuckers have all the money in the world, but they're miserable. Do you think they're just going to let us have fun? The Beastie Boys were right! *You gotta fight! For your right! To pa-a-a-a-r-t-y!!!*

Many of the comedians you might have known as the smart-aleky Lyft driver, or the snarky taqueria worker, or the mouthy bartender from your favorite sitcoms—who eventually got their own show?—well, they're not really comedians, they're employees of those dinosaurs. Sure, you might see them doing stand-up at the Hollywood Improv, but they'd never say 'fuck,' or have a controversial take on something. They're not real comics. They're just here to make sure you stare openmouthed at a glowy screen while the dinosaurs plunder the earth. They're here to make sure you're unhindered by complicated thoughts of resistance or revolution.

In return, these so-called comedians safely make tens of thousands an episode. The dinosaurs?—a billion a financial quarter, or whatever their fiendish, decrepit, rapey souls are getting off on in the days when you read this; hopefully you've killed off their evil, lizard-asses by the time you find this on a dusty, used bookstore shelf.

Showbiz assholes, the biggest sexual predators of all, outside of the Washington DC politicians, who are also puppets of the dinosaurs, dinosaurs whose names you probably wouldn't even recognize, but who really pull the strings in this country, are LOVING cancel culture. They figure they bought their freedom by sacrificing Weinstein. All of them are loving it—with their mediocre bullshit; while younger, better, more urgent, and truthful comics eat shit, even though they are actually the superior practitioners of the craft. The vanilla show-biz conformists collect ALL the money and viewership with their empty, nothing-to-see-here-move-along, PC, bullshit shows.

Cancel culture ALSO helps these so-called comedians strengthen their image in the public eye like it's a moral, rather than a wussy-ass, conformist decision, like the Ellens and the Lenos have done all along, even though they knowingly have several date rape producers on their speed-dial at any given time. They could have stepped in at any time, and did nothing but continue with their over-hyped, PG-rated bore fests. They did it for the money. Remember that. If cops that know about bad cops and say nothing are also bad cops? Then is Tom Cruise not guilty of more than just being a weird, creepy, little motherfucker? All of them. All of Hollywood. They got hard at the prospect of a meeting with Weinstein, knowing full well what he was. There are a million little Weinsteins in Hollywood. Trust me. The place should be raided by the entire military, if indeed the military's true purpose is to protect Americans. Just blow the movie producer's little luxury helicopters out of the sky, as they try to escape to Thailand and be a sex tourist until the smoke clears? That would be awesome. It's real people. Real sick.

A little bit of cancel culture actually addresses that. It's making guys like Weinstein and Cosby accountable. So that's the good part. But like Congress, they're trying to make the original bill unrecognizable by slipping a shit ton of pork into it. All this crap about stifling spontaneous behavior that might lead to any fun. They also want to get rid of ADHD Rick at your work, because he doesn't fit in with the sanitized, corporate, hivelike vibe in the workplace these days. All kinds of impertinent shit.

Trim that fucking pork down! Punish the predators! Fire the puritanical editors! Stay woke, but don't turn the movement into a joke!

–JC Scales

Living in Lower Fillmore During a Crack War

Okay, let me set out some vital details before we dive into the insanity. We are in 2001 San Francisco. After a year of slugging it out in the trenches, I got my first real room! It's just mine. No couch surfing, no girlfriend, nothing. *Ahhhh.* I'm here because in Santa Barbara I was a misfit and an unemployable weirdo. I'm not saying there aren't great people in Santa Barbara, but "worldly" isn't a word I'd use to describe them. I needed more. I've loved talking to the eclectic stew that is the SF citizenry over the last year. The same free spirit as the Santa Barbara crowd, but with more wisdom; the California is here, but it's not *just* California.

I guess I should start by saying I'm an adrenaline junky and a cocky bastard in the best way. I'll prove it to you. The main disadvantage of being an adrenaline junky and a cocky motherfucker is that half the audience would prefer if you crash like Evel Knievel, which, as a grand attempter of the near-impossible, your stupid ass often will. Greatness is built on a foundation of failed attempts. You only have to win **one** big one, babies! Ten would be better.

Seeing their joy when you crash is the worst, but when you *don't* flip over the handlebars—when you *do* pull it off!? The look on their faces is worth all the times when you *did* crash. Pulling a crazy stunt is the most incredible feeling there is to me. It's like the high of drugs, combined with the satisfaction of accomplishment, multiplied by everyone thinking you're hot shit and wanting to blow you. It's a potent potable indeed.

It sounds like macho bullshit, but once you've felt it, the bullshit is anything that doesn't end off of a ramp. What that ramp is, is up to the adrenaline junky. Who knows, the guy that died the most pumped might have been a Scrabble champion. For me, it's insane sexual situations, riding a 20-foot wave, bombing hills on a skateboard, running from the cops, or kicking a bully's ass. It's making the dive bar into my theatrical *and* my comedy stage. It's everything, all at once. So, here comes the jump, and, "*Fweeeeeeeeee!!!!!*"

We hobbyists of the extreme share a set of basic emotions: that daily need for the feeling of weightlessness and peak excitement. Just like nymphos need orgasms, we require that boost from cheating death. How much dopamine can one experience at once? We're all trying to break the record for sustaining a maximum adrenaline high. Does a two-year, uninterrupted adrenaline high at its highest level before your heart explodes sound good? That's what I'm going for. I guess you'd have to die to have achieved the maximum, so yes, in many ways, I think I'm trying to croak of excitement. Now it sounds weird. Why am I doing that? It must be an addiction; only an addict would pursue what is likely to end in death. So what rehab do I go to for this?

If I can say just one thing about my being a cocky motherfucker: If your style of cocky pulls energy out? It's called arrogance. I'm a cocky motherfucker, but I try to lift the spirits of the weak and abused—and anybody with a proper sense of humor, to be honest.

Now here I am in San Francisco, searching for like-minded pirates of the Dopamine Sea. I interview them all by telling them a story about myself first, you know, to get them talking? This story-sharing attempt either works, or I have a good listener. I search out my potential shipmates in seedy establishments across the city. I try to figure out what is the thing that happened in their life that drives them the most, that gives them strength. Then, I try to figure out what happened in their life that's keeping that first thing from achieving its full potential. You can triangulate those two points with the gleam in their eye. Now you have their trajectory. It might not be possible to map out a person's soul in a single conversation, but my theories have panned out quite a bit.

One of the only upsides to always being stuck in *fight or flight* mode due to multiple childhood traumas—another good thing to know about me—is that you are a quick study on human behavior. Your brain mistakenly thinks your life might depend on figuring out what the people near you are thinking, so it gets pretty fuckin' good at it. I creep people out sometimes when I respond to thoughts people are telegraphing with their eyes and mannerisms; how they clutch a bag in their hand, how often they look at the ground, the skin around their mouth.

My subconscious picks it all up and spits out the algorithm without me even trying. It arrives as a hunch. I've gotten off of planes partially knowing my seatmate without ever speaking to them. Of course, I can read people wrong, but it's rare. This knack allows me to understand human nature on a level very few people can approach. Being able to turn it off would be nice, but it's proven to be a fruitful talent.

I like interesting people, and I'm resentful if they bore me. *In this fantastic world, with all its possibilities, you chose the role of* ***boring conformist****? How is this choice so popular?*

It may sound antique, but I guess I believe in honor. A decent amount of people seem honorable here in San Francisco. They are seeking the truth and don't just accept everything the news tells them. They have the critical thinking skills to analyze evidence that may come from closer to the horse's mouth than what Brokaw is breaking down. Then, they take this information to the streets. Honor is what you get when you add courage to common sense. I suppose it'll be what trips me into my grave, but at least I'm surrounded by other people who feel the same.

So, I'm in luck! This... is where the intelligent freaks end up. *If* they can get that magical rent—I did! I slowly scraped, scrambled, and mostly scammed my way into cheap rent in the middle of the city!—Thanks, Tim! Also, I wrote, filmed, and acted in my first dark comedy! Not bad. I'm feeling pretty badass in the year 2001.

This is a place where my brains will be valued, and my oddities forgiven—celebrated even! Most of society just doesn't appreciate wandering, abstract daydreamers like me anymore. Here, everyone has backpacked across Southeast Asia, worked on a fish boat in Alaska, or *something* adventurous. People's eyes don't get big here if they see a tiny person or a lady in a muslim scarf.

In most places in America, people like me struggle. This is our *Shangri-La*. I'll be appreciated for what I'm meant to be in life, not forced into a job I hate forever. I've struggled at all my jobs so far. Partly because my stubborn brain won't even allow me to understand them. I wasn't able to monetize my abstract abilities, like some of the Asperger's kids and other types of people that, at school, would be labeled as *'the weird kids.'* I'm not sure what my exact fuck up is when it comes to the workplace. ADHD seems like it might be a good fit. Getting diagnosed was for rich kids when *I* was in school. San Francisco is where a *weird kid* can thrive. I made it! I won't have to live a life of anxiety and depression for not being a willing, or even an able, little *conformist*.

I tried to fit in; I really did. Seems to me the world's always trying to force me into situations that I can't excel in. They say the mysteries of the universe lay in vibrations. Well, all I know is I'm vibrating too fast—let me move at the pace of the city at something I'm good at! That's all I want. Growing up in an isolated beach town was great for idea development. It's time to make the stories come alive.

Also, I seem to always need to be in a perpetual state of euphoria, and it's simply not sustainable. Here's where I have no problem with attention span: being cheered on by the keg party crowds for a nutty stunt, going fast, gobbling down whole pints of Deep Chocolate Peanut Butter Hagen Daz, getting drunk, doing cocaine, and having risky bathroom sex with bar skanks. I have to fit at least four of these activities into every day, or I start getting depressed. It's tiring to be a slave to adrenaline, but it's been that way since I was a kid.

I've whipped the reaper so many times he took his sickle to the pawnshop. I hear he's collecting souls with a tattered fishnet now. I've beaten the most generous bettor on my dead pool by over a decade. How much longer can this go on? Who thought I'd live this long? Now what? When people ask me how I'm doing, why can't the answer just truthfully be, "Pretty good."? Why do I always have to be so fucking ***"Awesome!!!"***?

It'd be great if my brain's ability to seize upon insane situations bled into seizing some financial opportunities. If I'd been able to do *that* so far? Warren Buffet would be taking his naps with my balls in his mouth. But instead, I just have this lunatic in my brain telling me to do crazier and crazier shit all the time. The inner dialogue is so loud I've never heard a thing a boss has instructed upon me. Just gibberish comes out their mouth the second I clock in somewhere. Fuckin' *"Goo-goo-gaga."*

Luckily, I've always had the gift of gab to get me through my inability to concentrate on things that don't interest me. Thank god for this silver tongue and my handsome face. I look like if Matthew McConahot had a straight nose and had a baby with James Franco and Scarlett Johansen.

I've managed to float through a series of workplaces—barely—on these two traits: looks and charm. However, it quickly becomes clear at every job that I'm not suited for working on any sort of *"team"* or *"family."* I also don't have the seed money to start my own thing yet. Gotta *fake it 'til I make it*, I guess. But, do you know what's not fake? These sweet Scarjo lips on my face. Can someone please escort me to the office of the female version of Harvey Weinstein? Oh, it's Oprah? Never mind. I'll keep grinding, I guess.

In 2001 ordinary people are primarily still just using the internet for Yahoo Mail. Cellphones are becoming ubiquitous, but they're still those shitty flip phones. You can see that people here in San Francisco are getting addicted to this thing called "texting." They cause cars to screech in the crosswalks, oblivious to their mortality. People in their 20s think they can't die. They have to believe that to be willing to live in the high homicide neighborhoods they can afford. Look at them, subconsciously hopscotching feces and heroin needles, mainly focusing on texting their roommate about the chore wheel on the fridge. They only vaguely realize they're risking hepatitis C, destroyed sneakers, and being flattened like a pancake by the 22 Fillmore bus, all at the same intersection.

The I-pod just came out, which is actually a pretty cool device that allows you to carry around what used to be your record collection in your pocket. We have no idea that in a decade, our lives will revolve around I-everything. Just in case the hipsters may have been able to *hear* the Fillmore bus running them down while they text, they're listening to Weezer on their I-pods. They could be dead before they even get a chance to be all, *"I-fucked up!"* It turns out hipsters *can* die, the city just doesn't announce their deaths, and they use their mangled, skinny bodies to feed the buffaloes in Golden Gate Park. This lack of funerals helps to fuel the poor hipster's self-images that they are immortal. In addition to being willing to live in high homicide neighborhoods, this allows them to be stupid enough to deliver packages downtown on bicycles all day for slightly above minimum wage.

The boyband fad is finally dead, and long may it fester and rot. As revenge, terrible music in the form of raves has killed most guitar music in the city. I'd rather have the boybands back and call it a draw.

We're in a bit of a recession because the dot-com bubble turned out to be overinflated, and it popped like a tire on a spike strip. This has put the city's population numbers down a bit to where it still feels crowded, but good crowded, like a decent comedy show. Not like you're in Costco on a Saturday. There are still parking spots available; without meters if you know where to look. Not that I care about that, since I just sneak on the bus or walk everywhere. You can once again rent a room for less than a thousand bucks; also, if you know where to look. With the techies recently vanquished, things are looking up again.

The Haight Street bus comes down from Golden Gate Park into downtown, and the 22 Fillmore goes to the Mission. These are not the fancier bus lines in the city. They can be a bit stabby. SF heavily subsidizes the local busses because half the citizens don't pay to get on. Counterfeit *fast passes* made at Kinko's by the more enterprising crackheads cost ten bucks, and they last all month. If you don't have the ten spot, just do what I do and sneak in the back door when someone comes out of it. Long ago, the bus drivers gave up trying to enforce fare-paying because they gotta focus on the road. They don't want Sailor Dave to reach in his pants and chase them around the 14 Mission with a handful of bum fudge. It's hard to time the stoplights with shit on your lip. Specific busses are like little Shutter Islands on wheels. Those drivers don't get paid enough if you ask me. At least give them some war patches to put on their jackets.

Some of the city's worst busses stop at the nearest intersection to my house, but at least they're free. I'm set. My house is in the middle of the X marks spot to get anywhere good in the city in 20 minutes. That's 20 minutes door to door, and I'm downtown, Golden Gate Park, or one of the world's great taquerias in the Mission District. One extra bus, and I'm in North Beach in 30 minutes. Pretty awesome.

That single aspect of just the impeccable burrito access in The Mission is worth moving here alone! I like the taquerias with an edge. For the cheap burritos, you gotta go where life itself is cheap, where even the hipsters need a protective group to cruise down there. You see a taqueria with, like, a dog with a purse in its mouth walking out? That's the fuckin' place with the dope *carnitas*! *Pop! Pop!* You might even hear gunshots. Dab your finger on that red spot. The one on your shirt, make sure it's not blood. It's not. It's that bomb ass 24th Street *pico de gallo*. Fuck yeah! Another Saturday night in The Mission. El Faro forever! Lower Haight is crack infested, but it's a short bus ride to everything.

The hints of the technological clusterfucks to come are faint in 2001. It still feels like the late 90s. The city inhabitants are a decent mix of working class young people struggling to make it in the big city, poor people that the city hasn't managed to move out to Bayview and Hunter's Point yet. And let's not forget the ubiquitous yuppies who like everyone to know they identify as a "liberal." If you identify as a "liberal," it just makes me think you probably live in a bubble. I'm used to these types in Santa Barbara, but they really take it to another level here in the Bay Area. I'll describe them because they pretty much control the city these tales take place in. Let's call them *bumper sticker liberals*, so we don't get them confused with the good people who actually live by the word's actual meaning.

Am I liberal, am I conservative? Mostly what I am? ***Trying to get to work***. I think this is how most of the people who work the *regular* jobs around here feel. Who has time to label their political views? We just hate republicans more than the democrats—who we also hate. Poor people don't think any politician is going to do anything but take their money.

Many Bay Area liberals feel a little guilty about their money, but not so guilty they don't get Himalayan sea salt scrubs and caviar dolloped flatbreads all the time. These manicured Melindas make up many of the customers I'm going to be compelled to try and satisfy over the next decade. When you're starting out in show business, your day job is pretty much *service industry scrub rat*, aka, getting shit for the liberals. These fuckin' people. Tell me you're a punk-rock-anarchist, a skateboard-socialist, or a working-class-agitator. That's the politics of the regular people.

And just so we're clear, I'm not talking about people who act under the word's true meaning; the minority of folks who drape themselves in the term. "Liberal," to 'be open to new ideas,' 'live and let live,' and to 'look after the poor.' I'm talking about these fake ass motherfuckers; they got the "Save the Amazon" bumper sticker, but all they do is *order* the Amazon. They got the "Free Mumia" bumper sticker, but they call the cops on Black people. These douchebags want the public credits of being "Social Justice Warriors," but they ain't really about that life. These are the people who will think Hilary Clinton is the most extraordinary presidential candidate of all time, and they describe the Palestinian situation as "complicated." As a punk rock skater who showed up here in the 80s, I saw through their bullshit in five minutes. Liberal is usually some elitist shit parading as decency but failing whenever it's tested.

I have a message for these fake, monied liberals: anger is one of the only things that's ever changed anything, which is why you hate it. If you want to thrive in the Bay Area, everybody better be real calm and polite, or you might scare the money. The last thing they want is a lot of change. They're winning! Any significant changes would likely threaten that. Photo ops. That's what they want. Photo ops of them clamoring for change that they would call the cops on if it actually happened.

Sure, they'll let you smoke pot or get an abortion. The only thing the yuppies care about, just like all the other rich pieces of shit, is, does it inhibit the flow of capitalism?

So that's like half of the populace around the Bay Area these days; you may know them as Shitlibs, Democraps, NIMBYlibs, or Mercedes Mother Theresas. The undesirable half of city inhabitants: monied liberals and their bootlickers, along with a manageable contingent of techies that didn't get swept out after the tech bubble popped last year.

Of course, there's a better half here, thankfully: the tattoo artists, bike messengers, musicians, college students, bartenders, immigrants, and poets, which create the culture here in the city. And then, there's the poor, who struggle and suffer as an example of what will happen if we don't come up with all the money the city wants.

The new President, George Bush Jr., is garbage, but what else is new? Politics is a parade of rich white boys playing flesh chess with the lives of the poor, who mostly furiously beat their chests for the right to be the next sacrificial pawn. Their guts will be splattered in a faraway desert for nothing more than some monetary gain for the elite. Maybe the Pentagon can clear their shelves to justify another massive budget next year. Could it be that the rich just get a chub by brainwashing their *human capital* into walking into the meat grinder smiling? Whatever the reasons, there's some twisted shit out there. Gotta be clever to sidestep it, kids. Don't blow it.

I wake up one morning in my room in the poor people's neighborhood, next to the projects, to Sandy the Speed Freak in my room, yelling, "The Twin Towers have just been crashed into by airplanes!" This bitch has had some crazy delusions since I moved into her chilly Victorian house on Haight and Fillmore a few months ago, but this is *banana-splitzo*. I knew she was headed to Crazy Town when a few nights ago, I found her and her Jack Russel Terrier twirling and twisting naked on the bathroom floor. There was a tipped over gallon of GHB soaking both of their hides. Sandy continued to wail out her orgasm, going on its third hour. This is the hidden price of $300 rent in The City.

At any rate, here she is now, screaming in my room just a few days later. I'm supremely hungover, and it's well before noon. Absolutely unacceptable. I jump out of my *hobo-chic* bed, ready to scratch her eyes out. Instead, I look at her, and she seems less tweaky than usual. Her thin lips pursed across her cottage cheese textured face, self-dyed, Joker green hair with neon green drips still running down her temples. Her beady little eyes speak with utmost seriousness on top of her pointy chin. The tiny girl with a loud, piercing voice.

I go to look at her TV upstairs if only to end this interaction. Brophy's dial-up modem computer and her TV are the only objects in the house that occasionally give news of the outside world into our Lower Haight bubble. Well, aside from the angry project kids that creep in from the Western Addition to rob us and try to sell us crack. Do you think Sunnydale Projects or the Hunter's Point neighborhood has the toughest kids in the city? Nope. Right in the center of San Francisco, Western Addition, where the old *jazz district* had Dizzy Gillespie, Louis Armstrong, and all the other greats touring through and playing every night of the week on Fillmore Street, back in the decades surrounding WWII. The jazz is gone. Now it houses the meanest little fuckers this side of East Oakland. The rent is cheap, so *fuck it* if so is my life.

Coming home from work at the fine dining restaurant at night, I'll commonly pass a dice game up against Kate's Kitchen's black, shiny tiled wall. Kate's is the home of the Flanched Flarney Garney, basically a massive breakfast sandwich that comes with home fries and all the sugary ketchup you can squirt on them. All this for $3.75. The waitresses don't try to hide their disdain for you if you order it. Its utterance by a "cheapskate customer" almost guarantees a tip of less than a dollar. It's a big hit among skateboarders, gutter punks, and other Raggedy Andys. The waitresses mumble as much to each other as they deliver the ticket to the chef's spinning wheel of grease.

Once Kate's Kitchen closes for the day, their storefront is used as a premium sell spot for crack. I have to walk by it every night and tell them I'm not looking to score. They begin to tire of this nightly inconvenience and start giving me mean looks as I pass into the darkest part of the street. That's where I'd be an easy mark for a quick beatdown and a mugging.

If one of the hoodlums is winning too much at the dice game, the other two might signal the other one and jump *that* guy. No honor among thieves with this crew. This area has a long history of gang activity. From my porch behind a tall iron gate, I see uncles coach the new gang members in a cycle that continues through the generations. They teach them to be heartless, to see generosity as a weakness, to demand loyalty but never give it back, and to be ruthless no matter what. They learn to enjoy cruelty as a thrill, to celebrate Scarface, and shit on superheroes.

Sometimes, as I walk by them, they'll punch me and laugh even though they know I live here. But I still refuse to cross the street unnecessarily, walk midblock, pass Nikki's to the pizza place, and cross quickly to my gate, bypassing them. I guess it's what I get for moving into one of the worst blocks in the city. Haight Street, between Fillmore and Webster. Gang turf. Not whiteboy day, unless you're spending money on dope, which I'm not. Ok, now I am.

I feel like I start buying a twenty rock on Saturday nights, so they'll stop sucker-punching me the rest of the week. Usually, it's a 16-year old that I could easily whip. But wait, he has four friends, one likely carrying a rusty pistol that may or may not fire if I try to defend myself. It's that possibility of the pistol coming out that keeps my famous left hook in my pocket.

It's more likely that I make those first few purchases simply because I like drugs—all sorts. When you are surrounded by an element, it's only natural for that element to start to bleed into you after a while. Ask any prison guard. I've smoked crack a few times at this point in my life, but it's never been like a *Saturday night thing*.

Ok, where was I? Oh Shit! Sandy wasn't lying! There they are; the tall, skinny skyscrapers are smoking at the tops. They repeatedly show clips of the planes hitting the buildings on loop, punching neat little holes into them, shooting out smoke made of plastic, drywall, wood, and flesh. Me and Sandy stand there, her quiet for the first time ever. It feels like a dream. September 11th, 2001. The 90s finally ended that day as those buildings rumbled downwards into their own basements. This is definitely the new century, and we won't be turning back. The Pentagon meat grinder has gotten hungry.

Working for Chef Michael Mina

I now work at Aqua, a fancy downtown restaurant that spends 100 Gs a year just on flower arrangements. I check my tie that my roommate tied for me in the window's reflection, straighten it, and analyze my shoes for any scuffs before going in. It's really amazing how opposite I look from the place I just came from. I bullshitted my way into fine dining by memorizing some menu items and saying I could be quiet unless spoken to, move quickly but elegantly, and anticipate the diner's every need.

I'm a food runner. Basically, I do everything for the waiter. He just has to shine the silverware and bullshit that there is a faint burnt saddle leather aroma in the Super Tuscan, which has to be lightly coaxed out of the glass by gracefully swirling it. One would do best to analyze its garnet hue mid-swirl, up against the light, and stare at it in spiritual contemplation like your scoping a Goya at the Prado. He's totally full of shit, but the customers eat it up. A bunch of rotten grapes, and you're paying three times what you are for the steak. What a joke. I'm in awe. *I* could do this!

Out of the view of the customers, as they shine the silver for the next turn, they tell racist jokes to each other, and describe the terribility of the hair plugs on the *old money* guy at table 144. The guy that's been kept alive by his live-in doctor for ten extra years so he can convert a few more rainforests into some fossil fuel annuities.

"Did you see the tits on table 106?" says Hannibal, the former busboy promoted to server. Promoted so that false hope can be instilled in the other busboys, that they may someday make $300 in tips per shift, but only if they work really hard. Truth is, a restaurant is tough to get promoted in. Once they have you trained as a busboy, runner, or hostess, you're going to stay there. With all the turnover, you are more valuable in your original position than as a dime a dozen waiter or waitress.

You almost have to catch the manager watching torture porn with a methpipe in his mouth to get promoted to server or bartender in a fancy restaurant. These motherfuckers make 100 grand a year and golf with the customers. Do you think they're just going to let my skate rat ass start poppin' bottles for Andre Agassi?

"How can you not? They're popping out of her shirt. I have some lipstick in my locker the exact color of her areolas." responds Hagatha, who was hired because she looks like Julia Child. The busboys love her because at the after-parties she makes herself easy to take advantage of. Forget seeing a busboy during the rush if *she's* working. The hostesses think they're too good to fuck the busboys, but Hagatha prefers them. They tell her she's beautiful and leave her little snacks. With her big Julia Child potato head, her street value in Connecticut was limited but in Oaxaca? The bigger your head, the more revered you are. She is their queen, and what she lacks in wine sales, she makes up for in turning her tables over once the guests leave. It looks like a goddamn Nascar pit crew over there.

Meanwhile, Jason, the closet racist from Orange County, who considers this job beneath him, is stuck clearing his own tables during the rush. He can often be found whining to the busboys, "If you guys don't like this job, work somewhere else." He always has wine stains on his overly starched shirt trying to reset the tables in time. How do you say, "Oh, it's not the job we dislike, it's you," in Spanish?

Nicholas, a famous actor with an influential showbiz uncle—terrible clue, because, "Oh, that's all of them"—is at one of the restaurant's only circular tables. He's doing a five-course menu with drink pairings. Glasses will soon create a spinning comet effect in yellows, pinks, and purples.

A few minutes after sitting down, after the five lucky diners commit to the most expensive package the restaurant offers, the first wine in the series, a grapefruit colored glass of rose, is silently whisked to it's preordained position just above the knife. Seconds later the lobster salad course arrives. The waiter seamlessly steps back after one of his famous bullshit descriptions. Me and four other food runners, in choreographed ballet, gently swoop our plates perfectly across the fork tines. All but one of us align the middle of the plate with the tip of their noses. Nicholas gives us a slight eye roll and a look of, *You can drop the fancy shit. I just got a blowjob in your bathroom from one of these Asian prostitutes, and I already forgot which one it was.*

Banjo, the chubby, adorable, gay Filipino runner, who sweats profusely due to his 100 percent noodle and lumpia diet, is a quarter of a second late on the drop again. Ben, the grey-haired, bodybuilder, gay waiter, had stayed back against a wall to watch. He keeps his collar so tight that you can see how annoyed he is by how red his neck gets. Banjo has to scurry back to the kitchen, cowering his head underneath Ben's evil eye and his Sangiovese-colored Adam's Apple.

We all get in the kitchen to bring out the entree course to an eight top. We've been warned at the preshift lineup that Chef Mina is in a foul mood. His top-selling dish, the Ahi Medallions, are off the menu permanently. The reason is that their shape, two cubed potato shallot cakes sitting next to each other with Ahi and *foie gras* stacked on top of them, was not just in the form of the Twin Towers; it's a well-known fact they were an homage to them. Also, the PETA people are back protesting the *foie gras* by showing the guests posters through the windows. Signs picturing geese with plastic tubes jammed down their throats and force-fed grain until their liver swells and suffocates the other organs, killing them. Mmmmm, *delicioso*.

The eight food runners on shift arrive in a perfect line to the chef's right, waiting for the following table's plates to come out. The dining chatter is replaced by silence, perhaps a light clinking of stainless steel or the stirring of a *roux*. Chef Mina is standing in front of a wall of tickets looking through the pass at the cooks. Chef is a rising star in the food world and no longer actually does any cooking himself. He mainly just coordinates the serving of the tables and strikes fear into the hearts of his staff. He pulls a ticket and places it in front of the bigger ticket the cooks struggle to get out simultaneously. One of the newer cooks is dragging two items that the large table needs. Chef mutters quietly, "Dammit," as he shoves the ticket to it's new place on the extended clip. The new cook's shoulders can be seen tensing under his *beyond white* chef's coat. His back is to us, desperately trying to make his Diver scallops crisp up faster on the edges. A few lightly muttered "Dammit,"s was all it took, along with the knowledge that the chef was staring at the back of his head all night, wishing it would explode. We found that poor guy talking to himself in the *walk-in* later that night. After that, we never saw him again.

His parents wasted $50,000 on Cordon Bleu cooking school, and now they're getting their kid back like he just got back from Afghanistan; shaky hands and stuttering. "What the fuck?" says dad, "You're not an executive chef yet?" Half of these poor kids will hack it for a few months and go running to the university like their mom originally wanted anyway. The other half will become kitchen savages that can plate an eight-top on the fly. It won't matter if there's a critic in the dining room. There will be no emotion on their face, or tension in their grip. They will rapidly turn masterpieces of Michelin quality through the pass for the chef to inspect. Perhaps the chef will wipe a speck of demiglace off the rim. The speck may have never even existed. Chef always finds little ways to remind the cook that he wasn't quite perfect. Wouldn't want these guys to get enough confidence to start a competing restaurant, would we? Every employee must be beaten down regularly, so he doesn't get any ideas.

The fine-dining restaurants of San Francisco just eat these cooking school kids alive. The .com bust put all the rich people in a lousy mood, and numbers are down in the fancier restaurants. You can feel the extra tension added to the already incredible stress of the restaurant's typical baseline. The quality, consistency and coordination fine dining requires is not really humanly possible night after night. And if the chef misses your mistake, don't breathe a sigh of relief yet; the rich, asshole customer has been trained to spot a broken sauce since he was four. Rich people love sending back food. More than they love filling the air in poor neighborhoods with mercury. If I had a nickel for every time, I was snobbily handed a supposedly dirty wine glass that was actually fucking immaculate? I'd be richer than them. Can't argue though, you have to run off around a corner and pretend you got a new one, then smile real big and apologize as you come fast, walking back with it. Not once does a customer say, "This is the same glass." But, of course, that was never the point. The point is that I am at their disposal, no matter how ridiculous the request. I'm their servant simply because they were born in a better zip code than me.

After a few months, this shit starts getting old. The busboys have it the best. They don't really have to talk to the customer except to ask if they can clear something. God help you if you don't get permission first to try and clear a rich bitch's chardonnay glass. Even if there's just a single drop in there. She'll freak as if you just got her emergency transplant liver stuck in a traffic jam. But if she starts berating the busboy, he just pretends he doesn't speak English and wanders off. They make the same amount as the runners—about a hundred bucks in tips on a Friday—for half the stress. You have to be highly *on it,* though. When the hostess sees the guests walk out the door, she's already calling out the name of the next party for that table. If you're still straightening silver on there when they arrive, the manager will react as if you cunt-punted the Queen of England as she walked in the door.

Fine dining is a ridiculous game where, if you're a good little lap dog, the customer will flip a few extra coins at you on his way out. Being rich isn't enough for these people; they get off watching the poor try to please them when the poor *really* should be attacking them. Fine dining waiters should smash the pompous heads of the rich. Smash them with the silver trays they instead serve up their dignity in little slices on, night after night. Pathetic. Better than the coliseum days, I guess. Today, rich people have to settle for torturing waiters and simple, two-man basement fights between their gardeners. Rarely to the death. *Fuckin' Rome had lions and a dozen tigers eating poor people... in a god damn stadium*, the rich guys think, as Hector loses an eye near the earthquake supplies.

I gotta get out of this shit, and quick!

Here's what fancy restaurants and show business have in common: the focus on youth has nothing to do with the audience's preference. That was all manipulated into being by the leaders of specific industries. Fashion, show business, restaurants, they have young, beautiful people as the face of their industries because that's who the bosses in those industries are exploiting and trying to fuck. Fucking that youthful beauty with their gross, diseased, corpselike bodies, crushing it up and snorting it like unstepped on cocaine. The job is the bait. Those poor hostesses think sucking a dick for some server shifts is a good deal for her. She should be getting HER dick sucked. When society wakes up, these pieces of shit will be hunted back to the Philippine jungles where they first started committing their crimes. I, for one, will be scalping cocks like Geronimo on a new moon.

Drinkin' and Smokin'

They usually start cutting runners around nine pm, so I have plenty of time to go to the bars after work. I live in the middle of a goldmine of dive bars and dance clubs in the Lower Haight. Nikki's Haight Street BBQ is directly across the street, which does not serve BBQ at all. It's a dance club. I did see someone smoking some meat in their mouth in the bathroom once. I decided I didn't have to take a leak that bad after all. There's Molotov Cocktails, where when you walk in, you are blasted with a potent smell of fermented puke. This keeps the yuppies out. All the Europeans go to Mad Dog in the Fog. There's Noc Noc, with their weird Dr. Suessy bar stools, and Salvador Dali meets Dante's Inferno aesthetic. Toronado, with the best beer selection in California. The Top, where club kids go on nights they don't want to party in a warehouse. All within a stone's throw of my house. It's like the universe wants me to drink. It's a working-class party neighborhood. Everyone is spending about $40 on Friday night, and you can get in a fight for trying to bum a smoke off a non-hippie.

I start the evenings at the Spanish-themed, Movida Lounge, drinking sangria. Lyle works here. I know him from back home in Isla Vista. As long as I tip him five bucks every few drinks, he keeps my glass full. As a poor man, I've always relied on bartenders to kick me down a good deal if I keep the bar entertained. Bartenders get tired of having to be the entertainment monkey and psychologist all the time. If a guy can shoulder half the load, he's often going to get drunk for cheap. He's likely to have enough change left for a slice at the shitty pizza shop that is synonymous to dive bar neighborhoods. That doughy crap that is intended to sponge all the toxins from your belly.

The other bar I go to, near the panhandle, four blocks from the famed Haight and Ashbury intersection, is called Storyville. A hip-hop club.

Good old Doorman Gabe, also known to me from Santa Barbara, is a bartender now. I have the same deal with him that I have with Lyle. Throw a fiver on the bar three times a night, and I can get drunk. Storyville is great. The gangster vibe is slightly less than medium. You have great acts on the weekends, rap entourages that are racially diverse, DJs that mash-up rap with heavy metal, bands that mix turntables with drums and guitars. I make friends with the performers and even sing a song sometimes. I will dance my ass off, and groups of Black girls will chant, "Go whiteboy! Go whiteboy!" It's like a drug to hear them chant that. None of them will make out with me, though. Filipino B-boys flip and spin up towards the ceilings, carterpillering and windmilling into the audience's heart. What a place!

This is the San Francisco I love: Diverse and looking to party. I know I described my neighborhood as a crack and party neighborhood, but there's more to it than that. There's plenty of families around too. You could have a band just practicing in a front yard, a family will just start BBQing hot links next to that, and next thing you know? You got a little impromptu daytime block party going on. Everyone is such a unique individual; it's not like a collection of homogenized clicks. People will accept you and be interested in how different you are. This is the honest San Francisco. A true melting pot of misfits that don't give a fuck about anything but having fun. The crack thing is an issue. Coming home drunk with tip money still in my pockets, I start buying a 20 rock more than just on Saturdays. It's becoming an issue. I love to feel that unearned adrenaline rush. The Black and Asian girls at Storyville won't fuck me, and I'm not freaky enough for the ravers and punkers in Lower Haight. I could go to the Marina, but then I may as well have stayed in Santa Barbara. Could it be? I'm now the one that's too vanilla? Shit. Santa Barbara convinced me I was an unresolvable freak. How did this happen?

I have a terrible year, sex-wise, and I become so incredibly lonely that I turn to sucking dick. A glass dick. Some people call it a crack pipe. I hardly make any money as a food runner, so I'm limited to one or two 20 rocks a week. I'm not skateboarding (too many hills and deadly busses), or surfing (water's too freezing in Norcal), or having sex (my confidence lately?), or any of my other trusty adrenaline sources. So, for lack of any alternatives, crack is a reliable source of trash dopamine. It only sort of works, and for fleeting moments, but it's something.

The rest of my time, I'm at Ed, the Editor's house working on completing my movie. I have to get this done. Living in a crack-torn block is dragging me down, however cheap the rent is. I haven't talked to anyone from my old life in months except for my brother, who sends me money when I get desperate. That's the lowest, borrowing money from your kid brother. I'm supposed to be loaning *him* money. Trying to establish yourself in The City is not easy. But I'm a tenacious little cockroach, and I have cheap rent.

After what seems like months of sitting in a musty apartment with a grumpy chain-smoker who just cracks the window a few inches because we're in the middle of a long rainy winter, the movie is done. This guy Ed the Editor, has spent the whole time proving that he knows more about making movies than me. Hollywood just didn't understand his ideas because they were too brilliant and were considered niche. Even MTV used him to gain success and threw him away like trash. He asks me questions he knows I don't have the answer to, and I spend half of the $25 per hour I'm paying him to school me on shit that I fucked up or didn't know. I guess it's fair since I'm only paying him half the rate he wants. He does save some problems with cleverness. We even go out and film some more stuff with *his* camera to fix a few holes or janky transitions.

Thanks for everything, Ed. That winter felt a lot like going to the frame shop with my old man, sitting there with the window barely cracked, satisfying the Osha regulations for kids working in a smoke-filled environment, getting told I don't know shit. I still love you, Ed. You were less cruel about it all than dad was. We finished it. And your bitter humor was pretty funny. You made the movie better than it would have been.

Finally, Some Fuckin' Sex!

Then, my luck turns. With the confidence of putting my movie in the can, my crack intake finally lowers before it becomes a habit. My sex life lights up! I start visiting other parts of the city, and I have sex with two Asian girls in the span of a few months. Exotic for a boy from 80s-90s Santa Barbara. One was a one-nighter, which is fine. Don't even remember her name, just the feeling of gripping her coarse, thick hair strands in a bunch and ramming her face down into the pillow as I came.

The next girl I meet is at Murdoch's birthday party: Nozomi from Hiroshima. A wacky artistic girl who just bounces around with the energy of a *tootsie rolled-out* toddler. She's tiny and always smiling, wandering over to anything along our path to study it with excitement and wonder. Unfortunately, Murdoch has invited her to his birthday. He has the hots for her, but fails to make a move at the party. So I end up on the bus with her and fuck her this very day. Big vagina. Surprising for a tiny Asian girl. Bus pussy *does* tend to be a bit larger than average, but this is ridiculous.

Before the folks at Big Vaginas Are People Too, come after me? Let me just say that I believe that **all** vaginas are beautiful. I'm just looking for a good fit. My ideal vagina is medium-sized, so as to be somewhat snug, on my just above medium, *regular,* white penis. If the pussy could slightly veer to the right, just short of six inches inside so my bob tip could flick flack off the wall on its way past? That would be great, but totally not required.

Having grown up in sports, and being institutionalized as a rascally youth, where we were forced to shower in large groups together, I can confidently tell you large vagina'd girls that there is a dick out there just for you. One out of 20 dicks is what you would call 'big.' Don't think of yourself as having a giant vagina; think of yourself as being in the top fifth percentile for cock. There is nothing wrong with you. Insecure guys who feel that all vaginas should fit them are just mad and want you to think you have the problem.

On top of the genitalia mismatch, Nozomi also has a skin flap over her butthole. It's like that thing at the edge of your ear hole? Like a little cartilage skin flap? Maybe it's from being born near Hiroshima? At any rate, that isn't a solution to vagina looseness. I'm scared she'll sneeze or something, and the flap will snap shut like a valve. A guy could lose a dick that way.

We fuck around for a few weeks, and I break up with her. Then, out of guilt, I buy a self-portrait she painted of herself. There's a love letter on the back of it—or maybe its a *fuck you* letter—in thin permanent marker. (Anyone know Japanese?)

A few weeks later, I'm sitting on the front steps drinking a Sierra Nevada and looking out at the chaos on the block. I look up at the second-story window of the place across the street and catch the old lady that's always up there staring at me. She doesn't look away, and I wave. She waves back. The breeze brings news of fried fish and recently rained on garbage to my nostrils. I will never forget these things because they are a part of a fantastic moment.

As I sit there lazily daydreaming, I see something that's impossible. It must be part of the daydream. Cassie, my most fervent teenaged fantasy, walks by! She's like a Pfeiffery redhead but with Basinger lips. What?! "Hey, Cassie!" I yell. She stops and instantly recognizes me. Of course, she does. I had the worst crush on her in Isla Vista when I was 17, and she was 19. At the time, it seemed a chasm of age difference. I'd always be following some older girl around back then. It usually didn't happen, but now, the age difference doesn't seem to matter; I'm all growds up! We go up to The Gold Cane in the Upper Haight and drink cheap, sugar-filled, happy hour margaritas until we're drunk, reminiscing about the good old days. We end up in the basement of my Victorian, where there's an old couch that has probably seen many dirty dealings. It's almost dark in there, but for a dusty 40-watt bulb in the ceiling, which gives off so little light, it's as if we're in a scene in Godfather Part II. Cassie asks me, "Did you know that if you chew Peppermint Lifesavers in the dark, you can see sparks?"

"That's a new one to me. You got any?" I say.

She pulls out half a pack with the tin foil wrapping spiraling off. "I sure do."

We both pop in a lifesaver and start chomping with our mouths open, looking in each other's gullets to see if there are any sparks. I think I see one just before the Lifesavers are gone, and I start making out with her. She seems like she's waiting for it. Her lips feel as impressive as they look. When I used to masturbate to her I'd finish by picturing her eyes rolling back, and that beautiful, full, bottom lip, quivering in erotic ectstacy.

Next thing you know, we are in my room, trying to take each other's clothes off as fast as possible. I see Cassie's tiny apple titties and start sucking her prominent nipples that sit in the middle of her pretty, cotton candy-colored areolas. I fumble for the condom and quickly get my smothered cock into her tight, wet, red muff. Geez, it's tight. It's like sticking your dick into Chinese finger cuffs. I try to get balls deep, but it's like it's trying to squeeze me back out. Good thing I'm drunk; I'd have jizzed my load when her tiny tits came out. I'd thought about this moment for years, and now it's happening! A childhood fantasy made true. I'd made out with Amy from the Beach Shop in a taxi outside the Beach Shack, but this is different. I'm sealing the deal!

To gauge how amazing this experience is for me, you must know this girl was one of my most pined-for and lusted-after girls that I'd ever been obsessed with. 17-year-old obsession—the most potent kind! And now, a dozen years later, I'm fucking the shit out of Cassie, the perfect amount of drunk, where I'm still hard as shit, but drunk enough to not bust a nut too early. Invincibility factor times ten. It's as if, for most teenage fantasies being fulfilled, Daisy Duke has come alive, hops off that Dukes of Hazzard poster, pulls the tiny piece of denim covering her *wonder hole* aside, and whispers your name. She then flips her beautiful brown hair from the nape of her neck to the front of a shoulder, solidly planting her knees into your Star Wars sheets to prepare for the monster fuck of her life. She pushes her delicate love oyster out towards you as she arches her back, with a light, anticipatory moan. **That** is what this moment is for me.

Soon, Cassie is whimpering, stretching her neck back in an arc, rolling her eyes back, just like I'd imagined a hundred times before. I gather myself for a final flurry of sliding my tenderloin in and out of her curly pork barn. We both bust at once.

I sleep as a champion. I wake up, and Cassie is gone. I think it must have been a dream, but there it is on the table, her number.

Things are turning around. Crazy how a lonely year can make you forget who you are and take all your confidence and joy. We indeed are social creatures. I'm back, baby!

Fuck this Fine Dining Shit

I'm out in the alley, where the food delivery trucks bring all the butter and filet mignons in the back, and Chef Mina himself is about to grill me like one of his filets. He just pulled me out here from the kitchen at the beginning of service. "Where did you work before?" he starts.

"South Park Cafe," I say in my professional tone. *Somewhere better than here,* I most likely communicate with my eyes, unable to help it.

"Oh, I like South Park Cafe. Do they still have mussels?"

"Yes, black mussels and *pomme frites,"* I say, wondering why I ever quit there. Then I remember that after the first tech bubble burst my already slim, daytime bartender tips there were halved. Why do the jobs you can actually tolerate never pay enough? I so loved that easygoing Chef Ward. You did your best. You just didn't want to let him down because you loved him so much. I miss showing up in the mornings and making myself a cappuccino in the quiet, going into the kitchen for milk, and seeing the two early cooks making the blood sausage. One guy would be stretching open the pig intestine. At the same time, the other food prepper expertly pours a mixture of pig's blood, apples, and onions into it. *Boudin noir.* So good. Ah, to be back at *the bistro.*

"Did Chef Ward let you work the dining room with two-day stubble?" says Chef, ripping me from my fond remembrance into this new Financial District hell.

Well, yeah. The other front-of-the-house guys were French and didn't shave **or** *wear deodorant. They'd talk about your wife's tits in front of you, assuming* *you don't speak French. Goddamn French waiters have it so easy!* My thoughts are probably betraying me as my lip stiffens at finally finding out what this is all about. A trip into the alley with The Chef is usually a *this is your last chance,* type of thing. When you get back, everyone looks at you like you just got diagnosed with pancreatic cancer. If you come back at all.

"No, Chef," I lie, knowing this is the only thing I can say if I want to work through this shift.

"Ok, well, just so you know, I have the same standards, or higher, than he does."

Yeah, okay, buddy. I think I am no longer trying to mask my emotions, trying to save my dignity, even though my words are that of a sellout. "Yes, Chef, I understand."

He turns back to go into the restaurant, and I follow at a safe distance. Then, he sharply turns around and says, "Where are you going?"

"Well, there's a s-six top getting plated." In a chickenshit attempt to impress him, I blurt stutter that I was keeping track of what should currently be happening on the line.

"No. You need to go down to that end of the alley, go into Walgreens, and buy a razor. You have 5 minutes." He points towards Walgreens like he's sending a dog outside for puking up grass in the corner. I think about spitting on him if only to visualize his expression as my throat lubricant dribbles down his bird nose. I then punch and break that beak in my mind's eye. He smirks at my fractured masculinity. My anger must be evident now, as my mouth trembles in anger. I stand there, frozen, as he walks back into the restaurant.

"Fuck!" I mutter as I start toward the razor section of Walgreens. It's the end of the month, and I'm already going to be $50 short on the rent. After dry fucking my upper lip with Gillette's cheapest in the window of Mc Donald's, I get back to the row of runners at the pass, where the food comes through. Chef doesn't react. A whole new six top worth of entrees are about to come up. Everyone looks surprised to see me, but they are ambivalent. Isn't getting fired being *freed* from fine dining?

I'm not suited for this work; carrying giant bowls of steaming

Shabu Shabu broth, lit up with Sterno underneath. Sterno is a napalm like substance that could very well engulf the mayor in flames, but only after I scald his cock and balls with the broth first. What will the Russian thugs he's sitting with think? I look clumsy as I scissor the butcher string off a Rainbow Trout, *French serve* its belly open with a spoon and a fork, then pour in the *caper beurre blanc.*

Elvis Costello, Robin Williams, Charlie Rose, Andre Agassi, Quincy Jones, George Lucas all look at me a bit sympathetic as I fumble with the ramekins at their table. It's like they're seeing what could have happened to them had they failed to make it in showbiz. I think my bloodstream is usually missing its first drink of the day by five pm. The tiny espresso saucers vibrate in my big, shaky hands. *Tsk Tsk*, their expressions go, like they're watching a horse get shot at The Derby.

Not Dennis Miller, though. He looks at me like, *Is this clown going to achieve this faux Sisyphean feat, or am I going to have to do this motherfucker like the Pinkertons at a labor strike in an uneven calendar year?*

And not Kim Catrall either. She looked at me like a rack of ribs on the 4th of July. Can't really blame her. I look pretty much like a mash-up of James Dean, Vince Vaughn—prime Vince, none of that puffy face shit—and Paul Newman. Four percent body fat. At 29, I'm in my motherfuckin' prime. I make sure to be in between her and the door as she leaves, in case she wants to slip me her hotel key at the Pan Pacific. No dice. She's on the arm of some producer-looking, clown. Won't anyone rescue me from here?

One night, I'm filling the soup *amuse* pot with lobster bisque from a burbling cauldron that a cook just handed me. The chef likes to turn and face me, as I choose the *no looking back second* where you begin the big pour into the second container. Flip your wrist wrong, or hesitate, and you get a half-pint of it on the floor. You'd be surprised how much area eight ounces of liquid can cover, especially if you fuck it up during the rush. Even though like I said, I'm a shaky motherfucker in general, my hands magically never do at that moment. I would **never, ever** give this fucker the satisfaction of dripping any onto the floor. Then he could go, *"Pffffft,"* a little mouth fart of prefabricated disappointment, before turning away, disgustedly. That's his classic move, the *disgusted turn away.*

All the customers get a free little espresso cup full of soup as they sit down, as a free offering, along with their olive bread and organic farm butter. These people often sit down hungry and angry. So it's a good idea to get some cuisine into this hedge fund manager's wife before she starts grabbing at our sleeves as we walk by. "My blood sugarrrr," she bellows as if she's dying. The original, "I can't have glutennnnn."

Tonight is lobster bisque. That means there's a bunch of big wigs coming in. The pharmaceutical industry has taken over the city for their convention. The big-pharma bosses are all screaming at their secretaries to get a reservation here at Aqua. Chef Mina's star is rising in the food world at lightning speed, and the rich assholes all want to see what all the hubbub is about. We even have an extra long lineup to discuss certain VIPs and how they should be treated with even more kiss-assery than usual. People we should be murdering need our lips pressed into their asses even harder.

So my plan for this particular convention, since I'm in control of the soup amuse, was to give them a little of their own medicine. I was going to dump an incredible amount of microdots of LSD in there on the first turn, when the whole restaurant gets seated in our opening 45 minutes.

Once they were all good and tripping I was going to go in there with a Ronald Reagan Halloween mask, shrieking, "We did this to ourselves!!! We DID this to OURSELVES!!! Ahhhhhh, marble-julip-juicy-TREEEEEE!!!!!!"

A week ago, I would have ventured it. Then, I was depressed and didn't feel like I had anything going for me. But now, with a finished movie just waiting for a venue to have the premiere at? And the knowledge that Cassie will be back in my *stabbin' cabin'* soon? Can't risk prison. These decadent pieces of shit would bribe the public defender to throw my case. Remind the judge of those pictures the Israelis got of him in that hotel room in Tokyo with his fellow diaper-wearing friends. I'd go to the electric chair. I have a future now!

I think about this and other ways to exit the high end dining industry while mixing tartare tableside for the worst of the worst. Ladies whose faces look as if they'd deflate like a tire if you touched them, their bony bodies flying up into the chandeliers like a hissing, corkscrewy birthday balloon. Already speed dialing their plastic surgeon as they touch back onto the ground. "Fuck! He's in Cabo! Call the airport!"

I've mixed about 800 of these tartares tableside since I got here, and frankly, I'm sick of it. How many times per night do I have to mix a raw quail egg into a pile of Ahi tuna, garlic, pine nuts, Scotch Bonnet chilis, minced Bosc pear, mint chiffonade, and Himalayan sea salt? The pungent, pleasing aroma of the sesame oil hits the noses of the table's guests as my mixing spoons go *tink! tink!* on their plates. A manager waves me towards the kitchen with urgency in his eyes for the next big coordinated drop. He quickly pretends to check his cufflinks and smile as a jet-setting sex predator passes him.

I actually like this manager, Brian. His sole job is to wander around the dining room and charm the shit out of everyone, control the flow of the dining room, and comp champagne and appetizers to the VIPs. Never does a lick of actual work. Golfs with the customers. I should hate him, but he's too charming. Smooth as butter. His face is beautiful, like a lotion commercial or something. His fingernails are manicured, his suit is silky as his voice, and his soul is dead.

I walk into the kitchen to a plate flying across it, barely missing a waiter, and smashing on the wall, "Get OUT!!!" screams Chef Mina.

Oh, did I say it was always quiet in the kitchen? It is when the chef isn't screaming at a guy. Tonight's victim hangs his head and walks out; all the way to his car, and we never see him again. If he's smart, he'll finish trade school. First, I imagine he's going to get drunk at his neighborhood bar and curse the bastard chef. Around midnight, nearly every bar in the city has one, maybe two waiters sitting quietly at the bar, showing their resting bitch face to the mirror behind the whiskey bottles. He sips his Fernet Branca and plots the chef's untimely death.

The waiters get shit on by the whole restaurant; the customers, the bartender, everyone. You see, there's a huge wage disparity between the busboys, regular cooks, dishwashers, food runners, barbacks, hostesses, and valets. If they all ever got together, they could bring down the restaurant. They'd get more of the tips *quick* if they started sabotaging business in the millions of ways available to them.

But they don't. Why? Because of the people who really make all the money in a fancy restaurant; upper management, owners, investors, the chef, and in the hectic places like this one, the chef's number two, the sous. They have given the low-paid ones, the entry-level college kids, and the Latinos someone to hate: the waiter. The busboys are told that the waiter plays golf at the same courses as the customers. They tell the hostess that he has season passes to Squaw *and* Heavenly.

Rich people have been turning the poor successfully against each other for thousands of years. There are sure-fire ways to play the basic emotions of the common man, and they have figured them out. That's why you hear about a lot more civil wars than revolutions.

The expensive general manager jumps in on it too. Gotta keep up appearances and keep the hate on the waiters, and not themselves. Throw an emotional rib kick at the waitress that didn't fold enough napkins last night. Maybe fire a motherfucker for being late. Keep 'em scared and running towards the silver polishing area.

The assistant managers don't get paid much either. Slightly less than the waiters when you account for tips. They have to survive partly on waiter fear, and it tastes pretty good to them. These are the evilest bulldogs in the place. Brought up from our ranks usually, and promised a juicy general manager job in the restaurant group should they be effective enough at backstabbing and licking the guys' balls above them on the ladder.

I know all of these things. I see how they are playing us against each other, yet I still hate the fuckin' waiters. Until I become one, that is. Not in fine dining. Fuck that.

Why would I even *want* to be a waiter, you ask? Simple. It *is* the money. But the waiters aren't rich. More like, lower middle class. To the impoverished college students beneath them, they look like millionaires. Maybe the food runners should hate them a little, but, I mean, lower-middle class is not worth hating a guy for. Until your salary entitles you to hunt people for sport, you're still salvageable.

At any other job, as non-college graduates, we'd make less than half the money. The bosses know we'll let the rest of the restaurant use us as a punching bag for this supposed double wage we're supposed to be making. They allow it because they need to deflect the hatred by the insufficiently paid workers, the grand majority of restaurant employees, from them, onto us. On a certain level, as servers, we understand and accept that. We're young enough to handle the stress for a few years until our nerves start getting destroyed from it. As young people, we feel like we're on our way somewhere else in life, somewhere better. With that last factor, a human can put up with a lot.

Getting in and out of restaurants while you are in college can be very rewarding. You can graduate debt-free! And I'll take late-night conversation at the dive bar with Greg the line cook over Dan the psychology major any fuckin' day of the week. So get in and out quick, kids. Think of it like living near a toxic-waste dump. You enjoy the financial benefits of tips or cheap-toxic-waste-dump-rent for five or six years, and bounce before your balls start glowing—I'm talking to you, Treasure Island.

It's only when the industry has beaten you down for a few decades when things get super depressing. Look into the eyes of your next 60-year-old steakhouse waiter, up above his ratty cummerbund and his waxed, grey, saloon keeper's mustache. Those eyes tell of a sadness unknown outside the killing fields of fine dining. His hopeless peepers practically beg you to snatch the prime rib knife from his sad hands and free him from this torturous realm.

Back to Santa Barbara

I finally have my movie premiere in The Mission at Artist Television Access. A bunch of people come. It's glorious! This is the first time I've had a celebration of my art. An event! Way better than lugging around a duffel bag full of T-shirts in the hot sun. People seem to enjoy it, and we all talk and reminisce afterward. It's a perfect blend of new friends and Santa Barbara people. It's okay, I guess, but after that, I just feel like, *Whatever, I guess that's it.* I don't really feel that passionate about undertaking a new project. It seems like a lot of work for what you get at the end, a one-night premiere, and then back to the grind. I'm an adrenaline junkie. I say as much to the guy who played Nelson in the movie, Kellicut is his real name, and he says, "You should be a comedian. You're a bit dark but a good writer." I'd never actually thought about it. The rewards *are* immediate, the intense laughter of the adoring crowd? *Hmmm.* A seed is planted.

As my weariness at work ferments my soul, I am developing a crack habit at home. I never crave it until I'm five pints of beer in, and now when I go home, the guys at the dice game call me by name. I hide last night's leftover tip money from myself inside my housemate's books in his room. I'd never go in there while he's sleeping, would I? He has his dog Homer in there. Even if Steve's own snoring provided me some cover, Homer would certainly bark, right?

It turns out Homer doesn't bark when I go into Steve's room to get my money for crack. Steve wakes up anyway and says the only thing he really *can* say is, "Uhm, what the fuck are you doing in here?"

Researching Columbia?

So begins my downfall at Sandy the Speed Freak's house. I've started bringing around Deaf Tom, who is a scraggly homeless skateboarder. He often will come looking for me after midnight for a place to crash. One night, he keeps ringing the next-door neighbor's bell; over and over, they point to my house and tell him I'm over there. It's a half-hour before he gets it because he's deaf and comes over to ring *my* bell until *I* wake up. I let him in my room to sleep on the floor. Just before dawn, I find him pissing into my *ghetto blaster* radio. Now, the whole row of Victorians between Webster and Fillmore are gunning for me. One of the dice guys comes looking for me one day at the house saying I shorted him three dollars on last night's 20 rock. Steve doesn't have to eavesdrop on the conversation because all the noise from the front gate funnels in acoustic perfection, down a long, narrow hall, right into his room. After that, Steve tells me they all want me to move out. Shit. Should I just move back to Santa Barbara? This crack neighborhood is starting to absorb my spirit.

This question is clearly answered when we get a bill from the landlord, a 90-year-old dude who owns half the block and gives everyone a good deal. The bill is for $10,000. Apparently, Sandy has been putting our rent money in her speed pipe for a year. The old guy is just now putting a polite note on our door. After she goes down to his office and does something that he forgives the debt for, all is well. We just have to pay him directly now. I can only imagine the Hoover vacuum routine this bitch did on this old man's cock. Fuckin' Viagra has given all these old fuckers new life, I tell you. A hummer is a hummer, and a gummer is a gummer. It could be from a tweaker, or it could be a grand*mother.* Ain't nobody's mouth safe on rent day. Landlord's got a *stiffy*, and he's almost double of 50! Get Hoover lips down here; he's starting to eye ME!

This is too weird, and I've already bought my bus ticket back to Santa Barbara. Time to regroup, think about taking things in a different direction, maybe take the plunge back into the city next year, or maybe LA. Perhaps San Francisco isn't the jam. Who knows? I find myself on the Greyhound within a few days, pulling into that familiar station on Chapala and Carrillo Streets. Sweet home Santa Barbara.

Punching Skinheads at Giancarlo's House

I've been back in Santa Barbara for a few weeks and have settled right back into my old habits. The only difference is that, between key bumps and trying to hustle college students for drinks at pool, I'm scribbling down jokes in a ratty notebook or on some cocktail napkins. I'm going to be the next George Carlin once I have a hot ten minutes written down. This cocaine is telling me I'm almost there! Comedy Store in Hollywood, here I come!

I wake up on people's couches and dig in my pockets and their cushions to see if there's enough for a large brewed coffee. *Come on, two dollars!* All I find is the soggy napkins containing indecipherable writing that I'm convinced display genius of the *insane laughter* variety. Jokes so hilarious they could elicit howling from those guards with the furry, tall hats at Big Ben. The ones that aren't supposed to react, even if you taunt them? Well, once I do *my* act on them, they're getting fired. For now, as I uncrumple the bar napkins, it looks like the unknowable language of an ancient and advanced culture. Infinite potential, but as of yet, worthless. Am I trying to draw pictures of the jokes on some of these? Is that a kangaroo on a moped? What the fuck does "sazzle priss," mean? All right, I'll figure out a proper method. A voice recorder, maybe?

The Wildcat has become a full-on, LA-style dance club. No pool table anymore. That's a deal-breaker. How does the criminal element know where to gather if the dive bar doesn't have a fuckin' pool table? And the Madhouse is closed down. Corner Pocket? Dead. I've only been gone for two years. The new century has a strong vibe. I don't like it. So I hole up at The Sportsman, where I know people and where it still feels like the old Santa Barbara that I know how to thrive in. The bartenders quickly realize that I'm going to be a bad influence in their establishment. They decide to control my drunkenness by charging me for all my drinks.

They even cut me off once my volume level gets louder than the jukebox. This is bullshit. I'm 30 now, and people no longer find my *ring leader of chaos* routine so *cutesy cute*. Downtown Santa Barbara in 2003 seems like, after a long run of out of control behavior by all, it's time to chill out and take some deep breaths. All the destroyed bathrooms and sidewalk street fights have taken their toll, I guess.

Maybe I should go hit up G-Money in Isla Vista, and crash in his mold cave until I can't stand it anymore. My brother Auggie has a cabin on Los Padres Forest property in the mountains, Paradise Road. How he scored that, I have no idea. This guy just comes up with excellent deals no one else can get. He has my gift of gab but not the shady reputation. Is that how this works? You have to have the good reputation too? Well, shit, this town is on to me then. So I'm taking life lessons from my little brother instead of the other way around? Damn. Better finish my work and get out of here again. I could hole up at Auggie's cabin, but this poses the problem the teepee did. It's just a little too far from the action to use for anything but wound licking after a three-day drinking binge.

I'm crashing at Thadius' girlfriend's house downtown until one of her friends blows me on the couch, doesn't swallow, and leaves a swirly pool of opalescent cum on the cushion. Jen freaks when she sees it and buys a whole new fuckin' couch, delivered that very day. Are you kidding? Have you ever heard of *Febreze and flip*? I'm alerted immediately that I can sit on it but not sleep there anymore. Jen thinks I'm going to be squirting my seed all over the living room the second I'm not being supervised. So now it's *hasta la vista,* after ten pm.

Maybe it's not Santa Barbara that's gotten boring. Maybe it's that everyone I know is 30 or older now. They're all *rulesey* and *joblike now.* I'm not ready to grow up yet. My pleas fall on deaf ears, and more and more of my crash spots are closed for business after nine pm. Do I have to focus on happy hours only to survive in this restricted climate now? Be tucked in with an imaginary blanket by ten o'clock? My brain doesn't even start coming up with good joke material until eleven.

My dilemma is solved one evening when we all go over to Giancarlo's house after The Sportsman to drink Bacardi and make his neighbors wish they were deaf. Giancarlo is the guitar player of a band called Creature Feature, a grunge metally local favorite. Giancarlo is a great frontman; gravelly voice, goateed, dread locked, and dressed in all black with black hair. Basically a mash-up of Rob Zombie and Shaggy from Scooby-Doo. GC, as we also call him, generally just communicates with his guitar. Not a huge talker if he's not singing, although, if you hear a big "Yeeeeeeeaaaawp!!!" or a "Railer!!" from near the front door, you know Giancarlo has arrived at the party. Since he lives only five blocks from the Sportsman, things often end up over at his and Luis' house. Luis that I used to scam pizza slices off at Pizza Bob's almost 15 years ago. Yes, it's a small town. You'd be surprised how small of a city 50,000 people is. It's kind of annoying.

It's a typical after-hours crew here at Giancarlo's this evening; skaters, musicians, surfers, record store employees, college students, alcoholics, tweakers, and stoners. Oh, and tonight, some random skinheads.

After a few minutes, one of the skinheads taps me on the shoulder, and says "Are you Scales?"

"Yeah," I say, hoping he wants to buy some weed or coke.

"Come out to the street, we're going to box," says shaved head, shit for brains. I must have beat the shit out of one of his little gang mates back in the old days. It couldn't be him. He'd've been twelve. I haven't scrapped with the skinners since Isla Vista, coming up on a decade ago. So I'm still on their shit list? Awesome.

"What? Really?" I say, frankly surprised. He walks out toward the street, past the hedges that border Giancarlo's yard. I turn to the crowd, who looks as surprised as me, shrug my shoulders, and follow this dude out to the street.

At the street, Baby Goebbels seems determined to fight and walks toward me with his fists clenched. *Ok,* I think. *Bam!* I fold the dude up pretty quick with a left hook. His buddy, a roided up, recent prison releasee, psycho looking dude, starts rushing over to tap in for his buddy, who is now sitting on the ground, feet out and spread apart, holding his now bleeding nose. *Fuck this, I'm on a nazi per night diet, you guys.* This other dude looks like 230 pounds of methed-up prison yard fury too.

I smartly run. A few blocks up, I decide to hop a seven-foot fence and fall off the top from fatigue and drunkenness, breaking my ankle. It's the first time in my life when I completely snap a bone, meaning it can't be fixed with electrical tape and whiskey. How can this be the first time I'm going to the emergency room for myself in over a decade? Fuck, I'm agile and lucky, I guess. I'm wailing out in pain, and the cops come, guns drawn. We're in the fancy part of Santa Barbara, so they assume it's a burglary. They seem to believe my story and call an ambulance, which takes me about two blocks, later charging me $1,600 for the favor. Good luck collecting that.

This lands me up at Auggie's cabin, after all. For a long rest with my smashed-up ankle. No booze or cocaine, just a few pain pills, which run out all too quickly. Just me, my sister, pregnant with her first of five children, and my poor mother having to wait on the both of us. Auggie is always off working and staying down the hill most nights. I rely on weed and coffee to write my jokes, think about being a more successful human, and heal. Life did this to me to sit me down, to save me from myself. It's up to me to use this time wisely. I swear to myself I will.

There is a TV with cable, and I start watching the hour of stand-up that Comedy Central plays each day. It drives my sister crazy, and she complains during the punchlines from the next room. She's all huge and cranky, and I'm all pissed off because it's the most essential thing in my life right now. Only an hour a day. My manila envelope is full of scraps of ideas for jokes, and some have developed into actual bits. I manage to come to an agreement after she threatens to hit my leg with a broomstick, and I smash a coffee cup against the wall. One hour a day, no other TV shows, keep the volume down.

I discover comedians I've never heard of, like Arj Barker, Todd Barry, Patrice O' Neil, Doug Stanhope, Greg Giraldo, and Maria Bamford. I study them all like Donald Trump studies Mein Kampf. Their artistry is dazzling; the pregnant pauses, word economy, the abstract ideas they find hilarity in that the rest of us would pass up. I marvel at the expansive messages they can communicate with a quick facial expression or the way they modulate their voices. How had I not realized that this is what I am meant for in life? I'd done it in the dive bars for years, entertaining people for drinks, not recognizing my talents could be lucrative if funneled properly.

One day, I walk to the sink at the cabin, testing gingerly my fucked up ankle that is mostly healed now. There is a fox outside the window in the yard, just relaxedly kicking it. I stare at him for what feels like a long time, and he won't break eye contact with me. It's not challenging or begging for food or anything. It's more hypnotizing than anything. I start tingling. Is it? Is it Kit? My dead friend Kit, come to visit me, encourage me to once again follow my dreams? He's the same skinniness as him, and there's something reminiscent in the eyes. That's a thing, right? Kitfox? I get some raw bacon out of the fridge and toss it to him, still convinced it's Kitster. Eat up, old boy. You have whatever foxes do instead of skating to get to.

North Beach is Fuckin' Cray-Cray!

Soon, I'm back on the bus to San Francisco. LA isn't my style, and the Bay Area has world-class stage time for performers that are starting out and willing to pretty much give it away until they get good enough for New York or LA. In addition to that, San Francisco has some world-class comedy clubs in The Punchline and Cobb's. I decide It's best to develop here for a year or so until I'm ready to headline the major clubs in LA. Then, perhaps I'll help reboot the Beverly Hills Cop franchise, or whatever the fuck pays a few million to get me started towards shot calling my own projects. Three years tops, and I'm filming the big ones, on *my* terms.

I arrive in North Beach and go into the St. Paul Hotel, a boarding house where the whole floor shares the bathroom. $170 bucks a week. It's ruled with an iron fist by a Russian woman named Miss Kolnikov, an emotionless lady whose vibe does the opposite of hug your soul. "No Guests!" says a sign at the *check-in* window, a window that looks down the stairwell, a stairwell that I will try to sneak girl after girl up, and fail. Had I known that this lady would dedicate her life to stopping me from getting my dick wet, I would have gone back to Craigslist, looking for a place that I could spurt to my heart's content. Instead, I will be forced into the rub and tug joint next door when I simply can't go any farther without the touch of a woman.

North Beach is a neighborhood of vice, and I'm living under the thumb of a puritanical authoritarian. It's all dangling in front of my face, but the girls all either want money or go to *my* room. It's all strippers and bridge and tunnelers after midnight. Definitely not anything you would call "A nice, local girl." Every once in a while the forces that be will toss me an English lass with a hotel room. I've learned to never get in a car with a girl and go across a bridge. I'm not trying to wake up in Turlock in a trap house again, even if she did perform a whole Cirque Du Soleil routine on top of my meat wand.

I'm going to swear off the distraction of sexual pursuit so I can focus on becoming an overnight headliner. I do get a weird blowjob my first night, though. Fuckin' North Beach is crazy, you guys! I'm walking up a strip club block on Kearny, just before Broadway, past the Hustler Club, Crazy Horse, and a sex shop where you can jack off in a booth to vintage porn for a fiver. I'm tripping out because there is a car that crashed into a power pole with bullet holes in the windshield on the corner. Bystanders think the cops killed the guy driving it for trying to escape a DUI. I expect they'll just say he went AT them, and they'll all get a few weeks paid vacation. Everyone is just casually walking by the yellow tape like its everyday shit. I'm rubbernecking to see if the body is still in there. Soon, I walk by this silver Mercedes that's parked in front of a sex shop. There are three stripper-looking chicks in there, and one says, "Hey, you want your dick sucked?" I'm taken aback for a second, but I know an opportunity when I see one. The offerer of services appears to be a skinny, Appalachian-looking girl with a cute, birdlike face.

As I walk up to the car's window, I see she is about twenty-five and wearing a bathing suit. Also in the car are two other girls, a Black one with a big ass and a tiny waist, and a racially ambiguous looking one. Asian and Black combo, maybe? Intriguing. All are dressed in stretchy spandex and showing the product. They are confident because they own the means of production. Instead of relying on a pimp, they have each other. Three chicks with knives hidden in the car, and you're in there with them in close quarters. The Johns are going to be inclined to pay up, I figure. High bustability, though. They must be new in town and haven't made their way into the many strip clubs in this two-block area. Very new in town, like, tonight new. Florida plates. Sketchy. The sketchiness excites me.

Some of these girls can do this work and live a happy life. Most can't. I decide all these things about them in the two seconds it takes me to approach their German luxury cashier's window. S-Class, for SEX baby. One flashes me a tit now that they figure I'm on the hook. I have around $160 to my name. This feels doable. After two months cooped up in a cabin with my mom and sister, I've already popped a boner at the prospect of busting my nut in one of these girl's mouths.

"How much?" I say, trying to sound as poor as possible.

"$40," she says.

Seems cheap. Are these bitches going to drug me and take my kidneys? I guess I'll just keep my eyes open and be ready to elbow them in the throat if they get squirrely. "Ok," I say before quickly being let into the middle of the back seat.

In an instant, the skinny girl is applying the condom to my dick with her mouth. My dick is already at 80 percent blood capacity, so her job is pretty straightforward. She's slurping and gulping down there within seconds. I'm trying to focus on cumming, but dudes are walking by. It's clear what is going on inside the car, and these bitches are just acting like they're at their day job at the Clinique counter. Do they just blow the cops when they get caught every weekend? This is fuckin' bizarre. I love it.

After about four minutes, the girl stops and announces, "He won't cum."

"Whoah, whoah, it's a cock, not a teakettle. I was almost there, come on," I go to put my hand on the back of her head. She swats it away.

The tone of these girls goes from sweet to all business in an instant. The Black one goes, "You want to cum? 40 more bucks."

Now I get it. These bitches are getting two or three $40 payments from each dude. Shit. I'm sitting here with smurf nuts. I try to respect sex workers, but why they gotta be all shady and shit? I do *not* do this regularly. At all. The novelty adds to the excitement. "Ok, ok, but I want it to be *you* that makes me cum," I say to the Black girl. The skinny one is fuckin' fired.

"Money, Baby."

I grab two more $20s and hand them to her limply offered open hand. She pulls her silver, shiny bottoms around to the back of her knees and plops all that juiciness on my lap, *reverse cowgirl style,* and grabs my perky cucumber. She now uses her hand across the bottom of my cock to mimic a pussy wall, smearing the top half across her meaty pussy; basically titty fucking it, but with her vag lips. My *purple onion* juts out into the air towards her belly button with each heavenly bounce. A clever method to get a guy to cum without technically being penetrated. It feels very similar. She bounces up and down in a hypnotic rhythm that brings my cock to the moment quickly. I start my shivery convulsion as the other two girls keep a lookout for cops on the block. *"Uuuuhhhhhhn!!!"*

I'm done, and as soon as it started, I'm back out on the sidewalk. The girls turn back on the sweet talk for the ten seconds it takes to get rid of me, "Cum again. *giggle, giggle.*" What a place I've come to. I knew North Beach had a reputation for vice, but this is crazy. I think I'm going to like it here.

Soon I walk into a bar called Fuse and get a drink, laughing at how crazy that just was. Nestled in at the bar with a whiskey, I start writing notes frantically, trying to figure out how to make this into a comedy bit about how I'd probably be a stripper if I was a chick since I love being on stage and I can do a footlong line of cocaine. I don't look down on these sex workers. Yeah, there was an aspect of shadiness to it, but I trust them a lot more than a banker or a priest. The whole world is a scam; all you can do is minimize your losses. $80 for a shitty, fluff-hummer before a highly decent, pussylip, titty fuck is pretty solid. Eleven pm is prime time too. It *was* a luxury vehicle, I might add. Get your money, girls.

Do I work for the Eastern European Mafia?

I have to get out of the restaurants. So I go and look for a job in the bars again. I know this dooms me to drinking every shift since drunk people are intolerable unless you are also drunk. That's the reason I tried the restaurants; it seemed more sustainable in that respect. My choices for where to work are pretty slim since I'm shit with tools, I don't drive, and I suck at computers. I have to get a job that scores tips and a job that takes advantage of my gift of gab because, let's face it, workforce wise that's my only marketable skill besides this fine-ass face. Fuck all these minimum wage level jobs working at the farmer's markets or cleaning up trash in the park. I'd love them if they paid enough, but the non-soul crushing jobs never do. That's the price of working a job you don't hate in America; living in your car. Who can make it on ten bucks a fuckin' hour? I'm trying to **come up** in The City. I gotta make twice that, at least.

I put on the magic suit Motormouth Scott scored me and walk around town with a bullshit resume I put together. It contains a bunch of extinct Santa Barbara bars and restaurants. I can't put Aqua on there. Someone in the office would say I was great on the phone to cover their asses legally, and then they'd have that little rat-faced bitch Tony call back on a payphone to tell them I'm a seditious little shit that will orchestrate uprisings. He's not wrong.

So this is my new method to fill in the blanks on my resume, out of business spots with no one to call and check. It's not enough that my friends pounded in the final coffin nails into these defunct businesses by driving away "paying" business and engaging in black market comp deals with their employees. So now, I'm parading around their corpses, Weekend at Bernie's style, in 14 point type, on the cheapest printer paper money can buy.

Not that restaurants or bars ever call to check out your resume anyway. You just have to have it to present yourself. They mostly just look you up and down and see if you don't seem mentally deficient. If you don't have drool on your shirt, they'll throw you on the floor to see if you don't run out crying by the end of the night. A resume, a clean shirt, and a smile are all you need to get your foot in the door at most places. Half the dishwashers have pockets full of cocaine or meth and are wanted in Mexico City. That's where being named Juan Gonzales comes in handy. Is it that guy, or the other million guys named that? "Thin mustache and brown hair, you say? Somewhere between four feet and six feet tall? Thanks, ma'am, we'll let you know." Background checks are basically nonexistent in restaurants. It would disqualify half the experienced applicants.

I walk into one place, and I look at the mop-headed, bored-faced bartender. I tell him, "Hi, is the manager here?" They go loping off up to the office to get the boss every time. In this suit, I look like I'm going to rent the whole place out. I see their face drop when they see I'm just looking for a shift alongside them.

I meet Ivan, the owner of this Czechoslovakian-themed bar. We have a shot of Slivovitz at the interview, and I feel like this place could be fun. This guy is a character, always looking side to side as if he has a hit out on him, leaning forward like he doesn't want anyone to hear what he's saying to me. He leans in at the end of the interview and whispers, "You. I like you. I make you floor manager. You watch these guys, make sure they don't steal. Make sure they don't get too drunk or go to the bathroom five times for, you know, nose candy break. Regular manager stuff. You make sure the girls are having fun. That's it. $20 an hour. I pay you cash every week."

"Well, I don't use computers much. Word, but not Excel," I say, uncertain.

"No, no. Only **I** see the books for this place. Don't worry about that. Are you worried about that?" Ivan says suspiciously and does one of his side-to-side looks. This dude is shady, but whatever, I'll try it out. I have to study this guy. See what he's all about. Maybe try to do him as a character on stage. I'm worried about being able to play characters as a stand-up. I'm kind of like De Niro and Pacino, where I can only play myself? I just need practice. You can't have any holes in the act.

Ivan continues, "This suit," he touches the sleeve, "you have others?

You going to work Thursday, Friday, an' Saturday. Different suit for each night, okay? Come at eight pm. Ok, I got stuff I gotta do."

He gets up and follows a guy that just walked in over to the office. Co-owner? Shady deal? The other guy looked like an Eastern European mobster. Frankly, so does Ivan. Skinny and hunched, but for a slight beer belly and a grey blazer, black shirt, no tie. He smells like a stale cigar. Rosy cheeks, light blue eyes that always look suspiciously out past the crow's feet. Christopher Walken by way of Bohemia, but with curly hair. I should be suspicious myself, but like the car blowjob, I love danger and weirdness. I can't help it. I tell myself I'm a magnet for this shit, but I also seek it out. Nobody could self-magnetize this much ridiculocity.

I show up for the weekend shifts, and it's pretty straightforward stuff. It just uses the talents I actually have, unlike every other job I've ever had. All I do is make low alcohol *kamikazes* and give them out for free to the girls, drinking the strong ones myself. Make them laugh and feel special. Guys will tell me to tell the DJ what to play, and I'll go pretend to do so, really saying, "This douchebag is watching me to make sure I tell you to play Nelly or some bullshit. Shall we drop some Nine Inch Nails on their asses?" The DJ gives the thumbs up.

When the poser gangster looks over at me in reaction to a tune that is using power drills as its rhythm section, I just shrug my shoulders at him and say, "Fuckin' union DJs, man."

This shit is great. I'm Ivan's protege. We drink shots of Slivovitz and charm everyone who doesn't try to get the music changed. Usually, it's a steady flow of R&B and the more melodic, danceable rap. Prince, Blondie, fuckin' Abba, De La Soul. You know the drill, bachelorette party shit. We have a substantial upstairs used for private events, and I'm the point man for the host or hostess. I make sure enough ribbons are flowing down the curtains, or whatever. Easy.

I'm often out front with Ivan, yelling out to the foot traffic, "Welcome to The House of Love! Girls get in free on Thursdays."

I'll follow Ivan with a, "Look at these pretty girls. You like to dance? Let me dance with you. Czech Nights loves you!"

I do go on the dance floor a few times a night to light it up in my leather-bottomed dress shoes, which allow me to glide across the slippery dance floor. My ankle up into the air above my waist, extending my elegant *one-legged chicken dance* into a sensual corkscrew spin.

The Bachelorette parties love it. I pretend to want to save future brides from making a mistake. I beg them to stay single, and they blush. Ivan watches from the side and gives me a look of approval. He even looks impressed. *Butter faced* girls are made to feel like royalty in Czech Nights. I start to practice my Ivan character and even let it flow out on the floor once I'm confident. Then, one night, Ivan catches me laying it on too thick and appears at my side. "What is that? What is that you do? You make fun of me!?"

This is the first time I've seen Ivan annoyed with me. Shit. He seems like the cool kind of guy, up until he's not, and then people die. I think quickly like I always do, "Well Ivan, the bar is called Czech Nights… so I am Czech."

Ivan looks intrigued, and then, "Yes, this is great idea! You are Czech. Why don't I think of this? Ok, you follow me around. Watch what I do."

Now I'm following Ivan around, watching his movements closely so that I can copy them. He's explaining that, while my hand gestures are pronounced enough, they're too Italian. I have to "Stop pinching the dough" and start "Motioning to those I wish to know." Also, when I finish a shot of Slivovitz, I'm not making it look delicious enough. "The crowd looks like sometimes they are not looking, but they are looking!" he explains as if he's giving CPR lessons. These details are of the utmost importance, and now I'm stuck playing the Ivan character for 20 hours a week.

After a few months, I notice Ivan is off in the office with many different people each night. I start questioning this easy job. Am I just the fall guy for when the cops finally show up? I begin to feel like the $2,000 bucks a night the register takes in on the busier nights doesn't cover the expenses that a place with this many square feet—in a *primo* part of San Francisco—should cost. I'm starting to think this place is a front. I've seen some stuff that would support this. The bar business is not exactly a place where people with clean records end up a lot of the time. It's a cash business. There's a lot of wiggle room for money laundering or drug dealing. There is a laundry list of nefarious activities you can get entangled with in the club scene. I'm guessing our books say we're making a lot more money than we actually are, and that's why I'm never supposed to go anywhere near them. I also bet Ivan has an escape hole through the sewer or something once the cops raid the place, asking, "Who's in charge?" at which time the bartender would point to me.

Once the college kids go on summer break, I decide I've gotten all I can from this place, and it's time to go back to a tipped job. $20 an hour flat fee isn't cutting it. Sorry, Ivan. My heart will always be partly Czech, but the goodbyes I offer my jobs are strictly Irish.

Popping My Stand-Up Comedy Cherry

Well. I've written and practiced my comedy for a few months, and it's time to stop pussing out. I have 25 pages of jokes, and I'm pretty sure half of them are good enough to elicit laughter from a crowd—to be honest, it's more like four pages of workable material, but that's not bad for a total rookie. It's a challenging game where everything you say has to be genius. Unless, of course, you're a hack who just regurgitates remixes of other jokes to get Pavlovian laughs from people. People who reward you for feeling like an old sweater. Familiar, cozy, and unscary. That's not what I'm trying to do. I'm finally ready after three months of non-stop obsessing about jokes. I have multiple notebooks all filled up. I've been excitedly tapping night after night at my laptop, which is atop an ironing board. I dance and rock, side to side, with the timing of the jokes as I type them. I'm dancing these motherfuckers out, barefooted, and listening to the band Ween. I'm tamping out the weed roaches right there on the ironing board, then stabbing and jabbing the premises first, then the punchlines, then the tags. *Tappety! tag! tag!*

I try to write while sitting down at Peet's Coffee, but I get so excited, imagining myself on the comedy stage, that I sweep my arms into the back of people's laptop screens. I'm spastic as I enter the character I've created, which is me, but a more hyper, drunk, younger me? A playful tormenter that lets you off the hook at the end before things get too uncomfortable. Hints of madness where the audience is anxious about what I might do next. Like back in the dive bar days when I'd get the whole bar laughing, tightening, and releasing the madness, just at the right times, using my pool stick like a conductor's wand. I'm just going to channel that. If you can get depressed alcoholics that just finished a fifty-hour work week laughing, then these college students with their whole lives in front of them should be like selling bullshit to a voter. Easy as hell.

The only time I don't vibrate as I write is when I'm staring at a sentence, trying for ten minutes to figure out how to shave a syllable out of it, making it more phonetically pleasing as it pops out my mouth. I scroll and retool these 25 pages a thousand times. They must hum like a satisfied bluesman. I finally get to the point where I feel like any more changes would damage them. I better get on stage so I can stop scrolling through it again, and again, and again.

I've been non-stop fantasizing about doing comedy in real life, but the moment is too big, like staring at the sun. Will the laugh breaks be so long that I lose my way?

I think thoughts such as these as I climb the stairs to the Luggage Store in the middle of Civic Center, San Francisco. It's one of the filthiest, most degraded City Hall areas in the nation. Suppose you live in another part of the country and become unemployable due to homelessness, injury, or drug addiction. In that case, your city just might deem you "broken" and give you a one-way Greyhound ticket to San Francisco. San Francisco's skid row starts outside the mayor's window. It's a trick to fuck the liberals, "There ya go, buddy, they like helping people over there." Then they taunt us for having shit and piss all over the streets.

I've just walked through Night of the Living Dead, but as I reach the top of the stairs, I'm giddy at the knowledge I will soon be popping my comedy cherry. I see the host sitting at a table. He is Guy Branum, a humongous, hairless, gay baby man. His permanently furrowed brow hunts—constantly—for things it doesn't approve of, like an insomniatic shark; always moving and hunting with its judgement. He is somehow effeminate *and* a dominant alpha. It's rumored he was born at a Liza Minelli concert and was passed up to the stage, umbilical cord still dragging behind him, where they finished the night out with a duet. They say Guy spit on a hedge fund manager in the front row for not taking his hat off in front of Liza.

As I begin my set, he is standing in the back of the room looking at me with his arms crossed, and after every joke, he just shakes his head *"No,"* at me.

"How about this one then?" I reattempt. "Hey, you ever have that friend that wants to leave the bar five minutes after you get there. Every hot girl in town is there, and this dude is tugging on your shoulder like there's some magic party where Prince is performing and tossing out ecstasy pills from a giant, purple salad bowl?"

Now that I say it out loud, actually, in front of people, I realize that this joke sucks. Shit. Don't look at the fat, gay baby man. I look. He's now shrugging his shoulders, like, *Yeah, we all have that friend. So what?*

I look down at my joke list on the notebook in my hand, realizing the next one is stupid too. I skip it and try my best to continue to project confidence. I stutter out instead, "If s-someone steals my identity, can I make them keep it? I got some warrants."

Now he pretends to pull his flip phone from his pocket and dial 911, so he can report that someone here has 'warrants,' which he mouths at me as I begin to get annoyed by his theatricality, *Oh, Warrants?*

Fuck it. Stop looking at the giant, gay baby and get the jokes out, dude. I start talking faster, just to run through them and analyze the voice recorder later. I'll do one about my last relationship with the lawyer.

"My girlfriend groans quite often, that 'Justin, you're only happy when you drink,' and I'm like, 'THAT'S WHY I DRINK EVERY NIGHT!!!'"

Guy gives me a look like, *Alcoholism is sad, isn't it?*

I'm shook. *Keep going. Fuck this guy. Why do you keep looking to him for his diagnosis and opinion?*

"I pretty much raised myself, so the closest thing I ever got to fatherly advice was from a cop or a park bum. He'd always be like, 'Kid, come 'ere. Do you want to know how to be real persuasive in life? Always look at people with one normal eye and one excited eye. The normal eye reassures them that everything is gonna be alright... the excited eye hints at adventure!'"

This joke, which I know is good, gets a look from Guy like he's just spotted cat puke on his cashmere sweater. His lip curls up disgustedly like he's trying to keep a pencil held between that and his nose. Jasper Redd, a beanie-wearing, skinny, Black dude with a friendly face, is from Tennessee. He's sitting in the front row paying attention, although he's just laughing at my setups, but not the punchlines. Greg Edwards is laughing at everything because he's high on some edibles or some shit, and Arthur is sitting directly in front of me and dares to write in his notebook as I perform.

I decide to do some crowd work, "Hey motherfucker? What'chu writin'? You know you could learn more about comedy by watching me than whatever is in that rookie ass notebook. Let me guess, airplane food? Girls are weird? Ok, fuckin' Seinfeld Jr."

Little do I know Arthur is already hosting at The Punchline. These were the bullied kids, and now that they have a little power? They will remember with hatred any slight they receive from someone who is supposed to be lower than them on the comedy ladder. That's the main rule in succeeding in show business, kissing ass upwards fervently, and shit downwards always. Fuck that. I'm going to fuck these fuckers up with psychology so intense it's going to make The Art of War look like a *couple's therapy* book. Try me, sluts.

Ok, next joke. I'm getting a little endorphin rush from demanding respect, "How come when you hear a guy say, 'It happens to the best of us,' it's always a guy that's obviously never been the best at shit?"

Silence. My lip starts to get sweaty.

"So I got laid off my job a while back... and I was able to get this amazing thing called 'unemployment checks,' they said as long as I inquired about work, but didn't actually *get* the job... they'd keep giving me all this free money. *Great*, I thought. I always wanted to show up to a job interview with a ghetto blaster and my weenis hangin' out!"

"What do I plan on bringing to the table here at Java Jones? Amazing blunt rolling skills! Hey Pookie, grab those Philly wraps! This motherfucker wants to play!"

This joke finally gets Guy to bring up his splayed hand to shake it side to side in a *not-too-bad* motion. Greg and Jasper both laugh at once and on the punchline. I stupidly love Guy for a second like an abused wife loves her husband for doing the dishes that one time. Even Arthur has looked up from his notebook to give me a look of, *Now, that* ***might*** *be stage-worthy*.

Ok, the "Unemployment" joke is a keeper. Shit. Fuckin' finally.

On that medium note, I get off the stage and go to the Arrow Bar on Dirty 6th Street, but not before I get a #20 from Tulan: bird's nest style crispy noodles, shrimp, pork, beef, vegetables, and an orangish gravy sauce that one must assume is 75 percent MSG. I have to soothe my soul for the beating it just took. Fuck it. I better get an "imperial roll," too.

Of course, that big, gay baby man was going to hate me. I probably resemble every guy at his high school that pushed his books out of his hands and called him a "Poopdicked-manbaby-homo." Frankly, I look very unmarginalized. That's going to be a problem with some Bay Area audience members. I don't want to have to say, "Hey, I grew up in a teepee, and I was in a group home," to alert people to my *list of oppressed people's* credentials. I'll figure it out. Looking Anglo Saxon can get a muted reaction, is all I'm saying. I look like I should have my collar flipped up; how could they know I fucked a bunch of nazis up? Have you heard of *flag words*? I'm apparently, at first glance, a *flag person*. I saw the look on some of their faces, before I even told a joke, like, "Ah, nah." That was just the white girls.

What I *do* have going for me is that I'm authentic, a good performer, and a good writer. Ultimately, I'll be fine. The audience knows if you're not legit. They can smell it. If you try to act like you get pussy, but you're a virgin? They'll know. Collectively, they know. You can hear the judgment in the quiet, right after a punchline, even if you get a little laugh after like a whooshy gavel coming down. I'm as authentic as tamales from a short-necked lady with chipmunk cheeks. My life has been so crazy I'd never had to lie. Just report the facts and my reactions to them. That's ten comedy albums right there. I just have to dig them out and ritualistically practice the craft.

So, I listen to the tape over and over again. I try to figure out how to make this stuff funnier. *Does my voice really sound like that?* Ugh. I sound like I'm squealing. I go back to the ironing board, pick out which jokes to keep in and which new ones to try out. Now that I know how insanely brilliant every sentence has to be to get even a muffled laugh, my twenty-five pages that it took me six months of obsessing over look more like twelve now. It'll look like eight by next week. Even less than that the week after.

North Beach, Our Indispensable Muse

If you don't know, North Beach in San Francisco is one of America's great neighborhoods. The Brooklyn of the West Coast—way smaller, though. It's been a representation of low culture in its highest form since the Barbary Coast days. Back in the mid-1800s, the gold rushers would come into town from the Sierra foothills with their little sacks of gold. What the whores didn't take from them, the bars in the adjoining neighborhood, Chinatown, would.

You still have to climb down into the catacombs to get to those bathrooms in the Chinatown bars to this day, at Red's and Buddha Bar. In the old days, they'd get a bunch of gold rushers up at the bar in a row, and *shwooosh*, the old Chinaman barkeep would pull the trap door and *down* to the catacombs with you! Stomp on the ground up at the bar when you go in those places; tell me it doesn't feel a bit hollow under there. I wouldn't piss off the bartender, just in case. That's where the term *Shanghaied* came from, right in those very bars. Poor bastards would wake up with no gold dust on a ship to China. After two months, they had to work on the boat to get to China *and* back, just to get off the ship back in San Francisco again, penniless and sore as shit. Rough cut, Jacob.

Then, in the decade or two before the Summer of Love, the Beatnik invasion was afoot. Guys were lined up on the street with typewriters, offering new poems of your topical choice for a dime. All the greats passed through, even Bukowski, who wasn't a Beat but was what some of them aspired to be. Burroughs, Ginsberg, Neil Cassidy, Kerouac were always around, drinking at Vesuvio's or Tosca. Laurence Ferlinghetti himself would come out and get Kerouac in from the alley in the mornings, drag him into City Lights Bookstore, feed him a pot of coffee and some toast with marmalade. Then, old Ferli would set him on the typewriter, where he'd feel more natural. You could smell his puke in the alley between Vesuvio and City Lights for so many years the neighborhood just up and named the alley after him, like, "Hey, at least it's famous puke now.

I'm in Vesuvio one day, holding court at the bar, "Another thing our high school history school books were full of shit about: America getting Hitler. You'd think General MacArthur himself cut off the mustached part of Hitler's lip as a stamp-sized war memento. Not even close. It was the Russians who took Berlin. Americans didn't get there until two days later. I hear the Russians have Adolph's skull in a cardboard box in the Kremlin, just, like, sitting on a random shelf somewhere," I take a moment to soak up the interest and fascination from the rag-tag group of barflies. They're not hooked yet. "I hear at the KGB Christmas party they take it out and all take turns sticking their dicks through the bullet holes."

I get a little laugh from one of the old Beats at the bar and decide that's as high of a note as I'm going to get from the daytime crowd around here. So I walk out into the hateful sunlight, the hangover from last night now mostly dissipated. So let's check out the bar over here at the San Francisco Brewing Company. See if the drinkers are a bit livelier.

I breathe in the history of the neighborhood, as well as some random pot smoke wafting on the wind. I head a block down towards the famous Pyramid Building. I'm soon sitting in The San Francisco Brewery, which is pretty much unchanged since it first opened 100 some years ago. Jack Dempsey, the boxer, worked the door for a stretch back in the day.

My room in the St. Paul Hotel is directly above where I sit at the bar. It's possible Mark Twain himself smoked opium in my room before coming down here and whetting his whistle; maybe grabbing a mop-handle-legged prostitute on his way back up, only to be stopped by Mrs. Kolnikov's grandma. I chuckle at the thought of that, and I stare at my notebook, trying to come up with different names for genitalia. My initial plan is to be mostly clean and then get filthy for the last few jokes to demonstrate range. Finally, I get tired of staring at the page, trying to make the words appear. I look around the room for inspirational huffs of history.

At my feet is the original 1800s urinal/spitoon along the bar, a series of paddle wheel fans that run on some sort of ancient belt, pulley system trying to push air down at me from the ceiling: big, dark wood, and a vintage piano. There are corners in this room with the original dust still stuck in them.

The bartender, a large Irish man, named Shelly, is working the bar. He knows I can use another Jameson's and comes over. I say, "Shelly, what are some different words for genitalia in Ireland?"

"I'm a bartender lad, never studied much on genetics," he says, all *sing-songy*. He sounds like a limerick reads: fast and musical. I love Irish accents, even though I only understand half the affectionate insults they bestow on me.

"No, genitalia. Dicks and pussies. I'm trying to write some dirty jokes tonight."

Shelly is game, "Ah, ya mean the Irish Inch? The Maypole? The Yogurt Spigot? The Blinding Noodle? The Rump Splitter? The Glister Pipe? Mr. Peasby?"

"That's exactly what I mean!" I say, trying to write as fast as possible—Mr. Peasby—"That's great, now do lady parts."

"The Gee? The Bosca? The Catamaran? The Slip'ry Pit of Joy? The Fanny? The Honeyed Scabbard? The Faigheann Meala? The Lavender Hill?" He seems like he's waiting for me to say, "When."

"When, Shelly." I've scribbled as fast as I can and decide I'll possibly use anything good and legible. With my recently filled rocks glass full of whiskey, I sit and wonder how America can consider itself the greatest country on earth when it has so few words for our junk compared to other countries around the globe. I must take on this task as a matter of national pride. Lewis Black can have politics, and I will be a merchant of filth. For my last few jokes... or so.

The Brainwash

The Brainwash is a cafe / restaurant / laundromat / performance space / drug swap meet / place for the homeless to take a shit in a toilet and not the sidewalk—can the Brainwash owner please get a Nobel Prize for that? His name is Jeff.

It's named the Brainwash because this is the building where the Symbionese Liberation Army brought the rich kid granddaughter of national newspaper magnate, thee William Randolph Hearst. They brought her here after they kidnapped her from her home in Berkeley. Legend says a tunnel from the basement led across the street to Julie's Supperclub, later Radius restaurant. They'd move her between the two buildings when the neighborhood got hot. Little Patty Hearst was her name, in case you forgot. I wonder if they brainwashed her so much as they partied with her. What rich kid wouldn't want to rob a bank with a perfect alibi of being brainwashed into it? I'm not saying I know that's what happened, just a possibility. Rich kids get away with everything.

Nowadays, The Brainwash, in an attempt to get some money flowing into their registers, hosts low-end techies looking for free office space. These techies face their laptops into the wall, so they don't have to see any felonies. Construction workers come in for the ten-dollar Burger of Doom, a half-pounder cooked in the grease from the tequila-soaked bacon crumbles that will eventually get piled on top with a bunch of caramelized onions.

A few gutter punks are colonizing the house couch, trying to scrounge up enough train fare to get back to Berkeley. These bedbug delivery units will snatch any partial sandwiches that anyone who isn't used to eating 1,500 calories at a time leave behind. College students come and try to study in the chaos, drinking ice coffee with enough caffeine to kill an army of laboratory mice. The cockroaches and the mice roll around fat, happy, and unmolested. Goth rocker video game designers and wannabe, dot-com startup, CEO types come here to meet venture capitalists so they can deceptively appear to be grittier like they have their finger on the pulse of the street. A tweaker gets the 'no' nod on getting the bathroom code from Mikey, an African American, bisexual, hipster, cashier. He always wears a look of slight disgust, a flannel, and a black, pegged beanie. That formerly sweet boy has been turned hard by six shifts a week at the Brainwash over the last year. The tweaker made the mistake of not hiding the blow torch and broken lightbulb full of meth in his hand. Now he'll be forced into the alley, where other tweakers he owes hits to might catch him. Them's *the breaks*, Nathan.

People who live in the area do their laundry while imbibing cheap PBR pitchers for $3.99 or snacking on world-class onion rings. In the other room, connected by a doorway from the cafe, performance stage, and table area, the two dozen laundry machines and huge, submarine window style dryers built into the far wall. They display the spinning tie-dye and work shirts in a kaleidoscopic whirl that mimics the thought patterns of the average person walking around in here. There are also some video games in this room: a truck driving game with steering wheel controls, standard Galaga, and the greatest pinball game ever, Terminator II. Unfortunately, the glass of that poor pinball machine is mostly used as a table for felony drug sales.

We are in the middle of the industrial section of San Francisco, the warehouse district, South Market, where huge indoor pot farms, sex parties, and raves happen behind the windowless brick walls of giant buildings that sprawl out to the onramps to get on the Bay Bridge. The manufacturing jobs they used to provide have been shipped to China, so now it's cheap square footage, and a lot of it, for what the fuck ever you have in mind. You'd never know there are 1,000 people sweating and on Ecstasy behind the dank, dreary walls as you skate by. Tough people live down here, too; people who are willing to risk being murdered by a gang of roving junkies for the cheaper rent. Aside from open-air drug use, it's mostly a cinder block warehouse desert down here. Near 7th and Folsom, the Brainwash is six to eight blocks from where anything good happens. Centrally located a neighborhood *away* from lots of stuff: the Mission District, Civic Center, Downtown, the ballpark, Union Square, etc. So there's that; it's only saving grace.

Ten percent of the people at Burning Man live in this neighborhood. They believe in leaving no trace in the desert but overflow the dumpsters upon their return. What a bunch of broken junk their little festival creates. It looks like someone put the Muppet Show through a wood chipper. Once a year, they go out and do drugs in the dirt and have sex with random strangers, cosplaying the hippies they avoid eye contact with the second they reenter the city to rejoin their lives as code warriors for the hottest new startup. I relish the quiet week in The City when they are gone. I fantasize about a mighty dust storm swallowing them all up and leaving the crackheads to feloniously prowl their rightful, ancestral homelands.

Historically, South Market is where the manly lumberjack gays came to live back in the day, leaving The Castro to the more delicate end of the culture. AIDS decimated a lot of the inhabitants a few decades ago, and it never bounced all the way back. We have The Stud, The Eagle, and the annual Folsom Street Festival to remind us of that heyday. It's a little Mad Maxy over here. Let's just say you have a lot of freedom to wave your freak flag. I feel like you could be stabbing a motherfucker in the ear, and if there actually were any cops, they'd just slow down their car and yell, "Knock it off!"

The Brainwash is more of an outpost than a cafe/laundromat, a *weirdo-oasis* in the middle of nothingness. It's a great melting pot of culture, and I wouldn't have it any other way. The coexistence level is off the charts. An authentic slice of the old San Francisco. I just fucking love it.

It's July of 2003, comedy open-mic night. Among the customers are about three dozen aspiring comedians, many of whom look scared because they've never left San Jose before. Tonight they have timidly ventured into the industrial area of San Francisco. This is where the greatest open-mic in the history of open-mics occurs each Thursday night—overseen by your host with the most, Mr. Sugar Nasty himself, the Godfather of Comedy, Tonnnnnny Sparks!

I'm 30 minutes early but somehow still end up 23rd on the list. Shit. I guess I'll watch these guys perform. At my first show, the performers were pretty decent. This open-mic won't be like that. By the fourth performer, I'm outside asking the other open-mikers basic questions. Where are the best open-mics? How do you get a set at The Punchline? How dirty is too dirty? These guys love that someone newer than them has shown up, and they answer in their best comedy vet impressions, "Oh, The Punchline is tough. You have to show up every Sunday for six months."

The next guy segues in a beat too fast, "If you miss a Sunday, it adds a month. If you don't kill, that's another six months. If you get drunk, that's another six months."

Another guy that seems like he might be speaking from personal experience says, "If you don't wear deodorant, it's never."

The combined nervous energy of a few dozen incels that seem to suffer from mild autism creates an outside chatter that cuts into your eardrums like razors dipped in dog shit. These guys haven't been this excited since they won that Nintendo tournament. If I realized that night after night, year after year, I would be forced to listen to these clowns telling the same jokes, over and over, trying to perfect their best ten minutes; just beating the same lame material into the wall as if the banging of it against there will finally shape it into something good? I would have walked away. Comedy attracts a lot of broken people: incels, narcissists, and lawyers.

Jasper Redd has the right idea; he's off to the side, rocking his head to the music in his headphones, smiling up into the moon. Now *he's* funny. Jasper was a janitor in Tennessee when he decided to take a shot at the stage. He's doing quite well. His slow drawl and unique insights have gotten him far enough in a year to pretty much get a set at any show he wants.

I will come to love half of these other little guys. You can't blame them for being incels—the life chooses *you*. For the first year or two, until I can start getting booked at good shows, I will be immersed with these socially awkward basement dwellers. I can't imagine how many crumpled, empty cans of Monster energy drink they have piled up around their computers.

By the time I get up, I'm drunk. I intended to start with a three-beer protective layer, but I'm loaded after a several-hour wait. Tony, a cheerful, chubby, Black man from Mississippi, begins my friendly introduction. Inside him is the hate of a million rib-kicked Pitbulls. Yet, from the outside, he's the nicest guy you've ever met. He's making his whole living from this one open-mic. It's the most popular in the entire Bay Area, an open-mic with actual customers, non-comedians, some of whom came to see the comedy and weren't annoyingly surprised by it. He announces me with a, "Now this guy is popping his comedy cherry this week, so GIVE HIM... A LOT... OF LOVE!!! Come on, PEOPLE!!! He looks like mother fuckin' Jeffery Dahmer Jr. to me, but maybe he's funny. I don't know. These white boys scare me! Give it up!"

What the fuck? I think as he goes out into the crowd, demanding they cheer for the comedy virgin of the week.

Once I get to the microphone, it's silent again. So silent. The host just told them I might be a serial killer. *Shit.* I look out at the uncaring faces. One person is just typing away at a laptop in the second row. They've briefly looked up from their screen to see if I might be worth watching. I forgot I was supposed to tell jokes. I start with the new opener I wrote yesterday. "Many pro-athletes, before a big game, will actually abstain from sex. That's funny. I held out for three weeks just before this shit."

Laughs. Actual laughs. Not many, but enough to not die.

I finish with a tag, an intermediate-level move. "Bend THAT... Beckham!"

More laughs. At this point, nothing could keep me from pursuing this. The instant adrenaline I receive removes the alcohol buzz and replaces it with a feeling that I can only put in a mental drawer called "skydive-crack hit-blowjob." My eyeballs and brain feel like they're pure electricity. I'm off to the races! A few of the following jokes work; some don't. I'm not going to lie and say I totally killed. "Unemployment Checks" and "Excited Eye" do well. I finish with a few dirty jokes:

"So Brainwash, I was watching some movie or something, and one guy says to another guy, 'I used to rape guys like you in prison,' and the other guy got mad and wanted to fight. I was like, 'Dude, just don't go to prison. Wouldn't it be worse if he said, 'I used to rape guys like you at Trader Joe's?'"

"Haha." Who says rape jokes can't be funny?

"Because that's a place you gotta go! You know? For the sweet, sweet enchiladas!"

They love it. Of course, they do. We're in a cafe that tolerates open drug use and masturbation. This is the perfect place for dirty jokes. The comics that were outside have now come in to see what is happening. Audible laughter is something foreign to half of them. Tony gives me the signal to finish. I don't want to fuck that up and overstay my welcome like I saw some other comics do.

I go into my last one, "Ladies? Don't trust when a guy tells you how long his weiner is. He's lying and measuring along the bottom, where there's a lot of *grey area*, as to where the shaft ends and the scrotum begins. A very grey, cheesy area."

The house goes nuts as I stand there, braising my soul in their love. I suck it all in like silver spray paint fumes from a paper bag.

"Never SMELL!!!—the low-numbered end of a ruler. Some guy's been grinding it into his nutsack, trying to get an extra inch. Does it say five yet?!"

I mimic the mic as my measured cock, and put a ridiculous look on my face. They laugh. When I get off stage, there is a little row of incels there to high-five me. Tony Sparks himself is like, "This is your first week? You didn't move here from Seattle?"

"Nah, man, I did the Luggage store Tuesday and listened to the tape a hundred times. I mean, I was writing for six months and studied Comedy Central stand-up shows. I had a broken leg, so I had pretty much all day. That fuckin' Mitch Hedburg is something else, huh?"

Tony shakes his head from side to side, "That don't count. You ain't born until you hit *that* stage, and you was funnier than half them comics at The Punchline. No shit!" Tony says.

"Well, thanks." I'm on top of the moon.

Hoogs, a super good comedian that I *liked* tonight, is at the door, rocking his head up and down at me, smiling. He says, "Funny stuff, new guy." This simple sentence is all it takes to send me over the moon Jasper was staring at. An excellent comic telling me I'm funny. My old antihero self reminds me I enjoy that a little too much. My new self begins to subconsciously craft excuses for loving the crowd's approval so much.

I go home to listen to this magical tape where I **almost** killed—if it weren't for half my jokes.

Wait a minute? Where did the laughs go!? I'm listening to this tape recorder, and it only has like half the laughs I remember. On top of that depressing finding, the next three sets I do before the following Thursday are terrible. I'd say I bombed, but that insinuates there was a chance to blow. There are no laughs to get here. It's the same fifteen people as every other mic in town besides the Brainwash. They look at me, dead eyes, as I drop joke after joke, which all hit the floor with a thud. My tone becomes more uncertain of itself as I go on. I probably give up on perfectly good material, thinking this process means anything. I start to feel like maybe these depressing cafe open-mics do more harm than good, killing my confidence and making me give up on material that might be at least salvageable upon tweaking.

I can see how it might be helpful to a newbie to toughen them up, but I'm already so tough Sizzler would serve me on "All you can eat" night. My skin is so thick my nerves are fucked—I'm all shaky all the time. What I need is quality stage time with a real audience. Looking at the grim faces of the other open-mikers and openers is starting to bum me out. I've got to get to next Thursday at the Brainwash!

All I have is the tape of that last set there. I deliver my jokes pretty well. The liquid courage combined with the adrenaline balanced out perfectly into a comedy speedball. Timing, delivery, material? All fluid. I'm halfway to handling the craft already due to being the *master clown* at keg parties my whole teenage years and early 20s. Back when I was dancing for my biscuits, or in this case, shots of whiskey. My natural genetic storytelling ability is Irish drunk level, but where are the laughs on this fucking tape? I swear people were laughing louder.

Well, I'll tell you where the laughs went. Handheld tape recorders have directional mics, meaning they don't pick up all the sounds in front of it. Think of a skinny V-shape shooting out from the front of the speaker on it. That's all that it picks up. We assume it's like the eyes on our heads, and it picks up almost 180 degrees, and so we point it at the mic-stand like idiots, away from the crowd. If open-mikers knew this, they'd be only half as suicidal. Instead, we all go to our rooms, listen to the sets we are convinced we did okay on, and think, *Where are the laughs?* In our saddest moments, we convince ourselves we exaggerated the laughs in our heads at the time because we have to in order to continue doing this.

For years, until we finally get a professional club recording that's plugged into the soundboard, we are convinced we suck more than we actually do as if listening to your own voice on recording over and over isn't depressing enough. *Is that my voice?*

Show an open-miker this; you'll be their hero. You might save their life.

Who's this Whiteboy Living in the Chinatown Projects?

I'm trying to develop discipline and organize my life to be one of the greats in comedy. I'm only getting shitfaced like three or four nights a week now, in addition to cutting out cocaine and swearing off women. I love you girls, but you tend to require a lot of time and won't accept being the second most significant thing in my life. At least this is how it is with the crazy bar skanks I usually end up with—who I *love,* by the way.

I'm married to the stage now. The level of obsession I instantly developed during my second set, where I did pretty good and had a real audience, is so intense that no one would want to be around it. In showbiz, you don't have relationships. There are only personal assistants and the ladder upwards with the attendant asses to kiss at each rung, getting funkier and funkier on your lips, until you reach Harvey Weinstein. I'll have to be very clever to sidestep that part, but I will be. I'll be very clever.

My life goal is singular, and even things like brushing my teeth, eating, and texting coworkers are annoying. *Is this texting thing going to stick? It's garbage! I want to hear your fuckin' voice, so I know if you're lying.*

My preoccupation is thorough. I'm almost getting run over, lost in thought. I stop and sit on bike racks, and blown-out bus stops to jot down ideas that spontaneously pop into my head. I stab at the paper. I've always written sloppily like that with my hooked, left-handed style, that, with my frequent hand shaking, my recurrent anxiety, and the excitement to get it down before my ADHD chases another butterfly down the street. People probably look at my notes, and say, "Is Charles Manson here?" But if they could decipher those notes, they'd see the genius. If Miss Hinton, my fifth-grade teacher, could have just looked beyond the smudges she'd have seen.

I can't sit down at an appointed hour and write about relationships, tuna salad, or whatever is on the predetermined writing schedule. I can't work like Seinfeld. Stuff just pops in my head, and if I don't write it down quick enough, it flutters away in the wind.

That's another secret to writing funny: pot. I'm not saying most of my best ideas come within 20 minutes of toking off a joint, but that's what I'm saying. Comedians who don't smoke weed aren't as funny, with a few exceptions.

Girls can be hilarious. Not many of them have the wherewithal to be awkwardly flirted with by two dozen incels claiming to be comics for three hours at an open-mic, all just to get five minutes on stage. That's probably why female stand-up comedians exist in numbers smaller than albinos from South Pasadena. If you do have the luck to meet the elusive female comic, just know that she is very tolerant to a level of sainthood, and therefore already deserves to headline on the weekends.

In my bid to be a weekend headliner, I've made some positive changes to accommodate my new way of life: eating better, drinking a little less, getting rid of time wasters, and now I've got a new job and place to live. I'm living in the Chinatown Projects, baby! It's the very next building over from the St. Paul Hotel, but up Pacific, on the border between North Beach and Chinatown, across from Mr. Bing's, which becomes my new place to write on cocktail napkins and 99 cent pocket notebooks. The cockblocking Mrs. Kolnikov will have to listen to me getting laid from the next building over. Revenge is a dish best-served *doggy style!*

Mr. Bing's has a remarkable triangle-shaped bar, where the bartender has more room to roam around than the customers do. The bar's interior, designed in an era when San Francisco real estate was priced low enough where you don't have to utilize every square inch like Tokyo. Bruce, the bartender, is a character. He never remembers me, but he pours stiff. You can just feel Coppola coming up with script ideas in here. History oozes from the dirty walls.

A guy I know from the bars has a friend whose mom has an apartment in poor people's housing and moved out. Marco, the gangster, decided to keep the place and rent it out to white boys at a profit. Only $500 bucks a month and a view of the whole city out the bedroom window. Epic. I just have to pay in cash on the first. None of this, "Pay by the fifth, bullshit, *the first.*" I'm living with an alcoholic dock worker named Sean, who falls in love with any girl who will smile at him, always whining to me if she doesn't call him after a few days. How do I keep ending up with guys like this?

I walk the halls of this giant cement building, and the old Chinese ladies crane their bodies around in their wheelchairs to see who this whiteboy living in the Chinatown Projects is. I'm dressed in all white because my new job is at the Cheesecake Factory. White pants, white shirt, white shoes, white boy. Maybe they think I'm an angel, finally, come to take them to heaven. Or perhaps they think I'm an orderly come to take them off to the hospice to live out their final weeks. I quickly begin writing bits about things like this, and one about how "Rude cats better not fuck around because I'm living in the Chinese projects now, and we don't take no bullshit from little motherfuckers named Fluffy. Likely to get BBQ'd around here, Fluffers!"

The Cheesecake Factory is insane during the lunch hour. And look at this fucking place. It seems like if you gave a bunch of teenagers a bunch of Adderall and paid them to design in an ancient Egyptian motif, based only on what they know about Egypt from their American high school history books. They also have to mix in random pieces from a bankrupted Trump casino. Cheaply plastered Greek columns peppering a Rococo hell. Order the cheesecake slice first so you can slather the whipped cream into your eye sockets. Leave it there for the duration if you're smart.

I've been accepted there finally as a server, and they just throw me to the wolves after my training. The architect is a fan of customer seating but not kitchen size; between noon and 12:30 pm, all 200 tables are seated, which causes a ticket machine apocalypse in the kitchen. Even the Mayans, whose ancestors lived on *ayahuasca* and human flesh, get looks of fear in their eyes as the thin, perforated paper shoots out until the string ends in a pile on the floor. Guys are just making the dishes that are supposed to come out of their station as fast as they can, not even looking at the tickets, as the waiters come to pluck them from the pass. There's only room for 12 cooks back there—and they need 30! You can hear the urgency and stress in the meshed chatter of a million tension-filled voices from the kitchen and then out onto the floor, bargaining, screaming, violently demanding to have their needs filled first. "I neeeed bread." a lady whines, while the table next to her yells, "Hey, **we** were seated first!"

One lady is pulling on my arm, trying to get me to move her to a section without 'so many kids.' *Fuck, lady.* I'd love to get her out of my life, but she already ordered. I'd have to run to the kitchen and sharpie the new table number on, then transfer the table to their new server.

Ain't nobody got time for that shit. I can't yell at her, "This is a cake-based corporation, you dumb slut! Every child's birthday from The Golden Gate Bridge to Daly City takes place in here! Look over there. Kids! Now look over there. More fuckin' kids! I have enough birthday candles in the back I could wax every * in Greece you fucking pilled-up bag of whining, marmoset shit!" Management at the Cheesecake Factory frowns on that sort of honesty. If you can work at the Cheesecake Factory for a year and not smile when children fall and get hurt, you're a fucking saint. At least you're a better person than me, which, admittedly, isn't impossible.

Meanwhile, the kitchen is traumatized. Lady's are getting snapped toothpicks in their salads—even glass. The newest manager is in charge of table apologies and comps at all the tables. He will age ten years by the end of the holidays.

At the end of the rush, you can see enough food dying in the window to feed the Macedonian army. It never found a ticket to call home and will now be thrown out rather than feed the workers. A corporate rule, not to create a culture where we reward mistakes. That is unless I pretend to have a legitimate ticket. I stack up a pizza, a BBQ Chicken Ranch Sandwich, and a Bang Bang Chicken and Shrimp on one arm, pretending to stare at an old ticket I just plucked from my apron pocket.

I take it to The Cave, a dark room at the edge of the dining area where all the filth from service goes until after the rush. It's a habitat where roaches not only thrive, they evolve into even more unkillable creatures. Whatever the bug shit they use here is only killing us and seems to only anger the roaches. We fill sodas, make ice teas, and grab condiments for the tables in here. Also, we gossip about the tables. We wish them decapitation for the slightest offense and laugh about it. A good gallows sense of humor is required to survive in this madness. It's not personal; we just have to fantasize about the deaths of our oppressors to get through our shifts.

The Cave is also where the girls come after the rush to see what I've stolen to feed them after running around at marathon speed for four hours. "Oh, you got my pizza," says Amanda, the hot Native American girl. Totally gonna bang. She puts in her order to me around two pm.

The Cheesecake Factory can't possibly handle the number of tables it has during the rushes, but it tries anyway due to its corporate structure design. That's its shtick, "We offer everything and a shit ton of it, instantly."

Look at the goddamned menu. It's a phone book. Randomly associate 12 ingredients; it's a menu item at the Cheesecake Factory.

This all makes it impossible for us employees to arrange all the variables into the gourmet symphony that Union Square diners have come to expect, no, demand, since the first gold miners could afford a Hangtown Fry.

This uneven expectation vs. reality situation results in there always being 12 angry men and even more angry women in the establishment. Us servers are the face of the company, so they abuse us. They won't have Yelp to complain on for another year, but they **feel** it coming. These clammy-lipped, wannabe foodies can't wait to get all fuckin' *Siskel and Ebert* on the chefs with this fledgling new internet thingy, which, it is predicted, will soon be able to fling hate even farther than Rush Limbaugh's radio shows. Everybody will be a pseudo-expert on anything they please and will soon be given a chance to single-handedly bring down a business for having an off day. But they will have to wait for that until next year. For now, they have to get in all their digs before leaving the restaurant. It never ceases to amaze me how fairly decent people in most other parts of their lives turn into human garbage the second a restaurant hostess greets them.

I imagine the customers to be angry hecklers at a comedy club, and in turn, I destroy them with boomerang insults in my mind. So much hate, just to get a free avocado spring roll. Destroying them in my brain is one of the only forms of fun that isn't forbidden in the hefty employee manual that I was presented with after five days of training. On day six, I finally passed some college-style exams about the recipe ingredients, food safety, and steps of service. I'm then brought into the office to meet the GM for a minute and a half, where I'm given a congratulatory welcome wagon speech in the cookie-cutterest fashion you could imagine. Also, we are asked to sign a non-disclosure agreement that forbids us from spilling the big company secret: that the Cheesecake Factory has a team of scientists working around the clock to keep the world record for fitting the most sugar, fat, and salt into a single fork bite. Also, the portions are so big the French tourist families that have made the mistake of ordering an entire entree per person look shocked, as the plates are dropped in front of them with an ear-piercing porcelain *tink!*

The Cheesecake Factory has a reputation that all you have to do is complain about any little thing, and you get free shit. As crazy as it is during the lunch rush? Of course, they are going to fuck up at least one thing at every single table. That poor new manager, who just roves around the restaurant like the Oprah of hamburgers, "You get a free hamburger! And YOU get a free hamburger!" You'd think that he wouldn't have such a hard time with that, but they still hate him, even after he gives them the free food. They're angling for a gift certificate to come to get more fucked up food they can complain about in an endless cycle. Chislers and con artists come in here with their eyes squinting suspiciously, trying to get a free Chicken Madeira because the server didn't put enough lemonade in their Arnold Palmer.

This place sucks, AND we're all dressed in white. After Saturday's lunch shift, we look like a tie-dyed salmonella experiment. Off to the laundromat and to check Craigslist for anything besides a service industry job. There happens to be a lot of jobs available for people without college degrees in The City. All of them minimum wage or barely above. Shit.

The Punchline Comedy Club

In my second week of comedy, I go where they **all** say you have to go if you're serious about being a stand-up comedian in Northern California, The Punchline Comedy Club—the place Dave Chapelle calls "The best comedy club in America." When I get inside; low ceilings, only about 120 seats, a long bar along the back of the room where all the comics sit and drink two-dollar drinks. The comics most likely to get hired drink soda with lime. These fuckin' two-dollar drinks. Anything you want, it's like a trap. This business is connected to booze. I'm so fucked.

Multidirectional speakers allow you to continue hearing the comic even through laughter—the cocktail waitresses wading through the tables with loaded trays. The opener, a guy I saw eat it at the Brainwash three days ago with this same material, is now doing medium well with it. He smiles and soaks it all in. For a moment, just a little moment, the hole in his heart where his father's approval should have gone gets filled. The audience isn't a group of college students studying for finals that forgot it was comedy night at the cafe with the crappy coffee. These people came to laugh. The comics don't have to win them over from a starting point of annoyance or possibly hatred.

I can't get over the intimacy of the place. Jake Johanssen, a dynamic LA headliner, is just slaying these people. He stayed an extra night from his weekend shows to do Sunday. Most guys get on a plane back to LA on Sunday morning. This guy is a class act and will stay and talk with the comics for an hour after the show. Funny as shit, too. This place is incredible.

The last thing a real comic, who does it for the soul of it, wants to perform in is some mega-venue where you have to squint to see the back of the room. You want something more resembling a campfire, a personal conversation with a group of new friends, intelligent ones, which San Francisco has in spades. It's a little judgy if they disagree with your politics, but it's good training to get on PG—politically correct—network television, which is supposedly what we comics are supposed to want most in life. *Fuck that. I'm going straight to film. These guys can divvy up the sitcoms.*

The club has a reputation for churning out uncontroversial comics who know how to hit all the right prescheduled notes. You can count on Hollywood scouts being in the audience on the weekends, looking for local talent. This year Al Madrigal is the hottest commodity the club has produced. He will end up achieving an Eric Roberts level of fame. You'll recognize his face, but you won't know from where. Before that, it was Arj Barker; next, it will be Jasper Redd—who seems to find the inner sanctums of showbiz a bit disenchanting and disappears into obscurity. It's a shame because he's a great dude, which may have been the issue. But don't worry, here comes Kamau Bell and Ali Wong to put a platinum finish on the club's rep as a hotbed for marketable talent! That's a ways off, though. When I first show up, it's Al Madrigal everyone looks to as the example of, *local boy makes good*. He's proof that it could happen to us: a Tom Skerrit level of fame.

It's all very exciting, and you can feel the energy palpable in that back row of comics, who can't believe they just get to come in here for free—which is good because they don't have any money—and see all the best comics alive for free. Some of the local comics are lucky enough to have snagged a guest set, and you can see their lips quiver on the rims of their club sodas with lime, right before the host calls them up to do their absolute best seven minutes.

For headliners with a soul, the real goal is just to do stand-up. The TV fame is just to fill venues around the country on name recognition and not have to spend your whole day helping the club promote a medium-attended show. You just show up on Thursday morning, go to the local morning radio show, fuck around with those overly peppy idiots, and you walk around town drinking ice coffee and retooling the new bits in your brain. Then, you do the Thursday night show and kill because they all know you as the wacky neighbor on that sitcom. You wonder, but not too hard, if they're laughing at your jokes or the character they remember from their TV. You end up deciding it's the jokes. Who's going to call you a liar, one of the other comics? You'd have them blackballed.

After 60 to 75 minutes of that—unless you're Chapelle, who might keep you there until he's smoked three packs of Marlboro Reds—you go to the green room and let the openers kiss your ass for a few minutes, you go out and bum a smoke off the cutest girl in the smoking area, and you collect your blow jobs. Not a bad life, huh? You just have to make sure and get a Carson Daly Show appearance from time to time, and then you just go out and make people laugh a few nights a week, buy a house in Topanga Canyon and call it a life.

The American Dream, right? Well, the competition for that is about 100 to one in this place, and as you can imagine, the high school games are pretty thick with these nerds. Many of these guys got bullied in high school by guys that look like me, and they can't wait for a chance at payback; to become their high school bullies and surpass them. Do you think a woman scorned is the worst thing you ever saw? Try a nerd with power. These comics take one look at me and think, *Ah, we gotta get rid of this dude, he's going to make us look even goofier in comparison! I heard he might be funny too. Look at his skin; he's beautiful!*

Usually, I'd laugh at this—welcome it, even. I've always fed off of the haters and usually defeated them. No great things are ever gotten without a good contest. The problem is that some of these guys have a leg up on me already. They aren't so much competitive colleagues in a meritocracy, as they've gotten into the booker's mind, a young, redheaded woman named Molly, who *does* kind of look like if Molly Ringwald starred in a movie about The Summer of Love. Regular lips, though, not all lemon puckered. She is the same age as the mid-level comics who have gotten on Comedy Central once or twice, but they're still kind of nobodies in the business. So they need her—they need her *real* bad. I think she sees through it, but maybe she figures it's nice to keep them as a buffer between her and the new comics, many of whom have a bit of a school shooter vibe. These mid-level, one TV credit-having guys are the ones you gotta watch out for; they're on the ladder, but their position is not dried in cement yet. Instead of writing compelling material, their method to stay there is to just kick at anything beneath them.

This 27-year-old woman with Dave Matthews lyrics tattooed on her forearm is somehow a potential kingmaker in show business. You can guarantee *that* ass is getting kissed. Her mind is being plied with psychological ruses that even Machiavelli would say are going too far. The Prince has nothing on the brainwashing techniques employed by a *nobody comic* with a TV credit. Being famous is a crazier addiction than dope, especially for these nerds who never got over their dad's disappointment in their lack of athletic ability. These guys are **pumped** to get famous. And they're best fuckin' friends with the booker. The only booker in Northern California that can get you on TV. Can anybody say conflict of interest? *How the fuck am I going to crack this nut?*

The show ends, and I'm on the side of The Punchline where everyone smokes pot and excitedly talks about how to break into show business. I'm there with all the other open-mikers who wouldn't yet dare try to mingle or network by the front door or—jesus christ—walk into the green room.

Sirof, who started comedy two weeks ago as well, makes a play to be our leader. He's married to a hot girl named Sherry, also a comic as of two weeks ago. This proves Sirof has had sex with a pretty girl, so he has instant support among the ranks of white, incel, open-mikers. This demographic covers about half of the aspiring comics in the Bay Area. He stands before us, letting out a giant weed cloud from a pipe he didn't pack, skinny as a rail, Star Wars tattoos on his forearms, with a giant hawk nose, and Clark Kent glasses. Kind of like a Jewy Patrick Dempsey. He doesn't talk how he looks, though. He has the confidence and demeanor of a drill sergeant, "Okay, Fuckos! Most of you aren't going to make it, and I wish you knew who you were so that you could leave right now, and I'd never have to look at your face again. To the rest of you, if you want to make it in this business, this is what you're going to have to do..."

The incels edge closer; I go home to type jokes on top of my ironing board.

Well, if it Isn't Francis Ford Coppola Himself

Well, the best way I see to make myself useful in comedy is to get a popular underground comedy show of my own. Some of the other comics have shows, and it seems like an excellent way to get booked consistently. I'll call mine "Highly Disgruntled." It will feature the edgier comedians and will be low-lit, grungy, and subterranean. A bit of grit to contrast this sea of safe little Seinfelds. A show in the spirit of Carlin, Bukowski, and Lenny Bruce. I was never going to be a safe and sanitized comic, let's face it. I don't need a joke to be dirty or extreme to write it down, but it sure don't hurt. I refuse to censor myself. Fuck the networks. I look at South Park and Family Guy as examples of what you can get away with on TV, should I later decide that's a direction I want to take. Just animate that shit, and for some reason, it doesn't get banned.

These guys at The Punchline are a little too cheesy and PG for me. They can have that part of the market. I have to be able to get a little bit raw. It's my nature; it's where I come from; I don't know anything else. The public wants it, so fuck what the bookers and executives say. I'll slash through my own jungle.

I live in North Beach, where Lenny Bruce was arrested on obscenity charges for doing his act in the early 60s. Also, down the street is The Purple Onion, where stand-up comedy developed as a new form of entertainment from its early vaudevillian roots to just a man or a woman up there with only their soul to bare. Some of the greatest started grinding themselves into brilliance there. Richard Pryor, Phyllis Diller, Lenny Bruce. The Smothers Brothers had an album named after the place. Maya Angelou was a burlesque dancer there. North Beach drips with the history of not just stories but their telling. Robin Williams or Bobby Slayton could appear on the sidewalk in front of you any minute.

As I hit the sidewalks to look for a potential venue, here comes old Francis Ford Coppola himself, walking by me on his way to his offices on Kearny and Columbus. "Hi, Francis," I say, trying to be cool. He doffs his cap, and I take it as a sign of good luck for my search up past Vesuvio. *Of course,* my comedy room will be in North Beach. It's going to be so good Lenny's ghost is going to fuckin' haunt it.

I go up and walk around Washington Square, letting my good mood blossom further. I look over at the big Catholic Church at the edge of the grassy lawned park. It's funny that Joe Dimaggio and Marilyn Monroe had their wedding pictures taken on the steps right there, but they had to do the actual ceremony at city hall. It seems the priest inside wouldn't let them get married **in** the church. It seems the church's view was that Marilyn was a harlot and so shouldn't be allowed to have the pope's precious blessing. Then, after delivering the bad news, the priest went and raped a choir boy—what a world. Never trust a man in a robe, an apron, but not a robe.

Up on 333 Columbus, across the street from The Condor where Carol Doda's tits brought her along into fame, is a girl that looks like a red-haired Betty Boop, readying a brand new restaurant. For lack of a better title, she's calling it 333 Columbus. She seems super excited the moment I bring up the possibility of a comedy show at her business. "Yeah! Let's do it downstairs! Come on, and I'll show you."

I follow her, not believing it could be this easy. Fuckin' Francis, man. Fucker's good luck. Next time I'll rub his Buddha belly!

We get down there, and it looks terrific. Small round tables where you can sit the dining couples. A bar. I just need a milk crate-sized stage. The place is so small we wouldn't even need a microphone. Twenty-five people would make the area look packed. A perfect starting point for me to begin launching myself into stardom. It's like a little mini-Purple Onion down here. And on the very same street!

I'm at Kinkos making comedy flyers for my very first comedy show. I only have about ten minutes of workable material so far, so I headline some more experienced comics that I'd liked from around the open-mics and other shows. Within a month, I've seen 40 comedy shows and open-mics and performed at twenty of the open-mics. The Bay Area is an amazing incubator for emerging talent. Of course, you have to perform for peanuts, but I can't imagine a better place to be for a beginner. Once you've gotten as good as you're going to get, you move to LA or New York, but for someone developing, this is it.

I've selected Miguel Fierro to headline my first show. He's like a West Coast Dave Attel but with more anger. A depressive, sweet, yet rage-filled guy that loves to scream to you all about it.

I'm out all day passing out flyers to the tourists from Montgomery Street, all the way up to Fisherman's Wharf. I'm hustling tourists down the stairs, even up until I go on myself. It's packed. All the seats are full, plus a row of people along the back wall. They're laughing—my proudest moment. The plan is for me to go on and do okay, and we get up the headliner after about ten other comics have performed. This is a showcase. Traditional club shows are only three comics. Showcases are designed with more comics doing shorter spots because most of us newer comics only have five to ten minutes of non-shitty material anyway. Also, if each of those ten comics gets two of their roommates to come, we only have to rely on flyers to bring in twenty more customers, and you have a rocking show.

We look in awe at the headliners who can do an hour plus and finally get chased off by a flashlight beam being waved at them from the back of the room like a sweeping broom. "Okay, ten more minutes," they say, addicted to the adoration of the crowd like its crack. Most of us rookies don't fear running the light. We're glad to see it because we only have one joke left before our closer. If a guy sucks, you're not stuck with them for too long. If a guy is killing, maybe you don't give him the light for a while.

The Punchline comics have heard about the show and have come sniffing around for sets. First, here comes Kamau Bell. He sees the room is full and nods his approval at me. The fact he wants me to trot over and offer him a ten-minute set in the gravy part of the night makes me not do it. *Play hard to get. Fuck 'im.* Little do I know, when he leaves without getting a set, a permanent mini-grudge is set in motion.

Next is Arj Barker. Now, this fucker is getting a set. He's a local comic who has a half-hour Comedy Central Presents episode. I saw that special twice when my leg was broken. He is hilarious. I give him a set right before Miguel. I can't believe my very first comedy show features Arj fucking Barker, the headliner that would support and encourage me, while most of the other less established comics would shit on me for years. Shit downwards, always. It could be *their* job you're after. Hobble them however you can is how they figure it. I *will* take your stage time too if I *can,* motherfuckers.

I'm up there, doing some shitty host work. I'm just not a good surface scraper, like, "Hey, where do you work?" and then try to make that funny type of guy. That's what you need to be a good host. Sirof is great at that shit, and I'm a little jealous because a good local host can get on amazing shows right out of the gate. He's making them feel jolly, and I'm all, "Any cops in the audience? I have a question: Do you ever actually ever protect or serve anyone, or do you just exist to harass people who are already struggling with poverty? Because you're a fucking bully who has to attack people weaker than you and would never have the courage to take off your weapon belt and fight me like a real man?"

The English tourists in the audience are looking at me like, *Your cops have so many weapons they have a belt for them?*

"Okay, I haven't been tasered, so the coast is clear. So who wants to buy some fuckin' drugs?! Okay, enough of my bullshit, let's bring up one of my comedy heroes, Arj Barker!"

Arj comes up, shakes my hand, and seems like he means it when he says, "Good job," and starts performing in MY room! I'm sure this is just the good luck charm it will need. Arj opens with:

"So I quit smoking. I feel healthy, and I'm not tired. I didn't do it for health reasons, though. I quit because I'm tired of bad news about cigarettes. That's all you ever hear. Even if they discover something good, they don't publicize it. Like the FACT... that smoking seriously reduces the risk... of jogging."

"Hoidy har," goes a blotchy-faced tourist lady with an unlit cigarette in her fingers, tapping her knee nervously as this subject brought up a pressing concern of her needing to go outside and smoke. She probably hates California so far.

"They don't tell you that. It's always the bad news like they just found out that the Camel on the pack isn't really a camel. It's actually a horse, with a big old tumor growing out of its back."

There she goes again. She's going to light that fucker. I know it.

"I know it's sad, but at least that explains why it's always out in the desert by itself," now he goes into an Indian accent for some reason, "I tell you we cannot afford chemotherapy, put that beast *out* in the desert. And take me back to India; this is Egypt, I tell you. I don't belong here! You are using the wrong accent for this joke."

They can't resist his natural charm. Arj could read a vacuum cleaner manual and get laughs. He does a few more and gets off and thanks me. It's crazy how gracious some comics turn out to be and how dickish other ones are—it seems like a two-gear business.

I bring up the final performer, "So, it's time to bring up the headliner, my favorite local comedian, Miguel Fierro!"

Miguel comes up, looking calm and collected, "Hey folks, I thank you for coming, you guys are like family to me, and I gotta tell you I'm going through a little bit of a breakup." He adjusts his glasses and gets to shaking his head as the sympathetic women in the crowd go, "Awwww."

"Thank you, thank you. She had like a funny name, I know, I know, you're like, 'Gee Miguel, you mean like haha funny, or this dick tastes funny, funny?' but that's not the point."

"Hahahaha," they go.

"That's not the point. The point is that when you go through a breakup, people are always trying to give you advice, right, like they think they know what's best for you. It's like, I don't always want your advice. Like my Uncle Federico, he's all—*old Italian man accent*—'Miguel, women are like busses, you know? You missa one, try fucking a man.' What?"

Now they're coming alive.

"Uncle Federico? Please, get off. This massage is **starting** to hurt!"

After the show, all the comics are appreciative and excited about the room. The owner loves it! The chef, however, does not, this big, bald, Harley riding, recent prison releasee. He's all, "You only sold five dinner entrees. So now all those people are leaving to go eat somewhere else."

"Well shit, chef, they were drinkin' at least."

"I'm a cook, not a bartender. *And* I'm part owner. So…"

I was wondering what the rub was going to be. Little Betty Boop Jr. is just looking away now. I guess she's only got half power in this place, and I'm just now finding out. These fuckin' chefs, man. Never happy. "Okay, Chef, I'll have the hosts tell them food purchase is required. I'll put it on the flyers too. Sorry."

He accepts with a lip purse and a grunt. It's a done deal. The shows will continue. I paid the headliner fifty and made $100 for myself off the door. Next week we'll headline Brent Weinbach, a weird little freak who I love.

I'll Let You in Free

I have a weekly room in North Beach on a weekend night. This is fucking awesome. The offers to trade sets haven't exactly started rolling in yet for some reason. It's too soon, maybe? They haven't heard about it yet? I've got to get some more exciting gigs. These weekday cafe open-mics are killing my soul. Even if I could get three good gigs a week, I could be happy. I'll still do the shitty cafe gigs, but I need that Thursday, Friday, and Saturday trifecta, where there's a real audience that's excited to see comedy. I just want to look out and see excited and expectant faces instead of the haters at the Java Source.

Friday is my show in North Beach, and the Brainwash is on Thursday. I need a regular Saturday gig, so I go to the Mock Cafe on Valencia Street in The Mission. Plenty of foot traffic, but it's empty inside. What gives? All the bookers are doing to promote the show is a cheap ad in the back of The Guardian, where there are tons of other cheap shows competing with you. The slightest effort possible.

Meanwhile, hundreds of people walk by on their way to the dive bars that infest the immediate area. You got The Makeout Room, The Elbow Room, and The Continental Club, all within a few blocks. How is this room failing? I ask the booker if I can just let some people in for free to fill seats. He looks at me as if I'm asking to attempt nuclear fission with playdough and popsicle sticks. He snorts and says, "Sure," doubtful I'll be able to get even one wandering couple with no plans.

Next thing you know, I'm outside going up to the meandering college students, "Hey, you guys. I had a reservation back out, and I have a few rows in the back open. Our comics have been on Comedy Central and worked all the big clubs—I just want the headliner to have an audience." And then, those magic words every broke college student likes to hear, "I'll let you in free,"—works like magic. I have these kids filing in behind me like I'm the Pied Piper. And they laugh because they think they got in free due to a last-minute snafu. They feel like they are enjoying something of value.

These free showcases at the dive bars, where you surprise the regulars with terrible comedy, are mostly garbage. You have to charge five bucks or something. Or make someone think they got off easy by not paying, "Don't tell anyone. Shhh." I know this instinctively from my weed dealing days: you give someone something free with no strings attached? They figure you're a sucker that must need to buy a friend. Give them a deal; you still retain their respect. An audience that doesn't respect the show doesn't laugh as much. They might even heckle. I can't believe these comics have been given the keys to venues, and they can't even figure out some rudimentary basics like this. I can see that my talents are going to be quite useful indeed. I just need to be more patient. It's so hard, though, knowing what getting laughs is like and not getting booked at those shows. At the end of the show, the crowd files out. I never asked for a set. The bookers try to act like all those people were on their way in any way. It's funny that they are trying to act like they have the power card here. *Okay, we'll see.*

I show up the following Saturday and watch them wallow in emptiness and despair for about half a show. The six audience members, all awkward with the pressure of keeping these comics not suicidal by laughing at medium funny stuff delivered in a hipstery monotone that could excite no one, much less naturally drive them to laughter. The booker finally looks at me like, *Okay, see if you can do it again.*

I call his look and raise him a *Motherfucker. I grew up in the streets hustlin', watch this shit.*

I go out and do it again. None of the comedians have been on Comedy Central; they've been on the bus. These college kids don't need to know that. I said **our comics** have been on Comedy Central. I didn't say these **particular** comics. I mean, I'm technically not lying to them. Big-name comics crash the little shows all the time in San Francisco.

At any rate, the audience is in here laughing, and before, they weren't. I look at the booker, Tim, a surfer-looking dude that Guy Branum likes to introduce by saying, "This next comic is quite handsome, which doesn't make him a comic; it makes him an actor." I look at Tim point-blank and say, "Well, can I get a set then?"

He looks like he just got a weird bite of liverwurst and says, "Ok, I guess. Tight five, I'll give you the light at four."

Fuckin' sweet!

"You're up next," he says and motions the host over to tell him there's a last-second guest set.

I'm standing in the back of the 30 seat theatre, and I feel like it's the Apollo. I'm bouncing side to side off each foot like a boxer confined to his corner. I'm like Mike Tyson, ready to bite this audience's fuckin' ear off! With punchlines. I'm going to bite their ears off with hilarity. I have a weird urge to take off my shoes and my shirt. Here comes my intro, "This next comic is new to the game, but I saw him get a few laughs last week. Unfortunately, we were at a laundromat."

The audience laughs at my lack of performer experience. *What the fuck?* I go up and shoulder-check him slightly as he passes.

I walk onto the stage and smile, "He's correct, you guys. He saw me get some laughs at a laundromat last week, and I saw him bomb at the big-time comedy club the very next night." It gets a decent laugh, and I've dug myself out of the little hole the host made for me. "Hey, next time you see me at the laundromat, we can work on your punchlines while you fold my fuckin' boxers."

Another little laugh. They get the point. I'm *not* a little bitch. I didn't need to add that last part. *Don't go to the dark side. Respond, but don't escalate,* I think, just like the old keg party roast battles.

The host shrugs his shoulders in the back of the room like he's not impressed that I dealt with the situation appropriately. If I hadn't addressed the insult and plundered into the jokes, it would have made me look like a rookie. They would have turned frigid. Some of them are looking at me like, *Isn't this the guy that hustled us in here?* I quickly launch into my first joke, "The United States recently came in 13th place in a world happiness study. I was like, 'What!? You mean there are 12 other countries we haven't squeezed the joy out of yet?'"

Decent laugh. Nice! My happy chemicals begin to secrete.

"Screw you, Iceland! Number four on the list. How happy you gonna be when I come over there and eat Bjork, with a speeeork?"

A lighter laugh. I'm going in the wrong direction. The host is looking too happy. Did I start too weird? Okay, think quick. There is a little stairway to the right of the stage that 75 percent of the audience can't see due to an oddly placed support pillar in the middle of the room.

"I'm sorry about the awkward start, you guys. I'm just a weirdo, I guess. Hmmm. Okay, let's start over." I step to the side of the stage as if I'm going just to walk back on. Instead, I run quietly halfway up the stairway and jump over the rail, appearing to drop through the ceiling to everyone but the front row. I slam down onto the stage, "Heeeeeere's Justy!!!" I scream.

Maybe I just hadn't started weird enough. "Hey! Do you guys want to know why Jenny broke up with me? She said she didn't like that there had to be an audience when we was doin' the wild thing! I was like 'I told you, when I brought you to this park, that I **liiiive** HERE!!!'"

They laugh because it now seems I may live in a park for reals. I've gone insano.

"We had a little cardboard partition! Until you leaned into it and rolled down Hippie Hill into the drum circle! You said on Myspace you weren't high maintenance, JENNY!!!"

They go nuts. A spastic freak was what they needed to wake up in this sleepy joint.

I finish my set and go in the back to do a shot from the half-pint of Jameson in my back pocket. I sit there in the dark and inhale my victory. The host goes up and gets zero on an attempt at a joke. His credibility is shot. The next guy he brings up drones on in a poorly received monotone bit about how dating is hard. Fuckin' hacks.

I leave, satisfied and happy. I will return every Saturday for my guaranteed set, provided I help fill the room up. Club regulars seem mystified that I've rooted my way into a non-open-mic so quickly. They seem unhappy about it. Haha. Just wait motherfuckers.

Comedy at a Punk Show? Fuck No!

Joanne found out I do comedy and she invited me to do a few jokes in between bands at one of the punk shows she produces. I show up at the legendary punk venue, Thee Parkside, in San Francisco, and this place is off the hook. It's like the Red Barn in my hometown of Isla Vista, except everyone is 20 years older, and there's a bar. I haven't seen a swirling punk rock pit in a while. I realize I will have to turn up the juice in here if there's any hope of making this work.

Joanne introduces me to the crowd, and I'm up there, staring out into a choppy sea of indifference and hate. Kind of like a dive bar show, but worse. There's a threat to my safety lingering in the air. Here's an idea: most punk rockers hate comedians because we make fun of all the shit they feel angsted by. That is not something I considered when I told Joanne, "Why not? That sounds fun."

I feel a pit in my stomach start to develop as I launch into my first joke. In my best punk rock front man voice, I yell, "The government scientists want us to stop taking ecstasy, you guys! Because they injected some into some monkeys, and a few hours later the monkeys got a little bit fuckin' depressed. No shit! I guess when you go from 'I'm a furry rave puppet!!!' to, 'I'm a caged lab monkey, and tomorrow is electrode on the brain day!' you get a little down in the fuckin' dumps."

Silence. Hateful looks.

"What's next, Thee Parkside?! Are they going to give some heroin to some fuckin' rabbits?! And a few hours later, the rabbits are going to be all, 'Come on, Mom, give me $20!! It's for carrot cake, Mom!!' I wrap the mic cord around my elbow a few times like I'm tying off for a dose of toxic brown tar. 'I'm your son! We have the same ears, Mom!'"

The crowd full of former heroin addicts are more sure of their hatred now. So they start screaming, "Get the fuck off the stage!!"

"Where's the band?!"

"My brother died from heroin!! Fuck you!!!"

These punkers aren't like the ones I grew with in Southern California. These guys are all socially conscious and voting and shit. We were like, "Vote with a bullet! Fuck the system!" These guys are all, "You don't have to vote for the politicians, but at least vote on the measures!"

What the fuck? Is it because we're all older now, and many had second thoughts on our initial methods? Or are Bay Area punks different? I mean, these are the guys that beat up Jello Biafra at Gilman Street for NOT BEING JELLO BIAFRA ENOUGH!

They look at me, contemplating if I'm gonna get *Jello-ed* by the whole crowd at once or not.

I plunder on, "Hey, you ever start fucking a girl so stupid you figure it must be illegal?!!"

Next thing you know, there's a skinhead on stage with his dick out, pouring beer from a can of Olympia onto his greyish wiener.

There's a second stage mic for the backup singer that a girl with half a dozen face piercings has grabbed. She says into it, "**I** was that girl. Fuck this guy! Somebody fuckin' beat his ass!"

Now, in my first year of comedy, I've faced down some tough audiences, even feared for my safety a few times, but if I go on for a third joke, I might die today. Especially if I yell my rebuke of them, something like, "Awwww, did you burnouts forget what punk is?! That's right motherfuckers! I'm way more punk than you! Suck it! Which one of you fuckers has skipped a Nazi on his back across the floor of a pit before?! Yeah, that's what I thought. My friends ODd too, and I can guaran-fuckin'-tee you that some of them are laughing at that first joke from heaven. That's right fuckers! Punkers go to HEAVEN!!! It's not boring like the bible says. Heaven is awesome! And full of punkers!!"

They may like it. Maybe I would turn the tide and win these pierced Advil

addicts over. We'll never know because the other option is death in the parking lot. They seem set to drag me out there and gouge at me with their spiked belts and slash at me with their switchblades until I look like a rare hamburger with a bottle of ketchup squirted on it. So I go with, survive.

And that's the story of why I try not to mix comedy with music shows anymore. 'Try.' Some new asshole always re-talks me into it every few years, but whatever, a gig's a gig.

Brent Weinbach

During my first year of comedy, where I would consider myself an open-miker, I am blessed to see many comedy styles displayed in their highest forms. These impressive practitioners of hilarity, these genius entertainers drop punchlines with the deftness of a Dickensian pickpocket. I try and pick the genres I will blend in with my spontaneous instincts to eventually develop my shtick. My individual flavor that a slew of new open-mikers will, for years to come, be silently chastised for too much trying to copy.

Some of the comics I am fascinated with seeing live are Jimmy Gunn, Miguel Fierro, Bridget Shwartz, Arj Barker, Will Franken, Louis Katz, and Brent Weinbach. I try not to annoy them with too many questions when I see them outside. My immersion is total.

Now, Brent is a magnificent little freak of nature. Think cousin of the Addams Family that takes a lot of mushrooms and watches a lot of Monty Python. A skinny, half-Jewish, half-Filipino guy who looks racially ambiguous due to this rare pairing of ethnicities. This is what you want as a comic; to look mysterious racewise. You can engage in racial humor, which always kills. People will be like, "Well, he must be from the Azore Islands then. I can't tell." Brent can get away with doing impressions of the Black kids he is a substitute teacher for in East Oakland, "Look! It's Mister Wein**bitch**! 'Ey, look at dis muhfuckah's pants! 'Ey, Mister Weinbitch?! Yo pants is so tight... you fuckin' up MY sperm count!"

What kills for Brent could get me *actually* killed. That's only one small arrow in this guy's quiver, though; he's the real deal. Racial humor always kills unless you are a regular, *Anglo-Saxon-ass-looking* white guy, which is fine, considering historical events. Better than getting my throat cut for being an evil cracker. There's a universe of comedy out there, but it sucks not to have access to that barrel of reliable laughs. I will survive.

I'll slip shit in where I can. I'm not just going to let those rascally Costa Ricans off *scot-free*. I need a gimmick or something. Great material and powerful delivery don't seem to be quite enough.

Brent is slightly hunched in a parka and the European satchel bag he always carries around. He looks like he just walked out of a fashion shoot for a catalog aimed at Finnish, hipster, mountain shepherds. He's never done a drug—like our friend Salvador Dali—he IS the drug. I swear, every time I watch him, I have an acid flashback. He's like… amphibian or something. He's from the planet *Strange-o,* and I fuckin' love it. Absurdity at its finest.

Brent is a local comedian who is very dedicated to performing as often as possible. I see him perform, and he sees me perform several times a week. Brent nods to me subtly after my sets at the Brainwash, sometimes to signal that he doesn't hate what I'm doing. One night I'm psyched after he says, "Hey, that Jenny joke? That's one to put in the file for when you do your first set at The Punchline."

So, of course, when I score my first commercial gig, it's Brent I message on this brand new thing called Myspace. It's like Yahoo Mail but with pictures, and all your messages aren't to individuals; they're to the whole world. Because the messages aren't really **to** anybody, they're not a page long anymore; more like a short paragraph. Perfect format for comedians, and well, just about everybody, to tell their bad jokes to a guaranteed audience. Why sign up for an open-mic? Shakti in Mumbai says I'm hilarious and keeps asking for 'Bob and Vagine.' That must mean punchlines, right? As if the quantity of lousy comedy that TV sitcoms produce every year isn't bad enough, Karen from accounting has her wine glass full and wants to headline on my computer screen. By the time the TV show Friends comes out next year, she'll be ready to audition for the part of "Sassy coworker." It's terrible, this Myspace, and yet, I can't stop scrolling. It sure gets popular fast. You can be anything you want there. Reinvent yourself! It has a fancy dashboard control center that advertises you as your profile's unwavering president. Upload 10-year-old pictures with vaseline on the lens—no one will ever know you're a slob in real life, Kenny.

The kids love it, and the comedians have been having luck organizing and promoting comedy shows on it. I have been avoiding computers—all technology really—but okay. Soon, in an attempt to boost my comedy career, I'm scrolling through people's feeds and realizing that the sickness level in our society that I had a theory about hadn't gone nearly far enough. Newsy-sounding websites begin to pop up and post garbage stories with no factual basis. People will repost it with the confidence that Dan Rather told them himself. Aside from reuniting with the occasional long-lost friend, all this stuff just seems like trash. Hopefully, this *social media* thing is just a fad.

At any rate, here me and Brent are at the San Francisco Cat in the Hat movie premiere at The Galaxy Theatre on Van Ness Street. These people needed some comics to warm up the show. They book me sight unseen from Craigslist, which is good because I haven't figured out how to upload a comedy clip to the internet yet.

Brent is out there underneath the movie screen, and the audience has kids in it. It's the Cat in The Hat premier, so of course, there's going to be some kids, but the smallest of them, like five to seven-year-olds, have been placed up in the front row, so it's like *that's* the audience we should be playing to or something.

The hosts are a male and female duo; college-aged, one in a rabbit onesie, the other in a weird beaver mask or something. I don't know, it seems like they didn't plan this out much, and now Brent has got his forearm held out at these kids in the front row, trying to lure them into touching it. He's going, "Go ahead, touch it! Touch it!"

The hosts are visibly nervous now. The girl whispers to the guy, probably to look for the theatre's *rent-a-cop*. Then Brent yells, "DON'T touch it!" and the kids' recoil, laughing.

Phew! He pulled it off! Brent gets off stage, and the hosts look relieved. They give me a feeble look, like, *You have our hope and our faith.* I smile reassuringly at them and walk out. I open with my closer, so they'll be happy. "Hey, you guys want to know why Jenny broke up with me?!"

A few weeks later, I pay admission to see an original Brent Weinbach comedy show. It's in SOMA, down by the Brainwash. It's upstairs in this mazelike dwelling that seems like it was built by some acid heads with a lot of extra plywood. Pretty sure if there's a fire, we're all dead. Admission is five bucks, so fuck it. In one segment, we accidentally turn in on a rave seamstress studio that it looks like she's also living in. We wave at her as her electric sewing machine purrs away. We keep going and find the little room that seats about 20.

I even brought a date, a cute Mexican girl with a couple of half-hidden Chola tattoos. I met her on Broadway in North Beach. She says she's a professional dancer. I'm not a city guy yet, so I'm like, *maybe it's ballet.* She's pretty and crazy, just like I like. Brent gets towards the end of the show, and he's like, "Well, it's time to bring the brown," and he proceeds to show us about a dozen framed photographs of his shits. One is perched on a bed of lettuce; I think some had doll clothes on? His actual shits from his own asshole.

I didn't see that coming. Needless to say, I don't get laid. However, I have an expanded knowledge of what can be presented at what is billed as 'A comedy show.'

Bullshitter of the Year Competition

I've come up with a TV show idea. I'm not opposed to TV as a medium, just how it's generally used. Maybe I could *save* TV. Really, I'm just a storyteller. TV, stand-up, film, typewriters, and even Myspace are just ways to tell stories. Let's throw some spaghetti at this wall and see what sticks.

The Bullshitter of the Year Competition is pretty much what it sounds like. When I was a kid growing up in Isla Vista, California, we had a crazy amount of talented shit talkers. We didn't have cellphones or TVs. It was just us, living in the moment. It was a game for us just to talk shit until someone got butthurt. Twenty-five years before roast battling was even a thing, we'd already elevated it to a fine art. What if we make a structured Olympic sport out of that? An obstacle course of deception and insult mastery? It could work. Finding talented competitors would be hard to do after a season or two unless we start sourcing out of Ireland. Fuck it. Open an office in Kilkenny!

On the day of the event, it's me and the other judges, Miguel Fierro and Brent Weinbach. We will be scoring on an Olympic-style, ten-point scoring system.

I've wrangled a bunch of people from the improv community to be competitors. Comedians, I've found, like to say "Improv sucks" for the same reason rednecks are racist. The ruling class has to convince the lowest layers of society that they are at least better than one other thing, yet, it is also true that improv sucks. But, for the purpose of this tournament, their skill set works pretty well, I must say. We also have some open-mikers and a few brilliant civilian bullshitters.

In the first round, they come out one by one. One of us judges poses a situation for the bullshitter to wiggle out of: "It's WWII, you have three minutes to seduce Hitler and free the Jews," says Brent.

Andrew gets instantly effeminate, "Come on, Hitley, I heard your third ball is very handsome. You say you're a vegetarian, but I'm going to feed you some meat. Come on, do it for Bavaria! I'll shizer in your mouth. Oh, you're soooo tall. Does Eva peg you like I do? Just let the little Jews go, okay, Hitley?"

There's laughter. I salute the darkness on the other side of the stage lights that are blinding us at the judge's table, and there's an audience. About 30 of them, "Shit, there's an audience out there. I guess we'll have to be funny now," I say.

The judges are all writing tens and nines in judgment of Andrew's performance. They liked it. I average out the scores to 9.5.

Next comes Val Dorito. Now, to get some of the contestants to be willing to perform, I had to give them the questions in advance so they could prepare. With the key to the event being the spontaneity of the responses, how could I do that? I couldn't afford for any contestants to back out either, so I gave them all the answers in advance, the wrong ones. They'll either adapt or drown in flop sweat. Either way, the audience is happy. Fuck it.

I deliver the next question, "Val? You're at a job interview, and a crack pipe falls out of your purse. What do you say?"

Val is instantly pissed, "Wait, that wasn't even my question. Do you know who should win this? the competition itself. It's full of shit."

"Deal with it," I say, hoping she doesn't walk out.

Val is a pro, thinks a second, and, "Okay, well, that's just a straw. Do you not use glass straws? It affects the taste of your cocktails, and I only drink fancy cocktails. I mean, it *is* a crack pipe, but I stole it from my roommate because it's almost rent, and he can pay it if he can't find his crack pipes for a while-"

"But it's the fourth of the month. Isn't rent due on the first?" says Fierro, throwing a curveball at her.

"You never heard of a fucking grace period? With tits like this? Do you think I can't get away with paying on the 15th? Fuck you."

The crowd loves it. The judges regret giving the first guy such high ratings. We all scribble tens and nines again on our notepads before presenting the scores to the audience.

A guy named Brindley is in the lead by the finals. He's a clear genius, and we almost have to shoosh him so he'll stop coming up with escape scenarios.

In the final round, we hand each of the three finalists a handful of ice cubes. We've dressed up my roommate Sean—the lovelorn dockworker—like an Eskimo to hand it to them. He got the job because no one else wanted to do it, and he had the parka with the fur-lined hood, which is up and hiding his entire face. You can still somehow tell he's drunk.

"Okay, sell this Eskimo some ice cubes," says Miguel Fierro.

Andrew is first. He's a contender for winning because he went up the street with a witness to the strip club in a previous round and tried to convince the doorman to let him in free. The ruse is that it's because he has cancer, and he's never seen a real pair of boobies. It almost works, and Weitzman's relaying of how it all went down has people falling out of their seats. It's a new round now, though—the final round—and Andrew is about to lose that temporary luster he'd attained. He goes first:

"Look at this shit! High-quality ice diamonds right there, Son!" He does okay, but the audience seems to need more convincing since this is the final round.

Next is Val, "With every purchase of this high-quality ice, you get a fresh slice of pussy." She already used the sex card in a previous round, so the audience passes.

"Okay, here is our final competitor! This is for all the marbles Brindley," I say.

He holds out the ice cubes to my roommate, the Irish Eskimo. "Look! This stuff is magic. Are you aware there is an igloo shortage in this area? This shit is just little igloo pieces. Look, I'll build you one." Brindley gets on his knees and builds an igloo in front of us, and in our minds, we can see it. He gets up and sweeps his arm convincingly at the igloo in an attempt to impress the Eskimo, who starts rocking his head like he's finally interested. "What do I gotta do.... to get you **Inuit**... this igloo, bro!?"

Wordplay always gets a laugh, and this kills. Brindley is the winner, and I present him the trophy for the First Annual Bullshitter of the Year Competition. It's a large brass bowl with big handles on each side to raise up in victory. Inside the bowl is a cornstarched T-shirt that I swirled and dried into the shape of a soft-serve example of bullshit. Spray painted mud brown, of course. Brindley looks at the trophy proudly, and he should. He earned it.

We deem the show a success, and tell the audience we'll see them next year. I videotaped the whole thing. My plan is to edit it up into a pilot episode to send it off to NBC. My first year in comedy, and I have a pilot already. I've also been working simultaneously on writing my one-man show about growing up in a teepee in Santa Barbara.

One of these pots will boil eventually, and once *one* boils, it'll get all the rest to boil. I'm startin' a thing! Join me, or get the fuck out of the way.

Sperm Gets Cold When the Baby Souls Give Up

Soon after my first year in comedy has elapsed, I feel close to defining my perspective. The lens that I will filter all my ideas and make my material distinctive. So far, I'm performing primarily on top of coffee tables with no mic at crusty dive bars like The Uptown, located on Capp Street—arguably the filthiest street in San Francisco, a difficult contest to win. You have to battle these rough audiences to get even the lightest smatterings of laughter.

I decide I'm more of a quick set up, then punchline kind of joke teller, as opposed to a ranter like Louis Katz, the bespectacled and brilliant comedian that can do an entire 15 minute set on one idea. I've been having more success getting my ideas out in little 30 second spurts. In the chaotic environments where I perform, this is the most effective way to work. Grab their attention and get to the laugh quick, or they'll look back down into their 7&7s again, to sadly contemplate how to get away with killing their landlords and ex-wives.

You only have one chance at Pissed off Pete's Pool Hall. Don't blow it, or they'll all start yelling at you. Some of these fuckers can heckle too. Every open-miker should have three or four prefabricated comebacks. Because the 60-year-old cocktail waitress/cocaine dealer may realize you tell the same jokes every week. Maybe she'll decide she's funnier than you. She'll be waiting for you next week when you tell that shitty joke about your cats again. Some of the biggest laughs I ever saw were for the heckler. Like when that cocktail waitress yelled, "I hope that cat eats your fucking face when you die, you unfunny piece of shit!"

When that happens, you can't just throw back some cliche stock line that Milton Berle used. To give myself time, I'd throw out, "Did you hear they're making a sequel to Titanic? It's about your fuckin' heckling career." Even a medium-quality retort like that will get you a laugh and buy you some time while you size this piece of shit up. You have to be prepared to go in on them at the bat of an eye. Maybe attack their looks first, then their intellect, and finally, where their stupidity in life has led them to. Don't attack their mom or one-up them *too* much. It gives them the option to play the victim. After all, the fact you have the microphone, and you're trying to be the 'big pro-comedian,'—who is supposed to be able to handle hecklers without seeming angry at all. It can come off like a workplace power imbalance; you seem like too much of a bully. All they gotta do if you pull the whole cork out and go after their mom, is say "My mom died building mosquito nets for the war," in a weepy, hurt way—and you're fucked. I've seen it. The world is full of natural-born hecklers. It's easy to tear something down but hard to build it. Doing stand-up comedy is like getting coconuts thrown at you while you try to oil paint a masterpiece. It's fucked. And it better be a masterpiece, or they'll heckle that.

It helps that I've been getting heckled by the backseat driver in my brain since I was six. I don't let him win as much anymore, because in adulthood, I've learned how to roast the motherfucker back so he'll shut the fuck up for a minute. From crazies on the sidewalk talking to themselves to open-mikers that don't get out of the open-mic level. They never learned to outargue their inner backseat driver. You have to beat your inner heckler. Then, external hecklers are easy. After all, they're not inside your fucking brain, where all the best roasting files to roast you with are. So take heart open-mikers, you'll roast him into silence eventually. Be merciless. Stop *trying* to believe in yourself and *do* it.

Dive bars are the Big Apple of stand-up comedy; if you can make it there, you can make it anywhere. These people might be depressed alcoholics, but half of 'em are smart; they used to be somebody, and seeing you possibly on your way up pisses them off. If you're great? They'll eventually give it up.

Mostly the regulars that sit along the bar are just sick of hearing the same jokes for the third week in a row. They feel like a comedian should have fresh material each week. I see this and inject a lot of new stuff each time, staying up late into the night to do so, earning the appreciation of Salty Steve, the nine-fingered, retired union rep that seems to be the chieftain of the regulars. This is the grinder I've been sharpening myself on. I know I'm close.

Tonight I'm out in Langton Alley, outside the Brainwash, not a dive bar, but a dive laundromat, rehearsing my new material. Some homeless tweaker is concerned I might be trying to move in on his territory. A whole alley is quite an ambitious kingdom for one tweaker, but here he comes, Billy John, the Appalachian train jumper, swinging his cane at me, "This is my alley motherfucker!"

It makes sense how I deliver my material at the wall, pacing back and forth in the dark. I probably do seem like a hobo whose wandering eye looks to expand his own territory. Time to out-crazy this unloved ruffian, "EYES BOHORN IN DIS HERE ALLEY!!!" I scream in my own *drunk hobo* accent I use in my act, one of just three impressions I can do. This throws him. Being **born** in the alley *would* demonstrate a legitimate claim, would it not?

I rush into the Brainwash realizing Tony Sparks just called my name.

I get up there, "Hey guys. Fuckin' awesome neighborhood, huh?" I do a last-second switch out and put my Sailor Dave bit in front to reuse my hobo accent while it's still fresh, "Hey, you ever get in a bad street transaction and have to fuck up a homeless dude?"

Mild laughter, but it's something. Maybe rushing in here and dealing with that guy has my breathing off. Even something as small as that can throw off your timing. I plunder on, "What?! Motherfucker tried to sell me a three-month-old Street Sheet, man! If I'm goin' to be readin' poems about BBQ'd rats.... that shit better be fresh off the presses... Sailor Dave!"

This elicits slightly more laughter, but nothing to write home about. Billy John, the hobo landbaron, is outside the window, watching me on stage. He looks back down towards the alley's edge as if I'm still supposed to be there. He's in shock to see that I've now instantly appeared on the stage and am telling tales of his colleagues.

"Here's the poem I wish I would have read... in the Street Sheet that day," I scream, microphone in my pocket, as I go full alley-style.

I hold out my hand like I'm holding the skull in a Shakespeare play. Then, I bend my knees gently as if to be about to spring forward, "I know why the caged rodent SINGS!!!!... 'cause he knows I'm gonna BBQ him in a hole... with some TOBASKY and things!!"

I'm performing this to Billy John through the window at this point, "HARK! HARK!... I hear some whiskers in the dark. I did PCP in med school... now I live in a park!"

I really should be awarded extra points from almost being killed—or at least infected with something—two seconds before I got on stage. I instead get mediocre laughter from the third of the audience that's listening. "Fuck this shit! I did every salty dive bar in The Mission all week to get to this, and you're still going to shit on me? Nuh-uh, I don't think so!"

A laugh, a real laugh. I realize I hadn't used my inside voice, and I said that out loud. It was so real they liked it. It was an honest response. The audience knew they were being shitty, and now they're laughing because I called them out on it. They *want* to be punished for being bad. "Okay, how about this motherfuckers?" I leap from the stage up onto the cafe's counter, startling Phil, the curly-haired, bearlike cashier/DJ, AKA Phillie Ocean.

I'm up above them now, and I grab that aluminum lampshade hanging from a wire that's coming out of the ceiling. I point the light at the audience member in the third row on his laptop like I'm interrogating him. He's in the spotlight,

"Look at this motherfucker trying to look all-important with his laptop. I bet he's writing Harry Potter fan fiction!" He does indeed look like that's what he would be doing. The whole audience looks at him. He puts up his hands as if to convey, *Hey, why are you blowing my cover, bro?* They laugh because it's probably true. I wheel the aluminum spotlight onto the ever-present crackhead, "What brought you in motherfucker? The sound of the sizzle?"

The half of the audience that knows from direct experience that a crack rock sizzles when you smoke it laughs. The other half bristles, knowing I'm probably going to get to them next.

"That's not nice," says a Berkeley goddess mother, waiting her turn to tell a humorous story—with no actual punchlines—about living on

Wavy Gravy's hippie farm.

"Tony said I was funny, not nice," I say, as Tony shakes his head up and down, taking a break in the action to pick at some cheese fries.

"Fuck nice! I know your life is usually like the inside of a Cat Stevens song lady, but what about this neighborhood told you there would be nice things here?! You're a long way from People's Park. You're Little Red Riding Hood right now, and this is a room full of wolves, lady!"

They laugh at their predatory status and the fact that she *is indeed* carrying a wicker basket. Of course, it's got laundry in it and not mountain berries, and the hoodie is tie-dyed but close enough.

"I gotta try and make people who are dead inside laugh... audibly. Otherwise, I'm supposed to go home and cry because I suck? This is bullshit Little Red Mushroom Could!"

What did I just say? It's like something else in my brain is driving now, and it's just trying to keep the roller coaster racing. They laugh because nicknames. Maybe *they* could get a nickname. Some look almost like they're going to raise their hand, like, "Me next! Fuck me up next!" I oblige.

"Look at these sad excuses for comics. If you knew how much of their self-worth is wrapped up in if you laugh or not, you'd do what every girl who's ever had sex with them did and fake it! Laugh motherfuckers! You laugh like you're on acid, and you just saw a monkey fuck a frog's mouth!"

They laugh because they know it's all true, and now someone has addressed the elephant in the room. "Fuck this. Ya'll motherfuckers wouldn't know funny if it crawled up your assholes and started vibrating!"

"What do we have to do to get some laughs out of you pricks?" I continue screaming, "Because laughter, even fake laughter, is as close as some of these poor fucks feel like they're ever going to get to **real** love."

I pretend to get real sad, and the comics in the room do it for real. The little attention craving open-mikers do look cheered up some.

Someone is finally standing up for them. All the while, I've been up on the counter, pointing this ridiculous swinging light fixture at everyone. I start pointing out people with the light to mark the guilty before jumping back down onto the stage.

I take a breath and say, "I remember one of the great comedians saying 'You have to entertain the audience that's there,' well, obviously that motherfucker never performed in a laundromat in South Market, where the only 'audience' that's listening, looks like he just escaped from prison, then traveled through a motherfucking Lord of the Rings battle."

I enjoy a few laughs, including a shrieky staccato one from myself, before digging back in.

"He's not even here to do laundry; he was just walking by and saw me through the window. And he was like, 'I'm gonna take that bitch.' So now he's sitting there with his sweaty lip and his eyes bugging out in the front row, like, "Tell me the pain, Attention Boy! DADDY can fix it! He's all spitting a sort of orange foam out his mouth onto his tutu made of Scooby-Doo bedsheets?"

They're laughing now. The comics outside smoking and talking are coming in to see what the big hubbub is about. I'm starting to, what they call in the business, "Kill."

"And that's a good night at the Brainwash Cafe and Laundromat, people! How do I entertain **that** audience? I don't **have...** any... **orc...** riddles! Look, one of them is here right now, waiting to rape me in the fuckin' alley!" I point to Billy John, and he's so excitedly looking in at me that it does indeed seem like a dangerous situation for my butthole.

Kill, killing, killerington, the crowd goes. They love it when you even victimize yourself in your frenzy to dole out punishment. I can almost feel the wind in their laughter vibrate my curls. I'm a walking orgasm now. I can do no wrong. The brilliance just spews out, as if a god is speaking through me. I slash my way forward into the history books of The Brainwash. It's a greasy, frayed history book, but I'll take it.

"Fuck that!" Now they're just laughing at anything I say. I've only seen Patrice O' Neil and a few others be able to do this. To get them to laugh until they are in pain and have to stop for a second, one hand on their belly, and one up in the air, waving for mercy.

"Fuck that *entertain the audience that's there* bullshit! Have you fuckin' looked at yourselves?" They laugh at their pathetic state.

"I'm entertaining the audience I **wish** was here! You see this empty table? In my mind? Hot, streetwise, intellectual chicks....laughing their asses off....getting horny... they haven't been to prison... they don't **have** rabies. Instead of telling them orc riddles, I'm selling them DVDs and T-shirts! I'm getting crabs just by clicking on their Myspace profiles!"

The laughter is dying down a bit because, frankly, I think I pulled it all out of them. Should I do my new *wet dreams* joke? Maybe they just need the attention off them for a minute. Before I realize what I'm doing, I've launched into my "wet dreams" joke. I'm so greedy, and the buzz is already starting to fade slightly. I have to chase the dragon. I ***have*** to.

"What's up with wet dreams, everybody? It's like, Not only is my afternoon nap interrupted by boxers full of gizz... but the six-tittied mermaid I was trying to fuck ain't even real?!"

Smattering. Not nearly enough. Okay, this joke builds. Keep it up. Rough segue?

"Plus, you know that shit freezes ten minutes later. You can't just... fall back asleep. Ladies? You know that." I point at the college girl table that I'd until now spared, "How many times have you laid there all slathered in gizm... and your sternum turns to ice right after the baby souls give up?"

They laugh at the college girls, two who look horrified, and one giving me a look like, "Oh, yeah, slather me, you fucking *comedy stud*!"

"That's right! I said it! Sperm gets cold after 20 billion wannababies give up at once!"

The laughs are decent but less than that peak two minutes ago. *Why do I have to fucking notice that? Why doesn't the little critic in my head ever shut up and let me enjoy a moment?*

"Look at the girls not laughing! They have dry flakes of cum peeling off their chest right now."

Half the audience looks at me like they can't believe what they're hearing, the other half can't believe they're laughing at it, and cover their mouths in an attempt to trick Jesus. I leave the stage pretty much a king.

Outside, everyone is crowding around me to high-five me or offer me a toke off their pipe. It feels amazing. Susan Alexander, a corporate sales queen, talks about the new comedy club she's opening in The Tenderloin. She wants me to headline their first show. What? Oh shit, it's finally happening! It's going to be called 50 Mason, after the address. Creative. "Hell yeah," I say. And just like that, after a little more than a year of doing comedy, I'm an underground headliner. I just need to come up with ten more minutes before tomorrow night.

I go home and write, but I can't stop thinking about the feeling of killing. I try to replicate the feeling in my mind, but I can't quite get there. So I go and buy a $20 rock of crack, and for about the amount of time that I was up there doing it, I reproduce the excitement; an acceptable mirage. Just when I'm getting used to it, thinking I might be able to live there forever, I remember the feeling isn't permanent. By becoming aware of the illusion, I slip back towards everyday consciousness. I am again mortal as anxiety that the high is leaving arrives. I put in the last crumbs of the crack in the little glass dick and raise it to my lips like a little bitch, for one last chance at magic.

I take in the smoke, and for a second, I return. Then the thought of Hobo Bob simultaneously raising his crack pipe to me in a toast causes me to slip suddenly down into the muddy pit of a chase now reversed. I try to sleep to escape. No deal. I sit there, cold and clammy, grinding my jaw with my eyes closed, as the Nightmare of Hobo Bob unfolds like a skid row theatre production on the insides of my eyelids.

Ain't Nothin' Tender 'Bout the Tenderloin

That's how Dave Chappelle described the neighborhood I'm entering, and I can't think of a better way to describe it in six words or less. I'm about to show up to headline my first actual comedy club. Upon arrival, I quickly see why it's named 50 Mason. You'd never fuckin' find it without the address. There are no windows, and it's on a war-torn block. There's a vast junky residence hotel across the street, which shits out all its misery into the areas around where I now stand. From this hotel of vice, violence, and diabetes, murder threats are thrown down from the windows, and up from the street. Bottles break, cars screech, the smell is shit, piss, and soggy cardboard. This is the final tentacle of the Tenderloin's Northeast corner, poking into the heart of the *bougie* theatre and shopping district.

The Tenderloin ends at Market Street, The City's main thoroughfare, which cuts away South Market and The Mission at a strange bias from Union Square and the seven high-rent hills of San Francisco. Except at Sixth Street, where The Tenderloin crosses Market Street and extends like the octopus' big, coke pinky; its gelatinous nail fingerbanging its way into South Market's asshole. Good Vietnamese food, though.

A giant octopus of felonies and addiction plopped in the center of The City. Its name is The Tenderloin. In a city of microclimates, you never know what you're going to get from street to street. The way the winds whip from the ocean, down along the sides of Golden Gate Park, forming concentrated arctic funnels of collar busting hate tornadoes down certain blocks. 7th Street is a famous wind tunnel of doom. One block over on 6th, it will be calm. The Mission district can be 80 degrees on 16th Street, and you need two jackets by the time you get to 12th. One block can have a bunch of old money ladies in fur coats and emeralds going to see the musical Cats; the very next block over, you can have crackheads fighting in the streets with machetes.

I don't know how the tourists figure it all out in a single week. You need two, at least. Picking a tall landmark and heading towards it in a straight line can force you to cross many crime jamborees where "Melee" is the name of the game. You have to know the proper zig-zag to get anywhere. It's a great city once you get away from downtown. The grime is part of the adventure, I guess.

How would one describe the Tenderloin with a bit more nuance? It is a complicated neighborhood that is worth a venture. It's got the best under ten dollar meals in the country due to the immigrants of every Asian country cooking up spicy dishes in their molten woks for the drunken hipsters to enjoy. The Asian produce markets are the only reason this neighborhood even has any vegetables. Crom help you if you live in a poor community and there are no Asians there. If you're nice to them, they can even show you how to survive poverty.

I've had some of my greatest times in the bars here that drip with so much chlamydi—I mean character. Live bands, hot chicks, pool tables galore, hip art galleries, motorcycle gangs ripping through, every drug there ever was, unlicensed basement casinos, people acting a fool like it's Mardi Gras. It's a poetic bedlam that everyone should try once in their life to survive from lunch until the bars close. Extra brownie points if you walk all the way home afterward because you spent every dime in your bank account. There are reasons people risk assault to come here. And the whiskey flows. I'm surprised Anthony Bordain hasn't come yet to do an entire episode on just this neighborhood.

The Tenderloin is also full of suffering, murder, and other assorted death. This is where poor people live. In most towns, the blight is pushed out to the edges of the city. But the Tenderloin is in the center—the motherfucking center—of San Francisco. Stretching from City Hall itself into what should very well be one of The City's most expensive neighborhoods.

But it wasn't to be. The real estate is almost useless to the wealthy landlords around here because it's all early 1900s boarding house-style rooms where you share a single bathroom with everybody on your floor. There are some dilapidated ethnic food restaurants that can barely cover the already cheap rent. Then there are the bars where people get stabbed all the time. Even the techies know their limits and have so far only presented a limited presence here as homeowners and tenants.

So who lives here? A few of the more daring hipsters; whoever doesn't mind sharing one bathroom with a whole boarding house full of junkies and hustlers; anyone who doesn't mind living with rats and scabies walking across their balls like they own the place; and those unlucky fucks just getting out of prison.

You can score a room for like $700 a month. That leaves the crazies $200 from their 5150 checks for drugs and the little chocolate cakes they sell at the registers of the many, many liquor stores. These stores all sell crack pipes and crystal meth blow torches too. So if they get robbed, save your tears.

If a great fire ripped through the Tenderloin—and I'm sure they've planned it—all the rich developers would walk up to the edge of the flames and start jacking off into the fire, thinking about all the highrise luxury apartments they would now be able to build. In this case, I hope Satan exists so he can show up to collect all the sex offender souls as their abdomens pop in the flames. He'd be especially interested in the souls of the developers jacking off into the fire. *But they're not dead yet,* he'd think, before whipping up a great wind along Golden Gate Park's long, Northern edge, plunging the Pacific gale into the city to fan the flames and to blow the greedy land speculators into the fire. ***MMMWWWWUAHAHA!!!*** He'd go as their wicked skin snapped and crackled. The Loin burning down would be Satan's happiest day since the CIAs founding.

Seeing the scared looks on the French tourist's faces, get up to the top of the pissy escalator at the Bart Station at City Hall. I try to help them, but they never speak a lick of English. They pull out their maps frantically, in disbelief that they could be at the Civic Center—what in any city in Europe would be the town's crown jewel. Instead, it's a skid row! UN Plaza, the very place the United Nations was conceived... littered with shit and drug needles. This distraction in the sudden panic of the tourists might give the crack zombies a chance to grab the suitcase with the passports in it and run, so I just go up and point in the direction of Union Square and say, "Sun is gonna set, you better go that way."

Do you know why the postcards from San Francisco are all pictures pointing up at the buildings and the bridges? Because on the ground, half the place looks like if the Thriller video had been filmed in a toilet. But I love it. I love this fucking city.

"You lookin' whiteboy?" is something I hear several times before reaching my destination at mid-block. Yeah, I'm lookin', *lookin' to get the fuck off this sidewalk.*

I'm a half-hour early to meet the proprietor of the brand new yet dilapidated comedy club 50 Mason. Joe, a very UCSB baseball team looking dude, complete with the chewing tobacco-filled bottom lip.

Joe didn't check the zoning laws before trying to open a strip club here. Once that got shut down, he wanted to do it as a lingerie shop where the girls modeled the clothing. Essentially a sneaky strip club. Snake eyes again. So, as the last dying gasp of a failed business venture, he decided on a comedy club: comedy, the final coffin nail. I'm guessing Susan convinced him that the comics will work for practically free—which is correct—and the dream was born. Officially, Susan is in charge of promotions and booking the comedians. She does all the legwork while Joe pays the rent and runs the ticket table.

Susan is an archetype you will find in the lower levels of comedy: midlife crisis, corporate burnout salesperson, or lawyer. They know they have that silver tongue, and comedy seems like something less soul-crushing that would put that to use. She knows how to act on your desires right away and begins a hard sell you never see coming. She's half white, half Filipino, like Brent Weinbach. She has that racially ambiguous look, and that *big girl laugh* that convinces people on the verge of a laugh to actually do so, and ripples of laughter make their way from the back of the audience up towards the comedian. So, in that way, she's a goddess on those cold nights when you need a little extra help waking up the corpses. Whatever her corporate vibe is, the strategic big girl laugh almost forgives it. She's nice enough. She sees that the best way to get into comedy is to make yourself useful to it, and she's got endless energy to that end. She's chubby with long curly brown hair, big rosy cheeks, and a bunch of Margaret Cho premises with new punchlines. She's as fake as they come. She might make it in this business. I'm told I'll be paid $50, "If the audience shows up."

I've done my best to promote the show to the Cheesecake Factory servers, and about a dozen of them show up. Mostly college girls in their early 20s and a few gays.

It turns out I'm *not* their type of comedy. One girl is drunk and laughs too early, during that critical quarter of a second where the punchline is soaking into their brains, and here she comes with her cold water splash of a shrieking laugh too early. She's trying to help, so I can't, like, obliterate her. Also, I'm kind of the odd man out at the Cheesecake Factory, being the ancient age of 31 to them, and making this chick cry might make things weirder at work. Not addressing the situation, hoping it would go away, turns out to be a mistake. *You have to nip that shit in the bud, son!*

"You guys want to know why this country has such a problem with serial killers?"-*Shriek cackle!!*

"You sure you don't want to wait for the punchlines, Sweety?"-*Shriek! Cackle!*

"It's because we give the serial killers such great names! Zodiac Killer! The Night Stalker!"-*Cackle! Shriek!*

Fuck.

"Shit! If I thought you guys were going to give me a great name, like the Night Stalker? I'd take a fuckin' bite out of this guy right here!" I point at a guy with his arms crossed, who has looked pretty unimpressed so far.

I walk up to a bored-looking tourist couple, who it turns out are French. I think they thought that the tickets they bought were for a more theatrical production. You know, with costumes and stuff? I point at the wife, "Come on, lady! If you thought you could be called 'Death Mistress'!? You'd help me BBQ this motherfucker!"

A well-timed guffaw starts the bit's first real audience laugh from Susan. The French lady looks at me, like, *Bebeqew?*

"But maybe if we thought we was gonna get names like 'The Little Pink Panty Wearing Wussy Bitch Killers'? Maybe we'd think twice about it… Maybe he wouldn't look so fucking delicious!" I look at the intended prey, his arms still crossed in protest of any fun, brow slightly furrowed above his orange walrus mustache. I lock eyes with him and lick my wrist knob, down along the edge of my hand to my pinky knuckle.—*Cackle! Shriek!*

At the end of the show, all the Cheesecake Factory people leave without really saying anything. It wasn't the smoothest set of my life. With the girl cackling uncurtailed at the wrong times and letting it affect my delivery, I give myself and the show a C. The owner seems pleased enough, and I get my $50. Maybe all he cared about was that I got a dozen people to pay a tenner each, and he only had to give me a fraction of that back. For a block this shitty, the rent probably isn't that expensive. Between my coworkers and the French tourists Susan deceived, this guy has enough for a can of chew and a night at the Hustler Club.

Susan tells the open-mikers that if they want to get booked again, they have to bring some people like I did. She's 'not running a charity here.' The club model here is: Have a decent enough headliner and stuff the line up with newbies whose friends still give a shit about their friend's new hobby. They'll all come out once, and because their friend is only a month into the game, they will suck bad. Then, years later, once they get feasible at this, those same friends will rebuke the Myspace event invites, saying, "I went to see you that time, and you suck."

"I'm better now. Did you press play on the video clip?"

"It wouldn't buffer."

Shit.

This gig is what we call a *bringer show*. The first two-thirds of the show is usually pretty terrible until you get to the more experienced performers portion. It's a reliable business model if you only care about making small amounts of money.

I'm outside feeling all wound up, and one of Susan's corporate sales friends zeroes in on me. Like Susan, she seems about 40, and she isn't taking "No" for an answer. I have been good about not getting entangled in a relationship. I have been faithful to my promise not to get distracted, so I can focus on becoming the greatest stand-up that ever lived. But a guy's gotta dip his wick sometimes. So I let myself engage in one-night stands—at least it keeps me from chasing adrenaline with a crack pipe—provided there's no risk of it developing into something more serious.

So, we get to her house, and she's got all this voodoo shit around. She starts lighting black candles and shit. I'm a little creeped out, but I've fucked satanic whores before, and they can be pretty wild. Too scratchy, but wild. So *damn it, I'm in!*

We fuck hard, and she's speaking in tongues and shit while I ram her, eyes all rolled up in the back of her head. It's hot. She predictably does a number on my back with her nails.

After I cum, I go into the bathroom while she gets to her knees and bows before this Santa Rita altar, moaning, and chanting. Is she chanting for Satan to make her womb fruitful or something? I flush the condom down the toilet just in case. I can't afford for her to fish it out of the wastebasket and flip it inside out, playing *Casper the Friendly Kid Ghost's* inside her pussy with it, saying, "Fetaljuice! Fetaljuice! Fetaljuice!" into the bathroom mirror. Then, after I've all but forgotten, five years later, I get a knock at the door; it's a fucking Chucky doll, saying, "Dada? Let's play in blood!" Fuck that. I'm getting out of here before I wake up strapped to a sacrificial bowl with my wrists slit open.

"It was nice. I'll call you," I say on my way out, all *sing-songy.* I feel relieved to hear the door shut behind me. I knew you had to join the league of Lucifer to be in corporate America, but I thought your Beezlebub gear was just the embroidery on your fleece vest: "Oracle," "Sneeze.com," shit like that. This chick has all the accessories of a *bona fide history witch.*

What neighborhood is this? Where are the closest Asian noodles?

Confronting My Childhood Bully in a Bar

During the week, I'm still working day shifts at the Cheesecake Factory and focusing on getting on stage every night, no matter how shitty that stage time might be. This weeknight routine usually ends by nine pm, and it's back to North Beach. I'll play pool at Gino and Carlo's. I try not to hustle too much in there because North Beach is small, and you don't want to get a predatorial reputation. The citizens are very proud of their neighborhood here, and they are often found policing it themselves. Some old lady is likely to grab me by my collar and say, "Look at 'im. Cain't you see 'e's too drunk tuh gamble. That's prolly 'is kid's lunch money you're a takin'!"

I go outside to eat a square slice from Golden Boy Pizza and bum a smoke before going home to my room in the Chinatown Projects. I'm going to pound the new material into my laptop on my growingly wobbly ironing board, pausing to take in the view of the city in my $500 room. For San Francisco, this is a steal *without* a view. My saving grace in my financial life is I've always been able to sniff out the cheap rent.

On my way into the building, these two beat cops rush me, "What are you doing in here?" one says.

Good question. Ten pm, and here comes a whiteboy with a plaid, faux fur-collared jacket, walking into a building that everyone knows is occupied by ancient Chinese people who are asleep by dark. "I swear I live here. I'm subletting."

"From who?" says the other cop.

Shit. Saying "Marco" would seem like ratting, and I'm pretty sure Marco is a gangster. It's true; I met him through the strip club lined Broadway Street, which carries with it a criminal element. The bar I get most of my comped drinks at, Fuse, happens to be on Broadway, so I meet people from that element. The drug dealer boyfriends of the strippers like to have drinks in here. I know Marco carries a gun and has a particular colored handkerchief hanging out of his back pocket. That's a gangster, right? Am I being racist? I don't think so. And I'll be damned if I'm saying his name out loud to a cop. "Dario," I say, in a close approximation / compromise.

"Bullshit. Give me your ID. Empty your pockets," says the buff, bald Black cop.

"It's up in my room, I lost my California ID, and all I have is a passport," I say, emptying my pockets, which only have a bag of weed and some crumpled small bills.

"Fine. Let's go up there," says the fat, white cop, taking the weed and giving the bills back.

So I'm on this tiny elevator with these two cops. We're so close I feel like they can smell weed, booze, cigarettes, and flop sweat on me. I get nervous they're going to throw me off the balcony, five floors down into the courtyard. There's a very *Clockwork Orangey* feel to this. We get up there, and they look truly surprised that I have a key to the door. I show them my passport, they give me my weed back and leave, satisfied they put a scare into me. Assholes.

Sean comes out of his room and starts crying about the French girl I saw him with at Spec's last night. I'm not in the mood now after the ordeal with the cops, and I let him have it. "Sean? Do you know why no girls stay around you for more than a week? You're sullen. And they mean too much to you. You've known this chick for two days, and you're already picking out jewelry. Do you think they don't sense that? Cindy Lauper is right, Sean, 'Girls Just Want to Have Fun.' They don't want to be around some weepy sailor who is always staring out at the sea, composing sonnets. You're a whiny, needy ass, little bitch." That's weird. Why is he picking up a Bailey's bottle? That's a morning liqueur. *Wham!* This little fucker just smashed my forehead with a bottle*! Shit. Blood starts pouring out of a gash.* I'm enraged.

I grab him and pick him up. I consider throwing him over my ironing board through the window and into the cityscape. He's suspended, all 120-pounds of him, a tiny guy with a nose that's been smashed up several times, and now I see why. I consider his fate, then I just throw him onto my bed and whack him a few times until I figure equal damage is done.

He scurries out of my room, whining like the little bitch that he is. I crank up my computer and start working on a piece called "Roommates Suck," dabbing at the blood dripping out of my forehead every few minutes with a balled-up dirty T-shirt.

One evening soon after that, I see my old floormate from the St. Paul Hotel, Mr. Mottini, a dapper old guy that is an installment of the neighborhood. When he dies, a few years from now, they will have a memorial parade through the streets of North Beach for him. We should all be so lucky. You never know what kind of mood he'll be in. One day he's screaming at everybody; the next, he's giving out nice vintage jackets. A chill had arrived in town, and all I had was a thin hoodie and a flannel. "That's not proper," Mr. Mottini instructs, "An eligible bachelor in this neighborhood needs a decent jacket; this is San Francisco." Of course, Mottini still thinks it's 1965—don't anybody tell him. So, seeing me wear the same shit all the time, he gave me a dope-ass jacket that fits me to a tee.

So, I'm walking by Mottini around Mr. Bing's a few weeks after he gave me the jacket, and he starts screaming at me, "You been in my closet, asshole?! That's my jacket! Are you some kind of wise guy?"

I start to take off the jacket. I don't need this kind of trouble. Now, Mottini really starts yelling, "You son of a-" *pop!* His dentures pop out of his fuckin' mouth onto the ground. I try to use the opportunity to escape, but he holds eye contact while slowly bending down to grab them off of the Columbus Avenue sidewalk. Now he has them and pops 'em back in like this happens all the time.

"You want the jacket back, Mottini?" I have it off of one arm by now.

"No, you keep it," he says, polite as a peach. He then seems to drift mentally into a different decade. Maybe he's gone from 60s Mottini to 80s Mottini. He'll talk about businesses and mayors that have been gone for decades like it's today. Then, he'll just wake up and decide; it's *going to be 1972 today.* Next thing you know, he's down at the donut shop goin' "Look at this new pyramid building they built. What an eyesore. You hear about that Billie Jean King?!" Tomorrow it could be 1992. Wouldn't that be great? Fuck. I loved 1992, right up until I got busted for selling weed. Other than that? Stellar fuckin' year.

I walk away up the hill on Kearny towards Broadway, to Fuse Bar, thinking, *Time for a new neighborhood, the freaks have found me.*

An hour later, I'm still in Fuse, polishing off my third cocktail, calculating my funds, and in walks one of my childhood bullies, Brad. *What the fuck?* He's actually with a girl. *Is it him?* It's been about 12 years since I've seen him. He's with another couple as well, and soon the four of them are finishing up their first round. After the shock wears off and I convince myself it's him, I go up to them and say, "Hey, remember me?"

"Nope," he says, probably lying. The second I hear his voice, I know it's him. You remember the voice that taunted you—even more than the boot that kicked you. He's fatter and more haggard now, as many bullies are from the weight of knowing they're pieces of shit.

"Well, I remember you. This is my bar. Get the fuck out now! Hey, Anthony!"

My friend Anthony, a huge man, lumbers over in case this gets physical between me, Brad, and Brad's friend, who seems angrier than Brad. Angry that I've invaded their booth to settle old scores. I give him a look like, *I'd like that very much.* "Anthony, this is Brad, my childhood bully. You think he and his friends should get the fuck out of here?"

By 'my bar,' I mean the bar I'm a regular at; if he thinks it's my bar and wants to use that as an excuse to slink out, that's fine with me, but these fuckers need to bounce. Brad looks at me, looks at Anthony, and pounds the rest of his beer—of course he does—"Let's go," he says, and sure enough, they get up and leave. On his way out, in an attempt to save some face, he says, "Come out to the Avenues."

"Why the fuck would I want to go to the Avenues? The Avenues suck!" I say. The door guy laughs, sealing my victory.

The unmistakable look of a man that would kill you if he could. His girl tugs him away. And the moment is over. I'm overwhelmed with satisfaction. Shit. That was amazing! Punishing bullies is my new mission in life.

I go home to my ironing board and pump out three workable jokes just floating on that euphoria. Little ditties about tossing bullies from their pedestals. Short, concise, rallying cries for the everyday freak, nerd, or otherwise marginalized and pushed around!

Fuck the Cheesecake Factory, I Quit!

On the first of the month, I move out of the Chinatown Projects. A childhood friend, Dan, needs a roommate on 7th and Folsom, a block from the Brainwash, my favorite place to perform. I still have The Mock Cafe on Saturdays, 50 Mason seems promising, but 333 Columbus blew up in my face. I had let the other comics babysit it so I could headline 50 Mason and fuck that satanist. That was a mistake.

I show up the next week at 333, and Betty Boop Jr. goes into the office to hide from what's about to happen. I'm starting to think they met as pen pals from *his* cell, to *her* heart. She's as scared of him as everyone else. So, the chef stops cooking, comes out, and starts yelling about N-word this, N-word that at me. *What the fuck?* This motherfucker is scaring me. I don't need to see him with his shirt off to know there are "white pride" tattoos everywhere.

How the fuck did this guy learn the *mother sauces* in San Quentin? He's throwing up pretty decent French food into the pass, and I'm not selling any of it downstairs. I can see why he's a little frustrated. I **did** promise to sell food, and I thought I would, but comedy shows are full of cheapskate tourists just looking for a place to sit for a while. I don't know how to tell this guy I'm going to have a hard time pushing the $26 *Osso Buco* on Mary, the Irish retiree paying in change. We're selling the fuck out of beers, though, but this doesn't seem to matter to him. His huge, mutton-chopped face gets so red and angry I feel like I should back up a little bit and be ready for a bull charge.

His look is Modesto biker gang, but his menu is strictly *Lyonne. Ain't no gastriques on the yard, Wood! And this ain't the got-damned Rhone,* I say in my head, making sure to whisper it, even in my mind. "Look at these discount shoppers in this neighborhood, Chef," I actually say, as respectfully as possible without sounding meek, "A lady was making her own lemonade last time I was down there."

He says for me to get my mic-stand and amp out of there. So that's that. The audience is going to show up, not knowing the show is canceled. I hope when he tries to hand them menus, they all say, "Risotto? In the summer? You got any pizza slices and Budweiser, Broham?"

I ask the other comics what happened, and they just shrug their shoulders and say, "That chef is crazy. He said we 'better sell food to every table.' The host told them about the fuckin' risotto. They didn't want the risotto. What did he expect? We could have sold the fuck out of some buffalo wings. Is the guy too fancy for buffalo wings? Beer pitchers, maybe?"

"Wait. Sirof. You didn't tell him he should be serving buffalo wings, did you?"

His look is a confession, "Well, I just thought the place needed some pointers."

Fuck.

The losses come often in comedy, but other shitty opportunities always arise to take their place. In a dynamic location like the Bay Area, it's a great place for stage time as a non-famous performer. Plenty of reasonably good to shitty stage time to go around. The audiences are educated but a little particular. They laugh, but only if you're brilliant, and you don't use any designated flag words currently on their shit list. The whole politically correct thing has really taken hold here, and sometimes ladies yell at me that I 'should be ashamed!' I always say that I am.

With the varying quality of the shows, mostly shitty, I kill about once per week—usually at the Brainwash. The Mock Cafe is great, too, just not quite as reliable killwise. It's an audience of non-comics, though, so valuable as gold. I'll soon prove that killing at 50 Mason is possible too. It's enough, but I want more. My personality type always wants more.

Bye, North Beach. I'll be back in a while. With my new house, in a new, centrally located neighborhood, I'm thinking about a new job. The Cheesecake Factory is getting stale. It's 2005, and it's time to feel alive!

The restaurants have proven to be quite insane and dysfunctional.

I sometimes complain about my constantly chaotic life, but I sure do seem to seek these situations out. To work in this restaurant, I filled out paperwork and gave my social security number—to be in chaos. I must love the shit. Pursuing a showbiz job and working in restaurants go hand in hand. The sexual harassment you begin encountering in the chophouses will prepare you for your meetings with showbiz producers.

But all that's starting to come to an end. Creeps and weirdos have gone too far in the restaurant business, and the girls are winning settlements. This new work environment makes it challenging for just regular oddballs like me. The ADHD I suspect I have makes a lot of my social interactions weird, which in public I relish, because I can just keep swimming forward like a shark, leaving behind awkward situations that I'll never have to look at again. But at work—and it always seems like it's the same person weirding out on you because you don't interact with them in their required corporate handbook style—it's just not as fun anymore. The customers are always going to suck, but the coworkers can't suck too.

San Francisco is going corporate, and once you can label someone 'odd' in that sort of environment, it's a gimme to get them labeled 'creepy' a month later. Then you just need one girl looking for shifts to say she felt uncomfortable around him, and *blammo,* he's fired. The R-rated San Francisco of the 90s went down with those Twin Towers, man. It's like, becoming the opposite of what it used to be. I can't let that happen. I'm getting out of the restaurant business anyway. These customers are straight disrespectful, and I'm likely to pick up an assault beef. I need something less customer-y?

One thing that happens this year is Youtube is huge right out of the gate. Girls are getting modeling contracts because their video of them brushing their hair got a million views. Kids are dying trying to pull crazier and crazier stunts for video counts. The Narco traffickers in Mexico are posting beheadings faster than Youtube can take them down. It's insane what the internet is becoming. The whole world can come into your bedroom now, and if you finger yourself on your webcam when they do, some of them will pay you. You used to have to go out to the bushes behind the Greyhound station for that type of stuff. Shit is crazy, man. And yet, I know this is a way to get famous without dealing with the showbiz assholes. So I'm trying to figure it out.

And if getting your eyes raped by all that shit isn't horrible enough, autocorrect now tells us that we are expressing our feelings wrong. It's like a little bitch ass HR department for your very style of personal expression, something that shouldn't ever be fucked with; not by a boss, lover, family, nothing. Tell me how to fuckin' talk? Fuck you. You think I should say, 'ducking'? Duck off autocorrect! Doh!

Autocorrect! Because why should being redirected or told you're wrong all the time be limited to the voice in your head, the workplace, or a sexual relationship? Fuck you, you stupid fucking paperclip.

With everything changing so fast all around me, I get the terrible news that Derrick Plourde, one of the greatest punk rock drummers of all time, and my childhood friend, has shot and killed himself. Why is it always the unique ones that die while unoriginal, empty skin bags flourish? Don't do heroin, kids, not even once to try it. With all the deaths among my childhood friends and acquaintances, I've become numb to bad news by the time I hit my 30s. My protective shield is built, but not for this one—not for the undisputed master of the *Goletian dialect*. The guy was from Mars in such a beautiful way. Derrick was unique, but he struggled more. So immensely talented and therefore tormented with a brain that never quieted down. A brain that wouldn't rest. They get fatigued and start hallucinating negative shit if you can't ever turn them off. Poor, poor Derrick. I wish I could have been there with my hand out for the gun. I could have talked him out of it. I think I could've.

One day, I'm offered a chance to duck—that word again—out of this horrible Cheesecake Factory job when a table full of palm readers sits down. I recognize them from the upstairs and to the left of Vesuvio Bar, a palm reader spot. Three ladies and a preteen girl. They insist that it's part of their religion that women can only serve them. I'm allowed to take the order, but all the food and drinks must be brought to them by women. I am initially annoyed, but then I see it as an opportunity to get all these chicks I've been scoring dead pizzas for to work on my table for free. Some of them are noticeably chubbier from my efforts, and it's time I saw a return on my investment.

So, we do what they want because, as I remind my manager, "When it comes to religion, you can't fuck around lawsuitwise. Remember the Muslims they fed bacon to in Georgia last year?"

So everything goes smooth until, at the end, they order all this to go shit. The palm readers just put down an appetizer and an entree each.

Now they're ordering at least that much more to leave with. As they're finishing up their Cheesecakes, one of them lifts up a hair to my face that looks like her own hair. *Bingo*. Now I see what they're up to.

"Let me talk to the manager," the chubby middle Eastern lady with a mustache says, theatrical disgust shooting like a laser from her upper lip and eyes."

I've told you that Cheesecake Factory has a reputation for being easy to get free shit from, right? Well, someone told these palm reader gypsies, and now they've got the new manager on the ropes. I think he might cry. She's insisting that we did it on purpose, as revenge for their unusual request. She's placed the single, thick, black, straight hair in a baggy and is shaking the evidence at him. He goes to the *point of sale* monitor to start taking a bunch of stuff off their bill, as all their to-go shit starts arriving at their table, creating a mountain of bagged styrofoam on the center of it. The ringleader gets up from her seat to get a busboy to clear the dessert plates, "No, not that one," to make room for the growing pyramid of densely packed calories.

"What the fuck is that?" The beaten, young, Asian man who can't graduate business school fast enough, says.

"Their to go stuff," I say, beaten as well.

In the end, they get $300 worth of shit for about $80. The kicker? Zero tip. *I'm going to break these bitches windows*. After that, I put a recorded message that says, "This is Justin, I'm going to the hospital right now with chest pains," and I let the calls from the manager just go straight to that; let them wonder whatever happened to me like they give a fuck. They can fire *me* on a second's notice, but I'm supposed to keep fucking *them* for two weeks after the breakup? Homey, don't play that.

No one ever calls your previous employers in this business anyway. Also, I'm pretty sure the chefs have some issues with not showing at the parole office. That might *red flag* some employment considerations. The restaurant industry has always been 'don't ask, don't tell.' Bunch of savages with nothing but smoldering bridge smoke and farts swirling in their wake. Shit, the hostess? Even she prostitutes and carries a gun. Do you think she's cute? She'll fucking rob you. She'll snort Ketamine off your duct-taped body. In real life, she's the opposite of how she answers the phone. You gotta be tough to work in a restaurant.

In a post-apocalyptic war of the San Francisco industries? I got money on bar and restaurant employees. They'll be wearing the soft hides of the retail workers and Financial District hustlers as loincloths the first day. The bike messengers would give us a little trouble, but we'd overwhelm them at the edges of Chinatown by week two.

At any rate, I'm granting myself a little reprieve from service industry savagery: a mental health break and an opportunity to start fresh in some critical areas of my life. I feel like I'm on the verge of something great, and I need to clear some of the clutter, starting with Union Square. It's easy to avoid that area if you don't have to go there to work in that dystopian consumer hell. Any neighborhood with a Burberry store should be demolished if you ask me. Seeing soccer moms all cracked out on the Clinique counter is starting to affect my mood. Goodbye, Union Square. You are a bunch of plasticky bullshit that costs way too much. Shopping addiction has to be the lamest hangup in the book. I'd rather be in rehab for compulsively eating mattress filling.

Seeing Borat with Maria Bamford!

I go into AMC 1000, A high-tech modern theatre outfitted with several Imax screens. A stadium-style multi-plex that is on that part of Van Ness that used to be called Dealership Row. Fancy cars, as far as the eye could see—priced at a few thousand bucks each. Back when a high school graduate could support a family of five while stopping in for a new Mustang every few years, all on a union job. I feel that was stolen from me.

This movie theatre used to be the West Coast flagship Cadillac showroom back in the *big-fin* days. You feel small in the vastness of the display floor, walking across it after buying your ticket. Before you enter the escalators to go up into the building's many floors, you pass underneath the old Cadillac office, where the dealers would offer a cocaine-filled soda, or perhaps a frosty Manhattan cocktail to a Montgomery Street Mad Man. The office has an ornate, hand-carved, dark wood staircase leading to more dark, carved wood. After a quick signing of some reasonably straightforward papers up there, you had the glory of pulling onto Van Ness Avenue in this year's *Coupe DeVille*.

Now, standing in that palpable past, waiting for a movie ticket to see a movie where a guy puts homosexual moves on an unsuspecting Ron Paul, the dipshit Libertarian senator, I see something fantastic walk through the door. It's Maria Bamford, one of the most incredible headlining comics alive! She's with Molly, the booker of The Punchline, and Al Madrigal. Al has *asshole* so entrenched in his soul, they say that when he was 12, his dad used to let him fire people on the jobsite. He's gotten a few TV credits lately, so his bully-cock is extra swollen right now. He's one of these guys like Kamau Bell that act as the gatekeepers to The Punchline. Isn't this cute? The teacher's pet is being treated to a movie.

They start passing the ticket windows because they got their tickets already, *but wait, they're stopping*. Maria Bamford herself says to the line,

"Does anybody want a ticket? We have an extra one."

Before anyone can process what she offered, I'm already before her with my best puppy dog eyes. "I'd love a ticket, Maria."

She looks surprised that I know her name. She's mildly famous—the best kind. *Ah, to have an Emile Hirsch level of fame.* "Oh, here you go." She hands me my ticket, and I grasp it like it's the golden ticket for Charlie and the Chocolate Factory.

"Oh, of course, I know who you are. Everybody should. I'm a big fan, Maria. A big fan!" Jesus, do I sound like Kathy Bates in Misery right now? Handle yourself, Scales.

"Oh, that's nice, what's your name?" she says as we walk towards the escalators together. *Team cool kid* is visibly stunned and begins to flounder for some sort of attempt to stop this. They hurry behind us. Once we reach a floor where you have to get off, walk five feet to the left, and continue upwards in an opposite diagonal, Al blocks my path, "Don't sit with us, bro," he says like the punk that he is.

Molly has Maria on the escalator going up already. She doesn't hear Al's bullshittery. I could very well shove my way through him, but I would look like the asshole, and Maria is my hero. I don't want to cause a scene in front of her. So, I just say, "Yeah, whatever, Al. Enjoy the movie."

I let them go in front but keep somewhat close. It's not like Maria invited me to sit with them. It's a movie anyway; what are we going to do, talk about being neurodivergent? So when we get in there, I grab the seat right behind Al.

So Borat comes on, and we go on a journey. What a film! I had no idea what to expect. This fucking guy is a genius. I think the part where he tries to kidnap Pamela Anderson is staged, but it's hard to tell. It's like a one-man Jackass movie with some Monty Python mixed in. A movie-length prank video that has a costume budget and is loosely scripted. A series of public buffooneries that are so absurd you can see how they work by shocking an unsuspecting public. By the time the victims get over the jolt, it's over. Nothing left but for the camera to soak in the expressions of awe on their faces. I think Sasha (Borat) is able to use his fancy movie and press credentials to get backstage at some crazy shit and cause chaos.

I love it—never seen anything like it. Huge belly laughs the whole way through. I laugh loud and weird into the back of Al's head the entire movie and lightly kick the back of his chair a dozen times.

My One-Man Show

I've written and mostly memorized my one-man show. A one-man show can be similar to stand-up, but it's more of a long-form campfire tale with some laughs sprinkled in. Without explosions or violence in a performance, you can hold an American audience's attention for about an hour, so I'm aiming to come in at 59 minutes.

I quickly find one of San Francisco's ubiquitous underground venues to do the run of shows. Everything is on Craigslist; how did we function before Craigslist? I have no idea. Just a block over from Moss Alley on Natoma is a red brick building called The Omni-Circus. There is a five-foot-tall whale vertebra on the stage, and the seating is layered upwards like you're performing for Tina Turner in the Thunderdome. A wall of heads. Epic.

I book Thursday, Friday, and Saturday for two weeks in a row, and I hash this thing out, even bringing notes on stage the first few nights. The audience is patient, and we get to the meat of the thing eventually. It's biographical. I call the show The Goat Lady's Son because some people called my mom The Goat Lady, even though it was a sheep on a leash she used to walk around town with. The sheep had a Guinea pig living on its back, and my mom had made the Guinea pig a sorcerer hat one time, and she walked up to me in public like that. I didn't choose the comedy life, folks. It chose me.

All I have to do is take them on a skip through the lowlights and highlights of my life up to now, and they should be howling it up.

On the last night, my comedy hero—if I believed in heroes—Brent Weinbach shows up! Josh Keppel comes to tape it with an expensive video camera, and Motormouth Scott shows up. So does Joanne with a scraggly crew that looks like examples of the characters I'll be talking about tonight. Sometimes the audience is skeptical at some of my claims, and Motormouth, or Joanne, in an unspoken pact, stands up and says, "I was there! I saw it!" to calm them down.

(There are little pieces of this show elsewhere in this book, so I'll just say it's basically about living in a teepee in Santa Barbara. Hilarity ensued. Also, there's a book that the one-man show turned into. It's called *The Goat Lady's Son and the Child Gladiators of Isla Vista*. So, if you care, run get dat. They're saying it's pretty good.)

At the end of the last show, Brent Weinbach walks out and nods his head at me, his reliable signal that he liked that night's presentation. This subtle head nod is all I need to make it all worth it, but here comes more accolades! I feel like Kristy Yamaguchi skating through piles of roses at the Olympics. Sometimes, I worry that I'm getting more out of the attention than the spiritual benefits of creatorship and sharing. Of course, it's okay for a performer to receive both—fuck that humble monk shit, right?—but you gotta balance it out.

If the Bullshitter of the Year Competition was my TV show idea, this is for the movie. I'm building a full-service, multi-medium storytelling business. "Oh, you're a Vietnamese water puppet fanatic? *Boom!* Check this shit out!" My theory is that storytelling is storytelling, and you should be able to adapt it to different mediums as if it's an obstacle course challenge. How many *ways* can you tell a story? Even if you only tell it in one way later, the fact you put it through the process will make that final form more glorious in the end. The other forms give up their mojo to add to the final clay, paint, fireside story, or haiku. Telling the same story in different forms is the way of the master. Even though I was never able to make the teepee and sorcerer-hatted guinea pig material work consistently in stand-up, I feel like seven minutes isn't long enough to sell such a wild story. Not to an audience that just found out who you were when the host said your name—the fact that I tried made the one-man show it would be added to better. Leave room for experimentation. You might mystify an audience into a catatonic state sometimes, but it keeps things fresh and exciting. It guarantees you will stay supple and versatile.

My plan is to discover modes of storytelling no one has even thought of yet. As the Beats told stories in finger snaps and 'groovy baby's,' perhaps I will develop a way of storytelling so unique, it will make the wagging fingers of elder judgment turn back upon themselves. Countries will throw out their flags and tear down their walls, and we will truly become *one people* like Bob Marley wanted. Does that sound too hippie-dippie for someone called the Dirty Comedian? Well, I don't fuckin' care; that's what I'm trying to do.

The 16th & Mission Open-Mic

One night, I'm outside the Brainwash after a good set talking to Tony Sparks, and he's all, "Hey Baby, you seen that open-mic outside the BART station at 16th and Mission on Thursday nights? Starts in about an hour. Talk about chaotic environments. If you could do there, what you do here? Ah, shit, baby. You'd be declared a Jedi by Dave Chapelle himself. They's about 60 people there when I rolled by. They was into it."

"16th and Mission Bart? You sure it wasn't just a guy with a guitar that got himself a crowd?" I say, surprised.

"No, it was running pretty much like an open-mic, 'cept there ain't no mic. And get this, no list to sign up on. You gotta charge up right after someone finishes. If you tie with another performer, they roshambo it out. It's wild, baby. I'm surprised you ain't been down there already."

I'm intrigued, and after I finish my beer, I start making my way there, through the wasteland that is the SOMA to Mission route. If you make it past the freeway bridges that bisect the two neighborhoods, you have a chance of not getting mugged. I'm rehearsing my material out loud with my hoodie up, so everyone thinks I'm a funny crackhead, which isn't too far off base. I'm smoking about two or three $20 rocks a week. My habit would be considered pretty low-level to these professional freebasers. Crack makes my hangovers worse, but I'm still functioning at standard rates, which is 'pay my $400 rent no matter what,' everything else is fair game after that. Admittedly, my bar to 'adulthood' is pretty flimsy, but at least I'm not a furry fetishist… or a raver.

I arrive at this thing, and Tony wasn't lying. There are dozens of people watching the stage, marked in a geometric, circular design, expertly drawn in chalk. Soon, I will be bouncing around the edges of that chalk circle like an out-of-control spirograph. Performing now is Charlie Getter, performing a poem I must assume is called "Sweet Onion Salad." Charlie has appeared as if from nowhere, perhaps with foreknowledge of just the exact second the last performer's song ended. He pauses in sighed recoil, seems to become possessed suddenly, lurches forth a bit while cocking his head, and with a euphoric expression of a yogi attaining nirvana, he approaches his magical verses of gastronomic glee.

Charlie sports a raggedy Boston Red Sox hat and a blond goatee poking off of his chin. A slight beer belly paunch he's earned at a thousand happy hours where the hipsters are thin, and they never grin. There's a little grey in there, too, though he's still in his 30s. Those are the hairs that suspect the trouble he's in. His wild, excited eyes speak of an orgiastic madness. He licks his lips a bit and digs in:

"She bought me a bouquet of flowers, purple and blue…
I got some little stuffed animals worth talking to…
She brought some DVDs...
of John Candy movies...
& she made me a sweet onion salad...
It's raining, yes, and cold to bet...
and outside the weather does blow blow blow, but I'm feeling blessed, I am, you guessed...
cuz I got me a sweet onion salad...
there's an island in the South Atlantic named after South Georgia...
they say Georgia's all about the peach, but that's a reach...
Peaches won't grow close to Antarctic snow and in the south Georgia I know, they grow the finest of cloves
that she turns into sweet onion salad…"

Charlie pauses to scan us, to eat in our love. That love is half the reason—at least—that most of us do this stage performing thing. Not enough daddy hugs, I guess. He seems to be satisfied with the level of adoration, and plunges in again:

"Sweet onions ... sweet onions, warming up a poor man's bunions, turning hearts into mush that gush gush gush, like some three am lush…

calling, calling, that gush gush gush, like some three am lush, calling, calling...
telephones are weird detached voices over continents, talking, talking...
words beamed over satellites just right to a...
long green dress...
curled up...
under the Petaluma gloom...
She bought me some DeWalt tools on sale. Now I can drill holes underwater...
And I think if we don't be careful soon...
she'll be carrying a brown-eyed daughter...
but she'll be pretty, I think...
and work in a coffee shop...
and we'll give her a lovely and long and elaborate name...
but we'll call her Liz...
and the sun will shine and the dogs will run under it...
and I'll have... a sweet onion salad...
where cherry tomatoes will bob...
in the oil and vinegar, and the arugula...
will swim with the sweet onion slices...
and the fresh mozzarella, creamy and soft and warm as a long green dress on a cold Petaluma Monday...
someday... someday...
planes will fly and bringing people farther away and closer together
and someday... someday...
people will cry, peeling...
Vidalias under a cloudy sky and...
someday... someday...
I'll carry a basket of wishes under my coat...
and wrap it with a bow and hand it to you...
with a bouquet of flowers, purple and blue and a little stuft version of Winnie the Pooh...
and a DVD better than Caddyshack Two....
and some onions to turn into salad...
so sweet, they'll warm the cute bunions that grow on your feet...
that they will, and they will in a life as sweet...
as the onions, they turn into salad...."

Charlie retracts into his bow and slumps into the final stage of his exaltation. This guy is good.

The crew of raggedy poets, guitar players, performance artists, city college students, hash dealers, and psychiatric patients goes nuts.

Wow. I usually hate poetry, but this guy got me right off the bat. As I watch the performers, trying to get the courage to jump up there, I drink my whiskey from a half-pint and decide which jokes to do. I decide my longer bits or the weird stuff that didn't work on regular audiences might have a second chance at life here. The stuff about living in the teepee springs to mind. An exciting prospect. These kids are talented. I see a teenager named Julie rock a guitar and sing her goddamn heart out up to the moon. Another 19-year-old named Guinevere Q sings a hilarious song deftly as she strums her acoustic. Next, a guy named Carson comes up and raps. Someone just tells a fucked up story, then a guy comes up to smoke a hit of crack and yells at us silly crackers for trying to change the neighborhood. We're not sure if he scripted this out previously or if he's just freestyling.

All of this is happening on what is arguably the most drug-infested corner on the West Coast. What courage these kids have to try and make something good happen here. There's enough of them to discourage abuse from the regular clientele as we saw a minute ago. Some of the druggies like it and sit close enough to watch or even perform.

Shit, it's my turn to jump. I did it! No one is challenging me to roshambo. They're all looking at me, "Pardon me, if, throughout the course of the evening, I display too much confidence. But do not shrink away! I'm not trying to sap you of your energies. I'm trying to grow both of ours. They want us to act small so that we *will* be small, so they can be bigger than is their share. I have an idea: let's burn their houses down and chase them into the swamps!"

Ok, do a funny one.

"So, I was going to take a leak in the middle of the night at this girl's house because I'm a drinker, and I'm a little old now too, and so my prostate is more blown-out than Madonna's raggedy snatch. And trying to find my way in the dark, I smash my shin on the corner of her stupid bed. As if the extreme pain from that wasn't bad enough, do you know what she told me?"

"What!!" they all go.

"She said, 'Don't worry, everybody does that.'"

"Haha," they laugh at my excruciating pain and additional anguish.

"And it was how she said it, like 'Don't worry, E-e-e-e-verybody does that.' Like she was listing off all the names on a fucking war memorial."

"Haha."

"All the soldiers who fell in the battle of the gap!"

"Remember folks, handing a crackhead a burrito speaks louder than anything I could scream at you tonight. So consider me as your potential crackhead burrito recipient. I was sucking the glass cock right before I got up here. I love this corner!"

I motion a vigorous crack hit. *Shhhlllrrrrr!!!*

"Shut me up with *carnitas,* bitch!"

I do a few more weird jokes and get off. It's fun. I got a few laughs and bump half-pints of whiskey with some new friends that I meet. There's none of that high school game bullshit like at the comedy club. I feel more welcomed by these rag-tag spoken word poets and acoustic guitarists than I ever have by the comedy community.

Dave Chappelle's Cigarettes

A lot of the comics are nice to me. Like, half of them. Many even watch me perform, all wide-eyed and adoring at the smaller shows, and then give me the cold shoulder at The Punchline. They've been convinced that being seen talking to that dirty comic could hamper their chances at a fifty-dollar hosting gig at the premiere club in Northern California. The only game in town around here if you're angling for TV credits. TV credits are supposed to be all of our main desires at this point. Comedy careers are built by legos made from TV credits. So if you have a chance to stab your friend in the back for one, consider it a blessing.

Apparently, my style is too aggressive. Some of the senior comics are saying that Molly, the booker, might not think my act fits in with the club's vibe. This means that's what the senior comics are trying to convince her. Ever since I didn't run over to offer Kamau Bell a set at my North Beach show, he's been cold as ice. How dare I? So now, under Kamau's gaze, all my supposed friends walk by me to their usual stools at the bar without saying 'hello.' Well, I don't need friends like that, and so my circle is pretty small; a few unfunny comics that have character, and some funnier guys like Arj Barker and Brent Weinbach, who see that I have talent, and don't mind the weirdness of it. Some of The Punchline employees like me and don't give a fuck who knows. So that's nice.

I'm always here on Sundays, sitting on a stool up against the bar, waiting to not go up, drinking stiff Jack and Cokes made by my bartender/comedian friend Pappas. He's a skinny East Coaster who usually wears a black leather jacket and smokes like a refinery. He's got high cheekbones, pursed lips, and the complexion of a vampire. If the sun is up, he's not. He gets his whores from bad neighborhoods where the sex is so cheap every transaction is like its own little gender reveal party. He digs my comedy. Great dude. He'll be working the bar tonight, and the host will call his name to go on stage—and I guess *those* people aren't getting drinks for a while. Pappas is all, "Nothing I say tonight will ever be as funny as watching a fat girl fall down some stairs."

Sirof is already hosting all the time, so I get less hopeful about my chances when I compare my status to his. We started the same week, and he already has headshots and video clips on a DVD. These are to hand out to any Hollywood types that come to the club. Sirof's already profuse confidence becomes annoyingly grandiose as he chides me for my supposedly slow progress. He's excited to be able to ignore the fact that I get bigger laughs now that he looks better on paper. I have to admit; it gets under my skin a little.

Despite my lack of progress at The Punchline, I've been soaking up the comedy world here. The ins and outs of the business, who the underrated geniuses are, the stories too insane to believe. All the greats cruise through here, and many of them are generous with their time. One bitter headliner tells me, "Show business types could give a fuck about how good your material is or how hard you kill. It's your look and sound. Are you a programmable robot that can be made into what they think a focus group wants? Fuck show business, turn back while you can, kid." This story checks out when I see middle-of-the-road guys with squeaky, cartoon voices get opportunities, while geniuses like Brent Weinbach and Will Franken get nothing because they're neurodivergent types who don't understand business or how to schmooze. They are supposedly too weird or too niche.

Somehow guys like us need to get famous on the internet. I know this and yet still have no idea how to upload a file from a thumb drive.

Another thing I learn is smart girl comics are greeted lukewarm in show business, whereas girls who play the ditz? If you're, what we'd call "pussy forward"? Well, "Welcome to showbiz, sweety!" The smart girls like me, and I do all I can to help them. The biggest help I'm able to offer them is to try to be an incel buffer. I jokingly tell them to pretend we have beef, and they'd get booked more. The girls like me pretty well, like, half of them.

The minority comics like me pretty well. Guess who comes up to me after I tell a joke that goes, "I was out on a date with Janine! And she said, 'I have multiple personalities!' *Great,* I thought. Maybe I'll get gangbanged. I got gangbanged all right. Unfortunately, three of her personalities were big Black dudes."

Again, guess who would come up to me and tell me, "You shouldn't say, **big Black dudes**?" Mission Viejo Michelle or Laguna Niguel Danielle?

Spoiler alert: Both. The big Black dudes are the laughingest motherfuckers in the audience at that joke, so fuck off, Michelle. You ain't really *about* that life. Ever since you blew Li'l Bow Wow at your *sweet 16* party, you've been trying to claim ghetto status. That ain't enough. I didn't see you at the protests last month. Social justice usually comes with the word 'Warrior,' Michelle!

I mean, that joke *is* more trouble than it's worth because it's got flag words *and* rape, which is why I just **have** to tell it every night. I'm the one that gets raped, though. Does that help? Does context even matter anymore? Is absurdity proof of intent now? Some of the stuff I say is just stupid. I'm not one of those comics that wears a suit and uses words like 'pontificate.'

That being said, It's always these white, UC Berkeley-type kids complaining about my act on Yelp, or Google reviews, or what the fuck ever the bookers are mentioning to me. Some little Becky, or a skinny dude with fake, horn-rimmed glasses trying to get me banned from shit. I don't sweat them too much, but it's a shame so many of them find themselves at comedy shows. It's like the peanut allergy kid chowing down on a Payday bar. Why would you go to a comedy show if you are offended by almost all humor? When your mouth can't even smile, much less laugh? Aren't the comedians in enough pain?

What else? I know how to defend myself against hecklers now. That took some real attention and practice. The places you try to do shows in your first few years are brutal. You gotta be prepared. After a few of them almost got the best of me, I decided to put some effort into being *over-prepared* for the situation. First, I wrote some custom, savage burns that *sound* improvised and on the spot. That's what the audience wants, something off the cuff, spontaneous, improvised, off the top of your head. So, always try to actually *be* off the cuff first, and if it doesn't come, you fall back on the prewritten burn that *sounds* spontaneous.

Also, I nickname them right off the bat, it's quick, and it could be anything, even something stupid. One time there was a young crowd that didn't get me, and some kid started talking shit; I was like, "Look, Porky Boom Boom, don't you think you're biting off a little more than you can chew here? Seventh-grade playground roasts aren't going to cut it. Look, this guy's still got a fleck of white-out on his upper lip. Are they letting high schoolers into this show? Stay in school, kid, come back to me when you get a fuckin' GED."

You know, shit like that. It doesn't have to be amazing quality even. Nicknames kill, they're easy, and your quick entry into the game surprises them, puts them back on their heels enough for you to go right into the next insult. Now they're stunned. It's yours to fuck up now. She who quickly establishes the upper hand rarely loses. Make all the insults sound like you might have actual foreknowledge of this person, or make it based on their outfit, face, or what they said to try and verbally dominate you. It just has to be plausible by looking at them.

It's good advice to everybody—not just beginner comedians—to have a page of insults written on a page and memorize it for the hecklers *and* the bullies of regular life. Write them yourself—or, in the case of bullies, feel free to borrow insults from this book, just keep it off the comedy stages—or copy them from the internet. Beat up bullies with your mouth, it's safer, and if the bully hits you, no one can say the violence was mutual. They'll go to jail, and someone will bully *them*. Maybe that's what it takes for them to reflect on their behavior.

You can also do what I used to do if they want to get physical. Some guys won't take the roast. Why take a beatdown if you don't have to, right? So, when they approach, put your hands up in the air by your shoulders like you're giving up, but very quickly, spring forward, and palm their nose flat into their face as if you are trying to push it out the back of their head—practice on a tree branch that's about as high as a bully's nose. That should pretty much drop them. If you succeed, they won't bully you, or anyone around you, forevermore. If you *don't* succeed and get your ass kicked? Well, it's good to get a moderate amount of beatdowns in life. You might want to invest in a taser.

With hecklers and bullies, it hardly ever comes to that, though. You just gotta get some laughs from clowning them with prewritten but spontaneous sounding insults, and you've shifted the momentum back in your favor. Then, your brain will start spitting the improvised gems again—if your nature is so inclined. Otherwise, stick to the script, but without sounding scripted. Practice in the mirror, it worked for Travis Bickle.

It's hard too because you're sitting there looking at the heckler—okay, back to just hecklers at comedy shows—and them and the audience are looking at you, it's quiet, and every second feels like an hour. Your lip is burning. They're all waiting for you to say something funny in response to the heckler, when really you'd rather smash him with a trash can lid, like, "You dare interrupt my brilliance with your drunken belligerence? Try and shame me in front of all these people?" And you can't be too ruthless or even *one-up* them too hard. You have to pretend you appreciate the opportunity for the banter. He gets to be a shit bag, and you have to be a good sport.

I mean, should there be hecklers at comedy shows? I don't know. Half the time, it can help. The other half, you were unable to save the performance yourself, and they just kind of shit on it as it passed them. Is heckling fair? Who expects fairness? I don't know, fuck it. I say let 'em talk shit. It's *gonna* happen from time to time anyway. If there's enough dead air while you're up there for them to start a conversation, maybe a little crowd work is what they require. Some nights they want to talk. It's usually not even a heckle, just a clumsily asked question. Some comics are so scared they might have to go off their little scripts that any sound the audience makes that isn't appropriately timed, supportive laughter feels like heckling to them. I feel like most comics were bullied, and the stage is where they finally take back control. And now the bully even found them here, even in their happy place. That fleeting five to seven minutes each day, where *they* get to be the champion. It fucks some of the poor little guys up.

Fuck it, Dave. If they're rowdy, the long sociopolitical rant might not have worked that well anyway. It can wait for the intellectual Tuesday crowd. You always have to be ready to mix it up with the *piss and vinegar* audiences. It can be very rewarding.

After completing my third year in comedy, I've seen firsthand that joke theft is real, but if you just write every day, you'll be done with it by the time they steal it. It's crazy how casual people feel about joke theft the higher up you go in the business. There's a real 'whoever gets it onto TV first' mentality. This highly benefits the guys who've already made it and shits down the throats of those of us down in the crab bucket. Fuckin' Morgan Freeman himself said in one of his Actor's Studio interviews, "I'm a great thief. If I see something another actor is doing, I'll steal it." ***What the fuck did you just say?!*** Samuel Jackson shouts inside my head when I hear that. This is Morgan Freeman, the grandfather of America, saying this. You can only imagine what these other pricks are up to. How protected your intellectual property is depends on how many lawyers you can afford to retain, which, if you're performing at the Punchline's Sunday showcase, that number is probably zero.

At the open-mics, the incels whisper about how all of our best jokes are being told on the road. No one is there to call them a thief in Tuscaloosa. LA comics will watch us all at the Punchline showcases, and next thing you know, someone's closer is on Saturday Night Live. Some headliners are unscrupulous and will jack a few jokes from the local openers once they are safe in the next town. Carlos Mencia is just doing what dozens of other headliners do as matter of factly as buying a farmer's market eggplant. Many of these guys got into the business because their uncle is somebody, and they couldn't write a punchline that could even make some surfers on *mushrooms* laugh.

Do you think show business nepotism ends with movie roles? Shit. Pauly Shore's mom owns the *gawtdamned* Comedy Store. The rich kids need the poor kids to steal ideas from because when your whole life is rolled out simply in front of you, you don't have to ever be resourceful or imaginative, so those muscles in your brains die by Jr. high. I mean, why don't people talk more about how The Rolling Stones stole most of their sound from poor, Black, Mississippi Delta musicians? It's because privileged white kids get away with too much. Ya think? They're so bold about it. I guess we just don't question it anymore. The British Invasion was precisely that; they invaded those poor fuckers in the Mississippi Delta and raped and pillaged their concepts and their riffs. Comedy clubs are the same shit. So, I just write jokes every day. Steal a few if you need to, losers. I'm already writing better jokes than the ones you stole anyway. You won't be able to deliver them crazy enough to make them work anyway.

It is staggering though, I'm over 30 years old, and the rich kids are still trying to take all the best shit for themselves. I survived all this shit, and they're still at the gates of everything, checking everyone for *poverty PTSD*, like being able to afford the best bikes, guitars, surfboards, and lessons weren't enough of an advantage. Yet, you still manage to compete, and they stick you in the rib with a poisonous shiv right before the big dance. All you've done is vaccinate me from your poisons with your thousand little stabs, you little pieces of shits. Bring it on!

My struggles continue, but the booker puts me up often enough to stay interested. The offer for paid work at The Punchline just never comes, though. It can't be because they think I'm not good at comedy—I've killed the last three times in a row I went up. I keep hanging around because Dave Chappelle could walk through the door at any second. Management even keeps two packs of Marlboro Reds in the safe just in case he does. There's also the unlimited cocktails for two bucks that keep me coming in. I mean, shit, you can't expect me to be sober for all the local comics doing the same shit all the time. Maybe management forced the bartenders to tell them how many drinks I'm putting down every Sunday. They think I'll be too drunk around the headliners.

I don't need booze to perform, but it usually doesn't hurt. I need it to arrive at the gig and bide my time until I perform. Once the mic hits my hand it all goes away; the anxiety, the ADHD—I can't concentrate, like, at all, unless I'm fascinated by the subject or activity, is the main issue. Try explaining that to a fucking employer. Once on stage, I become *performer Justin*, supremely confident, almost invincible. The waiting to go up is when the intrusive thoughts of self-doubt show up. Alcohol shuts those up for long enough to get up there—I'm also really self-medicating with alcohol and have for quite some time, for a lot of unresolved childhood trauma. I mean, if you wanted to lay me on the Psychiatrist's couch right now.

Performer Justin is protected. He's going too fast for the intrusive thoughts—Felliniesque horror films written and directed by my mind's backseat driver—of, among his other greatest hits, terrible things happening to people I love. I'm perpetually trying to go a million miles per hour to stay up ahead of the distracting thoughts. I know it's you, backseat driver! I fucking know it's you making the intrusive thoughts. You are a two-trick pony: nightmare premonitions that never happen and backseat heckling. Fuck you! What a little bitch you are. I notice the intrusive thoughts come faster the more I beat you in our morning roast battles. Your desperate last attempts to keep control of me will be in vain. I understand you now. You are a pathetic loser with no resume, just a seat in my brain and a megaphone. You probably don't even have legs! A parasite who is frustrated, I'm learning to make my blood bitter. Suck it, parasite, suck my bitter blood until it poisons you.

Pauly Shore Can Suck It

I see that the San Jose Improv is holding an open audition for host and feature spots. So I get into a carload of comedians, and we show up there. There's the general manager and his assistant manager named Hollister. This guy Hollister is using all the Cliff's Notes, comedy club manager moves, trying to get all of us to feel blessed we have an opportunity to work for almost free. He does this with quotes like "This will be great exposure," and, "Oh, well, maybe I'll call this guy instead, are you sure you can't do the Saturday shows for $50 a show?" or, who can forget this classic? "Oh, I forgot to sign the check? Oopsy."

These comedy club assistant manager types are often comedy groupies that sucked at—or never had the balls to try—comedy themselves. Now they relish the chance to be an authority over people with actual talent to be able to punish them for being better than they were. At least until you get a name, then they instantly stick their tongue up your ass like a hummingbird at a syrup feeder. Until your career reaches *hummingbird tongue* level, your ass is grass.

It's a chance for these guys to be around the craft, even if they weren't good at it. They are the lapdogs that cater to the headliner's every need—like what Puffy used to do in the hip hop business, before taking it over—"Do you need anything else, Mr. Dick?" They claim to be friends with the headliners. They'll try to show you text exchanges they have on their phones with Larry the Cable Guy when they're drunk, thinking you're impressed. I'll, unfortunately, deal with this guy for the entire year of 2007. It's work, I guess.

I find myself on the stage of the San Jose Improv, housed in a historic theatre built in 1904 by the guy that invented Monterey Jack cheese. Big, old school marquee outside that advertises the weekend's headliner and any significant locally produced weekday shows under that.

The original bricks create the wall behind you. The floorboards look original too. They creak in the empty theatre as I take command of the mic. I'm suddenly up there dressed in a suit, to no audience, to do my "tight five," as they call it in the business; your absolute best, cleanest, most repeated five minutes.

I look good. Harvey Weinstein would definitely want to roofie me. This is the best first impression you can make at a show business audition.

"Hey! Full house tonight, I like it. Hey, so I was in the park the other day, and this kid's ball rolled up to me. So I threw it back to him, and the kid's mom got all mad at me. It was almost… as if the kid had never even *played* dodgeball."

The crowd doesn't go wild because there isn't one. The GM uncrosses his arms, a good sign, maybe? I do a little crowd work on some nonexistent front row customers, "Damn, lady, save some guffaws for my closer. And this guy over here looks like he's at an autopsy. Liven up, buddy. They might start cutting into ***you*** next."

Crickets, the only choice available.

"Hey, remember that song by the Beatles that went, '*Lovely Rita, Meter Maid*'? Isn't that sweet? A meter maid. She's lovely. Obviously, these guys never came to San Francisco and took a look at *our* meter maids. That song would have gone a little more different: '*Angry Nancy!! Devil Whore! Ate her own babies for Breeeaak-f-a-s-t!*"

Wrong city. We're in San Jose. More crickets.

I can't tell if they like me or not, but I'm the only one they summon into the office.

"That was one of the best auditions we've ever seen for a host spot. You did great!" says the assistant manager. The GM is standing behind him, nodding in approval. This would be the last nice thing Hollister ever says to me. I guess they want to make sure you've bitten the hook before they start jerking you around.

In the coming weeks, I will come all the way down on the train to make $50 performing for tech company corporate buyouts. You're supposed to just do a few jokes about their company before launching into your regular material.

Those go fine because I have plenty of jokes that are clean or can be easily cleaned up. So I bite the bullet, telling myself I'm not selling out; I'm just compromising until I earn a name in the business.

Soon, I'm featuring for Pauly Shore on the weekend, not hosting, featuring. Nice!

Pauly has all the employees of the San Jose Improv come to work two hours early for a meeting about how he needs to be addressed and catered to. Get this; HE is the speaker at the meeting. Haha, what a douchenozzle.

I blow him off the stage every show, and by Saturday, he comes up to me in the separate green room I'm assigned because the opener isn't allowed to be in the same green room as him, and he's all, "You're stealin' my gravy bro, too many dick jokes, bro."

This fuckin' guy. So, I go to get on stage that night, and I'm like, should I just let his little bitch ass win? And I decide, *No.*

The host mispronounces my name. I could get a laugh by correcting him because half of any audience that shows up for Pauly Shore is a bunch of little rats and would reward me with a smattering of laughter for selling out my own. I pass on that opportunity. Fuck it, let them think my name is Skyles. It's San Jose *and* a Pauly Shore crowd, maybe throwing these people off my scent is the wise maneuver. The host also announced me as an SF comic, and I look hella caucasian. So, I better start with an *I grew up in poverty* joke before I start torching *them.*

"So when I was little, when it would rain out, all the other kids would come to school with their fancy little rubber boots, you know what I would have to wear, Improv?"

"What!?" they say.

"Bread bags! Rubber banded over my shoes. They didn't even match half the time. I had one 'white' foot and one 'wheat' foot!"

"Hahaha," I add a girly giggle to their laugh, and they love it.

So let's do a joke like I understand the neighborhood I'm in.

"Improv!" I know the venue I'm in. Check. "I was across the street at the bar over there after last night's show? And there was a bunch of buff dudes acting like they were tough or something? And I was like, 'Look, *tech bro,* how tough could you be? You live in San Jose.' *'Oh, man, we ran out of Red Bull last week and had to use Rock Star to put in our vodka!'* Get the fuck out of here, you pussies!"

"Haha."

"Improv? I was recently standing outside a club much like this one, enjoying what I felt to be a highly delicious cigarette. And this Huuuge dude came up and bummed one off me, right? And I'm skinny, so of course, I had to fuckin' give it to him. And as I was lighting his cigarette for him," I extend out a shaky phantom lighter, "I notice he has like 15 teardrops tattooed on his cheek."

It gets quiet because there are a couple of guys with tear-drop tattoos in here. "And I go, 'Oh, so I guess your the big fuckin' crybaby!'"

They go pretty much nuts. Except for sad boi, cry baby tattoo in the third row. I look at him and go, "Awwww, do you want your fuckin' Finding Nemo blankey, Holmes?"

I might get stabbed later, but self-preservation has never been a concern of mine when it comes to having a good time—*Bahdoop a doop doop*. Keep skipping with another short one. "So, I was fantasizing about choking my landlord, right?! Just chokin' the fuck out of him, and I was like, 'Wait a minute, I live in a van.'"

"Haha."

"When I was born, I was four pounds, Improv! My mom said I shivered for the first six months of my life, like a wet, tiny, blue-lipped Chihuahua. Now the Pro-o-o-o-blem… with bein' a blue baby, is that after that you *hate* the cold. Any other torture I could withstand. Even if Osama Bin Laden himself was threatenin' to drive nail through my weenis! I'd just look at him and laugh. I'd be like, 'I'm from San Francisco

Osama, we pay money for that shit! Let me go pick out some jewelry for my little rhinestone cowboy!'"

"Hahaha!" I motion in a hand circle and some hip jerks to indicate that the cowboy lives a fortuitous frontier life in my pants.

"But if he took that same nail, put it in the freezer for ten minutes, then rubbed it on the back of my neck! I'd be like, 'Sorry, mom! They made me blab about the chicken pot pie recipe! I had to tell 'em about the extra corn!!"

"Hahaha."

"I'm killing this guy," I say, pointing at a guy in the second row. "What the fuck is **your** problem?!" I ask another.

"They say!"

"Hahahaha," goes one guy insanily, most likely from the last joke hitting him finally.

"Hey, chill it out bro, the punchline is up the road a bit."

"Hehe."

"They say... that the higher income and the higher education a woman has, the more easily she reaches orgasm. No shit. If I were making 200 grand a year, I'd be squirting all over everything too."

"What?" they guffaw in disbelief that I'm saying the things I'm saying.

"When asked if this was true in *her* life, Condoleeza Rice bit four people in the fuckin' face. And then she came… six times. On the sixth orgasm, that fuckin' gap in her tooth started whistling."

"Holy shit!" Someone says above the considerable laughter. Ok, let's get filthy.

"When I do finally get elected Supreme Court Justice… I'm going to judge each crime based on the interestingness of its perpetration. For instance, if **you, sir,** embezzle old people's retirement funds? Extra prison for lack of originality. But if **you sir,**" pointing at a different guy, "convince a girl to let you go anal... because you told her your dick is allergic to pussy juice?"

They, of course, laugh. I'm getting tired of explaining these parts, so just assume it, okay? I'm a motherfucking stage pimp. They laugh all the time. *Capiche?*

"Amnesty, you get amnesty for that. Fuck it, if you find a girl that stupid? You get a free fuckin' Cadillac!"

Wait, the laugh wasn't that big. I should not have been cocky just now. Shit.

"Hey, motherfuckers! Laugh it up. Pauly is on next, and if it's not perceived that I'd gotten you all enthusiastic enough? *I* get docked. Laugh it up, **chuckle butts**! Daddy needs to get paid so he can get laid!"

Ok, there's the light. Let's bring 'er home. "Improv? The largest porn industry in the world is right next to Hollywood in the San Fernando Valley. Do you know why it's so close to Hollywood? Because once Hollywood abuses you and crushes your dreams… a bus pulls up, like, 'Come on Jenny! You're going to your new home. Except instead of sucking dick *for* a part, sucking dick *is* the part."

Gasp.

"You're going to love it, Jenny! 'Do they have cocaine there?' Even better Jenny, all the meth you can butt-chug!"

I then go into Pelican Beaks, my trusty closer, which always kills, and take a bow. Passing Pauly at the big burgundy velvet curtain, he looks at me like someone would look at a piece of white, furry dogshit. I crushed it with no name recognition, something he can't even do *with* name recognition. This guy is the epitome of Hollywood, rich kid, nepotism. Suck it, Pauly.

After the show, Pauly tries to get me to control the lines to his merch table, which he sits behind as if it's an iron throne. He wants one line for people to buy signed 8x10 glossies of him and another line to do pictures, "But no cellphone pictures! It has to be a real camera!" he barks at me to enforce. Cellphone pictures with celebrities are ubiquitous on the internet now. The prettier celebrities are complaining they don't look hot enough—at least not without their images being studio manipulated before they hit the interwebs. *How will we give every high schooler in Calabasas an eating disorder if the photographs of our asses aren't digitally altered before the manipulatable kids see them?* Why Pauly would give a shit? Who knows? You'd think the blurrier the pus bags underneath his eyes are, the happier he'd be.

A person comes up to me while I'm deciding if being booked at this club again matters enough to humor this sad, *yayo* destroyed, muppet head. This fan says to me, not him, "You were hilarious! Can we get a picture together?" This drives Pauly mad, "Lines are getting squirrely bro!" I look at the guy with his cellphone out, ready to take a picture with me, and say, "Sure, let's go outside and get the theatre in the background." I look at Pauly like, *You were gonna' complain about me anyway. Fuck you.*

Pauly Shore is the ultimate jibble-jabble troll doll that would do best to climb into his musty wack hovel in the '80s and leave real comics to handle the jokes.

Suck it, Pauly, just suck it.

Making the Cancer Beanie Lady Laugh

I'm staying out of trouble. I haven't fought anybody in years, and I'm staying away from damaged bar sluts—I do miss them. All of these life changes I've undertaken are to focus on becoming a great headliner. I have broken down and had a slew of one or three-night sexcapades that I'm able to sever in time before it becomes a distraction. When I go home with a girl, I can avoid the temptation of getting a $20 rock, which is the other way that I can finish Saturday night with a bang. One last chance to feel the adrenaline I get from the stage. I have some hiccups when it comes to violence. Some people just kind of beg to have their asses kicked, and I seem to be a magnet for them. I managed not to choke Pauly Shore, so I figure my game is getting stronger.

The first time I brawl with someone since that skinhead in Santa Barbara is a quick, random *one-off* that really has nothing to do with me. I'm in a bike messenger bar on Folsom called Cassidy's. A dive bar with a few pool tables, a jukebox, and filthy bathrooms. My kind of place. I'm sitting there making Rachel, a rosy-cheeked, busty, brunette bartendress laugh. I'm chipping away at my four-finger pour of Jameson's, and this crusty dude comes in and buys a beer. When she gives him a dollar back, he says, "No, I gave you a twenty!"

"Bullshit," says Rachel, used to this sort of shit. She drags the wrinkled five back out of the old school register and wriggles it in front of us.

"You fuckin' bitch, I'll kill you!" the guy screams and starts climbing over the bar to try and do exactly that. I grab him by the shirt and pull him back down and, since I must assume this is attempted murder, as he stated, I don't hold back. I use my left fist to smash his nose flat into his face. He'll be blowing out cartilage chunks from distended nostrils for weeks. I half expect him to just be dead with how hard I hit him, but he is an enterprising little tweaker. He lunges at me with his fingernails, trying to scratch my eyes out. *Splud!* I mash his nose in deeper—did some just squirt out his ear?—grab him in a traditional bouncer grip around the collar, and another lock around his elbow, pushing him towards the door so fast he trips and stumbles to keep up, disabling any attack he might try to launch. Before we get to the front door, he tries to wriggle out and get his little Gollum claws on my face. *Chock!* I ram his head into the free postcard rack that's just ads for local businesses. I try to knock him out with it, to no avail. A few dozen postcards spill out onto the ground. This guy was clearly outside sucking on a meth pipe to get his scam courage up, and now he's like a little tweaky Hulk.

I manage to get him out the door, and he proceeds to rub his face all over the front window, marking it in a crimson, biohazardous graffiti. He's making devil noises at us and laughing. Me, Rachel, and John Brown just sit there watching him, wondering if he's going to throw a manhole cover through the window or something.

Enough bike messengers are aware of the situation now, so I figure it's safe to wash this hepatitis blood off me. It all happened so fast. There are still people in the bar that didn't realize what was happening until this guy started in with his demonic window performance. Now everyone is looking in disgust as this guy spreads enough disease blood on the window to kill us and all of our future children. Rachel seems less fazed by all this than me. I guess when you are the sole employee of a bike messenger bar in South Market, you're just glad most of the blood is outside.

I finish my glass of whiskey and almost successfully wave off another. After all that, I go home, looking down the alley to see if tweaky Hulk is down there. Nope. I look up into the light-polluted, starless sky and think, *Well, it's going to be a while before I have to pay for a drink in that bar again. Wouldn't it have been amazing if E 40s "Captain save a Ho" came on the jukebox right that second?*

The second fucked up situation happened shortly after that. We began our evening at the Greenroom, a small-time comedy club in The Wharf. All tourists, all the time. The first six comics in a row bomb. Those of us who haven't gone up yet are whispering to each other about why that might be. The audience is fucking ancient, for starters. Sometimes the club will offer an entire cruise boat free admission on the weekdays in the hopes they buy some drinks or nachos. The margins in the comedy club business are slim to nil, and you have to crawl after every dollar. The owner and the employees are often comedy superfans, or they wouldn't do it for the peanuts you make in this business. Unless you're at the very top, that is. The highly mediocre Jay Leno gets paid; we all get played.

At any rate, it seems like one of *those* discount crowds, and the comics are going way soft on these old sunburnt people. They're doing their most agreeable material, just aiming to get consistent smatterings of laughter so they can avoid being depressed on the long drive back to Pleasanton.

There's a lady with a cancer beanie in the front row. This is not the show you imagine when you are excitedly cobbling together your first open-mic jokes. It's as if we're on a game show called "Comedy Ironman," and they designed it to be impossible to win because they don't even have the prize money if someone does.

I go up and scan their faces to decide which of my potential strategies to unleash. The tame shit hasn't worked; these people survived The Depression. They **want** it rough. At least that's what I'm about to gamble on—it's the only strategy that hasn't been attempted. This might be their last chance at a laugh so roommate material probably isn't going to work. I'm just going to talk about what a dipshit I am for a minute. Everybody loves that. Then I'll go into some shit about how things are 'fucked up nowadays, and weren't they better back in the day?' Old people eat that shit up.

"Hey folks, I'm what you may know as a *yoouung* person. You know us annoying fuckers, always texting on our phones, playing video games, asking to not be crushed by the weight of the ridiculous bills you guys keep inventing."

"Don't you guys own all the houses? What's up with these fuckin' rents, guys?"

Ooops, I forgot to trash myself first.

"Haha," one guy goes. That's all I needed.

"That's right, buddy. Remember when you got out of school and rent was $100? Then you walked right into a union job that paid 30 to 40 grand a year, right?"

"'Bout that," the guy says, going along. That's great. Don't jerk the pole. I'm the perfect amount of buzzed: three Jack and Cokes with a light layer of food under it.

Focus.

"You guys got to drive a new Mustang off the lot for three grand, straight to your house you paid 30 thousand for, all on a high school diploma. Do you know how much that shit costs now? 30 grand. Yeah, for the car. Just for the fuckin' car."

They laugh, thinking about how they figure they had it best. *Don't make it too mean now; you got a little groundswell.*

"For the house, you gotta sell your soul to corporate America. Ain't no union around to save you nowadays, Sonny. And that's why in 40 years the average salary is still about 30 grand. Except for my car costs what your house did, and my house would cost more than all the money you've ever fuckin' made. That's a nice little trick you guys pulled. But, of course, that union stuff all got labeled as communist by *you* assholes! Interesting."

A lighter laugh. I shouldn't have said 'assholes,' should have said 'guys.' Okay. Stay at them.

"Well, what was it back when you had it, Fred? I think it was 'American worker unity' back then, but then the government told us it was too expensive for my generation, so now it's 'communist.'"

Crickets.

"Fuck you; it's communist! You guys had it, and now *we* want it. Fair's fair! If that's communist, to not be afraid all the time if I'm going to find myself on the streets with a $20,000 doctor bill for my busted leg. If that makes me a communist..? Well, then call me Ho Chi Fuckin' MIHN!!"

They laugh. The elderly audience gets it because, subconsciously, they have the same fear. Ah, the first real laugh of the whole night. Okay, it was a rough first date. But they know I know who they are, and now they know a little about me. *You were just laying a foundation.*

"Where's the landlord guy that was laughing in the beginning?!" I rush over to him.

"You lower those fucking rents, Ralph!" I shake my fist and squint an eye like I'm in a Popeye cartoon.

"It's just a duplex," says Ralph, proving I pegged one if not all of his income streams. This gets a laugh. He's a big old guy with a walrus mustache and a pinky ring. If he's not from Texas, I bet he hunts there a lot. *Should I go in on that?* Nah, once you do too much crowd work, you can't get back to regular material. It's an *improvised experience* at that point, and transitioning back is too much emotional gear switching for them. One more light roasting of Ralph, and it's back to the jokes.

I appeal to the audience, which is lightly chuckling, "This guy is charging two grand per college student to rent bunk beds in a bathroom! On Craigslist, he called it a 'spa-like environment.' What the fuck, Ralph?!" The fact that I named him Ralph makes it funnier. They are loosening up—another decent laugh.

Let's do a few jokes these people can relate to. Let's start with rapid memory loss, "Hey, you know when you're in a conversation with a group of people, and there's a new guy there? And he's pretty fascinating, but you forgot his name, and when he goes to the bathroom, you just pretend you forgot how to say it? You're like, 'How do you *pronounce* that guy's name again?' And they're like, 'Bob.' It's never Lucretious or some exotic shit. It's always, 'Bob.'"

A smattering. *Okay, do a top drawer joke. Don't fucking lose them! Death. These people are close enough to it to be getting Christmas cards from the reaper at this point. So what's a good one about death?*

"Folks? If you don't make plans for your belongings, then when you die, it all goes off to Goodwill. Why then, do they call it 'Goodwill?' They should call it 'Didn't even fuckin' have a will.'"

They howl for the first time. They laugh and spit in death's eye, like the Americans they are. Maybe offering them healthcare would be an insult. What are they, pansies? I keep the bit going while it's still hot. "These pants right here came off a guy named Grandpa Jenkins! Two bucks! I don't even care the pockets are haunted. All they do is steal change and blow wind on my balls. *Whoooooooo! Whooooooo!*"

They are primed up now. Let's do a dirty one; one they can relate to. "Hey! You ever be eatin' out a college chick and pull a muscle in your neck, but you don't want her to know how old you are, so you just throw the injury into the dirty talk? 'Oh look, I'm the hunchback of snatch! Can Igor have some *poonanny*? Igor looves the *poonanny,*" I hunch my shoulder and bulge out an eye while I shuffle towards the lady with the cancer beanie.

The crowd of sunburned retired cops and bank managers laugh their asses off, loving me for reminding them of their last business trip.

The cancer beanie lady manages a bit of a laugh as I pretend to be a hunchback, trying to eat her out. I kind of have to address her, I mean, she sat in the front row. Why would she have sat in the front row if she didn't want the comics to address her obvious condition? I mean, this lady looks like she's losing her fight. It's really sad. I want to make her laugh. I need to.

Now, if I do go in on her, and she doesn't laugh, then I will maybe be chased out of this building. But if she *does*? It will be like a blister of stress popping. It will bring down the house. It all hinges on if she laughs or not. Comedians are gamblers who gamble on the emotional reactions of strangers. Well... fuck it. It'll sew up my performance one way or another.

"Ma'am?" I say to her.

"Yes," she says quickly as if she wants to interact. *Nice!*

"I just have to know… when the Make a Wish Foundation called…" I milk the scared silence, taking the risk of all risks.

"Why the fuck would you wish for *this* bullshit?"

She laughs. Oh fuck, *praise be*, she laughs. This single laugh releases the steam that had built up the whole night so far and bewitched the other comics into confusion.

I pretend to be her on the phone with the Make a Wish Foundation, "Hello? Yeah, I want to go see a bunch of people that are worse off than me. Oh, the comedians are even more miserable than usual? Book it!"

They howl. They howl long and hard.

"Look at her!" I direct them to do what they've been scared to do. Look at this poor struggling human directly. They knew she was there, but after the first glance, they did what the other comics had done: ignored the elephant in the room. Uncomfortable at the challenge of it. They just couldn't take the risk.

"Look at her cheeks! They're getting rosier!" That indeed does seem to be true, as she laughs even deeper now. "You can just see the white blood cells gangbanging each other. Keep going, lady! We're going to beat this!"

They've all laughed themselves insane by now. So I say a few other things and get off. One of the greatest things I will ever see in comedy is that look on her face; of having laughed and feeling the dizzy endorphins of joy from that, the appreciation of her struggle being acknowledged.

Ok, we're finally to the part where I get in a second physical altercation. Later that night myself, Carney, Cash, and Cash's girlfriend Stacy are in the yard of this massive house on top of Russian Hill. Eric says it's been empty for years. Most likely an item on some faceless foreign investor's portfolio page. The yard is pretty big; we could just claim we thought it was a park or something if we get busted. Anybody this rich needs to share their yard with us when we get drunk, end of story. "We should break-in, and live in there," says Carney, who then climbs onto the roof and starts breaking into the skylight.

From the circular, cascading fountain in the yard, whose edge we've been sitting on drinking beers for 20 minutes, we watch Carney getting us a house to squat.

"If we make it for two years, I'm pretty sure we own it by *squatter's rights,*" I say.

"Get in there!" goes Cash.

"We'll crank up the fireplace with some furniture," I continue in anticipatory excitement. Stacy giggles at us jackasses. These are some *down for the revolution* kids right here. Half the comics have never been away from their mother for two nights in a row. I'm pretty sure these guys have hopped trains cross-country: anarchy, *circus hobos*—raised by bikers.

Awesome. They make me feel like a punk rock skate rat again—a feeling I miss.

Cash got into comedy because he street performed his own show for years, doing magic tricks, curbside pyrotechnics, stapling shit to his chest, whatever the children clamor for. He's pretty funny, has a natural swagger on stage that can even sell his more mid-shelf material. Carney, I don't know well and will never see him again after tonight.

Stacy is a bartender at Vesuvio, at the bottom of the hill we're on right now. This pretty much makes her a god. She's super pretty, and no one can believe how this hyperactive, skinny, weird-looking lizard boy, street performer has scored her. He is entertaining, but she's *really* good-looking for him. Perhaps a good sense of humor really *is* what women want. Bummer, since most people are so goddamn unfunny. Is *this* a factor in the rise of the incels? Shouldn't we be happy for the weird-looking fuckers that get hot chicks? Instead, we whisper, "He must have cocaine."

So, we're out there laughing and cheering on Carney, cracking our second beers, and I'm thinking, I should do shit like this more often. Skip the cokey dive bars and just hang with people in foreign investor yards. Move into them as we need.

I think it's time to get a girlfriend again. I'm kind of feral out here on these streets with no one to account to. This right here, though, feels great. Who knows? Maybe we'll be homeowners soon if this squatting thing works out. I'm just kind of grooving, thinking about stuff like that, and enjoying the crisp winter evening.

Next thing you know, some fuckin' guy comes bursting out of the house yelling, "What the fuck are you doing in my yard!"

Holy shit! This completely contradicts the mellow squat vibe we had going. We run away laughing, and as we're hopping the fence to the street again, this fuckin' guy comes ripping out of nowhere. As Stacy is jumping over, he grabs her leg and makes it, so she falls in a flip onto the sidewalk six feet down, where I myself had just landed a second ago. *Thud.* She lands hard onto her hip and breaks her pelvis. She's whimpering immediately. I hop back over the wall, enraged. The guy is there with his wife, and I punch him hard enough to knock him out cold—looking at the picture of his purple eye, swollen shut, in court a week from now will be a great pleasure.

His wife screams and maces me. I'm so angry that it has no effect on me. I eat so much habanero that pepper spray is like seasoning to me. I rise up and growl at her like a spicy, Sonoran jaguar, and she runs away.

I jump back over the fence again. Stacy is in bad shape.

Reeeeepewww! The cops are here already. Fuckin' rich neighborhoods, man. Cops are there in less than a minute. In the neighborhoods I usually live in, the 911 operator answers, laughing. Carney gets away, me and Cash go to jail, Stacy goes to the hospital.

Bummer shit. Not for Cash. He can sleep anywhere and has. I'm 34, and my shoulders hurt from a life of tossing and turning. Sleep doesn't come easy for me, even in expertly designed scenarios. Cash is there on the floor snoring within an hour of getting to the drunk tank. I recently discovered an amazing invention called memory foam, and I'm missing it right now. Two pillows would be awesome too. Maybe a fan to make some white noise? This is not optimal. How did I survive a youth with regular left turns into bullshit like this? Prison would kill me now just from a lack of bedtime accessories, to say nothing of the constant rapes.

The drunk tank brings back a little PTSD from the old solitary confinement days. I'm feeling a little jittery and on edge. My hands are shaking again—*Snore!* Eight or nine hours later, the guard finally comes around and calls our names. Cash doesn't move quick enough for his liking, and he says, "I'll be back in a few minutes." Cash is back snoring again in seconds. I consider stomping on his head. It's two hours before the guard comes back. We eventually get the charges dropped. The judge looked at the hospital papers for Stacy and the photograph of the antique shop owner's face, "Let's just call this a draw," he essentially stated.

I can't believe this used to just be a regular Saturday night for me. It seems like anything I do after getting pumped up on comedy ends in ruin. I'm just too amped up. I can't just go home and just watch TV like a normal fuckin' person. I need, like, a knockout pill or something. Something more potent than whiskey and weed. Those sleeping pills are weird. People take them and start sleepwalking across the city at night, prostituting and shit. I heard about this girl who would wake up with piles of money and didn't know where it came from until they traced her movements with surveillance footage. Found her sucking cock in the alley across from her house. Fuck that.

Technology Hates Me

It's 2007. For years, I will be reminding my customers that 2007 is one of the best years in California *pinot noir* history. Monsanto now owns almost as many politicians as Exxon/Mobil. As a result, I can now taste the ammonia in random food bites.

It's about to be discovered that the banks fucked over home loan recipients with fraudulent deals that had exploding interest rates buried in the fine print. I think, as a society, it's time to start reading the fine print, folks. There's a reason it's fine, and it's not because it's a Brazilian teenager. Somehow this fucks over the entire global economy, but since the banks are 'too big to fail,'—whatever the fuck that means—instead of being jailed, the bankers get billions in taxpayer bailout money *and* take everybody's houses back. That's a weird fuckin' result. At any rate, this means we poor folks have to live with being even more poor for a while—what a bunch of shit.

2007 is also around the time Britney Spears shaves her head and tries to beat a paparazzi with an umbrella. People claim it's a sign she's gone nuts, but I say it looks like she's getting better. Cue the "Leave Britney alone!" kid. He's fuckin' right, too. We should be protecting her, not from drugs or psychosis, but from her greedy fuckin' dad. But, unfortunately, everyone is too busy eating popcorn because the only thing America likes more than its ammo clips these days is a good old celebrity train wreck.

Also, this year, disabled veterans are beaten on the capitol building steps for protesting the Iraq war. At this time it is America's view that whatever grievance you may have, you cannot disrespect the Capitol Building, one of capitalism's most powerful sympto—I mean symbols! Can you imagine what the authorities would do if, like, some actual militia members with harm in mind tried to rush that place? I mean, if this is what they do to disabled veterans who are mostly peacefully protesting, *jeez Louise*, it'd be a bloodbath, wouldn't it? Right?

Don't worry about politics though, Keeping up with the Kardashians is here to make it all better, creating a cult of rich kids, and even worse, poor kids who think being rich is cool. That's the show: being rich. Who would have thought blowing Ray J would lead to anything but multiple trips to the clinic? The Kardashian kids' dad got OJ off on murder, so you just know they're good people, right?

Oprah recently dragged James Frey over the coals on her show for lying about significant events in his memoir. The public started getting hungry for doxxing. The hunger for his blood was so overkill. It was weird to me. I'm all for keeping memoirists honest but come on guys, he's a writer. He's already suffering enough.

There's something about the public's new ability to condemn an individual to the point where that person can't even get a cup of coffee in public anymore. They've gone crazy for blood. It's like a replacement for feeling powerless to do anything about life's real problems. With the internet now, everyone's voice is powerful, especially the hateful ones! A group of Napa Valley soccer moms can bring down an entire restaurant because the waitress had hair in her armpits. "Get her! Get her blood!" they shout into their keyboards in unison. If an outrage isn't trending, why bother? How will you join a *Twitter mob* and destroy a car parts store for having an "allegedly" racist employee? Back in the old days, you had to *believe* in the fight. You had to challenge a guy physically, tell him, "After school bitch!" and then risk getting an eye gouged out. Now you can destroy shit casually. Starbucks Corp can start a bunch of fake accounts and whisper on Twitter, "Peet's is letting their workers show up with Ebola fevers." Next thing you know, a flashmob of internet piranhas destroys Peet's. "All their lips were sweatier than Woody Allen at a Jr. High!" the reviews are saying. Peet's is like, "Ebola? What the fuck? How do we suddenly have negative two stars? Can you even *have* negative stars on Yelp?"

The internet sucks man. Throw this shit in the trash.

In an attempt to counterbalance all this shit, I'm headlining underground shows and growing a fanbase in 2007 with my *in-your-face-no-apologies-I-have-your-refund-stuck-in-my-dick-hole-why-don't-you-try-and-suck-it-out!* style. One notable instance is when I get a standing ovation for jumping on a table, unzipping my pants, and threatening the audience,

"I will leap off this table and give you a flying squirrel-style teabag!! You'll be blowing nose bubbles with my SCROAT!!!"

I tried to do long socio-political essays, but they just aren't for me. I can't do rants. The *growing up in a teepee* stuff usually only works in a one-man show format. The stand-up audiences just look at me like, *you didn't grow up in a teepee. Tell us about your bar sluts and roommates again.* They prefer it when I freak out like a man who's had enough, and he's gone mad in such a ridiculous way. This is the persona that develops in the chaotic rooms I come up in—the psychotic attention grabber. The material isn't that serious, but I think I bolster the confidence of the weird, the mad, and the forgotten. I think they go home and fall asleep with a smile on their face that night. Of course, I'd like to aim higher for my career, but that's enough for the time being. I have ideas on how to fix society. I'm just not that type of comic all the time. I slip in stuff.

The entitled San Francisco dining customers I meet in my day job give me all the rage I need to get ready for another night of verbally assaulting the tourists, hipsters, run of the mill college kids, techies, yuppies, and assorted misfits who need to keep warm in a dive bar or a laundromat on a windy night. Sometimes I see the restaurant customers AT the comedy show, later in the night. I hope they *tipped* me earlier. The nicer I had to be at dinner, the more savage I might be at the midnight comedy show. "Twenty percent is a starting point, assholes!"

By now, comics who have only been doing comedy for a year and a half are marching past me for spots in the big Bay Area clubs: Cobb's, The Punchline, and the San Jose Improv.

Some of the bookers don't like it when I give the audience tongue lashings. But, to be honest, most of the audience members love it. I told this lady her sweater looked like it had reindeer shit on it at a Christmas show, and she demanded to be put on my email list. My strategy is to just douche on myself for a while, then go rip up the audience a little. One out of ten times I go on stage, I'm a little drunk and overdo it. You want to *almost* overdo it in comedy, but not go past the line where they hate you. Or where you're not funny enough to match the brutality. It's a delicate dance. Balancing edge and hilarity is like Nikki Sixx loading a syringe; you try to get as close to disaster as possible without ever actually *achieving* it. The organic difference can be subatomic, but you cross that line? You can feel the air turn colder in the silence of the crowd's mass, psychically connected judgment of you, while you stand there, naked and unclean.

The only thing that can help the show continue successfully after that is if a talented host can clean up the mess by roasting you. It helps for that comic to just pretend he has another gig and leave the building immediately. I've been banned from several venues at this point for not only not leaving after turning the room to ice but demanding shots at the bar afterward—it's rare, but I've done it, and in this business, gossip travels fast and collects details faster.

I'm becoming a thorn in the side of the softer edges of the Bay Area comedy scene, and that's what I like. The easily offended, who in turn write innocuous, inoffensive material, then wonder why they can't ever kill; the instantaneous video uploaders who count up perceived social slights like White Boy Rick counts the years he's been in prison. Those comics are the **other** team: the hipstery, monotone, unfunny, fake-glasses wearing little bitches that won't let you laugh if there's a victim. They're the ones trying to make an enemy out of me. Them and their only Black friend, Kamau Bell. They're already kind of winning the battle because I always have to watch them struggle with their weakly punchlined social justice essays that are more meant to clap for than laugh at.

Bring it on, kids. I got all the paper flyers and flip phones you can handle. Do you want me to start a fire with two sticks right now? Take your internet and shove it up your ass. I'll NEVER get a smartphone! I'm gonna win! Teepee Boy is gonna win!

I don't intend to soften my act or, unfortunately, drink less. I'm having too much fun doing it this way, and every show I lose, I'm gaining two. The Bay Area in 2007 is the beginning of my heyday. People are screaming dirty shit at me from the city busses, and I'm pretty sure half the time it's because they recognize me from comedy. I'm on my way, finally, to a Gary Sinise level of fame. Let's be honest, with a mouth as dirty as mine, that's aiming high. Although Gary Sinise owns his own house, he can go out for a steak whenever he wants. If I can do **that** and get a decent message out to the children? I'll be happy.

I get too excited before a set, and I pretend the booze is to calm my nerves, but really it's because I have anxiety and have to begin drinking almost anytime I walk into a room full of people I don't know. If I could ride that three drink window; where I'm clever, friendly, and moderately talkative, everything would be fine. The problem is I'm also an extremist who doesn't know how to have three drinks. I gotta bet tequila shots every pool game, which I always win. Fuckin' idiot. So, that's why some bookers hate me, "Yeah, he's funny, until the time he's not," is a quote

I heard. The bookers that love me fuckin' *really* love me. I can get those tough audiences howling. Comedy shouldn't be so predictable and robotic, hitting notes like you're a violinist in a symphony. Comedy should be a bit volatile. Try convincing half the bookers that. People that have never even met me or seen me perform are snubbing my booking queries just based on reputation.

I convince myself it's the PC movement that's galvanized itself the last few years. The audience wants a little filth, but bookers are acting like FCC regulators, overriding the customer's desires. They're being little bitches to the internet reviews. I mean, the other nine times that I *don't* get too drunk? I usually really kill it—killing is good—I mean, if Sam Kinnison walked in here, they'd be falling all over themselves to suck his dick, but *I'm* not marketable?

Fuck these assholes trying to tame the raw art. Lenny Bruce would whip them like Jesus whipping a merchant in a church. If this is what is going to be the main aim of the PC movement; to kill humor, then I intend to be its grim reaper. I know that even a rape joke can be funny. It usually has to be *me* getting raped in it, but I mean... 'getting a blow job from Condoleeza Rice's gap in her teeth is like playing that game Operation? Don't touch the sides, or she'll wake up?' That's rapey *and* hilarious. So these are the battles I'm fighting. The audiences are getting a little more uptight every year, and I'm getting dirtier. Eventually, we're going to be passing each other in opposite directions. Do I wave or flip the bird?

Another reason the newer comics are lapping me is these nerds were born for technology. I often go up barefoot and don't even use the mic. It's my way of bringing it on all stripped down and primal. I'll just take the mic and put it in my pocket, then yell out the bits *rawdog* like a mystic shaman of filth. That's one of the things that drew me to stand-up comedy, the simplicity and the nakedness. Now you gotta have these social media invites down pat, and you gotta be able to fire off a video clip with no audio issues and of a certain length in minutes. Craig Borders got me a real show business inquiry, and I sent the lady a VHS tape instead of a Youtube link. Talk about *dinosaursus rex*. We live in the most tech-savvy region outside of Seoul, Korea, and I'm like Fred Flinstone over here. It all happened so quickly. Yelp is a thing now, so my shitty restaurant jobs are even shittier. If we get a one-star review, we have to show up 15-minutes early, then talk to the GM about it if the customer's description sounds like it was us. I'm a manager favorite, "But the lady wrote that it was a short Asian."

"The Asians here don't make mistakes," I'm notified, along with a write-up.

Mark Zuckerberg hasn't thrown Tom from Myspace into a pit of obscurity with Facebook yet, but he has his trunk loaded with duct tape and lube. Soon, we will be plasma bag dripped our opinions and endorphins through dings from our phones, *Ding! Ding! Ding!* We'll frantically reach into our pockets to see what the notification is. The sideshow scrolling of people's idiotic thoughts, their weak admissions. *Who are these people?* We think. It becomes so easy to just insult people on there and think there's no consequence. We're using it to vent our anger at the undeserving, leaving them to deal with our brain turds.

This new *like* button is an absolute shitshow too. It's what the average teenager now uses as the sole gauge of their value, like us comedians with open-mic laughs. *Leave the comedians to die, but at least save the kids!* The availability of social media on a cellphone should be illegalized before it becomes such a ferocious drug, but how can we know yet what it's becoming? It seems like there are some hurdles, but these bespectacled geniuses in Silicon Valley must be working on it, right? Yeah, right, more like working on how to make it **more** addictive. These assholes refer to each other as, get this, "Silicon Valley, Bad Boys." Hahahahahaha, fuck these guys. We should chase them down the streets and beat them with sticks.

The dinosaurs in congress have no idea how to even *use* the technology they are supposed to regulate, even if they wanted to. They *don't* want to. The concentration of wealth and power seems to me to be the main contribution of advanced technology so far; that, and the dilution of a human worker's value—just means fewer bribe envelopes to sort through for the *congressaurs*. Why *wouldn't* they wave it all through?

We're in trouble. Technology has only changed us a bit as of yet, but there are already fewer kids on the playgrounds because they're playing Call of Duty and Mortal Kombat, ripping off heads instead of playing outside. Soon, we won't notice they've disappeared because we'll all be scrolling *Facecrack* on our phones. These computers, which were supposed to be coming to save us, eat up our brains with trash.

Youtube is huge now, solidifying the vanity angle of computer life.

For example, 12-year-old girls are getting modeling contracts because the video of them combing their hair got tons of views.

George Bush Jr., our idiot president, has appointed the opposite person that should be in charge of every agency that might deal with these issues. So, that's fucked.

With the falling of the Twin Towers **up** went the Patriot Act, which allows unlimited surveillance of all of us, and now we all have I-(micro) phones in our pockets they can listen into at their leisure. Trust me, the government can turn your phone into an instant microphone into your life, as well as a tracking device. Orwell would be proud.

Technology hates me, not just because I'm figuring all of this trash about it out, but because it found out I'm related to my mom! It can still smell the teepee on me that she raised me in. It knows I want back on the grid so I can have a career on stage. But technology doesn't like when you shun it successfully for years at a time, and then try to, like, walk up to it like it's lunchtime at a high school, "Uhm, Technology? I didn't realize not wanting to be *your* friend meant the rest of the school would *also* not like me."

The plot for the movie Mean Girls is really about technology and teepees.

I don't mean that I just can't figure out how to use technology—even though that's part of it—the stuff just **doesn't like me.** It starts smoking and sputtering. Ask my friend Motormouth. He won't go in elevators with me. I think my body is fuckin' vibrating too fast, and the electrons fuck up any computers or machines it gets near. It's fuckin' uncanny, guys.

I've never been able to upload a video of my comedy without the computer crashing. Also, I've failed my driver's test twice because the car went Herby the Hate-Bug on me!

Even simple technology like condoms rip on my penis. I can assure you it's a completely unsharp penis too—no reason that should be happening. And I can't use sheepskin condoms because it might be a member of my family.

Technology despises me. As a matter of fact, if you're secretly taping this set hoping I go, Kramer, your video camera probably just died.

It smells the teepee! The Great Sheep Spirit's first encounter with sophisticated technology was trains full of cowboys shooting into the herd with Winchester rifles. As a result, the Great Sheep Spirit is **not** a fan of new fangled gadgets! Teepees and technology might as well be called Hatfields and Mc Coys or Whitney and Bobby.

They should be kept separate, okay? It's like Micheal Vick hosting a Lassie marathon.

I can't sell out on The Great Sheep Spirit, but I also see the need to have a freezer to put ice cream in. So you see what I'm dealing with?

While the teepee is in my past, I've always tried to hold to its ideals: to tread as lightly as we can on Mother Earth, to live as naturally as we can, and to respect The Sorcerer-Hatted Guinea Pig.

I fought the good fight for many years, folks, but they make it too hard. And when you **do** try to join the information superhighway for the first time at age 35? Technology looks at you like the doorman at the Viper Room looks at a group of guys with crooked baseball hats and no chicks, "Back of the line, K Feds!"

That's what you are if you have trouble returning text messages, or working an Xbox controller. You're Kevin Federline.

My little nephew doesn't understand that I can whoop his ass at Pac-Man. It's always, "I beat Uncle Justin at Mortal Kombat. Watch Uncle Justin. I'm gonna' rub your head in my butt."

"Screw you, Dae Dae! In 1984 I speared your mom's favorite dolly with a *dig 'em* bar! Xboxes can have accidents, Dae Dae. Oh yeah. Go ask your Ma about the wrath of Uncle Justy!"

So obviously, I have issues with modern machines, people, I'll admit it. I long for the days when if you had a cellphone, *you* were different. Back then, I took pride that I lived almost totally off the grid. Unfortunately, the sad truth is if you want to make an imprint in this world? You better learn to digitize your toes. Because when there's only one footprint in the sand? That's when god learned how to email.

I got wired up, folks. Society has made me its bitch. Now, I'm all stressed out when I can't call Jenny because her number lives in my cellphone that just died. I'm trippin' 'cause my website guy is too stoned to click or drag. The ghost of my old sheep taunts me in my dreams, people. "Bu-u-u--ullshit! B-u-u-u-u-l-l-l-l-shit!" He thinks I sold out on the teepee. Have you ever woken up and seen a ghost sheep floating over you? The fluffiness is horrifying! Guinea pig casting little spells on me!

It's just proof that I still belong in the teepee. All the white man's tools are working against me. I have to have a smartphone at least. Jenny won't respond to smoke signals. Society has regulated that she only responds to text messages, saying, "Totally raging party, bitches!"

I'm torn between a life of fresh night air and farm animals or electricity and vagina.

After much agonized internal arguing, I've decided I have to go with the side that has vagina on it.

Jenny? If I can figure out how to access my Facebook, I'll put an absurd picture on your wall. You know, to prove that I'm modern and evolved?

Pooping in holes is all behind me, Jenny! I promise this time. I'm sorry about what happened at your parent's house on Hanukkah.

(Clutch the air above your head. Fade to black.)

The ancient art of stand-up comedy went unchanged for eons, and now it's become one of the most technology immersed mediums there is. I'm fucked. But wait, one night at the corner of 16th and Mission, an amazing thing happens.

I'm there bouncing about the edges of the 12-foot wide chalk mandala that's on the bricks at the top of the Bart station stairs. I'm getting really into the swing of it, telling a joke that goes, "You know what I love about San Francisco, 16th and Mission? It's the variety of people in which to socialize with. For instance, I was just out on a date with this Hindu girl Sivrupti…and she claimed she was saving her body to love her many gods. And I was like, 'What?! That's like a hundred gods, you whore!'"

The savage ones laugh—about half.

"I want Jenny, the born-again Christian, back. At least she was just getting it on with Jesus. I can compete with Jesus. He didn't even shave and dressed in potato sacks."

And that's when it happens; this offended *bible beater* who was just randomly walking by heard me joking about her savior having sex. She comes walking up to me and says, "Is that right?" I look in her eyes, and they are that of a religious fanatic—the most dangerous kind! I start to put my hand on her shoulder to create space between us, but this stocky little bitch is determined. *Whap!* She's in such a hurry to sock me she doesn't even put her sandwich down. The meat flies one way, and the bread goes the other!

She runs away, and we are all left there in stunned silence.

Motormouth, who is in the perfect place to record it all with his video camera, goes, "What would Jesus do?" This gets a laugh.

I snap out of it and, in a deep-seated need to repair my ego, quickly go onto the next joke. After all, in ego terms, I just got socked like a bitch, by a bitch, while everyone watched. Even a *comfortable with my manhood* type of dude like me has to address that, but not so much that it seems like a response. I mostly have to just continue in a mostly unfazed manner. I say, "Ok, that's the first heckler to ever get the best of The Scalesman. Next joke! Which of you guys think that the girl's orgasm *and* birth control is something *she* should worry about?"

I gesture to the men in the audience.

"Well, I have great news. There's a new pill on the market just for you. How it works is it shrinks her eggs so little, your sperms can't find them. And how it guarantees she'll cum... is it shrinks her... until you have a big dick."

The guys realize I've tricked them.

"Look at the guys not laughing right now."

I dangle my pinky limply.

"Shrinky dink. Shrinky dink."

After my set, we rebuild the sandwich, and I take a bite to recapture any masculinity I may still have laying around on the stage. Not bad. Ham and cheese. Too bad it wasn't on rye. I could put a Bukowski reference right here.

A few weeks later, a clip titled "Watch this lady punch Justin Scales in the Face" becomes one of the first stand-up comedy clips to reach 50,000 views on Youtube.

I finally won a battle in the technology realm. This is great!

Burger King approaches me and asks to pay me to advertise on my Youtube page. I tell them "No" because I'm a principled little bitch. Burger King is bottom of the barrel like McDonald's. I'll eat there out of necessity, but be a spokesperson for them? Hell naw. I figure In-N-Out will come sniffing around soon, so I decide to hold out. I forget to ask Burger King what they were offering. What if it's a lifetime supply of milkshakes and onion rings? *Principles Justin. Stick to your principles.*

Kamau Bell
Mapper of All Molehills

Here I am again at The Punchline to watch the same comics do the same jokes every week. I've been coming pretty much every Sunday for four years or so now. I've gotten about eight sets so far and killed at half of those. But, unfortunately, I was too drunk for the other half.

One time I pounded five Jack and Cokes before my set, then I may have called an audience member an alcoholic drama queen—perhaps in an ironic twist of projection. I also may have implied that I thought I saw her having sex in a porta-potty at the Blue Grass festival. I didn't think it was such a big deal, people were laughing at it, and she shut up. So I guess the nickname I made for her was Marina Michelle? And I may have additionally stated that I was going to 'light her fluffy pomeranian on fire so that I could watch her try to stomp it out.'

At any rate, I think the animal lovers wrote a couple of internet reviews about it, and now it's been like six months since I got up. So I bring it up to Molly finally, and she's all, "Oh, it's been that long? Okay, you can get up next week, no problem."

So now it's next week, and she isn't here. Fuckin' Kamau Bell is the substitute booker tonight. *Shit.* So, predictably I don't get a set, and I catch Kamau out on the stairs towards the end of the show. I'm determined to launch a last-ditch effort to get my set Molly promised me. I've intentionally stayed at a three Jack and Coke limit to guarantee a good performance. My new shit has been slaying at the underground shows. I know it will work here. *Let me up. I'm bulletproof!* "Hey, Kamau."

"What's happening?" says Kamau, averting eye contact through his black-framed glasses. He's slightly hunched, somehow flabby and skinny both at once; Frederick Douglas afro, minus the grey. His dad is Black, and his 'mom is BLACK!' as he says in his act. His look confirms this. Nerdy, with a bit of Black militant thrown in. He'd be the guy in the Black Panthers that, like, would design the pamphlets. He'd just pack pepper spray instead of a shotgun. His act is a constant reminder to remember that we're also surrounded by microaggressions, as if worrying about the main ones isn't enough. Now we have to worry about whether gas stations in Beverly Hills should stock magnum-sized condoms in case any Black men visit. (That's not his joke, but it's kind of in the spirit of what he does. I'm not putting material by comics who might not like their characterizations in this.)

I say we focus on the big stuff, like holding violent cops accountable, instead of all of us separating into a bunch of micro-causes. "Save the dogs! But only the little ones!" How about not distracting yourself with petty bullshit like that? The motherfucking world is on fire. Who is destroying it? How do we stop them?—this is where the work should be for an activist comic, I would think. I'm not going to tell a comic how to write, but I think microaggressions are all about micro-bullshit. I'm guessing he's not a big fan of my little poopoo peepee jokes either, so it's not like some potentially great relationship is getting shat down the drain here, should this conversation go poorly. *Fuck it; I'm gonna say what I need to say.*

We just stand there for a second, on the stairs, outside the club, "Did Molly tell you that I was supposed to get a set? She promised me one last week."

"Nope. She didn't say anything about that to me," he says, seeming to take a little pleasure in the power imbalance of this conversation.

"Well, I guess you wouldn't just throw me up there, would you?" I regret saying instantly—too close to groveling, but I'm a junky for stage time. We all are. Every one of these comics will drive to Barstow on a second's notice for a $50 feature spot, and they'd sell you to the dog food factory to get it. Most comics are nerds that have never thrown a punch at someone, but they would rip out your entrails and eat them for a paid hosting spot in Antioch. It's the only preoccupation in a comic's brain: *How do I get more stage time? How do I get the bookers and the comics above me on the ladder to like me more?* This thought repeats in their brains until it terrorizes them, stealing their sleep and eating into the time they should be using to write good material.

"No, I guess I probably wouldn't," says Kamau.

That's it. I go a little crazy. "Yeah, no shit. Ever since, I didn't come running after you at 333 Columbus to give you a set. You should like me *more* because of that. But no, everybody has to kiss your guys' ass. It's like you guys are the bookers or something because you got Molly under your thumb."

"I gotta get back inside," Kamau says, starting to turn towards the door.

"Yeah, go. Just know that I know you guys wouldn't be all *besty westy* with Molly if she wasn't the booker." Kamau flinches a bit. Still, he can't meet my eyes. "She was a goldmine for you first guys that got here. Damn, bro, she's an impressionable young woman, and you guys just pulled out your forks and knives. That's right, buddy. You can't fool me, though." I've lost any control of my mouth at this point. I guess I'm trying to get myself banned so I can stop wasting my time here if that indeed is what I'm doing—and it seems I am. *But then I wouldn't be able to see headliners perform for free? Fuck. Why is life always an even break whatever you do?* Over four years? Sirof is featuring. He started the same fuckin' week as me. I hate watching all these guys that aren't even as funny as me getting up every week just to do a complete copy of their last performance. What's the point? We get it. You are a large man who loves his cats.

I continue my screed, "Look. You can't even make eye contact with me. What's going on around here?"

He makes eye contact so he can tell himself the things I said aren't true. Then he walks back into the club, leaving me out here pissed.

Later, he will say that I called Molly a 'young *girl,*' not a 'young *woman,*' and I think he even claimed my eye contact comment was a joke about his lazy eye. It seems like I'm gonna be on the outs at The Punchline. Fuck it. More time to focus on what's working, I guess, which is plenty. These other comedians are so wrapped up in The Punchline being the only local option to get your foot in the door of show biz. I try to focus on the fact that there are plenty of other meaty bones out there. However, the Punchline is the only place where the legend Dave Attell will see my leg cast and hit me up for some pain pills. One time I got to talk to Dave Chapelle after he walked away from an eight-figure deal to renew his groundbreaking show on Comedy Central. I *believe* you remember it. We did NOT talk about that. We chatted for a few minutes about the tiny town in Ohio that we've both lived in called Xenia.

I was there early one night; I think to tape a hidden cheat sheet on stage with the order of my jokes. You know, like a setlist? My ADHD prevents me from memorizing the order of my jokes, okay? Robin Williams does it. Did you think that shit is *all* improvised?—he might be an ADHDer himself. And so I put my cheat sheet up there, and there's the headliner, Greg Giraldo, eating nachos at the bar. He's the only other person in the joint. He sees me get big eyes, like I recognize him. He has that perfect level of Hayden Panettiere, medium fame. He looks familiar, but it's unlikely someone will start yelling, "Hey, you're Greg Giraldo!" from across the street. I'm sure he owns his own house. Aside from having that perfect medium fame I am aiming for, he's one of the most underrated comics of all time, top 30 of all time funniest comics. Yet, if you saw him in the street, you'd think he works at the pizza place you went to on your birthday. Fuckin' Greg Giraldo, eating nachos at the bar. I get a nervous look on my face, like, *Shit, he's eating.* Never bug a guy when he's trying to eat, piss, or fuck. He recognizes the issue and goes, "No, sit, I'll eat, you talk," so I mildly babble on for like ten minutes, and then he talks for a few minutes, answers a few of the questions, gives his opinion on a concept I mentioned I was working on. It was one of the only times I felt comfortable sitting at that bar.

I still want to see the great headliners perform for free and to meet them. Maybe I shouldn't have gone off on Kamau. Would I have done the same thing as him if I'd gotten here quicker? Perhaps. A booker for a place like this needs a buffer. So the incels don't crawl over her like a pile of brains in a zombie movie. She's like a hippy girl in her 20s—how she landed in this gig is a mystery to me—so she doesn't want to be all yelling at people, throwing up bans, telling the unqualified the cold, hard truth. Better to have buffers. I get it.

This stage addiction is all-consuming and can cloud your judgment. I guess Kamau was probably pretty pleased with that outcome. I handed it right to him. I wasn't even drunk. I'm not banned, but I'm not going to be a *club regular* anytime soon.

Showing Up at SF General Double Kankled

It's New Year's Eve. I'm at a big house party with the 16th and Mission crowd. Thank god for these guys. As we know, hanging out with the comics gets old since I see them every night at the open-mics and showcases. And these spoken word artists, rappers, digereedooists, acoustic guitar players, teen hobos, and college students have more heart than the traumatized comedians. Not so concerned with personal neurosis and ladder climbing in show business. You know when you go to happy hour with your work friends, and all you guys talk about is work? Times that by ten when hanging out with comics. For going to bars and stuff like that, I hang with the 16th and Mission open-mic guys. They have a general knowledge of the world at large. They have welcomed me, as a group, way more than comedy ever has. Performing on the corner is way less stressful. I can improvise and try out new stuff of any medium. I'm more relaxed, not concerned with getting a big laugh every 30 seconds.

I love my other shows too: Club Deluxe, every Monday, Brainwash on Thursdays before I hit 'the corner.' I pepper in other stuff onto that, and I've got a thing going on here. 50 Mason died already, but venues come and go pretty fast. I headlined a lot of shows there. Thanks, Susan and Joe. I've carved out a niche here in the Bay Area, despite the two-thirds of the bookers who don't want raw aggression or filth at all. Many audiences **do** like it, and they're not getting it in many other places. So, after a little more than four years in the game, your boy's got a decent following. I can send out an email and get 40 people to show up to a show at this point. If the venue itself can draw 25 more, we have a rockin' show. It's going to be 2008 at midnight. I just have to avoid any self-imposed devastation. Five years is when you're supposed to hit your stride in comedy, and things start happening for your career. I feel it; this is my year. The year I blow up.

We're all standing there by the open bar at the New Year's Eve house party, at one of the 16th and Mission open-mic kid's pads, having the time of our lives. I've downed four shots of Johnny Walker Black Label in the very recent past, and I'm in a storytelling mood. Some kids who are just coming onto their acid get a little freaked out by my hyperactivity and go downstairs to regroup on the stoop. I'm telling some of the people who didn't make it to the street corner to perform last week about the funny drama that happened while they were absent, "A guy hated my performance so much that he went looking for a trash can. By the time he gets back with it comedian, Greg Edwards is on stage. This guy, who was so offended by me, just dumps the trash all over the stage, spreading it out nice and thin, and he says to Greg, 'That was for the last guy.'"

I allow a beat for laughter from my small but mighty audience.

"Well, let's just say that was the last big laugh that happened during poor Greg's performance."

After refortifying myself with a few more shots of Johnny Walker, I decide to wander around the house and end up in a room where some people I know are smoking a pipe. Awesome. I accidentally cut in the circle as I step into the only available space in the small area. I grab the pipe and hit it.

Unbeknownst to me, the pipe has DMT in it. These kids get wild over here. I already have had the pipe in my mouth and am torching it before anyone would have been able me to slow up. I hand the pipe off to someone that had their finger up in the air to me, mouth opened, but never started. *Oh well, that's what you get for smoking out of pipes without knowing what's in 'em.*

The combination of the DMT with the amount of whiskey I've just consumed in the last 20 minutes short circuits my brain. I wander over to an open window for some fresh air. As I look outside into the sky, no less than four of the universe's mysteries are revealed to me. Someone says, "Scales, I walked out this window across that ledge last week. I bet you could do it."

I'm like, "Oh really? Well, **I** can fly motherfucker. What'chu think about that?"

His dinner plate pupils seem to agree. So I grab a salt and pepper shaker off the ground, one of those wooden, twisty ones that an Italian waiter could murder the chef with, and a real metal sword off the wall. I want accessories for this stunt. I start out the window, intending to, I think, walk across the ledge to the other window, about eight feet across. Then I will pry the opposing window open with the sword and apply pepper to the length of the sill before crossing its threshold, surprising the people partying in there into giving me a line of coke, which will balance out the DMT and the tequila. I'm turning drug use into an Olympic event, didn't you hear?

So I'm headed out there, and my puffy Dickie's jacket gets me stuck in the first window, and I pop out a bit, and too late, I realize I popped out a little too hard, and now I'm falling forward. I have a choice to make: I can either try and twist around and grab the side of the window frame and risk falling backwards if I miss, or just pick a spot on the ground and take it like a man. I use up a fraction of a second too long deciding for the side twist option to work anymore. I've picked my spot.

"Ahhhhhh!" The pepper shaker drops at a slower rate than me, and the sword hits before any of us 25 feet below. *Clang!* This probably startles the acid twins on the steps. But wait. *Slam!* I hit the ground as perfectly as I can, not hitting my ass and injuring my spine but shattering both my feet. My heel bones both now resemble a run-over, albino Rubik's Cube. But I don't know that yet.

I'm so fuckin' high and drunk I think maybe I just sprained my ankles or something. I try to get up, and that just isn't happening. The acid twins run off down the street shrieking. No one sees them again for weeks.

I lay there in pain as people poke their heads out the window. Soon I'm loaded into a car on the way to the hospital. "No, take me home. It doesn't hurt that bad," I lie. I don't want to go to the emergency room on New Year's Eve and be the biggest New Year's Eve idiot—the guy with his dick stuck in a bowling ball sighing in relief when I arrive. Fuck that. Plus, I'm scared of SF General Hospital. I asked the nurse where my pain medication was in a rude tone last time, and this fucker looked at me like, *I can kill you in your sleep, bitch.* "Just take me home, and I'll hold out until tomorrow. After the *New Year's Eve party, idiots rush* is over."

So they take me home and get me on my bed. I sit there, watching my ankles swell up to the size of grapefruits. I call my brother and he's at the Pan Pacific Hotel with a girl. His night pretty much went the opposite of mine. He's not exactly happy to hear from me. We drive to St. Mary's Hospital because I'm afraid to go to SF General, him calling me a fucked up alcoholic the whole time. Poor kid. He sure picked a family to be in. Between me, our sister, and our mom, it's a miracle all his hair hasn't turned grey from being the normalest of us. He's also the glue that tries to keep us all together. Bless his soul.

St. Mary's is happy to take me in, put me to sleep on morphine in their expensive bed, and tell me they don't have the expertise to fix two shattered heel bones two days later. They then try to bill me $50,000. All that after taking their wheelchair back once we reached my brother's truck again. What the fuck?

When I get to where they *can* fix me, at—you guessed it—SF General, they say I should sue the shit out of St. Mary's for that kind of service. And that's why they aren't scared to fuck over poor people. We can't afford a lawyer for shit like that. Be nice to take money right from the pope, though. It's a Catholic hospital, so I'm not surprised they fucked me, even though I'm way older than they usually prefer. I *am* poor and have pretty lips—the Catholic Church's total *go-to*.

So begins another difficult stage of my life. I'm stuck in my house. I finally realize how loud my upstairs tweaker neighbor is, and they begin construction on a huge building next door. I'm in a wheelchair and can hardly ever leave the house. The sons of the El Salvadorean family next door carry me up and down the steps a few times, but that wears out after a while. It takes me 40 minutes just to take a shit. The hallways are narrow so even navigating the house in my wheelchair is impossible. I end up crawling around the house like a two-armed salamander. I'm four months away from crutches. This is garbage.

The internet I was poaching suddenly has a password required. Crazy how quickly we all just migrated to putting everything through that wifi signal. Without it, you're nothing in 2008. I'm too broke right now to pay for all the wiring and modems for the wifi, much less the monthly bill. I refuse to trade in my flip phone for a smart one. I'm trying to stay mostly unplugged in my life, but damn are they making it harder and harder to do that anymore. Soon it'll be legal to pay your employees less if they refuse to be part cyborg. It's all going to shit quicker through technological innovation. I feel like I'm the scientist in the movies saying, "No, don't blend that pig DNA with the human DNA. We already have Roseanne!"

How do I not even have a radio? Just books and construction noise all day. Trying to write jokes is impossible. The morphine does allow for some creativity with its ultra relaxation. Still, it's not my usual method of writing, which is drunkenly fixing new material I just performed earlier in the night.

People check in on me and help out for the first few weeks. My mom stays for a while but has to go off and tend to my sister, as usual. My brother fills up the kitchen with non-perishable food and takes off a door, so my wheelchair can get through easier. By the time you close in on your first month in a wheelchair, it gets pretty lonely. My roommate even tiptoes around the house now, so I won't ask him for shit.

Now that I'm home 24 hours a day, it becomes apparent that my upstairs neighbor is not only a tweaker, but a gay prostitute who is using our building as his fuck office. He seems to be a 'your safeword has no power here' type of man-slut too. He'll just violently toss out the cock-struck Johns to wander the stairways of our building high on meth, looking for stray cock they might be able to suck.

One time one of them wanders into the construction site next door in broad daylight, yelling up at Steve's window, "Steve! I love you, Steve! Please give me your cock, Steve!" There are guys in hardhats out there that have no idea how to deal with this. This shit doesn't happen in Fairfield, where they drove in from to work. There's no concrete being poured they can bury him in. "Steve! I want your cock!" I've pulled the curtains back and angled my wheelchair for a better view. I'm hard up for entertainment these days, and this is pretty good shit. An hour later, the cops come and get him. He gets wild and starts trying to spit on them until they put a beekeeper net over his head and tie him to a Hannibal Lecter dolly / seat thingamajiggy.

This is the year Steve's house gets wild. The same year I'm stuck indoors for the first half. I hate this shit. The tenant laws in San Francisco are so strong there's nothing the landlord can do. They just tell us to document everything. Meanwhile, I'm a captive beneath a meth circus.

Over the next year, his customers will knock on the back door, naked from the waist down, and ask for pants. He's stuck back there in the backyard. He'd never be able to navigate the pitch-black basement to the street. I have to let him walk through our house, and yes, I give him some pants. Another guy walks right **into** our house because I forgot to lock our door and arrives in our kitchen looking at me expectantly because he's only just met Steve on the internet with only a penis pic for reference. He thinks **I'm** Steve! He is, of course, pleased with the look of what he thinks is the product until he sees I'm in a wheelchair. Then his face starts screwing up, confused.

I slither up the stairs and beat on Steve's door, yelling, "You motherfucker Steve!" He pulls back his curtains and laughs.

This is how things drag on for months. Then, I'm able to kind of get around better and book some gigs. Steve starts feeling bad for me and takes the password off his wifi again. I might just make it out of this.

After a month or two, I can get onto the stage at the Brainwash and the street corner open-mic. I just have people carry me up the short step on top of the Club Deluxe stage. I'm back, babies! The crowd loves it. Being that I'm in a wheelchair, my anger is more justified. I can be more threatening, but they know it's a hollow threat now. I'm clearly marginalized—a *must* for Bay Area audiences. They fuckin' love it! Other comics are saying, "This is what you needed for your act. You should get paralyzed for real!" and they say it seriously. To perfect your act, there is no price too high for them. Plastic surgery, intentional self-hobbling? It's **all** on the table. And it's true, now that I have more of a disabled appearance, rather than that of the typical, white, labor-exploiting colonist, the Bay Area wants me more. This is why I always wanted to start with the *growing up in a teepee* material, to wash off the white land thief look. But like I said, half the time, that material didn't work because the audience is giving me looks like, *Nah, you don't look like you grew up in a teepee, I don't buy it, but now you look like you fell off a building, so that's pretty good.*

We are ground zero for the PC movement here in the Bay Area, and without that *marginalized status badge*, your anger has no merit here. I hate that shit, but I didn't exactly turn it down during those months in the wheelchair. The audiences are here to listen for flag words and clap if they agree with your politics. Unfortunately, half of them don't even remember how to laugh because jokes usually have what they've been told is *problematic material*. We can't support victim creation, even in joke form, say the socially aware college kids these days.

The old school comics from LA and New York are having trouble getting laughs out of these young audiences these days, so they make a disgusting and filthy movie called The Aristocrats in protest. It doesn't help their cause, but the protest probably makes them feel a little better for a while.

Times are changing. Less is thought to be funny anymore by a growing number of people. The bookers want us comics to cater to them, follow *their* rules, and narrow our scope of topics to be more palatable to an audience with a huge list of emotional allergies. *Don't trigger Marin Michelle!* She has eight internet profiles, and she'll go on Yelp to complain about you with all of them! Of course, no booker would say this out loud, but with their profit margins so slim and their internet ratings so important nowadays? You can see the safer comics getting booked more. They don't *have* to say it.

This is what I'm fighting. And quite well, by the way, because I just make the other half of the audience that doesn't have a stick up its ass laugh twice as hard to make up the difference. It kills the ultra socially aware kids to see me kill, and I love watching their faces wrinkle up in disgust while I perform. A lady once got out of her chair and yelled, "You think that shit is funny? There is nothing funny about getting blowjobs from the mentally disabled."

"Your boyfriend doesn't have a problem with it," I say, expressionless, pointing at the equally sour-looking guy next to her.

The ensuing *oofs* and *gasps* my response to her gets are worth more than all the laughs in the world. The look on her face allows me to achieve a temporary comedy nirvana. What some of the bookers try to punish me for is what *I think* makes my aura glow.

Folsom Street Fair

I'm at Motormouth Scott's house in The Mission. About six of us are pre-partying for Folsom Street Fair, doing key bumps of molly and coke. Also, because we are nuts, we're doing mushrooms and drinking. Scott's marriage to the doctor exploded a while back, and he's back to his old ways with a new bachelor pad that has more pot plants in the closet than shirts.

I'm dressed like a pirate, in red felt, assless chaps. I've recovered mostly from my injury, but I'm still on a cane. I had metal put in my ankles, so I figured I'd get a nice one. Sterling silver alligator handle. I have an eyepatch and a pirate hat. Scott has taken a picture of me, printed it, laminated it, and now I'm wearing that as a necklace. It's all pretty ridiculous.

The doorbell rings, and it's the casual lover of the girl who I was just making out with on the roof. So I go out to see who it is, and I get a pretty shocked look on this Egyptian cannabis dispensary owner's face, "Hey, we were just beating Motormouth with a wiffleball bat. He's all tied up and ready to go. You want to come in?"

"No-no-no-no-no!" he says, waving his hands frantically, backing up on his heels as if I'd just broken out of a sarcophagus. He practically runs down the block to get away.

I go back in and tell them who it was, and everyone laughs. Scott loads up his new $20,000 digital video camera, and we're about to go down to the festival where I'm going to interview the freaks. Folsom Street Fair is a mile-long sideshow for bondage freaks and other assorted kinksters, furries, fisters, and fuckboys. It's quite a spectacle.

The big thing now is webisodes, so we're going to make a webisode out of this. I have the Bullshitter of the Year Competition, my comedy album being edited as we speak, and my one-man show so far. Between those and these webisodes me and Scott are going to make, one of these pots **has** to boil. I'm determined to adapt to the digitization of storytelling. No one can fault me for not putting in the effort. I've sworn off having a girlfriend, work as little as possible at my real jobs, and I've been going full-bore at this for about five years now. I'm good at it. I have millions of ideas, and I put in more hours every workday than Ryan Seacrest. How can I fail?

Scott is my official videographer, and Keppel is a news reporter, so we use his station's expensive equipment to tape a lot of stuff as well. We have hours of decent footage. Little do I know that that video on Youtube of the lady punching me is one of the last clips I'll ever see come from Scott's camera. You see, Scott loves to tape stuff. Not so much for the monotony of the editing room. His mountain of tapes are poorly labeled, and to find something specific, it would take a year of sorting through his homemade porn and probably other shit you'd need therapy after seeing. Whatever, we're having fun, and a few competent people are taping and photographing me. Lee Stoneman also captures a lot of gold. Thanks, guys.

We show up at Folsom Street Fair, and the main drag is three blocks closed down between 7th and 10th on Folsom Street. In front of the Brainwash, at the start is a stage with a rock band composed of Drag Queens. They are railing against the breeders, and they are getting drunk, pounding on their drums, and screaming into the mic, strutting around effortlessly in stiletto heels and sequined dresses. "Stick it in her tuna salad. Listen to this fearsome ballad!" they wail.

I see Bubbles, a bearded transvestite I know. Total gender mashup. He's riding around on roller skates, Daisy Duke shorts, and a Marilyn Monroe wig. I offer her an Altoid dipped in LSD, and he pops it on her tongue and disappears backwards into the crowd after one last white-buttoned tongue flash and a wave goodbye. I pop one myself to fortify myself against reality. Ok, let's do this.

We wander in deeper, and there's a cum wall. A bunch of guys are tugging their scrotums and beating their meats so they can spray their jizz on a wall of pictures of the entire GW Bush cabinet, who, heading into their final year, have succeeded in destroying the entire country of Iraq and a good part of America. There are pictures of Carl Rove, Cheney, Colin Powell, Condoleeza, and GW himself, pasted to a wall, all dripping with mother of pearl from the balls of Earl. Gobs of it.

Scott tapes it and turns the camera to me. I interview the closest guy to me, "Sir, what's the filthiest, most *homoey* thing you've seen today?"

This camera is enormous, so we have an air of legitimacy to our broadcast. This thin fairy sees he's on TV and fixes his hair, a glittery constellation of curls. "Well, I'd say this wall is pretty faggoty. I mean, notice how Condoleeza has hardly any jizz running down her face? And Karl Rove over here looks like his jowls are just **full** of cum? He's going full Godfather with it. That's faggoty as hell."

"Faggoty. What an amazing word. Do you mind if I borrow that? I will only use it out of love," I say.

"Well, in that case, you can squirt it up your asshole. Toodles," says this fantastic human before prancing off to catch a passing friend.

Satisfied with this, we wander on, past the guy on his knees with a sign around his neck that says "Human urinal," past the lady tied to a cross getting her pussy whipped with a medieval-looking leather whip. There is actual froth flying off her pussy, and she is moaning with pleasure. All of this is happening in broad daylight, in the street, in front of a carpet store.

We go into Cassidy's to whet our whistles and play a game of pool. The bartender tells us to play at our own risk because the felt is soaked in squirt from a girl that was just getting fisted up there. I push in the quarters.

There are furries, transexuals, leather boys, Burning Man yuppies, ravers, goth dominatrixes, and a guy who thinks he's a horse in there. The drinks go down fast.

"Sir, can you tell us what is the nastiest, most depraved, most faggotiest thing you've seen today?"

He quickly responds, with 100 percent certainty, "You."

The Big Homecoming Show in Santa Barbara

Evil Farmer is having a Santa Barbara reunion, and I'm going to do a set during their intermission! The show is going well! We're at Soho, and there are 60 to 70 people in their mid to late thirties in love with the moment because they haven't seen each other in years. Not since when everything was perfect. For the time being, we are all transported from the George Bush Jr century back to 1990, when the most significant problem on our minds is where the next kegger is.

Everyone is smiling, and I'm only drinking beers. There's no way I can blow this. Ari Gorman, the bass player, signals to me that he will bring me up after the next song. The song ends, and he fucking mumbles my intro. Never let the bass player speak into the microphone folks, it's like putting Gweneth Paltrow in control of the BBQ.

So, I jump up there and start my routine, right? All the faces are smiling. This is going to be great! My big return to the hometown to show I'm a big San Francisco comedian now. They're going to be so proud and laugh so hard.

I launch in confidently, "I know it's hard to believe I've suffered enough to even be a comedian. I'm tall, handsome, obviously... fuckin' **loaded** with charm!"

I feel like their smiles are fading. Audiences don't like to be *surprised* with comedy. So I speak louder into the mic to hold their attention, "And I'm **hung** like the guy in Ryan Seacrest's screensaver!"

The audience looks mystified, *Comedian? There's comedy? Am I going to be included in stage banter? I didn't bring my stage banter! Am I going to be expected to laugh right now?! Ahhh. I need to psych my way* ***into*** *that for a day or two. I'm clamming up now!*

The manager instantly appears in the sound booth and shuts off the mic. I continue yelling anyway, and the audience, being signaled this performance is unsanctioned by the proprietors, wanders off, half of them probably thinking, *I see Justin hasn't changed.*

I keep on going feebly for a few more jokes, my spirit broken, and then just end up standing there, silent, and—I imagine—sad looking.

Fuck. Goddammit, Ari!

It looked like I'd just jumped up on the stage and commandeered the mic, like a drunk fraternity brother at a wedding reception. The intro was undecipherable.

In a final shame, I get off the stage, and Clark the Vulcan comes up to me and says, "I thought you said you were going to be funny."

Ouch!

Never mix comedy with music, folks, unless it's like, a charity event or something. You know, where the guests expect a multitude of speakers and performers? Just throwing up comics unannounced to fill that dead air where the next band is setting up is dicey. I've seen it work, but only like twice. And the comedian was either a local celebrity or on the flyers.

When will I learn? I'm a stage whore. I have to admit that. Comedy is a delicate art, and the ambiance needs to be a certain way for the audience to get into it. They have to be kind of... coaxed into it. And then they have to plan on it. Finally, they buy the tickets and begin steeling themselves for potential abuse by the host. Sitting in the front row at a comedy show is like swimming in an icy lake. You have to go through a period of shock first; then, hopefully, you become engorged in the exhilaration.

You can't just surprise them with it. This complicated recipe is what makes it so gratifying when you can work it consistently.

The most famous clubs look like ordinary buildings on the outside. The true magic is something about the inside. It's hard to explain how the chairs, the stage, where the bar is, how high the ceiling is, the neighborhood it's in, the capacity—about 120 people tightly packed in towards the stage is best. It all matters, and the variables are made or broken on a subatomic level. It's like certain places just have the architectural *feng shui* and some sort of unknowable magic. The Punchline and The Purple Onion have it. Cobb's doesn't. Bill Graham

Auditorium doesn't. Some venues just fuckin' have it, man. The Fillmore, The Independent—they just have it.

Being an edgy comedian, I'm stuck at venues with support poles in the middle of the room and motorcycle gangs roaring by. How do I start getting better stage time consistently? The one or two good gigs I get a week lately are just enough to drive me crazy. Take me to rehab!

Doug Stanhope

So I'm there scrolling Myspace, checking out people's profile songs and shit, reading about people's day, looking at pictures of their lunch, and confessing to their *bunny burner* tendencies. I get a message from someone claiming to be Doug Stanhope, arguably the greatest living comedian. A brilliant filth master who can fluctuate between distended hooker holes and Keynesian Theory in the same performance. He says he's watched the video clips on my profile, and he's pretty impressed. I've managed to tape the material about growing up in a teepee with both a believing *and* enthusiastic audience and posted it. It took me a week to figure out how to post clips on Myspace, but I did it. (I bribed an open-miker to do it in exchange for a showcase set somewhere, if I'm being honest.)

"Haha, real funny, Al," I respond, thinking it's my comedian roommate, Al Gonzales. I go on the profile and see that he has thousands of friends. It's not a fake profile! ***Oh, fuck!***

We start chatting, and he's very nice and encouraging. So I work it real slow for a few weeks and pop the question, "How's about coming to San Francisco and doing some shows with me?"

"Sure," he says.

Well, to say I'm over the fuckin' moon would be an understatement. It's my favorite comedian. Guys like him got chased out of the business after John Belushi overdosed in the hotel above the Comedy Store. And after Sam Kinnison fake crucified himself on a real-ass cross at a comedy club, Bill Hicks died, Pryor lit his head on fire smoking crack, and a few years ago, Mitch Hedburg died as well. The cocaine and heroin have worn off, and the resulting bodies have piled up. The ironic partnership between grief and comedy is now in plain view. Stand-up has always been a haven for whackos and misfits. The tragic stories have been rolling in too rapidly. They tried to make some changes back in the 80s. The comedy club manager union had a meeting and decided they'd have to stop paying all the comedians in cocaine. Make things a little more network-friendly and tame. I hear The Hollywood Improv had to call Pablo Escobar personally and have him turn a plane around. It wasn't enough, and nowadays, they are just trying to discourage guys who they think will end up breaking everyone's hearts. I look like one of those guys to them, but what they don't know is that I'm a cockroach that's going to live forever.

Guys like Stanhope are unicorns in the *new technology century.* Misanthropic filth merchants like him have to trick showbiz into giving them some mild fame, then bite their hands for it, but by then, it's too late to blacklist them. They have enough name recognition to fill a venue just off of flyers stapled to the light poles in any medium-sized town in America. *I just need a Liev Schreiber level of fame. Something to staple to a telephone pole,* I think to myself.

I plan to become Doug Stanhope's protege. I would never have considered being a protege for someone before because I'm such a cocky shit. Still, between the nuts and bolts knowledge he has about DIY comedy careering—he's both *outside* and *inside* of showbiz—and the brilliance of his act? Yeah, I'd be his protege. Fuck it. For a year of road tours opening for him, why not? I'd learn a shit ton.

So it's all ready to go at the Club Deluxe, a classy jazz joint that's spitting distance from the corner of Haight and Ashbury. Luxurious booths, little cocktail tables. There's a stage you'd be hard-pressed to fit a whole band on, lovely honey-colored wood panels backing it, rippling grains of amber twisting throughout it like a Kansas wheat field in a beer commercial.

The bar area is along the back of the room, where it should be. You can see the performance floor through a sporadic wall that comes down from the ceiling and breaks for a few feet to give you a view of the show, picking up again below to create a counter for people to put their drinks on. There is a row of stools along that, with room for a walkway between those people's asses and the barstools up against the actual bar, which, if your performance is good, they will turn their stools around to watch you. This bar area allows a psychological barrier of protection for the more timid audience members. The real action is as close to the stage as you can get. You want to be able to smell the flop sweat, maybe even get some of it on you, before the next comic comes up and hopefully kills.

I go and pick up Doug at the Oakland airport, asking him how the cavity search went. "Medium," he says.

A few hours later, we're in the sporadically used kitchen in Club Deluxe, drinking Corona and tequila, waiting for my roommate Al to finish warming up the crowd. Al is the comedy booker at this venue. Al is good at the parts of show business that I suck at, and vice versa. I was unsure of making another comic a roommate, but I must say, this balancing act we've got going has been advantageous. I got him in the door with some bookers when he first got to town, and he's basically the mayor of stand-up around here already.

The crowd is laughing. I nail my set down so that I can do two different sets at 20 minutes each and never repeat a joke between the two nights. I want Doug to see that I have enough material to headline if he passes out drunk before a set or something when we tour.

Hanging out with Doug is, well, depressing. The guy answers my questions in short sentences, and maybe I'm asking him too many of them. Eventually, we're just standing there kind of quietly. It seems like most of the headliner's brains are just too big. The world's horrors won't let them relax. I nervously make some comments to fill the dead air, and it's getting awkward. I don't know; maybe he wants to think about his new material before bringing it out there. Maybe I'm bugging him. I tend to spontaneously ramble on due to some defect in my brain. I need another shot of tequila.

I look through the western saloon doors that separate the kitchen from the performance floor area. There are about 80 of them out there so far. They look excited. Al says my name, and my face is suddenly in the lights.

"You ever have a guy say some bullshit like, 'This is going to be beyond your wildest dreams.'? I don't like that. Last guy that said that? I grabbed him by his fuckin' shirt and yelled, "I don't know, my dreams are pretty fuckin' wild!!!"

This joke never really kills as an opener, but it's quick and gets them listening. Some of these jokes are just for me too. Too weird to live, too good to die.

"I used to date this girl named Flo. Some called her Heavy Flo, which is weird because she was skinny. Hmmm? I loved her! So much that I once spelled out her name in cocaine... to prove my love. Her full name was Florinda Rudolpho Perez Fuqua. When I got to the 'q' in 'Fuqua,' my nose exploded!"

They laugh, not realizing I've done something very similar.

"Club Deluxe! I was at the Bill Graham Auditorium recently, and the band's singer inquired, 'Is that person ok?' I guess someone got dizzy near the side of the stage and needed to sit down or something.' So I was all, 'Fuck 'em! Let's rock and roll!' And that's the night I realized how uptight San Francisco is. Three hundred people turned around and looked at me like I'd walked up to an albino and asked, 'Hey, what's up, super-cracker!?'"

"Haha."

"Where's all my bleeeotches at!"

Ok, now we're just getting stupid.

"You ever realize your new upstairs neighbor is not only a tweaker but a shitty bass player?"

"Haha," they all go because they are all either a tweaker, a bass player, or sitting next to one.

"Four in the fucking morning, and *Doooong! Dooooong! Dong!* After a month of that, I'm like, 'Well, I could kill them. Or, I could just become a tweaker too. I hope I can play harmonica shitty enough to be in their band!' I turn the mic sideways and up to my mouth: *Blllerrrfff! Blllerrrrfff!*"

They laugh because my life is all fucked up. I continue to offer myself on a cross to their glee, which, weirdly, helps me.

"Men? You know how when you're taking a leak, and a guy comes up next to you and starts talking to you? I don't like that! Like, bro! Can't you see, I'm trying to take a leak... on this truck?"

"Haha," the street pissers go.

"Well, why'd you park it on Haight Street?!" I say to the Haight Street bar audience.

"YOU'RE LUCKY I DIDN'T POOP ON IT!!!!"

This is probably happening to someone in here's car if they parked anywhere nearby, but they laugh anyway, not realizing it. Okay, let's turn it filthy.

"You ever be going out with a girl so stupid, you figure it MUST be illegal. Should I have felt guilty about sticking my dick through the bars of her helmet?" wait for it.

"Hahahaha," goes half the room in unison—the sick half.

Now for the tag/act out. I put the mic down to my dick, forcing it to mimic it, and scream, "Here comes the magic yogurt stick Becky!!!!"

That joke was pretty fucked up, huh? Well, I consider myself to be a reasonably happy person because I allow myself to process my trauma through what some people might call, 'inappropriate humor.' By 'some people,' I mean people who either could afford therapy or people who ain't been through shit. When it comes to how I deal with MY shit, they can shut the fuck up. My mental happiness is far more important than their fake valor. None of them are here now, judging from the level of laughter. Hear that? All that trauma, laughing its ass off? That means they're not in pain for once; those are the people I work for. If my jokes offend you and make your dick shrivel up to the point where you're peeing inside yourself? Well, then you're the motherfucker that I'm probably talking about in the jokes.

"My father told me once after I showed him a clip of my comedy, 'Why can't you be more like Sinbad?' My dad's a prick. Anyone else in here got a prick for a dad?"

"YEAH!!!" goes a bunch of 'em. Who would have guessed daddy issues would be a goldmine here? Lucky me!

"One time he saw my cousin and me eating pudding pops, and he said, 'Looks like you're suckin' on some jail dick.'"

Getting a Doug Stanhope audience to gasp in horror is one of the great achievements in my comedy history.

"And yo mama jokes hurt worse when it's your dad tellin' 'em. When he says, 'Yo mama's labia is so purple, Prince wrote a song about it?!' It hurts."

They give it up. I'm floating on their love. This is better than getting a blowjob while knowing you have a joint and a leftover, half burrito waiting in the fridge. "Ok, thanks, guys!" I walk off stage as a champion.

The two shows at Club Deluxe go great. About 100 people each night shoved into the tiny venue. You couldn't have flicked a bottlecap in any direction without it flying down someone's laughing gullet. After the second show, I rescue Doug from the adoring mob, which makes him uncomfortable, and we get down a few blocks to Aub-Zam-Zam. It's a tiny martini bar operated by an eccentric old guy that you can order whatever you want, and he just makes you a martini. If you don't like it, he kicks you out—like the *soup nazi*, but with martinis. Also, The Doors, Hendrix, and Jefferson Airplane used to hang here. We are right in the thick of Patchouliville, probably not Doug's favorite scene.

This fucking hyper, red-headed chick that works at the Brainwash came to the show. *Why did I fucking tell her?* Her head exploded when I told her about the show, "Doug Stanhope!? Oh my god! He's god! He's a genius! You know him?" I should have snatched the flyer out of her hand right then.

Doug's fans are fanatical. It's got to be annoying. So now this redheaded chick with a pointy chin and freckles is chasing after us. She actually comes into the bar with us. *Fuck.* She's about to ruin my chance to finally bond with Doug. *Fuck.* After we finish our first drink, this bitch hasn't even stopped to breathe. Just jabbering on and on. You can almost see where her jawbones connect begin to glow red.

Doug says, "Ok, I'm gonna head back to the hotel," and he pulls out a wad of cash and pays me $200 for both shows and says, "Thanks, you got talent. You're definitely my San Francisco guy." It's not a tour, but it's something! I featured for Doug Stanhope for a few shows! That's pretty awesome. Going on an airplane for 100 audience members per night was a generous favor to us from a guy of that stature. I'll take it.

Shit. I'd have done it for free. At the very least, it's going to look great on my resume, and Doug Stanhope saw me perform. I know that because when I looked towards the swinging kitchen doors, I saw his silhouette there. He could have easily stayed in there and worked out the new material, but he didn't. He came out to the edge of the room to watch me perform. And I killed it. Fuckin' awesome.

He walks out the door, the red-haired chick, Alice, going, "Wait, I was going to suck your dick."

He's gone.

I go back to Club Deluxe, and Doug has left a plastic bag full of his DVDs and CDs. A big pile of expansive brilliance. I'll call him in the morning and try to return them to him. So I do, and he says, "Just keep them, or you can bring them to the San Jose Improv tonight."

"Ok, I'll bring them," I say excitedly. Doug hangs up before I can blab anymore.

He just offered me a guest set, right? Shit. I decide that he did and get ready to go down there. That little shithead Hollister went around my back. Hollister emailed me begging to get him, Stanhope. He must have heard the news I got some shows with him. He never called me back for more shows at the Improv because Pauly Shore probably complained that I was snotty or some shit. Whatever. Fuck the clubs, man. They exploit the non-famous comics, pretty much all of them, so I wasn't exactly in a hurry to bring this guy Doug Stanhope, although Doug would make them give me a set. I would kill and then rub it in Hollister's face near the bar. Why am I so fucking vengeful against this guy? He represents everything that is wrong with the comedy clubs, that's why. So, I bring up to Doug that they want him to add a day to his stop and do The Improv. He's like, "Nah, I don't do the Improvs anymore." Well, apparently, Hollister groveled him into it.

Doug can pretty much guarantee any venue that if they give him the entire door covers, then at least 300 severe alcoholics will descend upon their bar and drink every drop of whiskey and tequila they can pre-stock. At $20 a head? That's going to be at least several grand per show for Doug. That's good money. Everybody wins. Why would he let a comedy club collect the door and then hem and haw about how much he gets? I fuckin' love this guy. I'm going to model the first part of my career after him, and then I will get my life story made into movies.

I got shows with Doug Stanhope within four years of doing comedy. What can stop me?

Hollister must have promised him the entire door. So I hop on the CalTrain with the techies that work in the city and live down there. We finally get to Diridon Station, and I'm like, *Ok, 62 South Second Street, where the hell is that from here? I hate San Jose.* I see a Yellow Cab and start running for it. I had bet wrong on how long the train takes, and the show has got to be more than half over by now. I clutch the plastic bag full of Doug's merch as its sharp-cornered contents bang off my thigh when I run.

Three other people are closer, and they get there first, "62 South Second Street," they say.

"That's the Improv! give me a ride, you guys, I'm performing!" There are now four people in the car if you count the taxi driver. I'd be willing to sit bitch in the back, with my feet up on the hump. It could work. One of the guys pokes his head out the rear door, now half-closed, as I arrive at the cab. He looks me up and down as I put on my best, *I don't smell or anything* smile, and he says, "You're not Doug Stanhope," *Slam!* and the cab takes off, leaving me there pissed. It takes five minutes for another taxi to show up. It seems like a year. I finally get to the Improv. Neil Hamburger is up there, awkwardly telling jokes in his nervous, shaky style. Nice! *There's still time to get a set.*

I see Hollister trying to cut the distance between me and the stairs on the right side of the lobby. He knows if he can keep me from getting to Doug, he can stop me from getting a set. Hollister said some bullshit on the internet a little bit after the Pauly Shore shows; the shows that had left a nasty taste in my mouth, so I flamed his ass—exposed him for the asshole that he is. *Fuck you motherfucker.*

Now, if I could get a guest set from Stanhope himself and kill? Right in front of Hollister? His hate just feeding my performance? Well, I think that'd be a very Merry Christmas to me.

I'm going to beat him to the stairs without having to run. I would resent fate if it made me run right now. But alas, stairs are his enemy, and I can fast walk/shuffle pretty quick at this point on my pin and plate studded heels. Once I'm on the steps, he knows he's beat. Hollister slows his jog before his heart rate gets out of control, and soon I'm knocking on the green room door. Inside are Doug and the GM talking, "Hey Doug, I brought your merch to sell after. You think there's still time for me to get a set?"

Doug looks surprised and impressed. "Shit, you made it. Yeah, sure. Can you put this guy up next?" he looks at the manager, who seems confused as to how to respond. On the one hand, I wasn't as much of a bootlicker as they wanted to work here as an unfamous comic. On the other hand, I just brought Doug Stanhope into our region for them to book. And I did it because he was impressed with my work and wanted to do shows with me. My resume has suddenly bulked up since those shitty Pauly Shore shows. The GM is stuck. "Well, if you want to give him a set."

YES!!

Within minutes I'm on the side of the stage, and the host brings me up. I grab the mic and yell into it, "Ok, where's the motherfuckers that just left me at the train station?!"

I soon find them laughing their asses off and in shock that I wasn't lying. To the crowd's glee, I just eviscerate them for being shitty samaritans who are going to get some well-deserved instant karma. I just absolutely burn the fucking room down for about ten minutes. Killing isn't even the word. I walk off stage to a finally smiling Doug Stanhope. This smile is the greatest payment I could receive. Thanks, Doug, for lending your support to an underdog and letting him in on some pretty badass shows.

PS Fuck the Improvs

He Had His Dick in My Face

Keppel has brought his camera down to interview people about the crisis-infested corner of 16th and Mission, the open-mic we do there each Thursday night, and also what they think of my comedy. It's for a project we're working on.

First, he's got Potholder, an acoustic guitar player that plays comical folksy numbers. He's dressed like he's going to audition for a West Coast remake of Midnight Cowboy, and boy, aren't we in the right setting down here on the corner for that? He's got a strawberry blonde Lemmy mustache, leather cowboy hat, a blazer that is the color of over creamed coffee, and a cutely askew neckerchief. His face is cheerful and friendly. He's a great guy. He's trying to answer Josh's questions about what this outside open-mic is on a drug-infested street corner, but huge motorcycles keep blasting by.

Josh: "So why do you come out here?"

Potholder: "Well, there's usually nothing better to do on a Thursday night, except come out here and drink beer in public and try and entertain the people who pass by or came to see us."

Josh: "Are there many comedians that come out here?"

Potholder: "Not many good ones," he gets a good laugh out of himself on that one. "There's only one that has my heart." Oh, maybe we *are* rebooting Midnight Cowboy. "This is a hard venue for comedy. You have to be really funny, or people are just staring at you."

Josh: "What would someone see if they came down here on a Thursday night?"

Potholder: "Something unique to San Francisco, I haven't seen many things like this around other places. We don't try to make money off it, there's nothing pretentious about it, there's no sign-up sheet, we just like to come out and drink beer on the fuckin' street corner."

Josh: "And finally, when was the first time you saw JC Scales do comedy?"

Potholder: "I saw him here, and he was definitely funny—sort of—as far as I can remember. I think he did some, like, *Goat Lady stuff*."

Josh: "Is he like a thorn in your guys' side, or like a companion?"

Potholder: "He's one of us. And he's the only comedian ever to be one of us. That's weird. We never took a comedian. He fell out of my window once."

Josh: "What do you think's gonna happen with Justin?" *What? Like I'm gonna die, Josh?*

Potholder: "He will become a supernova and ascend to the comedy heavens." *Oh, so you think I'm going to die too? Ok, why don't you guys suck it? Next!*

Next, we have Charlie Getter, a giant walking smile and fountain of goodwill. He's got rabbity front teeth in the middle of that big smile, and it's all surrounded by a blond goatee. He always wears a worn baseball hat and, most likely, a hoodie. Tonight's selection has letters spelling out Lake Tahoe across the chest. He is very talented yet humble in manner, but the sparkle in his light blue eyes is confident. Cocky even.

Josh: "Tell me what this is about? I heard this is kind of a brainchild of yours."

Charlie: "We used to have a poetry reading at a coffee shop that went out of business, and so we ended up here. People were like, 'That's crazy, people are getting off the train, they don't care.' But they do. In the summer we get beautiful crowds, but in the winter it's cold, and they rush by us. And it's horrible and wet. But we come every week, rain or shine.

So you know, that's what we are, and that's how we do it. For a little bit of time, we reclaim public space for two hours on a Thursday night, and we're out here."

Josh: "When was the first time you saw JC Scales?"

Charlie: "Scales stumbled out on this corner. I met him on this corner, and we saw him, and he did a set, and he blew everyone away. And now he's part of the crew."

Next is Guinevere Q, a teenage genius from Chicago. She plays her acoustic guitar songs as if she had some stand-up material and fashioned them into laugh-inducing ditties instead. So smart. Old soul. Bigmouth; literal and figurative.

Always smiling with her brown, ponytailed hair loosely tied. She wears these rectangular Ben Franklin glasses. If someone told me they didn't like her, I'd ask them, "What the fuck is wrong with you?" Salt of the earth, that kid.

Josh: " What is this all about?" (It's hard to hear her response because Charlie has gone straight from talking to Josh to the stage, and this guy is even louder than me.)

Guinevere Q: "I've been coming here every Thursday night. I come here for people like Charlie Getter and Scales, all these cats. It's art in its rawest form. Hecklers are coming out of the woodwork. This is an impoverished neighborhood, a lot of crack deals go down, but when we're here, crime decreases, we often have quite a presence, you see? I'm here to see if I can handle a rough crowd; I've been heckled, things thrown at me, spittin' towards me, and also the most inspiring moments where people were diggin' my thing. I'm here every Thursday for the last three years, testing stuff out, pushing the limits, and meeting other artists."

Josh: "And when was the first time you saw JC Scales perform, and what did you think about that?

Guinevere Q: "The first time I saw JC Scales was at the Brainwash actually, he had his dick up on the table, and he was writhing in front of me. I thought, who the fuck is this guy, and why does he think he's a comic? And then the next thing I knew, I was laughing hysterically. He had some bit about growing up on a sheep farm or some shit, and you know, he's got issues with his parents, which I think is hilarious. Anyone who has issues with their parents, who brought them into this world, that's just comedy. So uhm, that's the first time I met Scales, was at Brainwash, he was standing on top of a table, and he was rubbing his dick in my face, and I thought, you know, this guy knows what's up, he's a genius. That's comedy."

Ali Wong

A while back, this new girl showed up, and before she even had five minutes of workable material, everyone talked about her like she was going to be the next big thing. She's instantly groomed for success at The Punchline. Ali Wong, a four-foot-tall Chinese girl with nerd glasses and a dirty mouth—didn't even have to do a full lap on the open-mic circuit. So this is what Northern California has decided to produce this year comedy-wise. I'm a little pissed; I gotta be honest. I've been here years earlier than her, and I'm repeatedly told I'm too dirty. And now this chick comes along talking about how there might be bugs in her pussy that will chew up her baby's face and make it look like Seal's. Are the bookers wagging their fingers in rebuke of her? No, they're insanily palming their cheeks and going, "She's god! She's god!"

What the fuck? Don't get me wrong. She's gotten funnier after her first year—you have to give new comics at least that long before you gauge their potential ability. It's a long game, comedy. They say it takes you five years just to find your voice—Tony Sparks said I was born with mine, but whatevs. They tell the open-mikers it takes an average of 20 years to be a decent headliner. I think they say that mainly to discourage the unserious or the disturbed, though. Finding encouragement in comedy is like trying to find heroin at your grandma's. You end up smoking the *coffee nips* for a placebo high. Not in Ali Wong's case. She's been getting her knob polished from day one, and after less than two years in the game, she will leave a showcase before performing to find another one that suits her better if the audience isn't *giving it up* enough for her liking.

All the Punchline regulars do this. They get three or four sets at The Punchline every week and cruise out to other stuff, but only if they think it'll be good; this is a great way to keep your confidence high, which *is* essential in comedy. After a lousy set, it can take a few days to recover. But unless you slash your way through those tough crowds, shaking them by their ankles until the laughs fall out? You'll never be a great one. And it's ALL I do. Hell, I can't even **get** booked at the easy shows. I'm so used to fighting for every laugh that I forget to turn down the playful antagonism a notch when I get a rare set at The Punchline. The audience raises their hands like, "Hey, we laugh easy, chill," before I make the adjustment; hopefully.

So Ali Wong started out watching me from the back of the rooms, all wide-eyed and adoring. Much like *all* the newer comics do initially, before they are whispered to that I'm out. I'm too angry and dirty. *It's okay for you, Ali, because you are a short, Chinese female with glasses. You are a widely castable net of a pre-approved Bay Area set of demographics. You will be the hero of us. A hero who loves to talk about her pussy. That angry white boy shit Scales is doing? That's Brooklyn shit. Scales should move to Brooklyn. Don't be his friend, Ali. It'll cost you. He's the competition anyway. Think about it. Dirty jokes are a niche market. There's only room for one. Hobble him. If you get a chance, hobble him.*

First of all, fuck moving to Brooklyn. I have rent control here. The landlord can legally only raise that by like two percent a year because it's an old shitty building. Location location location, but still, it's a shitty old building. I have a three-bedroom house in the center of San Francisco for $1,200. It looks like I'm dying here, kids. And if that's going to be their attitude about me, I think I'll stick around just to piss in their slushies.

In comedy, Ali Wong walks right by me, straight into the premium greenrooms and an Oliver Stone movie. Yeah, it sticks in my craw, I'll admit it. Wouldn't *you* be pissed? Not at her, I mean, she's just trying to get her hustle on like everyone else. You can't be mad at someone for doing what you would do yourself. Maybe *I'll* get a second look because of *her* success.

A third of the bookers love me, so they make Ali Wong go right after me in the showcase lineups to prove that I am clearly the superior choice. If there can only be *one* dirty comedian from the Bay Area, it should be me. Nope. Even though I get more laughs than her consistently, she will be christened as *the dirtiest allowed* to be presented to show business this year. I have to learn how to upload video clips, man. That video clip where I got punched fizzled out at around 60,000 hits. If I were tech-savvy, I'd have just re-uploaded that same clip every two hours until one of them snowballed me into stardom on Youtube.

That's the other way to get your comedy career moving. One Bay Area comic, Anjelah Johnson, was able to skirt around The Punchline when her bit about a nail salon got a million hits. For now, I'm still going to the Punchline on local comedian showcase Sundays, and while all the other comics are doing their tight seven that they would be presenting to NBC, Ali Wong just uses it to fuck around and try out the new stuff. She's already got it made in the shade. I'm jealous; clearly, I'm a little jealous. This is bullshit.

I don't resent her. It just pisses me off. So, you CAN be dirty. You just can't be an angry white male? Everyone's been trained to search out the exits in case I pull out a gun or something? Are you even listening to the words I'm saying? I'm the opposite of that. I try something closer to the subdued stoner delivery that some hipsters use to present their inauthentic, unfunny material and even faker Clark Kent glasses. It just doesn't seem authentic. I'm embarrassed I even tried it for a spin. I'm not a spaced-out stoner. I'm a student—not a copier—of Bill Hicks and George Carlin. They yelled. I like it. Should I wear a see-through plastic jumpsuit, so the audience can see I don't have a gun? I could tape my *weenis* back out of view on church nights.

Maybe it's the novelty of a miniature Asian girl with glasses doing it? Or is it just not *angry whiteboy day* in The Bay? The woke ones who rule things at The Punchline can't say it's not *angry whiteboy day* in The Bay because it would be anti-woke to be racist like that, even against angry white boys. Maybe they have to say it's because I'm too dirty; the networks would frown if I were to be thrown up at an *industry* showcase. It's never an HBO executive in the audience. It's always the networks with all their half-baked sitcoms. Let me at the HBO guy!

At any rate, I perform with Ali Wong a lot. She's nice enough and funny enough. I don't get the frenzy about her, though. The material is above average but not outstanding. I do take refuge in the fact that I leave few laughs left for her to scrape off the stage when she does go after me. The competitions and the showcases are all pretty much mine. I wax her like it's personal. I don't think it is. I feel like I have to prove a point to the other people watching. I'm not trying to discourage her. I just need it to be known. Deep down in my soul, I need it to be known.

One night I probably take a little too much pleasure in shutting Ali down in the Yo Mama Competition at Club Deluxe. They're always stupid, one-time, throwaway jokes—it's best not to overthink it—but it was nice for her to have to come up onto the stage and at least look me in the eye while I beat her all roasty style. No ill will, I just know I'm funnier. (Come on, Netflix! I'll do it for half. Fuckin' half of what she got, man! Does anyone know anyone over there?)

Kankled Again

I'm starting to lose focus around this time. I'm past the age of 35, older than anyone from the old neighborhood thought I'd get, including me. The parties are charging a cover on my brain and bones now. I didn't really budget, longevity-wise, for this. Now that I've been in the city for a while, all the bartenders are pouring me heavy. My star has risen in comedy to '*notable underground headliner who can wake up even the coldest of crowds, but you have to get him up there within an hour of his arrival. Otherwise, there's a 50 percent chance he'll get drunk and torch the crowd too much.*' I know, it's wordy—probably not going in my bio.

I can pretty much just show up at a lot of the showcases and get a last-second guest set. Sometimes we have to go all the way out to Vallejo to perform, but once the booker agrees to give my ride a set, I can pick from dozens of open-mikers who have cars with heated seats, bottled water, and weed for the ride home. I don't get stoned before I perform because I lose my place on the new stuff, but if I can manage to get stoned on weed enough *after* I perform, I don't feel like scoring a crack rock at the end of the night. I need to get a girlfriend again to clean the gutter off me, is what I'm thinking.

Interesting things are happening in comedy. I forgot to tell you, that girl, Angelah Johnson, who got famous on Youtube for her impression of a nail salon employee? She became a cast member on Mad TV from that. I knew you could skip all the showbiz middlemen! This is proof that Youtube can help a performer get a level of fame where they don't have to sign a shitty contract with some slimy Harvey Weinstein type. She goes right from this video clip onto a comedy TV show. Not bad. I need a fucking intern reloading that video of me getting hit by a heckler. Where are the tech-savvy interns? The bad news is that *I* would have been crucified for this same impression of a Vietnamese nail salon employee.

It seems like PC culture is a little bit random in who it decides to prosecute. *Hmmm. I wonder what the criteria is?* (analyzes his reflection in a window.)

One night I'm headed to a show where the brilliant impressionist of everyday people, Will Franken, is headlining, and I'm racing on my bike to get there. I've already done two sets, and I'm going for the hat trick. If I could end the night by killing it right before Will goes up, then sit at the bar with a Manhattan to watch him send up Marin soccer moms and your neighbor? Well, that would be amazing. I'm thinking this as I'm racing down Kearny about to plunge into North Beach, between the Bank of America building and that little Chinatown park. I'm crossing Sacramento Street, and *BAM!* A truck comes out of nowhere, T-bones me on my bike, and my ass goes through the windshield. Then the truck hits its brakes, sending me flying up and through the intersection. I'm already on the ground before I realize what happened. I try to get up, but my foot is shooting off in the wrong direction. *Uh oh.* Someone runs up to me and sees my flapping foot and says, "Do you want me to call an ambulance?"

It's a valid question. The richest country in the history of the world, and the average citizen, when injured, has to ask themselves, *should I just fold up my leg like a beach chair and ride the bus, rather than incur massive debt for an ambulance ride that will cause the foreclosure of my personal American Dream?* I have zero credit and zero assets they can confiscate—the poor man's only advantage—so I say, "Yeah, call an ambulance!"

They call 911. I consider dropping my ID down a rain gutter and giving a fake name to avoid the mountain of hospital bills I'll ignore.

The ambulance gets there and loads me up. The poor Asian guy never gets out of the car because getting in a car accident while Asian in America is an onsite conviction for him. He was scared of the Financial District pedestrian's finger-pointing. I'm pretty sure he ran the light but did he? He must be drunk, at least. All the drivers after eight pm are drunk down here. I was in a hurry, and my mind was already at the end of my destination. Having performed twice already, I'm more than slightly buzzed. I don't know, did *I* run the light? For now, I blame him.

In the ambulance, they start their questions to decide what sort of treatment to give me, "Do you have insurance? Do you have an ID?"

They want my identity before they even crack open an ice pack. I give them my wallet, now scared, under the bright lights, ankle killing me beyond belief. *Just give me some painkillers man, my world for some painkillers.*

We get to the hospital, and they take the X-rays. Surprise, surprise, it's a tib-fib fracture. *No shit.*

I'm sitting in their bed, wondering how much per hour they will try to bill me for. And the traffic accident cop comes in and asks me a few questions, but really to see if he can smell alcohol on me. I was riding my bike and wearing a hoody downtown. He *must be one of those scummy bike messengers*, is what his mustache would be thinking if it had a brain instead of donut crumbs in it. He gets the whiff he was looking for and leaves. I'm found at fault and will receive a $3,000 bill from the Asian guy's insurance company, along with the hospital bills I will drop into the recycling after I make sure none of it has my Social Security number on it.

I now have snapped both ankles and shattered both heel bones. It should balance me out, right? Plates and pins in both. I can't work for a while, that's for sure.

Within a few days, after all the other comics have heard I went to the hospital yet again, Justin McClure messages me about headlining the Purple Onion. It's to be a benefit for my fucked up ankle. Nice! That will give me a chance to tell you all about my eventful hospital stay.

Headlining Two Weeks After Being Run Over

The place is packed. People that didn't get seats fast enough are crammed up against the walls. This will be a great night in my life, despite being all smashed up. This place is **the** history of comedy, from Lenny Bruce to Phyllis Diller to Robin Williams on through to Zack Galifinakis, and now me. You feel the history the second you walk in the place. A hidden dungeon of vice. Who knows? Maybe pirates used to come down here to watch X-rated sea shanty shows. The Purple Onion has steep marble steps down into what *had* to be a speakeasy back in the day. You *feel* that Barbary Coast party spirit down here; it's safe to laugh at the dirty jokes because Jesus can't see down here through all the pot smoke and sarcasm.

The terraced seating accommodates only about 60 people, with room for 25 or so others to stand. Everyone is packed in tight, feeding off each other's body electricity, creating a charged-up *Tesla coil* of laughter.

There's a bar and a big Purple Onion sign in orange and purple, providing the stage's backdrop. A cocktail waitress is rushing around with a tray full of drinks. You can feel the excitement in the room. This is everyone's big night out, and I'm to be the conductor for a symphony of chaos. I love it!

I will perform booze-free in a rare occurrence. I've decided to sit in Jackson's wheelchair on stage. Between the wheelchair and the pain pills, I should be slowed down to somewhere between a politician returning a text to a lobbyist, and a punk show by the Dwarves, (who I believe played this venue slightly over a decade ago, during the Tom Guido, garage punk era.)

Ok, here comes the host to bring me up. The other performers have warmed up the crowd well. The host is the highly capable Sammy Wegent. He grabs the mic and says something like, "And our headliner, folks, is coming to the stage. He was run over by a car on his way here just two weeks ago. So give it up for Mr. Justin... **Scales!!!**"

The crowd is going nuts. It's full. They all showed up to support my idiot ass getting run over by a car. Sometimes I really, really love this world. I hobble up in my hospital gown and with crutches. I stack them against that beautiful, shiny, purple, and orange sign over bricks that backdrops the stage. A stage that *can* fit a four-person band if it has to, but they'd be snugger than in the van they slept in getting here from Wisconsin. It's plenty of room for my antics, even once I get off crutches.

I'm wearing big grandma sunglasses because I've been sitting in my room for two weeks straight, taking a bunch of pain pills, and writing this set. I haven't trimmed my nails or showered in a while. This is my third bad injury in about as many years. I look like shit. One hundred sixty-five pounds, and I should weigh 180.

The stage lights are kryptonite to me right now. And frankly, these are the first people I've seen other than my brother and mom since I got home from the hospital. My lovely assistant is Jennifer, who I know from a pot trimming scene in Potter's Valley. She notably won't fuck me. Not that anybody would want to right now, due to my raggedness. She puts my pills and water on a stool by me and makes sure I don't fall over transitioning from the crutches to the wheelchair. As she goes to leave, I look to her and say, "Thanks, Sweet Ass," and she gives me a look, like, *You wish.*

I turn, finally, to a sold-out crowd. *Holy fuck. I'm sober.* I only took my morning set of two Vicodin and just been raw-dogging the evening time. I just doubled up on the Advils and figured I'd white knuckle through it with a clear head. Anything but alcohol on stage for me? It doesn't work. Punchline deliveries have to be timed to the tenth of a second. Alcohol only works because it's a perpetual state of being for me. At least at night time. After two Vicodin, I'd probably be all, "Oh, what's this? What are *you* guys doin' here?" *Ok, shut up. They're all looking at you.* I begin:

"Yeah, it's true, Purple Onion, I was on my way over to this neighborhood to inseminate the masses with love, joy, and laughter, and a car ran over me and broke my fuckin' shin. And that's not all people. Two years ago, I fuckin' fell out a window drunk, and I had a sword in one hand and a pepper shaker in the other." They laugh because the visual is morbidly poetic and slapstickily hilarious. It covers your whole comedy tongue. "And I shattered my heel bones."

They seem hesitant to laugh at what indeed must have been agonizing. So I let out a staccato, high-pitched laugh at myself. This releases them, and so they laugh too.

"Yeah, that's funny. Haha. And two years before that, I knocked out a skinhead and broke my ankle trying to climb a fence. My ankles have had more surgery than Madonna's pussy."

A weaker laugh because I wrote this shit on pain pills. When you're high on pain pills, some things just seem funnier. It gets better. Stop complaining.

"Never broke a bone until I was 30. I'm not even that crazy anymore. It's like I'm getting charged for shit I did in '92."

Chuckles and giggles.

"Or is it this? We all have a guardian angel until we're 30, and if we were real assholes to him, on his way out, he sicks a demon on us. It's like the office equivalent of when you quit your job, and you rub your balls on the boss' phone."

"Or, option three: is the highest-selling voodoo doll of all time, the Scalesman voodoo doll? They *do* hate me in Haiti. That's why call it Haiti, not Likey."

"What's up with this, though, Haiti?! You're poking the doll a bit low. My mouth is up here. You CAIN'T… kill… The Scalesman!"

"You think they call me The Scalesman because I'm **not**…a superhero!?"

"Fuck. I know so much about pain, Morrisey calls me for song lyrics."

"My ankles have seen more metal than a Motley Crew groupie's beaver!"

"God damn it. I… EAT… CARS!!!"

"You think I look bad! Well, I know a truck that's looking pretty fucked up itself. Bent up steering rod... twisted up... transdermal vibricator. Ok, I don't know shit about cars! But shit was cracked."

"I got windshield glass in my asscrack right now!"

"When I got to the hospital, they jammed a rubber tube down my weenis hole!"

"I ATE BROWN JELLO!!!!"

"You're not even supposed to survive San Francisco General Hospital once. Three-peat bitches! Three-peat!"

I get a small applause break—nice!—and take a quick drink of water.

"SF General sucks! The nurses wear gang bandanas! It's the only hospital I know where you can go in with a broken ankle and come out with malaria! There's been a few budget cuts. This is my life. How do you think I got this funny, sir? Do you think punchlines just float into my head as I'm sitting on a cafe patio with some guy pretending he's French? No! You have to harvest golden punchlines from your side with a rusty butter knife… and then simmer it, for years, in regret, melancholy, and broken bones. Until finally, it's ready to make a bunch of people who are dead inside... laugh." I motion to them.

Laughs and claps.

"That's how you get on Letterman, folks!"

They're laughing decently. I go for my pill bottle, which is actually TicTacs, gobble down about four of them to trip everybody out. I then throw the whole bottle out to the crowd, assuming it will disappear forever.

"And on a side note, if you ever see me after the show, feel free to not come up to me, and say, 'I thought you were a stand-up comedian." I wag my head back and forth, sideways, like how an idiot would talk.

"What's the other one they like? 'It'll be a good source of material.'"

"Fuck you, buddy! You know what else would be a good source of material? My fist in your fuckin' dome. Welcome to Club Cripple!"

"At least, when I was 30, I knew who my enemies were. It was people. I knew who to punch. But how do you run a beat down on bad luck? Catch a black cat and ram a rabbit's foot up his ass? Neighbors ain't gonna like that!" I scrunch and contort my face absurdly.

"It's gotta be bad luck too, people. It can't be Karma. Even *I'm* not **this** big of an asshole."

They laugh and laugh. I've got them now.

"So I'm rolling down the street, riding my bike, trying to get to this show, and BAM! My ass goes through the windshield, I fly up in the air and do a couple of spins, hit the ground"—A bottle breaks in the trash can at the bar, almost perfectly timed to mimic the breaking windshield. When you're in the zone, sometimes the room itself starts helping you tell the stories—"break my leg, and there are people everywhere, and I'll I can think is, *Fuck. This is going to be embarrassing.*"

They become quiet. Occasionally in stand-up, quiet is what you want. This is one of those times.

"Big tough guy, screw my leg. I don't want people to see I'm a mortal human. Wouldn't want to take comfort from a stranger." I put my hand up as a shield, "No, no, I'm too macho," I say, wriggling down into Jackson's wheelchair.

"So, I get on the ambulance, and the guy is like damn, guys that snapped both bones in their leg usually pass right out. And I'm like, 'Dude, are you like, trying to tell me I'm the big winner tonight? I'm all for looking at the silver lining in shit, okay, but there's only one silver lining to this situation buddy, it's called four milligrams of morphine. It's in that drawer right there. I remember from last time!'"

They laugh. I mean, look at me, I'm still in my gown and hospital bracelet. It's like I came directly from the hospital. This performance is as authentic as grits brought to you by a lady who called you "Hon."

"Why do I always have to fuckin' train the morphine guy!"

Jennifer, my lovely assistant who I'm failing to try and get laid by, appears to have had a date join her. She has let out an extended, high-pitched giggle that goes on and on.

"What's up with the hyena gangbang back there?" I say, unable to muster any more meanness on such a pretty girl. Chicks I'm trying to bang, bringing dates to shows I'm headlining is a fucking deal breaker.

"The doctors that fixed me last year are like, 'Oh come on bro, you again? Ok, we're going to put a titanium rod from your knee to your ankle. And I was like, 'Dude! I always wanted to be Wolverine, the X-man. And now look, is this some sort of sick joke, wish fairy? I'm not laughing.'"

I laugh, ironically, because no one else is. Okay, don't lose them. Shit. Where's the comic book nerd to say, "Actually, Wolverine's bones were made from Adamantium." I could get a minute of howls from going after *that* guy—no such luck. I plunder on.

"So I wake up after the surgery, and there's a kid in my room. Cecil, 16 years old, and he's been shot 13 times. It was two weeks ago in Western Addition. Three kids got shot. And he was the oldest one, at 16. And, so, I stopped feeling sorry for myself right then."

So quiet you can hear the refrigerators hum.

"So, his buddies came in one day, and the way they had the curtains hung up, they didn't realize I was in there, and they start naming names and shit, like, talking about when and where, not that I heard any details because I'm freaking the fuck out in my head, right?"

Even quieter. You can hear the roaches fucking now.

"And I go, *Oh shit, they're going to realize I'm in there, and that they then have to kill me!*"

The laughs start up again.

"What am I gonna do, pretend I'm sleepin'? Nah, they're not gonna buy that. So I came up with a plan, I pretended I was asleep, and then I pretended I woke up in pain, 'AHHHHHH!!! MY LEG!!!! MY FUCKIN' LEG!!!!'"

Quiet again. Okay, let's start shifting out of storytelling mode before they forget what laughing is for the dirty jokes coming up. I'm not telling stories about my asshole getting bloody to silence.

"And all those little fuckers ran out of there like murder was on sale!"

Laughter and claps. Oh, there they are. Okay, good.

"I'm telling you guys, you take a comedian with medium acting skills… and put them in a life-threatening situation? They'll turn into fuckin' De Niro!"

Laughs. Good. Okay, we're heading back to the setup punch stuff.

"That's what they should do for the next Lindsay Lohan movie, put a bunch of wild ferrets on top of the fuckin' camera. Bitch'll be puttin' Meryl Streep to shame in a heartbeat!"

Hahahaha, they go.

"The worst part about all this? Is that nobody I know loves me enough to jam a suppository up my ass. I had to do it myself. You can't just go first knuckle either; it'll pop right back out. That shit hurts. Your ass doesn't want stuff in it, okay? So guys, next time a girl says, 'It hurts,' listen with compassion. Keep trying, but listen."

After I finish out the hospital stuff and fucking around with the crowd. There are some sweet moments where I reveal to the audience that the pills I'd been crunching in my teeth the whole first ten minutes of my set were TicTacs, and did a guy in the front row want some, not that his breath had been a problem for me, but he did seem to be abnormally spaced from his date. Another time I tore into the Guy

Jennifer brought, saying, "Loosen up the tie, Wall Street. It's a fuckin' comedy show!"

After that, I devolve to my 15 minutes of filth, and we call it a night. I couldn't think of a better way to spend an evening. Seeing those faces made me rise to the occasion, even though I couldn't have my liquid courage. I never needed it. I just think I do. I'll remember this set perfectly, instead of it being like a semi-hazy dream. That's a plus. Sobriety feels weird but good. Almost like a high in itself because it's so unfamiliar. Too bad I won't make a habit of it once I recover.

Justin McClure, the show's producer, gives me the whole door, which is $700. What a fantastic human this guy is. So needed, and my biggest comedy take yet.

What a life. I've indeed taken a lot of hits. But did I die? No. I don't think I *can* die. Or I would have by now, right? I'm a little Cucaracha. This injury isn't as bad as when I shattered both my feet, either. I'm feelin' shitty because it was only two weeks ago, but I'll be back on the streets in a month. It is true; I heal like a wolverine. If you told the doctors that fixed me on the sword and pepper shaker incident that I was on my feet for 12 hours a day within a year? They'd laugh. But, **heeeeeeere's Justy!!!!**

Tourettes Without Regrets

A punk rock, bartending, South Bay comic, Rachel Warner has scored me a gig in a mega show in Oakland called Tourettes Without Regrets!

I've been delaying my attempt to try and describe this event to you because you have to be there to believe it. Nothing I could write could do it justice, but if I can convey just half of what it feels like in there, it should be sufficient to blow your mind away.

Think of a sexually charged Jerk du Soleil, if you will. Seven hundred screaming teen and twenty-something kids of every demographic you can imagine, from Too Short's nephews to white girls named Becky. There is sexual energy everywhere. Anybody could just start fucking anybody else at any second. You feel it in the air. Also, a little tickle in your balls. A knowingness. A rotating skit/game show, Fear Factor episode of sexual deviance, and mayhem. "Who wants to come up here and make some puppet porn? Your lackluster energy has pushed me into a state of just looking for weird whack material at this point!" yells our host, Jamie DeWolf, a verbally deft, fedora-wearing, red-goateed, black-clothed, red-tied ringmaster. He conceived this sexual convention of misfits and thrill-seekers—the show where an audience member might be the night's biggest star.

Over the next year, I will make my bones here by becoming a three-time dirty haiku champion of Oakland—a listing on my resume I'm particularly proud of. Here's a sample of my wares: "I like Brown Sugar! Nubian Booty Princess! Give a cracker joy!" Haiku number two: "Civilizations! My stiff cum rag contains them! Civilizations!" All right, that's enough. A year after that? I will become the first *resident comedian* in Tourettes Without Regrets history.

There are sexually explicit rap battles, do or die challenges that might incur an STD, or maybe an emergency room visit. There's a battle rapper named Jelly Donut that is dressed like—you guessed it—a jelly donut. "I might be filled with raspberry, or I might be a peanut butter fluffernutter. One thing you can be sure of is after this rap battle, your rep will live IN the gutter!" The Saurus has maintained a nine-month winning streak and will be going to the world rap championships this year. His rhymes are multisyllabic, and they say his mind is photographic. Syzygy goes up against Butterscotch for an epic beatbox battle. Perhaps Infinite will beatbox alongside Brent Weinbach as he does his comedy act. You just never know. It's all a crazy mash-up limited only by the fertile imaginations of the participants. What is going on in Oakland, man? Why don't I come out here more often?

The hours of restlessness that Jamie spends thinking of fucked up shit to make these people do, no, pay a cover charge to do, must number in the thousands. I don't think the guy sleeps. He's a man on a mission, but it sure ain't from god!

Naked squirters on giant steel hoops hanging from the rafters, spinning high above the audience in celebration of their airborne tits, which look enticing in their gravity-defying juxtapositions. Furries with the assholes ripped out of them from their misspent breaks work the floor preparing for the next skit of entertainment. Along the back wall of the room, girls do molly bumps off their house keys and position their tits out for everyone to admire, or if you're nice, perhaps jack off onto. I have found my personal Disneyland. This place is amazing. A deviant, sex ninja, whorehouse extravaganza.

Jamie directs the mayhem across the stage in rapid intervals like the master showman he is. The country's most dangerous redheaded stepchild. Black sheep of the Dianetics Cult. He is L Ron Hubbard's actual great-grandson! He escaped as a teenager, and he's been speaking out against their brainwashing ways as a spoken word performer ever since. They harassed him and threatened him until he just snapped, "Fine, try to kill me then, pussies!" They finally gave up and left him alone after realizing he couldn't be intimidated.

A true *dirt purveyor* in the vein of myself; brothers from another mother indeed. What an opportunity to make a show like this my home. I head towards a perch to watch it all after introducing myself to Jamie, who tells me to "Hang tight, you're going later in the show."

In a lonely craft, that of eloquent filth, I have found a brother in arms. I just have to crush it tonight. I'm sure I'll be able to flourish here. This show was built for me. I get to the bar and almost forget

I'm not drinking due to all the pain pills I'm still on, "Bottled water, please." When you fall out a window with a sword in one hand and a peppershaker in the other, then put your ass through a windshield the very next year, you begin to rethink your drinking habits. Also, I've been enjoying waking up and remembering my sets, which I don't blow any of drunk. That's good. That's real good. Look at all these rowdy people, though. *Shit. I need a drink.* ***Don't do it.***

Up now on the stage are two people Jamie has plucked from the crowd as contestants, victims, or martyred innocents; it depends on how you want to look at it, I guess. First, we have a huge Black man with a trucker hat and a quadruple X, airbrushed T-shirt that says, "Cornbread, Da Bom," on the front. He looks like his rocking crib doubled as a meat smoker. If this man handed me a BBQ plate, I wouldn't question it. Some guys just look like they know how to work a grill. And then, next to him, we have a women's studies major at Cal Berkeley, Becky Blakely.

So they are looking at Jamie as he cuts open a plastic bag full of bloody pig hearts and cow tongues, dumping them with a *Skkklllrrrrch!* at their feet. Cornbread, we are to find out his name is, has a look on his face, like, *Yall want me to smoke those?* And Berkeley Becky is trying her best not to look terrified, but it's barely working.

"Hey! Pull that trash can up into the middle of the audience," Jamie barks at one of his furry assistants. They are all dressed like truck stop squirrels, parole badgers, and delinquent bears. The inside of their costumes, I will find out, smell like stale pussy, ass, and rodent barf.

The owner of the Oakland Metro comes up onto the stage, saying, "What the fuck? Is that shit real?" and looks at the blood beginning to pool up underneath the low-cost alternative farm parts.

"Oh, we're just going to play a little basketball," he says to the guy. "Hey, this is Tom, the owner of the Oakland Metro, everybody. Say 'Hi' to Tom!"

Tom faces the crowd and gives a worn smile that looks to have seen too much in its life. "Hi, Tom!" we yell. He is looking to Jamie for any sign of uncertainty so he can cancel this particular event. It's farm animal blood that will be splashing all over the crowd, possibly into their mouths. This is California, after all, and there are insurance liabilities to worry about. Jamie doesn't flinch, and Tom has to settle for a promise that no blood will be flung towards the ice wells at the bar. Jamie gets excited that the boss seems somewhat okay with this. Before walking off the stage, Tom, the proprietor of the establishment, grabs the microphone and says, "We're going to be counting these pieces as they leave the stage, they all better be accounted for later," and, after wagging his finger at Jamie, he just walks off. Now, if you're at a party and the homeowner or bar owner doesn't consider shutting it down every 15 minutes, did you even party? Or was it more of a mixer? A gathering of fellow citizens?

I'm pretty sure that Jamie laughs at the end of every first Thursday of the month when his show hasn't been shut down in its middle by an authority of some sort or another; him finally dragged off to the nearest loony bin or prison. It's just all so shocking you don't quite know what to do, and that's how he gets away with it. It's all over and done with before you can rediscover your faculties.

DJ Fuck Off fittingly starts playing that Nine Inch Nails song that sounds like a pumping heart as the two contestants look down at the hog aortas they are about to try and earn $50 by scoring baskets with. Becky gets a steely, determined look on her face. *It's on.*

After pig heart basketball, a girl with a blond bob cut comes up and does a striptease. In the end, she's just standing there in her undies, trying to twirl her pasties, but her titties are too small, and she's trying to chew gum at the same time. The look of concentration on her face is so intense as to be angry-looking. Finally, she ends up just taking a bow and trots her skinny little ass off the stage to claps and cheers. She tried her best and exposed almost every nook and cranny of her body. I clap for her too. Whatever her skill level, that's at least worth something. From skit to song to whatever, you never really know what you're going to get. It could be brilliant, or it could be a meltdown of sorts; you just don't know, and that's half the fun. It's a four-hour show, so yeah, there's going to be some random filler here and there.

Now Jamie has the microphone and says, "This guy has been blowing up in the Bay Area. He hasn't even been doing comedy that long, a very strange man. Give it up... for The Scalesman!"

I start hobbling up on my crutches, in my hospital gown, and my giant grandma sunglasses. I'm still pretty fucked up, and steep stairs are my main enemy in life. Nevertheless, I manage to hobble up to the stage without help.

-I'm so happy this last trip to the emergency room didn't end in a wheelchair this time. That novelty wore off quick—on me, not the audience. I'd have to roll the wheelchair up to the sides of the stages and tip it over sideways until I fell into the edge of it. I'd have my back to them as I tipped over and would just stay that way, never turning to face them; somehow, this makes it funnier, the anonymity of the victim. I would milk it for extra laughs as I jerkily, slowly, agonizingly crawl to the mic and pretend I can't reach up to the microphone like the stand is bolted into the stage or something. I'd stretch my hand up all shakily towards it, just barely out of reach. They laugh, those sick fucks. Who says you can't joke about the disabled? To those who wanted me in a wheelchair forever because it made my angry white man act a little funnier? Fuck you. Anyone with a proper appreciation for ridiculocity and chaos should be able to see I'm at my peak when I'm partially broken but still able to struggle and lash out a bit. Crutches. I should be permanently crutched.—

I finally get to the edge of the stage. Jamie starts my intro, "Come on! Make more noise than that, you little assholes!"

I finally take the mic from Jamie, "So you guys like dirty shit, huh?"

"Yeah!" hundreds of kids yell back.

"All right, I'm going to start it off easy in case there's any pussies in here that need to be coaxed. Maybe give them a chance to leave if they want."

"One of the first things I learned when I moved to the Bay Area, Tourette's Without Regrets, is that you should be very careful when ordering a teabag. You might just get Earl Grey himself."

A decent laugh.

"Plop! Plop! Fizz! Fizz! you got old man nuts on your chin."

Ok, they're getting into it right off the bat. This is going to be great.

"My father told me how a man should deal with his emotions. 'Never cry, son, because tears are made out of the same shit piss is, so crying is basically pissing on your own face.'" I've wedged the crutches into my armpits and given myself room to shuffle around a step or two side to side between where the crutch rubber hits the stage. It's keeping me from leaping around the stage in a blur. I'm whipping the mic cord like a snake at them.

"Remember hand mirrors?!" I yell, modulating my voice ridiculously.

"Our mom's all used to have them. Do you know why you don't see them anymore? Because every guy in this room would be like, 'Hey, I wonder if I have an ugly *poop pinata*.'"

A good laugh. I pick out a victim in the audience—a white dude with a shaved head.

"Trust me, American History X, you do. Tell him!" Now I'm motioning to the poor girl with him.

"Tell him. Your shit-smeared puckered starfish makes 69ing barely worth it. Tell him. Are those burn scars on your rectum? What the fuck is wrong with your asshole, bro? It looks like a stack of Funyuns with Sriracha squirted all over it!"

People start moaning.

"Shut the fuck up!!"

Now they start clapping.

"Don't fuckin' clap either! I don't need your charity! Don't you love that? When you try to help a disabled person, and they tell you to go fuck yourself?' I never thought I'd *be* one of them."

They laugh at the broken man before them.

"I love my mother, Tourettes Without Regrets! I love my fuckin' mother! But she's too natural, man. I'm afraid if she ever gets real sick she's gonna try to heal it with, like, an herb pack or something. I once saw her comb my sister's hair with a fuckin' pine cone!"

The audience laughs, especially the ones with hippie moms.

"You E-V-E-R hug your mom real tight?!" I yell, modulating my voice insanely again on the word 'EVER,' "and you try to feel around to see if she's got any titty lumps?"

Gasps and "*Whoahs.*"

"Oh! Well, I'm sorry you fuckers don't love your mom enough to cop a titty feel!"

"Wow," they go.

"Enough to give her a **Mom-agram!**"

I look to the side of the stage and see Jamie busting up. "You like that? I look back at the crowd. "Yeah, he fuckin' likes it. Of course, he does. I wrote it," I cockily say.

"Once, for a shot of whiskey, I ate a shoelace!!" I scream. "And I forgot about it until two days later when I looked in the toilet and saw two poopy nunchucks!"

Groans and laughing.

"Attached by what appeared to be the world's biggest tapeworm!"

"Oh my god," goes a girl. *Just wait, sweety.*

"You ever be jacking off so hard you accidentally punch yourself in the nuts!"

Haha.

"Why would my most sensitive pieces be placed right next to something that needs to be twisted and beaten in the morning?! God is a fucking idiot!"

Art Degree Dana boos amongst the groans.

"Fuck you! Fuck you. You fuckin' pricks! Like you can do anything more to me!" I say as a challenge, motioning to my hospital gown and emaciated calves.

"Assholes, you fuckin' assholes!" Jamie is laughing from the sides.

Someone flicks a bottle cap at me from mid-audience, and it sails up and hits me. The audience goes, "Ooooooh," as if my credibility and authority have been challenged.

"Oh, that's funny. I grew up with a guy that could flick a bottle cap into your forehead so hard he'd make it bleed. And he's dead now. Do you want to try that again fuck face?! *Hahahahaha,"* I laugh like a demented hyena, and the threat has passed. They laugh a little, enough to move forward. I just head into the next bit abruptly.

"Usually, when I get run over drunk or fall out a window, I'll quit drinking for a little while. Let's call it a 'loosely scheduled break.' And I gotta tell you, folks; people don't want to let anyone stop drinking. Like 'Why don't you drink? Have a shot!' I used to be polite, but now I just tell a motherfucker, like, 'You want to know why I'm not drinking right now? Because I don't want to end up fighting with you, then hugging you, then making a pact with you to go to fuckin' Coachella.'"

They laugh because half of them already bought this year's tickets.

"Another reason I'm not drinking? Is one time I ended up in a van halfway to Vegas, I woke up and some homeless hippie chick had her hands in my pockets digging for change, but what she found was a hackysack with a PULSE!!"

"Whoah," goes someone in disbelief.

"We didn't even go to Vegas. We ended up at some nuclear war protest in the middle of the desert *outside* of Vegas, with nothing to drink but warm Sierra Nevadas and LSD." I go back to that old reliable well and start in on the poor shaved-headed guy from three jokes ago. "American History X! Have you ever sat in a port-a-potty in 105-degree heat, high on acid, trying to take a shit for an hour?!"

American History X confirms that indeed he has, by shaking his head up and down.

"He has! Remember! Remember the spiders down there talking about dividing up our nutsacks?"

He's laughing and shaking his head. Yes, he does remember.

"It was fucked! Why won't I drink? Stupid. You got any more questions, reporter Jimmy?! Ask me why I don't jack off on Christmas Eve anymore."

"Why!?" goes the crowd.

"Because when your little brother comes down to bring Santa's milk and cookies, and he sees that? You're not his hero anymore!"

Okay, let's start thinking about bringing this home. "I'm not going to say I get laid a lot, Tourette's, but I've seen more pussy than Stevie Wonder hasn't. I ain't squeamish either, ladies. I'll use my tongue to tie a knot in your fuckin' tampon string!"

"Ewwwww," goes many, *"Owwwwww!"* goes a lady suitor.

"You seen them milk mustache commercials? I got a deal like that, but with Tampax."

"Oh, nooooooooo," the poor audience cries.

"Yeah, me on a billboard with a bloody mustache like Jamie DeWolf at breakfast." Jamie does indeed appear to have a goatee so gingery that it looks dipped in period blood, dried, then dipped again.

Joanne Rawkmom is here and yells, "Goleta!!!"

"That's right, muthafuckah's! I'm from fuckin' Goleta!"

"So this fuckin' bitch told me she didn't want to fuck me anymore because I look too Aidsey. I was like, 'What?!' I'm a comedian, they pay us in fuckin' Snapples.' That shit better be strawberry-kiwi DeWolf! You guys want to know some stuff I've eaten out of comedic poverty?"

"Yeah!" they yell.

"Top Ramen burritos! Last week I had to use the lubricating oil from my hair clippers to fry a fuckin' egg! I had to eat cereal with ants in it because I'd already poured the fuckin' milk! Over here, dude from The Goonies, you ever try to pretend that ants are just poppy seeds that bite?"

"Hahahaha," they go because this huge dude with a slightly coned, bald head does look like he came out of The Goonies. He laughs because he's clearly *going* for the look.

"I'm fucking starving! Ladies! I don't care if your snatch looks like a dead spider clutching a piece of fucking pastrami."

"Oh my god," they go, as I hold up a clawed hand with insinuated lunch meat crumpled up in there.

"Oh fuck," they go again, still not done being horrified.

"You show me a can of spaghetti sauce, and I will take you to O-town, bitch!" I turn away from the beautiful girl in the front row and say, "She's wet." I see an angry face over here, point at it, and say, "And *she's* pissed."

Time to launch into the closer, "So I was masturbating to the sound of my neighbors fucking! And I realized it was just a baby crying!"

They thought I couldn't take it any farther. They were wrong.

"Fuckin' baby! Trickin' me! But I got *my* revenge!"

Suddenly, I've cast my crutches to the side, and I rip off my hospital gown, and I'm standing there naked, except for a baby doll strapped to my dick.

"Congratulations, it's a girl!"

"Fuuuuuuuuck," they all bleat in resignation and shock.

-I will give you a second. You may need it. Breathe in-

Now, did I cross the line? Yes. Clearly, a line was crossed. Am I a pedophile? Of course not. But I *was* molested, and that joke is just an abstract way of me processing my grief from that abuse that I suffered. If we don't make fun of the things that have terrified us, we will be owned by them, is my approach to life. I don't know, man. It's just one of the ways I deal with my trauma. From the outside, it might look peculiar the way some people choose to process their grief. Your comfort level isn't the issue though, their healing is.

As long as no one was actually molested? Fuck it. You should be able to deal with your issues however you want in the interest of healing, provided you don't hurt other people in the process. I draw the line at child molesting jokes about specific kids, like, if you have a kid, no one should make a joke about molesting that kid. Of course, they are free to, but that parent should also be free to knock them the fuck out.

This was a generic, fake-looking babydoll. There was a high level of absurdity to it. I don't know. Will I do that joke again in the future, once I've grown a bit and been able to rectify some of the tragedies I've been a part of in healthier ways? Maybe, maybe not. I guess we'll just have to see.

Looking to Kill a Guy on Dirty 6th Street

One night at the Tempest bar, I'm losing at pool because some nights are just like that, and in walks Cassie, my childhood crush that I got to have sex with five years ago. Holy shit, she looks like she's been through it. She has giant scars on her face now. She says she was sitting at a bus stop near here, and a guy came up and slashed her with a boxcutter. She then tells me that she went out in the middle of the street and just laid down so a car would have to stop. I ask her if she would recognize the guy, and she says 'yes.'

The next day we walk up and down 6th Street because that's the closest place where a piece of shit like that would hang out in the daytime. We go up and down several times, but no luck. I have a hammer in my hoodie's marsupial pouch pocket. On 6th Street, during this era, the last four out of the previous five broad daylight murders have gotten away with it. So I figure, fuck it, I'll just put up my hood before I pop his head like a watermelon at a terrible comedy show.

We give up after an hour, and I buy her a lemon beef salad she doesn't eat at Tulan. Finally, she breaks down and just starts talking in broken sentences about how her pimp got her pregnant a while back. She had a Down Syndrome baby, and they took it away from her. She almost hemorrhaged blood to death during the birth, and it was like they didn't even want to save her because she was a drug addict. *Holy fuck.*

She had been prostituting since before she saw me on Haight Street that day before we fucked that first time at the beginning of these stories; you remember. My Daisy Duke. Back then, she would have gotten in trouble with that pimp for fucking me for free. I had no idea. She *was* dressed in a lot of vinyl. Oh man, how do I come across so much suffering? South Market is a fucking *third-world* country. I never know how to help these people except talk to them and buy them a sandwich or a drink. Can I find someone fixable, please? I could offer them shelter, but my house has seen enough tragedy lately, man. I was hoping for a break for a while.

We part ways, and she says she'll call me if she needs anything. I try to call her a few weeks later, but her phone is turned off—no response on Myspace. I worry about her. Should I not have parted ways so easily, brought her to a battered women's shelter at least? She didn't seem to have considered those avenues. She doesn't look to be living on the streets either, but she has to be close. How much can a hooker who has two big box cutter slices down her cheeks charge? Gotta be rough, to say less than the least. Maybe I should have been a less sensitive listener. I could have been more big brothery and preachy. Does that ever work, though?

How could a girl from Los Gatos who graduated UCSB fall this far? The cocaine got too expensive, so she transferred to meth, is what I gather from our discussions. I'm devastated. This girl was the Dukes of Hazzard poster girl of my teenage years but in real life. I just. What can you do? I don't have the tools to help some of these people. I feel like a failure, but I know I can't let it live at my house, or I'll soon end up like them. I need these vibes to be on the other side of a locked door when I close up for the day. I have to figure out a way to *help* these people. They don't want the food—a lot of them—they want $20, so they can get Four Loko, meth, crack, heroin, or pills. And now my Daisy Duke is one of them. It can get anybody.

Bangkok

I've sat by myself for many months with no whiskey, tequila, or crack in my blood—just a shit ton of pain pills from the series of injuries and a little weed. I used to break up the dive bar life by shacking up with a girlfriend, but I swore them off for comedy. My new strategy appears to be going to the emergency rooms and getting crutched or wheelchaired. Now that I say it like that, it sounds like a stupid trade. So what the fuck have I been doing with my life?

I've tried to figure out why I'm such a seeker of chaos and if there isn't a better way to live in a more sustainable calm. Now that I'm past 35, I've decided I want to see 40. When you're over a decade away from an age, who cares if you live? Less than five years? Now, that's visible on the horizon. Shit. To be honest, I like my 30s, even though my body feels all the skateboarding and shoulder stiffness. Maybe my 40s can be even better, mentally. With every self-caused catastrophe I live through, I'm getting better at impulse control. If I could make all my brains agree to be logical, I'd be unstoppable. The way my brain gets wiser, calmer, and more competent as time passes is addictive for a guy who's never done anything but think too much. As you age, you learn to trim the fat and not be consumed by anxiety over shit that shouldn't matter to you. The quality of the thinking gets better. Less frequent.

Swearing off women to learn comedy was also my downfall. Aren't they always the ones who have picked me up out of the gutter and cleaned me off when I get too filthy in there? There were a few times in the last five years I could have had a girlfriend. They drifted off after realizing I spend most of my evenings at open-mics and dive bar comedy showcases. So, did I even really have the choice to have a girlfriend anyway? And you have to choose to be married to girls or the stage. Depending on the intensity of your pursuits, life only has room for a guy like me to have one true obsession. It's not fair to the girls to shack up with them, but shit, at the rate I'm going, I'm gonna die soon. I need a good woman to save me right now... again. Because I'm a slovenly piece of shit, and I just can't do it myself.

My dead friend Kit, who visits me in times of hardship, tells me to go on a soul-searching journey in a dream. He never talks with his mouth; he just kind of transfers the idea in energy form with a slight smile, always ignoring my questions but never getting impatient.

So, I find a job trimming weed. It's something I can do sitting on my ass. The restaurants and bars are going to be out for a while as my feet recover. Two hundred bucks for every pound I trim. I guess this is my new day job until my comedy career blows up. Soon, I have $5,000, and I buy a plane ticket to Thailand.

After a grueling flight, we land in Bangkok. I find myself in the backpacking district where they herd all the non-rich Western travelers, which is, at any given time, ten percent of the planet's white kids who are in their early 20s, "Full Moon party, man! It's a religious experience!" *Get it the fuck away from me then!* Seven dollars a night for a room. Khaosan Road. The guy who designed the set of Blade Runner has definitely been here. A futuristic ghetto of vice and consumerism. All the T-shirts you can carry for ten dollars, plus a blow job for even cheaper from a lady with a forgotten sexual origin. Not bad looking, though, whatever used to reside in her panties—or still does. Fuck it. Should I play *penis roulette?* I *do* like to take risks. And if I'm being honest, I'd rather fuck a Bangkok ladyboy than a real woman from the Bavarian suburbs.

I don't partake. I'm looking for a real relationship. Something tells me what I'm looking for will be in the north of the country. My Lonely Planet book has a big chapter about a place called Chiang Mai.

I think I'll hang around this insane place, Bangkok, for a few days until I become overstimulated and head out. What a spectacle Bangkok is, mysterious and exhilarating wanderers for centuries. Looking at it is like trying to fit a quarter of the world's items into one peripheral view at once. It's just too much. The stores explode with flip flops and umbrellas. So much colorful plastic and tapestry that spins or waves at you in the breeze like the hair of a hypnotic siren. Piles and piles of plastic and T-shirts. They don't care because they have several oceans to throw it all into when it's outlived its use. When you're poor, and from Bangkok, recycling is the last thing on your mind, surviving until tomorrow is your only concern. Sell it all! If it breaks, throw it into the sea! The government doesn't seem to give a shit either. Everyone is making money a dollar at a time—keep the wheels of commerce spinning!

The Pad Thai lady with her street stall is a magician. Adding each ingredient at the exact instant her mother would have, tossing it all up in the air from her molten wok, to temporarily suspend, like a Salvador Dali painting made with egg, noodles, tofu, and sprouts, before all falling into a cardboard box for a dollar. Best dinner you can get on the planet at that price. Even two tiny Mexican street tacos cost more than that. These people sell their shit cheap, and if they don't have what you're looking for, they can get it. "Come 'dis way!" Tijuana prices look like a Beverly Hills boutique compared to this.

There are too many Thai people here and not enough money to split up, so everyone is scrambling, but not too hard; after all, they aren't capitalists. Your shift is ten hours in Bangkok, but once you drag your papayas to the side of the road, or whatever, you just put out a sign and kick it in the shade, do your other side hustle at night, when it cools off. In the hottest two hours of the afternoon, people ain't tryin' to run to go get you your shit like a poor, sweaty, piece of shit bellhop in Miami. It might take you 40 minutes to get your chicken skewers. The workday is like a social scene. Everyone in the whole country is smiling, bullshitting with their friend in the next food stall. Suppose your coconut scooter tips over. Everyone stops in the intersection and comes and helps you pick them up instead of honking. The old people, or the neighborhood mystic rambler, are considered equal neighbors. Not like America, where if you're odd and rich you're eccentric and interesting, but if you're odd and poor you're homeless.

Have you ever heard the sound of a million salespeople talking at once? Go to Bangkok, and get out before you go insane. You have to see it at least once. How so many people can live in one city should be the eighth wonder of the world. You can buy a personal monkey for $20! Indian kids drag you by your arm towards their dad's suit shop, "Hugo Boss, $100 suit, just fo' you. Let's go meashah!"

Tuk-tuks are the mode of travel. They have beefed up golf carts that let the wind of a thousand smells sail through your hair, leaving traces of all of it in there. The drivers barely listen to where you want to go. If they can get you into a preselected whorehouse they can make ten bucks. An entire day's pay! In Bangkok, a tall white guy with that fresh look is always being torn in multiple directions. By the time you get out of this guy's tuk-tuk, the path you guys took is going to look like a pile of funnel cake, which they have on Khaosan Road for 50 cents!

After four days in Bangkok I'm ready to plan my trip upcountry, towards Thailand's first kingdom headquarters. It turns out in the old days, it was too close to China's manipulative influence, and they moved it south, closer to the equator, where it gets so hot and humid no one wants to truck their sweaty asses down here, much less fight upon arrival. I get it. I've been sweating my ass off since I got off the plane. I hear it's cooler up north.

Thailand is super thin sideways but stretches northwards and southwards hundreds and hundreds of miles, like a long, curving monkey finger, trying to pick the nose of Malaysia. This beneficial shape of Thailand presents the traveler with choices of different terrains and climates.

One morning I pull out my Lonely Planet book and plot my way northwards into some cooler weather. My book is an 800 page, archaic, behemoth museum specimen. It sticks out even more, now that all the college students have their Thailand sim cards inserted into their miraculous and modern I-phones. A fully functional smartphone makes them almost invincible. It also steals from them the opportunity to figure out their trip with nothing but their spontaneous intuition and, only after failing that, a vast Lonely Planet manuscript; a voluminous index with outdated tour details and possibly *flat out wrong information*. They can just find a hostel on Tripadvisor.com and check-in from 700 miles away on their phone like fuckin' sorcery. Crazy. Very **not** Indiana Jonesesque, I must say. These new I-phone thingies are everywhere in Thailand, lighting up the open-mouthed and confused faces of Europe's recent post collegiates. They clog the sidewalks looking back and forth from their phone screen to a semi decipherable street address.

I thought I was chintzing out on adventure by getting the book, but these kids are ridiculous. Their whole experience pre-decided before they even got on the plane. *Boooooring.*

The smartphone kids look at me with my bulky Thailand book in the cafe like we're in a Bill Hicks bit, like, "Whatchu readin' fer?" Except its not waffle waitresses wondering this, it's 20-year-old English chicks; the drunkest, rudest motherfuckers in Thailand. The English are a plague here. By midnight they make the Australians look like goddamned debutantes. They leave that tea and crumpet shit at Heathrow Airport, that's for sure. Once they get off the plane, it's,

"Pints!" and "Buckets!" Buckets are a horrible concoction prolific in all of Thailand's tourist areas. They consist of bootleg Red Bull and a local Thai Whiskey called Sangsom. Buckets are served to you in an actual metal—possibly rusty—bucket, with enough local liquor to get you highly buzzed. Two buckets puts most—not all— English teenagers in the gutter. Once in the gutter, they will get their pockets picked by hungry orphans, which roam around the edges of Khao San Road, in little, barely seen packs. Once, I find a group of these kids gathered near a T-shirt stand where I just picked up a T-shirt that says, "Sorry man, I'm ladyboy." I start calling them 'fourphans' because they seem to rove in crews of four. Enough to overwhelm an adult, but not so many as to be highly visible. I offer them my leftover *pad thai,* but they all rush up with their hands palmed, going, *"Baht! Baht! Baht!"* I give them all the coins in my pockets, and they are gone in a series of puddle splashes and excited shouts.

Khao San Road and the rest of Bangkok is a trip, but I'm soon ready for something else. *Get me the fuck out of here.* According to my Lonely Planet book, I should take the midnight train and arrive in the morning at my new town, Chiang Mai. That leaves me one last day to kill in Bangkok, so I go and eat a mountain of chicken wings—at 25 cents a pop—to fortify me for a citywide journey of the *must-see* spots that I haven't hit yet. These people know their way around a fried chicken wing! This batch has a sauce of tamarind, ginger, and hot peppers, in a sugary, viscous goo. I order another round, and the lady pops about a dozen of them in to *glurgle* and *pop* in her ten-gallon impromptu street fryer. The health department seems nonexistent here. Thank god my stomach is more invincible than London Becky's smartphone. I could see someone with allergies, or an otherwise delicate composition, dying here—but not before leaving an atrocious Tripadvisor review. I sit down on a plastic kid's chair, keeping my backpack in front of me where I can keep an eye on it, while I munch away at my fried meat, tongue expertly digging between bones for thin strands of protein, in an attempt to impress my Thai, street food lady. I don't want her to think I'm a typical Westerner, here only to extract the vices that will temporarily titillate me before going back to my depressing life in a soul-sucking country. I'm a man of the people. All of them!

I still have the whole day to kill. I visit the Royal Palace, a vast network of temples and palace buildings with golden statues and Buddhas everywhere. Half-mile long murals, which represent millions of man—and hopefully women—hours, flowing out forever to your left and right in extreme, beautiful, infinite detail. A visual appendix of the mythology of the Thai kingdom. Famous artifacts galore! *Do you like giant gold Buddhas?! No? Well, come over here! We got a tiny little green one! It's the most famous fucking one, too!*

Tour guides lead their humongous groups around with big flags. Bottled water is a whole dollar, which, for Thailand, is exorbitant. I can feel pickpockets around me and keep feeling for the passport and money wad in my front pocket. I heard these clever little fuckers will razor blade your pockets open as they walk beside you. Not that anyone would ever be able to pickpocket me. If someone even slightly glances me from behind, I know their height, sex, and what position their hand was in **exactly** when it glanced me. This level of hyper-vigilance, which comes with unresolved childhood issues and the resulting lightweight PTSD, has its benefits, but it's mostly fatiguing.

In the thickest part of the prime time crowds, you just have to move with the groups; try to swim sideways in planned out lurches. Maybe with that and some luck, you can cleverly escape the riptide of Chinese tour groups, who move in lavalike flows, always following their tour leader's flag obediently.

Thailand is still a kingdom, an undisturbed monarchy for hundreds and hundreds of years. The only Asian kingdom to never have fallen to Japan, China, or the West. China is all up in their economy, though. There are other ways to bend a country to your will than militarily. China is a patient monster, and laughs at us Westerners as we panic about our insignificant, yearly quarters. These fuckers will wait for you to make a mistake for 500 years, dude. And when you do, they'll be ready. The constrictor only tightens a little at a time, but choke you it eventually will.

Among these types of ponderings, I take in all the huge and magnificent sights, finding little nooks to perch outside the throngs and taking pictures with my little cardboard disposable camera.

After the Grand Palace, I still have the late afternoon and evening to kill. So I take a sunset canal cruise through some of the many canals of Bangkok. I swear you could be a pirate on these waters. A complex maze indeed. There are little alligators in there too. The skinny Thai kids dive off the thin planked porches of their houses into the polluted canal. The tourists throw little coins off the sides of the boat for them to dive after.

When our fifty passenger boat pauses for scenes like this, an army of tiny vessels assails us to sell us snacks and plastic junk from the sides. They try to get the plastic into your hands from below, then won't take them back. This guy made his eyes sad, so I just had to pay him for the bootleg Hello Kitty keychain I didn't want. This old guy is like 80, shooting around in an 18-inch wide skiff on the currents, slingin' bootleg items from every corner of the Marvel Universe, undercutting his competition by ten percent, out paddling them by double that. Mr. Nok is a beast. Don't let the turkey neck triceps fool you.

The skyscrapers are pretty impressive and give you a clue as to the massive expanse of the city as we sail past them. A tour guide tells us about the buildings in bad English over a crackly loudspeaker. Snack bags blow off our boat into the canal in a rare breeze. I can smell sausage juice oozing out of the fat German guy beside me—even onto me—as he almost nudges me out of the boat with his back flap meat. We are all 'dripping sweat by the pint,' as London Becky would say. From the smell of the Berlin Bomber here, I'm guessing you could get drunk off it; eleven percent alcohol at least, coming out of him in tributaries, onto my shoulder.

You never really get a view of the whole mass, though, unless you go up in those skyscrapers. There *is* a rooftop bar called The Heineken Bar that the other backpackers were talking about, where you can look down on the whole of Bangkok. I never made it. Bangkok is flat as fuck. There's nothing to look up at except for *skyscraper row* here. You kind of just feel the massiveness in your bones when you're down in its details. The last reference you have is the memory of seeing it all when you came in on the 747 passenger plane, as it dipped its wing and turned for the final descent, pointing your head right down at it. Also, the number of scooters that let fly at a green light lets you know you are in a place of *dense population*. No hills. You're down in a humidity bowl, trying to look up at it, failing to get more than 30 feet out before sweat comes saltily down into your eyes.

It's finally time for me to leave Bangkok, and I end up at the train station. I get on after one last *tuk-tuk* through Bangkok. The train rocks me back and forth into a lucid dream state. I know that this journey of discovery will be fruitful. I will figure out how the Thai people find tranquility in all the world's chaos. Look at them, always smiling and looking humble, yet proud in their toil. I'll learn to slow my brain down and relax. To reduce my anxious thoughts, and just be. To control my impulses and stop being such a euphoria freak.

I'm on a search, too. What is my purpose? Is it comedy? Am I not looking through my philosophical lens in the right way? Should I write books? Go back to movies? I like the material I'm doing, but is it meaningful enough? I tried the cultural and sociopolitical ranting, but the audience just didn't seem to want to see that from me. They want me jumping around and acting crazy. I see the value in offering Friday night mindless respite for the working man and woman. An all too temporary relief from the bullshit of working a shit job. A chance to feel good on the weekend, before once again, pumping for the man. Shouldn't I be offering more? A blueprint to break the chains? Sure, I hint at it on stage, but are hints enough? I should be shining a light on his cuffs ***and*** telling him how to get the key, right? That second part is essential, is it not? But am I not making him feel *somewhat* courageous? By showing him a man unchained and gleeful in that freedom?

Is that freedom I present a blustery charade? After all, I smoked crack three nights a week for a stretch. I've been a marginal alcoholic for 20 years. I rob myself of a good amount of happiness by overthinking everything. Just because I don't take shit from employers and other authority figures, am I still not a slave in different ways? It's just little $20 rocks here and there, but still. Am I ineffective on a self-accountability level, even if I'm getting the laughs? Do they subconsciously know I'm partly full of shit?

As I go onto Chiang Mai, I ask myself the hard questions, rocking gently, side to side, with little train bumps.

It's past two am now, and my mind is still racing, searching for an epiphany that isn't there. I think about the horrible injuries I've recovered from the last few years. Is that not the main reason I've been so weakened? I shattered my heel bones. Fuckin' both of them. That's where all your pounds per square inch go, homey. Brutal. So many morphine pills. I don't get the morphine and heroin geniuses. I guess I'm just a *wake-up and go-fast* type of dude. Skateboarding and surfing turned me into an adrenaline junky. I feel a bit hollowed out by all the pain medication, but at least I haven't smoked crack in a year. Or much alcohol, since you can't mix it with pain pills unless you're an idiot that wants to wake up dead eventually. So that's good. I've stopped my worst habits and traded them for others. At least it's different brake pads getting worn out now, right?

I'm beyond battered. Not as hopeful or as confident as I've always been. Searching, feeling unlovable. I hit a wall in my writing. I didn't feel I produced enough keepers on the opioids. Kurt Cobain would be trippin'. I just stared at the wall half the time or yelled at Upstairs Steve or the construction workers.

The Morphine pills made me a little confused and nihilistic. I guess different chemicals have different effects on different people. Alcohol makes me hyper as fuck past the point where most others pass out. I once took a couple of Adderols and didn't feel shit. I think I'm going to pass on the pill thing from now on. My body chemistry has already had its choices made for it. Instead, I'll treat my issues with whiskey and tequila! If you don't drink, snort, or smoke it, then fuck it. *What the fuck? This is a journey of self-discovery!* Oh yeah, sorry.

So now that I'm mostly recovered, I only limp a little bit in the mornings until my kankles loosen up. I've gotten virtually zero cardiovascular exercise in several years. I'm fucked, man. I still feel so weak. I took the pain pills for months, but in 2008 (before the Oxycontin fiasco came to light), they just load you up on the shit. I got through half of them and just quit *cold turkey* once my shits started feeling like giving birth to an ostrich egg through a torn-up asshole lined with exposed nerves.

I'm here putting a lot of pressure on Thailand to offer solutions for my complicated issues. Many broken Western men come here, looking for answers that their societies just don't have for them. Sorry, but Thailand can only provide a fantastical voyage—a mirage of sorts—offer comfort, a healthier diet, and meditation. That's a lot, but it doesn't have all of those answers you need. The more intricate work has to take place inside yourself. We try to skip that last part as we chase a girl or journey that we are sure can save us.

Finally, I sleep.

Chiang Mai

It's morning, and out the train's windows are wavy reeds as far as the eye can see. There's a beautiful sunrise. I feel suddenly invigorated, even though there seems to be no coffee to be had. I get off, and it's not like Bangkok at all. It's not exactly breezy, but the humidity has been cut in half, and the air doesn't feel like it's on fire.

I'm taken to the backpacking district and find a private room for about $12 a day. I got my own European toilet and everything—go to Thailand, you'll see what I mean. The beds in Thailand, however, are all hard as a rock. This is disappointing to discover. I guess I'll have to get drunk enough to sleep on my back every night due to my shoulders being out of cartilage from a life of tossing and turning to the greatest hits of a brain that just won't shut up.

Now that I've gotten to a town where I'm going to stay for a while, I get real familiar with the local whiskey, which is actually distilled from sugarcane—so isn't that rum? Whatever. At least I'm safe from the crack. Baby steps. After a few slugs, I start feeling that old *mojo* stir.

Chiang Mai will be just what I need in life, a new view off the porch in a medium-sized town. After a decade in a big dirty city, I need a break. I'll go back to America at full strength, ready to achieve comedy nirvana. I'm close, but I need **some** missing factor that I haven't been able to identify. I can't stop until I've achieved *George Carlin level* brilliance. Maybe it's just a matter of unclenching my soul from this tension of my past. I've come here to learn to live in the now, to make peace with my unchangeable past. The people all smile here—and it's a natural smile, not a fake business smile. They know something that I need to learn.

I go back to the hotel for a nap since I got shit sleep on the train. I sleep happy. My spirit somehow knows that this trip will get me back and spry again. When I wake up, it's dark, and through the 12 pack sized cinder block window in the bathroom comes floating the guitar riffs and singing of a cover band playing Radiohead's "Creep." Is it a recording? No, it's a cover band for sure, but they are nailing it. I get up and begin to trace the whereabouts of the rocking sound. Haven't seen a band in a while. Shit. Did I go the whole year of my injury never seeing a band? I think I did. Well, there's part of the problem right there! I head toward the mesmerizing sound in a beeline.

Heaven Beach

I follow the sound down into a hodgepodgy open-air strip mall of bars, restaurants, and impromptu tables and stands. Everything from food carts to brick and mortar restaurants and everything in between. Dogs, an elephant, Thai people, and Westerners, all are swirling about, joyful and content. I know right away that I will spend a lot of time here. The happy party energy just grabs you right away.

I find the music leads to the inside of a bar at the end of the strip. It's called Heaven Beach. The floor is sand, like a beach. There's a pool table along the back wall. That's good. I can't be paying for all my own drinks if I want to stretch this money out. I will win some *bahts* and beers on that pool table in the coming months. The bar covers the entire wall down the left side. A middle-aged Thai lady named G, with shiny chipmunk cheeks, wavy hair with bangs cut in, and bright, happy eyes is there, moving quick to fill the drink orders. She, I will come to find, is the owner. We will be great friends. However, she will quickly put an ixnay on my drink weaseling ways. I can't help it. I'm just a drink weasel. It takes me so much booze to get drunk it would cost me $100 a night, five nights a week. However, I don't want to exploit the *third world* so I quickly resign to paying for half my drinks here. The English dudes will have to pay in pints on the pool table. Then I'll pay for my own shots at the bar. I'll tip, unlike these European kids, equaling everyone's karma out, right? I'm just redistributing the wealth towards the Thais and me a little bit. Stockholm Steve just bought a $600 phone; he can afford it.

Now that my plane ticket is covered, I have about $1,000 a month for everything else. This budget places me between the rich London kids that book their tours on their I-phones and a backpacker.

These poor backpackers try to spend as little as possible to try and avoid going back to their hometowns and putting on the rat race manacles for good. You can sidestep it for a year or two after—or instead of—college, but eventually, if you're not creative or determined enough, if you can't figure out a way to hack capitalism, the rat race gets you. This makes the backpackers budgeting a frantic affair: *Is 50 cents too much for fried tofu and peanut sauce? That could mean returning home a half-day earlier in the scheme of things. Should I just wash my own clothes in a monsoon pond?*

Fuck that. I want a scooter, rented by the week, a massage every other day, all the good foods this country has to offer me, and my own toilet that isn't a hole in the ground. My hole shitting days are over. I will have to employ *"monk robe strategy"* again, where you look like you also have no money. It's to keep these backpackers out of my stash. They get excited when a new face shows up flush, fresh off the train. When I give to people on this trip, it will go to local youths and their moms, not to Dreadlock Donny from Dublin.

They're always chewing their lips, rolling their cigarettes, and chain-smoking in nervousness about their budgets. I feel for them, but I'm here to have a good time. I limit my interactions with them if possible, stopping short of being a total dick. After all, I know about the uncertainties of life in a foreign country with no money. I did it deep down in Mexico. Some weeks were pretty garbage—however, I am an enterprising ruffian and wasn't delayed from agave splendor for long. You must have a pretty big reason not to want to go home to live abroad with few resources. Hiding from adulthood as long as possible *is* a qualifying reason, I guess. Good luck, Dreadlock Donny. Stop eyeing my chicken wings!

These backpackers compose about 20 percent of the people here at Heaven Beach. They left their backpacks at the hostel, but you can sense the little *ghost packs* perched on their backs.

Heaven Beach will be my office in the evenings, after I take in all the tourist sights in the daytime, eating healthy vegetable curries and papaya salads all along the way.

There are about 70 customers inside Heaven Beach: half Thai people, and the other half; Australians, Irish, English, and American kids, mostly in their early 20s. Little else. A few old pervs lurking on the edges some nights. Should I follow them later and see what they try to go do? I might. I might just do a little vigilante justice if I stumble onto the opportunity. These sex tourist predators make me mad.

I order a Singha beer and a shot of Sangsom, then talk to the lady owner for a second. I finally turn to look at the band as they start a Killers song. *Oh shit!* If you closed your eyes, you'd swear it was the actual band, but you look, and it's a bunch of five-foot tall Thai dudes. The band is called Nyok. They specialize in grunge and alternative. They do Nirvana like Nirvana does Nirvana. It's fucking amazing! The singer is a long-haired dude with soulful eyes and a voice that can go from *gravel* to *piercing shriek* in a heartbeat. They have enough material not to repeat a song for about three days. By the time you hear "Creep" again, you don't give a shit. Nyok will be the soundtrack of my trip here, and I'm okay with that. I buy the band drinks and play pool with them, and within a week we are all friends. I speak in such an animated and excited way, even the Thais who speak no English gather around to laugh at me. My slack is back within days of arriving here; my jaw isn't tight, my hands don't shake. I'm back, baby. I'm fuckin' back.

Getting a Massage in a Thai Women's Prison

In the daytime, I cruise around getting massages at places like the women's prison, where they supposedly get to keep the money for when they get out. I wonder if the administration costs the prison takes out is Susan Komen level. Nah, they probably give them half.

Strong grips there at the prison, just how I like it. A dangerous aspect to it, which I love. I want to whisper, "Hold me hostage. Let's get you out of here." I mean, what could these women have possibly done to get in here? They seem so sweet and dainty. Murder? Can I request a *crime of passion murderer*? You know **that** massage would be excellent. Do you know who else gives amazing massages? The blind. The college for the blind is instantly placed on my rotation along with the women's prison. In Thailand, a complete, one-hour massage is seven bucks. Are you kidding me? I hope these European kids are tipping.

I insist on overpaying everywhere to make up for my Western counterparts. Lunch is a dollar! "Please, take two." I get way too generous my first few weeks—especially when I'm drunk—before I do a little accounting and realize I better reel it back. Shit, I was even buying the backpackers shots last night, which cheered them up for a few minutes before they went back to worrying about their budgets and scratching their hair. I'm pretty sure I'm supporting the whole village during those initial honeymoon weeks. These people fill my heart with joy, and I'm glad to do it.

There's something magic in the tranquil, smiling, satisfied with little Thai people. Is it the Buddhism? It does appear to be the only religion with some salvageable parts. No, it's something more ancient. It feels like it's just the clay that they're made of. They've always been Thai. They've never been colonized successfully. Maybe that's a factor. Their diets are amazing. Is it all the components added up? They got it, man.

Whatever it is, they got it. And I want it too. Show me how!

I decide to get a haircut, and the lady fucks it up so bad I just get it shaved at the next place over, giving mean looks over there as the new hire buzzes away. Now I look a little like a monk. I'm going to be a partial Buddhist, an intuitional Buddhist, so I've got to look the part. I am soon dressed in the garb of the Thai people. Maybe some people laugh at me, but I want to live as close to Thai people as possible. I've already impressed them with my hot pepper eating ability and my fried insect snacking. They see I am eager, willing, and respectful. They quickly begin to accept me.

I ride my red scooter everywhere in the daytime, making my own wind for myself at about 30 miles per hour. The rent for my wheels is $15 a week, and the gas cost is negligible. I go out to the suburbs, outside the old city, to see how the regular folks live. Humbly—that's for sure—but always looking content, unstressed. One day I see my laundry lady washing the clothes in a trash-filled pond at the edge of town. *Is that? Shit. Those* **are** *my shirts.* Well, what did I want for three shekels? Who cares? I've gone from hopeless to happy in two weeks. Something about cruising around on a scooter aimlessly is just helping my soul. Thailand hangovers aren't as bad as they should be for some reason. Maybe it's all the papaya salads and having climbed out of the big poopy city for a long-overdue break.

One amazing place I find randomly on my meanderings is a giant temple on top of a mountain with a stupendous view of Chiang Mai way down below. I finally reach Doi Suthep, after about an hour of twisting and turning around, curves up into the clouds. Tour busses almost kill you coming down the other way, *'Look out!'* There are cows, elephants, and monkeys on leashes. Kids dressed in traditional mountain tribe garb. You can give them some change to take a picture with them, or they'll sell you a tiny bird in a bamboo cage so you can let it out to fly down the mountain. That's pretty cool, actually. Long rows of food and trinket stands.

Religious buildings are better in Thailand. It's more about the yard. You don't have to climb into the pews of guilt and ask bloody Jesus to forgive you for sinning so bad they had to drive a spike through his hands. I'm against all religions, but if I had to choose, I'd have to go with the Flying Spaghetti Monster or this chubby, smiling, Budhha guy; *they* seem fun. Not like this Mohammed guy that you can get killed just for doodling, or this guilt tripper Jesus, who has somehow stayed pasty white in the Middle Eastern sun. If we could just get rid of those guys, we'd be all gravy the way I figure it. Buddhism has that bullshit about taking pride in your suffering too—big red flag that it's just a mechanism for the masses to be content toiling for the ruling class. Buddhism has garbage elements too, but way less of them. The people are smiling real smiles. That's huge and a sign that the religion's sole purpose isn't meant to enslave people's minds. I think it's more to provide relief to inevitable suffering, rather than being a saddle to sit your self-imposed suffering *onto*—big difference. I always consider these things while looking at the awesomeness of a religious sight. I can't let it impress me too much. A motherfucker could get confused by the majesty.

After you mingle around at the bottom of Doi Suthep's temple steps for a while, you eventually have to face the steps themselves, hundreds of them. The lazy Westernerners are taking the tram up for about a dollar a pop. I can't do it, though, even in the humidity. I plan to go to the tourist places but not *act* like a tourist. The Thai people are taking the steps, so that's what I gotta do. *Ok, let's do it.*

Along the stairs are giant hand-carved Naga serpents protecting the grounds, long, skinny dragons with rhinoceros-type horns. I finally get up there, and it's incredible: pagodas; bells; windchimes; **all** the colors; temples; people of all heights and nations; statues; altars; murals of the story of Budhha; Hindu imagery too.

I eavesdrop on a tour guide for a minute as she tells the story of the sacred white elephant that was trying to carry a holy Budhha relic over the mountain but died in his attempt right on this very spot. So they decided to build the temple here, in honor of the dead elephant and Budhha. *"Thanks a lot, assholes, I would have preferred a lighter load and more breaks. Nice temple, though,"* I imagine the elephant would say to all this.

At the edge of it all is a marble patio with sweeping views of Chiang Mai off a steep edge. It looks like you could just sail right off and down there again.

After looking around for an hour or so, I feel like I get the gist of it all and settle in on a plastic chair and a kids table for a new dish I haven't tried. It's the regional dish that tops all the others: Khao Soi. It's a two curry soup with chicken and pickled vegetables, topped with fried wonton wrappers for some snap and crackle. You can't take any shortcuts on the curry, two of them, which the old lady pounds in a stone bowl with her Popeye forearms. It's epic. Oh man, I never thought my new favorite food would be a soup. I won't get all Anthony Bourdain on you with the flavor profiles. I'm just going to tell you to go to Chiang Mai and eat Khao Soi every fucking day that you are there. After soaking in the glory of a second steamy bowl of gastronomic perfection, I head down the mountain on my scooter, ready to coast if I run out of gas.

Obama Wins the Presidency!

I sit in my hotel room, sweating all over the mattress, drinking Singha beer. I'm watching the American presidential election. Thank god John McCain chose the batshit crazy Alaskan governor, Sarah Palin as his running mate. Holeee shit! He then let her talk on his campaign's behalf on the television a bunch of times. Hahahaha. What a shit show. It would almost be funny if it didn't affect our lives so profoundly, but fuck, American politics is a Nihilist's dream. This vice presidential running mate choice is the biggest mistake John McCain has made since trying to fly a fighter jet over downtown Hanoi.

The smooth as silk Barack Obama has become the USA's first Black president. I'm not as excited as everyone else is about him because he's yet another fucking lawyer. But, I mean, after eight years of George Bush Jr., the nation's first fifth grader president, I'd take a methed up wolverine whose platform included banning guacamole.

That's how American politics works. They brutalize you with one election cycle so that you'll just take any goddamned improvement on the next one.

I decide to go out and see if anyone else gives a shit about this development in Chiang Mai, and I find a unicorn—an honest-to-goodness Black man. I rush over and drunkenly high-five him. "We did it! Congratulations, man, we did it!"

He just kind of shrugs his shoulders and goes, "I'm from England, mate."

I Almost Died at Muay Thai

I'm going to go down to see some Muay Thai boxing, and I have an hour to kill, so I walk the entirety of Chiang Mai's famous night market. This place is like a classier, more controlled Khao San Road. It runs along the hotel district, where you can find the town's only tall buildings. It's the only place you get kind of a big town feel. It's definitely a bit of a shock, walking through the narrow walkway lined with stalls of beckoning merchants on both sides; hundreds of them. They have everything there. You could probably find a statue of Fatty Arbuckle if you look long enough. Bootleg Mont Blanc pens, Muay Thai boxing shorts, both of which I buy. There are vast food courts, tour package centers, massage parlors with sharpied signs that say "No Naughty" on them. This is to ward off the wicked European retirees looking for cheap hand jobs. It goes on for a mile or so. We tourists are run down this course like Pamplonian bulls while the merchants try to get our cash.

After eating a plate of fried oysters in sprouts, egg, and scallions, I head into the Muay Thai match just as it starts raining. I locate the waitress and tell her to come every ten minutes for the entire evening. I give her a 100 *baht* bill to let her know I'm serious. It's fight night, and I feel alright.

The roof is corrugated aluminum siding, and the rain is pelting it good, giving the room an ominous, Apocalypse Now feel. The music is some light, primal drumming, and like, a spirally zydeco washboard sound? A weird snake charmer flute too? It's making me feel a little shroomy, to be honest. With the pattering of the rain, it's quite hypnotic.

Muay Thai is basically boxing with all the extra karate kicks you can throw in. The first fighters are little kids. They don't hurt each other too bad. Then some local teens fight. It seems like technique-wise they are professional level already, but too skinny to do too much damage.

Then, after about a six-pack of SingHas and some nips off my Sangsom Thai whiskey bottle I snuck in, the main event starts. I'm drunk and ready. *Shit, don't they let a guy in the audience fight sometimes? I'll go in there.*

A Thai guy, skinny everywhere but his tree trunk thighs, and this huge, white dude with an actual-sized tattoo of an English flag waving across his chest. This English guy is a real mutant: three hundred pounds of questionably achieved muscle. This guy has a *full English breakfast* to warm up for his *full English breakfast; you* know what I mean? Big floppy ears that point straight out, permanently cauliflowered from getting beaten on by smarter, quicker fighters. Up above the cromag brow, the skull just kind of disappears as quick as it can, providing as little space as possible for a brain that doesn't need much; just enough real estate to provide for basic functions such as shitting and killing. The lack up there is quickly made up for in the jaw area. His jaw is so big and meaty I feel like you could just throw lamb shanks up into it, and the underbite would catch them. They announce him as "Big Ben," like the stupid clock tower in London. I instantly hate him.

After a few rounds of the local Thai guy just kicking the ribs of this guy with little to no effect, I start heckling. This is the point at which my cocktail waitress starts pretending she doesn't know me. "Fuck England!" I yell mercilessly. "Take down the colonizing trash! Big Ben?! More like **Little** Pussy!" I forget how loud I can be when I'm drunk. He definitely hears me, and towards the end, he darts a few looks at me, one time getting a direct kick in the ribs due to training his attention outside the ring. I laugh, "Haha. Pay attention, you cunt eared bully. Thailand can't be colonized motherfucker! Get his ass! Get that big piece of stupid shit!" I'm not the only one yelling, but I'm probably the one yelling the loudest over the snake charmer music.

After the fight is over, with a decision going to the local Thai guy for landing a million kicks that do almost nothing, I suddenly feel the shadow of a mountain behind me. It's the fucking English guy two rows back. Two-thirds of the crowd has already left. Soon it will be just him and me. Now's my chance, right? Haha. Fuck no. I get the fuck out of there as quick as I can without running like a *widdle bitch.*

This time it's his turn to laugh. I think he's used to it. He didn't seem that mad. I didn't insult the queen directly, or anything. I don't think. Did I? He was so obviously cast as the villain. I was helping him, right?

Isn't that what the hecklers at comedy shows say? "I was adding to the show?" Jesus, I deserve all the heckling I get.

German Asshole

Around Thanksgiving, a few weeks after Obama won, I'm entirely immersed, living as close to a Thai person as I can. I can only speak a few words because that shit is complicated. There are like eight different ways to pronounce a syllable, and while the Thai people are fun-loving and tolerant, they are big into respect. You don't want to accidentally call them an 'obese dog' when you're trying to compliment their noodles. Of course, there is a buffer on this for the drunk tourists because we have money, but that only goes so far. Problem tourists get kicked out of the neighborhood all the time. For the Thai people, making a social faux pas is a way bigger deal than us. They don't want to make people feel bad unnecessarily, or seem inconsiderate. Social standing in the neighborhood is vital. Once you get labeled as an angry drunk or a grifter, that's it. You might as well put out a beggar's cup or pack up and leave town. In my few weeks here, I've already started seeing these elements of the culture reoccur enough to create a case study.

My hot pepper eating abilities have helped me charm my way in early, even if I struggled with squid jerkies and frog haunches. I'm invited to go on lake trips outside town. This gives me great pride to go in the back of a pickup truck with eight other Thai people and some tag-along German guy who has been complaining that nobody likes him all day. Where the fuck did *he* come from?

Entering the lake parking lot, the driver doesn't slow down for a speed bump, and the two teenagers sitting on the dropped tailgate go flying in cartwheels onto the ground. If this German hadn't been hogging a prime corner, they would have been able to sit with the tailgate up. I'm starting to hate this piece of shit German guy who doesn't rush out to help them like I do. The kids are fine except for some knee and elbow scratches. I guess 80 pounds doesn't hit the ground as hard as 180 does. Maybe I'll test that theory later with this German guy's head on the way home.

We order a bunch of snails and crabs from a restaurant that's just built there on the sand. I go swimming and play water volleyball with my friends and forget about the German guy. Some of the Thai people feel bad and try to console him as he whines. Fuck that. I'm here to have fun. Who the fuck doesn't have fun in Thailand? This place attracts too many broken assholes from Western countries. *Fuck. Stay out of my scene, man.*

It's primarily Thai people here at the lake. If they leave the old city, the tourists usually just go to see the sedated tigers or the poor elephants that walk the same circular mud trail all day long with a different tourist atop its back on each loop. So everyone pretty much does that and then goes up to the temple on the mountain and takes pictures down at the city from the patio. That's about it. Most guys go to the strip clubs and never leave.

The bass player, me, and the drummer of Nyok are beating the singer and guitar player and some of their groupies at volleyball, which includes a few local kids and some European girls. One of them is Asian/Swiss, from the French side. Very beautiful. She's been here a week and is totally in love with the singer. On a 30-day visa, you have to go through all the stages quickly to make sure you get a decent heartbreak at the end.

All these naive love searchers are coming through, and the heroic Thais are trying to provide a sufficient fantasy for them, knowing it's not really real. All for free food and liquor for the duration of the tourist's stay, maybe a little more. There will be some email exchanges later, but they rarely come back. Perhaps a sob story about a stolen motor scooter will pry up a few hundred bucks on the international wire before everyone drifts away. The Western tourist will get a Facebook invite from a friend that goes something like, "There's word the Brazilian economy might collapse next year! That's where the cheapest ass will be!" And that will be it. Thailand will only be a memory.

The Thai people know this process well, and many will try to provide you with your required fantasy. It's a very subtle form of prostitution for *you*, but *they* have to actually fake feelings as well. The most savage aspect of the Western fantasy is that the Westerner has to *feel* like his fake love is real. It's that last part that ages the Thais who engage in this prematurely: constantly living a lie. They feel stuck doing it because they are financially more desperate than our American hookers, who can pull one 20 minute trick a day and get by if they want. Our hookers can mark up the *girlfriend experience* considerably. Living a lie is hard on the spirit, especially, I imagine, for the Thai people. Yet, the farmlands send in their prettiest girls to the cities each year, many hoping to get access to an English retirees bank account. Just like every other country, the rich take it all while the poor squirm for survival. I can't blame them for hustling any way they can.

It's not all bad, though. Look at us, all having fun at the lake. When the restaurant brings out the bill, the German guy skedaddles somewhere. He knows that it is customary for the male Falang (Westerner) to pay when you travel around with Thai people. It's usually like $25, so who gives a shit? Well, we have a two truck crew today, so the bill is $100, which, for that many people, is cheap for drinks *and* food. I'm going to kill this fucking German guy. He knows better than to try and go in the truck I'm in on the way back, but the other truck says that the Westerners have to go in this one because the regular Thais live in the suburb. So he climbs into our truck to a less prime seat upon a wheel well.

As we enter Chiang Mai, I pull out a pack of cigarettes I bought drunk last night. The German guy actually asks for one and starts to even reach over for one. *That's fuckin' it.* I say "No," and put the pack away. I look at the traffic in front of us. The second it turns green, I spin the motherfucker backward off the side, grabbing his shoulder and also lifting him with my other hand by the back of his knee, backflipping him perfectly to his feet again so he at least wouldn't hit his head, just before the truck takes off. He tries to stab his heels into the ground and regain his balance, but he falls backwards onto his ass.

He gets up all mad like he wants to fight, and we all laugh as he starts getting smaller in the distance. I toss the pack of smokes at him, knowing once we're out of sight, he'll probably smoke them. These German dudes, who, after a lifetime of bottling up their emotions in the rigid society of Frankfurt, finally get to where no one who they'd consider a peer is observing them. Their feelings explode outwards like springy fake snakes from a pranky peanut can. Frankly, it's gross. These are the motherfuckers jumping off the taller buildings over prostitutes that didn't love them back. Good reason to stay out of the hotel district—bouncing Germans.

This particular German is out of our lives now. Sonny Boy says, "Bye asshole," and waves to him. Lek says, "Amazing," and looks at me adoringly. The Thai people have to be patient with these assholes since their personal economies often rely on them. Straight from the tourist's pockets into their hands is the closest thing most of them have ever had to reliable income. They'll laugh if justice gets served from someone else, though. I went all day without pounding that guy. For me, that's pretty damn good. What was the term I used, *situational Buddhist?* At any rate, you can't expect me to be a full-blooded Thai after three weeks. Fuck that guy.

The Mighty Mekong and the Hair Salon

Well, I've been here with the Thais for a month, and it's time to hop the border. You see, one of the secrets to Thai happiness is that they only extend limited visas to Westerners, and you can't own property here—If you're some rich business guy, there are ways, but aren't there always for those assholes?—If you're a regular guy, you have to put it all in your Thai wife's name. Then she takes it all when you divorce three years later. Talk about nation-building. For every shitty block with blown-out windows in London, there's a *resulting* block full of shiny, brightly colored bars, restaurants, and hostels in Chiang Mai. Thailand is a little shady that way.

You can see them, 75-year-old English retirees crying in the gutter, suddenly bankrupted. It reminds me of when I was 11, and I saw some snowbirds in Laughlin, crying in the parking lot of the Edgewater Casino. Crying because it looked like the husband gambled away all their retirement in an overnighter at the craps table. She was trying to comfort him, but all he could say was, "Winnebago is almost out of gas. Winnebago is almost out of gas."

The only difference is these old English guys got swindled by panties. The panty casino, if you will. It's all Viagra's fault. These guys could have just sat on their porches through the retirement years with uncomplicated thoughts, but they just had to pop the blue pill; try to take one last *meat stab* at glory in an exotic land. It just proves that the thirst for adventure never dies; you can only numb it for a while. That's why people with Alzheimer's wander away; in a moment of clarity, they try for one last adventure, but in a cruel return of fate, they get confused again within two miles of the house. I understand that, **but** old befuddled guys **do not** need to be chasing around youthful pussy in their twilight years. First of all, it's disgusting to look at. Second of all, these poor fuckers have deteriorated mental faculties and have been out of the *pussy mindfuck game* for 20 years. They can't possibly defend their bank accounts—or their hearts.

Why would the Thai authorities stop it, though? It makes their country more prosperous. Viagra has been the best thing to happen to the Thai economy since the Vietnam War. You can buy bootleg versions of the shit at the register at 7-11 or walk right into any pharmacy and walk out five minutes later with the real shit. In the decade since Viagra's availability, Thailand has gotten **strong,** as strong as a retired Smelter from Liverpool's cock on a Saturday night in Chiang Mai. Take a look at these fuckers too. Gross lookin' creepy pieces of shit, walking around with girls in their 20s. Even younger. It's just not right.

These poor girls. Most of them are just trying to send money back to the farmland to get grandma some cancer treatment in Bangkok. Maybe something else dire. Most of these poor girls have a reason to put themselves through this. Too much poverty and a surplus of beautiful girls. What to do? *Let's make an industry out of it and call it tourism!*

After three weeks in the country, you get used to it. Sometimes, I just have to let the guy *see* that I am disgusted by him. I'll kind of lean into his direct path and curl my upper lip in disgust. Yeah, he sees me. *Pretend you don't see me all you want, fucker. Just like that girl pretends that she's somewhere else when you fuck her.*

Some guys *do* find love here with a younger woman and can manage to treat them like human beings. It's not *all* bad. Usually around the ten or so years difference mark? A 70-year-old man has no business with a 20-year-old woman. "You could be her grandpa, you sick fuck," I said to a guy. You *do* see young Thai women with older Thai men too. It's cultural. The older a thing is here, the more revered—all the old guys planned it that way! Older guys are seen as more financially stable here, which is, let's face it, a big reason as well. It seems like the patriarchal mindset is global. Gross.

So, it's complicated. You see some shit that just goes too far, that's all; I can't *not* say something if this guy looks like Winston Churchill with an Ebola goiter, and he's with a girl that's so pretty she could turn Lucy Lui into a cutter. He's making her walk ten feet behind him in subservience too? It enrages me—such a striking image of *white power on vacation*. The power imbalance of it all is jarring. Because of poverty, a model quality girl with a beautiful soul has to fuck, cook, and clean for a diseased Grinch. What the fuck kind of world are we living in? It gets you when you see it up close, man.

Thailand is a fantastic place, but **that** thing takes a minute to get past. It's not constantly in your face, but it's more than occasional. So prepare yourself, but don't deny yourself a trip to Thailand over it. The place has so much more to offer.

I am sucked into one of these poor fuckers' lives one day when I'm getting a haircut. He comes dragging his ass in and starts whining to the lady that's cutting my hair, "Where's your sister? Her phone is off."

"She don' like you no mo'. Divohce you. When she leave town last time, she no leave town. She watch you! She watch you, fuckah!" says the lady cutting my hair. I can feel the scissors getting a bit wiley. This is not going to be great for my haircut. I consider telling her I need a bathroom break, but I need to hear this story. I guess I'm going to get my hair butchered into absurdity for some juicy dirt. I'm not happy this guy is getting destroyed, but this is a cultural phenomenon I must study. And yeah, I'm an eavesdropping gossip whore. Fine, you want me to admit it? Most good storytellers are, so *zip* it.

"No, no. I just had some guests over. We didn't do anything," he lies. I'm Judge Judy right now, and this guy is lying like a pope after summer camp. A Thai woman and an old English guy have so little in common culturally. There is no reason they would be in a house alone together in a social situation. She would have to be providing a service of some sort in exchange for money. You should have used the *cleaning lady excuse,* bro. It also just sounded like a hollow lie when he stammered it; lookin' at the ground all sad like he thought he lost $100 down there. This guy is fuckin' toast.

"She got pitchas. You kissing dat lady. She on yo scootah, howding you tight. Divohce baby. She divohce you!" says the lady, as she snips too much off the sides.

Oh, just fuckin' shave it again!

"Is she going to take the house?" he's starting to figure it out. He just starts crying now, realizing he's going to be financially destitute.

She finishes up, I and get out of there, leaving her to try and get rid of him herself. My lips are O-ringing at the heat of that tea; my hair butchered, yet again. Is that why the monks just shave it? Self-defense?

I feel bad for the guy, but how stupid can you be? Fuckin' Viagra, man. You should have left that genie in the bottle. When you're English, as you age, life makes you just absolutely too ugly to fuck. Take the hint, lads. These 20-year-old Thai girls look pretty depressed, some of them. I'm pretty sure your soggy, ancient *spotted dick* has something to do with it. Jesus. Look in the fucking mirror naked, Woodruff, of Wales. Would you want *that* heaving and sweating on top of *you*?

Okay, enough of that horseshit. I suppose that's my sermon on retired seamen of Southampton's semen. Feel free to use it if you want to shame a guy. Just don't try to say the title five times fast. Now, if you remember how I told you about Thailand's other main strategy to keep the Westerners from getting too big a toehold in its country? The Thai wife keeping the whole house, or bar, or restaurant in the divorce instead of just half of it? They just don't let you stay very long. I was able to get just a 30-day visa, and I have to cross a border into another country before being allowed to hop back over for another 30 days. Then, if I remember correctly, you have to leave, for like, six months, or a year? Good idea, Thailand, if you're going to let the *white devil* into your country at all. Some of these guys have a different wife in each South East Asian country and just keep hopscotching around until their balls rot off.

At any rate, I decide to make an adventure out of it and take a speed boat up the Mekong River into Laos. Laos is a communist country where it is rumored they will cut your head off for possession of even a joint. Then they'll hang it from a streetlight as a warning to the others. I think they might have even banned that Journey song, the one that talks about streetlight people? It bums the bar customers out.

I take a bus up to the topmost part of Thailand and get into a boat about two feet wide. Within minutes the Australians are white-knuckling the side of the boat. Let me tell you, folks, when the Australians are scared? You know shit just got lit. The Mekong is like a fuckin' mile wide with catfish so big they say they'll pluck a kid right off the river bank. There are substantial fucking logs twirling and swirling in 20 foot wide whirlpools, which you can feel trying to suck us in as we pass their edges at 50 miles per hour. You can hear the motor strain at its peak, as the guy driving in the back looks unperturbed, even entertained, at the Australia fear, which is a rare product indeed.

Me and this Thai Dude from Bangkok are at least doing a good job of hiding our terror. I've embraced the Budhha attitude of accepting what is, and I don't stress too much. This guy takes this route twice a day, right?

Once up, once down to get back home? He seems relaxed. Maybe that's the opium? We stop on a sandy bank to take pisses, and the driver goes straight to hitting a mysterious pipe, solving *that* mystery.

Holy shit! Some water buffalos just walked out of the bushes and are looking at my dick like they want to start nibbling on it. I get a little piss on my pants trying to deal with the situation, and now the boat driver is laughing.

We get to a riverside restaurant on stilts and order some noodles. It's like a four-hour ride, so we take some little breaks for the Aussies to change their shit-filled underwear and so we can fuel the economy of a remote village. The waiter tries to sell us opium and bootleg Marlboro cigarettes. The food isn't bad; not very protein-heavy, probably like how they eat. Meat is for rich people around here. The cows you see along the Mekong are too skinny to eat anyway.

We finally get to Luang Prabang, Laos. It looks like a poorer Thailand, and indeed, their language is similar enough to understand each other. I let the Australian teenagers drift off and attach myself to my new friend, Jakapong. He's a tour guide from Bangkok. He grew up there. He takes Thai people in groups to places like France, England, and America and makes sure they get from place to place and don't get human trafficked. He's got a big, warrior-like face that reveals almost nothing; sandblasted wood. He talks in thoughtful, short sentences as if the words cost him a buck each to say. It's not that he doesn't have functional use of English; he went to college in England, I'm to find out. He's quite the Liverpool soccer fan—a not rare enough quality in my recent circles, frankly. Fuck Liverpool, man. I don't know who their coach is or if Ronaldo is on their team, or whatever? I'm just saying that for the people who wear that team's jersey abroad? It's usually not a good group of people. That's all. (If saying this costs me some book sales in northwest England, I don't give a fuck. Get yourselves to-fucking-gether when you travel, people.)

Jakapong's backpack and clothes look European style but not fancy or brand new. Also, he took the tiny speed boat up the river so he couldn't come from *that* rich of a family. I peg him as an upper-middle-class kid, like many kids from the Goleta hills I grew up with. That's the best place to come from; not rich, not poor. He has a nice digital camera with a video feature in it, and we go looking around for stuff to photograph and video.

We find a stadium with a bunch of Laotian kids playing. One of them is missing an arm from a landmine left behind in the *secret wars* when the US left after Vietnam. The Americans took some of the Laotians who helped them back to America but left the rest of the country here to face Hanoi's wrath for having supported the Americans. We find an old tire with a rope attached to it, and Jakapong directs the kids to pull the littlest kid on it while he videotapes. They get her going fast and good and whip her down the running track that circles the field. The little girl is laughing her ass off, spinning in a circle. When Jakapong rewinds it for them to watch, they all climb up on our backs and scrunch in to see themselves. They've probably never seen themselves on video before, and they go nuts laughing and pointing. It's a great moment there in the old soccer stadium.

Later, we get the traditional local massage and go up a long, steep set of ancient-looking steps to a temple on a hill. We view the nearby, vertical smoke tendriled, jungly hillsides, with other temples on them that probably have people looking over at us.

The next day, Jakapong goes off to Vien Vieni, which features *inner tubing* and college-aged kids getting drunk. I'm good on that and wave to him as he goes deeper into the interior of the country. I rent a scooter and navigate old rickety bridges and villages with scraggly kids stopping their play to watch me drive by slowly like I'm from Mars. I smile and wave.

I meet an anarchy monk, who convinces me to buy a pack of cigarettes off him, which he then smokes two of. He talks in his language to me as if I understand. He seems to be complaining about how boring and bullshit being a monk is, but at least you get fed a little bit and have a place to sleep. I look at him like I understand, which I think I do. When people reveal their feelings to you, I feel like you can understand if you try, even if you don't speak their language. So I just respond to this guy in English to support him. He seems to be going through it at the temple right now. "Yeah, man, that's crazy; they gave that little kiss ass Sip a spoonful of honey on his rice? Sip is a little bitch. You know he's miserable if he needs the approval of the head monks that bad—to be kissing all that ass? Just for a little spoonful of honey? Fuck that guy."

He seems to appreciate my words, and I give him a handful of Laos money before we part. I give him back the barely used pack of cigarettes too. I only smoke on a drinking binge, and I'm trying to be lightly spiritual on this trip.

My one splurge in Laos is when I go to their Michelin-rated restaurant and get a five-course meal for $25. BBQ beef tendon, curried pork rib, tealeaf salad. It's good! Amazing actually. Not pretentious at all, except for the table of Belgian people next to me.

I give up on spirituality after dinner and get drunk at a bar before the curfew, at which time everyone has to go back to their hotels and stay there. It's a communist country, and they are serious about some weird shit like curfews. And the paperwork. They scrutinize the shit out of all your papers like if they fuck up, it's *their* head that goes in the stoplight basket.

I buy some weed from some sketchy kids across the street from my hotel. Fuck it. I don't like to be told what to do, so I jam a towel under my door and roll a crude joint out of a Lonely Planet page. The seedy, shitty weed gets me a little high. The thrill of risking a beheading gives it a speedball aspect. I get a little giddy.

The second morning I head back to the boat landing and buy a ticket for the next boat out of here. It seems like the fast boats leave every hour or so. I grab breakfast at a riverside restaurant with a bamboo patio that you feel bending as you walk across it. "Coffee, orange juice, eggs, and toast, please." I'm right there at the edge of the balcony watching the boats go by. A married couple from Germany at the next table befriends me. "You American? You look American," the armless man in glasses asks me. He's shoveling in his eggs from a fork that's wedged into his toes. His English is perfect.

"Yep," I confess. I fuckin' do, too. It's annoying sometimes.

"Obama, huh? No more Bush. That's good!" the curly blonde lady beside him says.

"Very good, indeed." I raise my orange juice in jubilation of the fact being spoken aloud, "No more Bush!" I meet their eyes, both in turn, to not jinx the toast.

He looks at his orange juice with its straw. I feel stupid raising a glass to an armless man, but he laughs to let me know it's okay. "We're on the next slow boat, back down. Will you be getting on?" The slow boats are big, less dangerous, and you sleep overnight, arriving in

Thailand the following day. Kind of like how the train from Bangkok works on your way to Chiang Mai.

"No, I'm on the fast boat. I'll let Thailand know you're coming back so they can hide the liquor," I say, unexpectedly funny for my coffee not working its magic yet.

"Oh, so you're a crazy fucker, huh? You know they don't report all the drownings, right?" the guy says, in between footed-egg-forkings.

"Well, I'm about to get on it. Thanks for telling me now," I joke. We laugh. Germans have a sense of humor. It's just really dark. Look at the fairy tales they write. Pretty sure kids named Hansel and Gretel are from Germany, you know what I mean? And that was a story that was happy enough to export. I have no idea what the bedtime stories are like in Dusseldorf itself. We talk a little more. They are from Berlin, and they are having the time of their lives. This guy looks it too; outright bubbly at nine am.

We soon part ways. They try to pay for my breakfast because they think I'm taking the dangerous way home out of poorness. But, I just like to pay the lower rates for the adventure, to be closer to the people.

I give the rest of my Laotian money to a kid at the boat landing, and his eyes almost pop out. He looks side to side to make sure no other kids see and pockets it. He does look like the kid refugees I shared an elementary school with; Pseud Lok, Khamsorn, and La—the ones who got out. This is where they were before I met them at Isla Vista Elementary School all those years ago. What a trip. I'm guessing their journey between the two places was a lot different than mine. I hope your uncles that stayed are okay, Khamsorn. Goodbye, Laos.

Banging the Swiss Girl in an Orchard

We finally get back to Thailand, and I get my well-earned passport stamp. I'm good for 30 more days.

That very night, after Heaven Beach closes, we all load up in trucks and hop on our scooters to go to the owner's house for an after-party. It seems like these people just drink, smoke cigarettes, and party. The police are harsh on weed, and the tourists are too chicken to bring their own coke. Columbia is far as fuck away, and people seem to be really scared of Thai prison. Beneath all the smiles, there is a terror of punishment for getting caught with hard drugs. No one I've met here is into any of the hard stuff—not even weed. I guess for a good reason. There's a backpacker hippie town called Pai, where you can get mushrooms, but I haven't made it over there yet. That could be cool. To be honest, I haven't craved anything else but the sights and pleasures Thailand *does* offer anyway. When cocaine *does* creep into my thoughts, I just ignore it for a few minutes, and it goes away. Absence is a good thing. Also, the injuries went a long way in breaking up the little habit I was developing. *Thanks, injuries?*

We get to the owner's house, and it's a palace. The maid starts setting up an iced bar for drinks and putting out food. What the fuck? This lady got me to pay for half my drinks all last month by playing *monk robe strategy,* where you look poorer than you are so mooches don't plague you? I thought I invented that shit. Nice! I would never have guessed. I mean, the bar is packed every night. What was I thinking? Of course, she's flush. We rage all night. Different musicians play acoustic guitars by a fire in her huge backyard. Everyone is smiling and having fun. Blankets are brought out by this indefatigable maid, who is still running around refilling stuff and cleaning stuff up into the late-night hours.

I try to slip her a 100 *baht* note as a tip, and she waves it off.

Eventually, we all go to sleep on the house's couches and patio furniture.

I wake up to an epic sight. This estate is situated at the edge of rice fields that stretch out forever onto the perfectly flat landscape. Over the fence, only little packs of palm trees break up endless, light green rice shoots. At one corner of the humongous backyard is a mini fruit tree orchard. We all start drinking again in the morning, unanimously unable to handle the responsibility of an open bar. There's a keg, bottles of soda water, and Sangsom. We all start chugging it, and soon the party is as loud again, but a little more raggedy. The stout maid appears. She continues maintaining us, setting up more food, and rather than discouraging more drinking, bringing more ice. The bar is closed tonight, so there's nothing else that needs doing.

Soon Lek, the guitar player of Nyok, is arguing with his girlfriend of the week. Finally, he tells her he's done with her and to leave him alone. She cries for a minute and then gets mad. She points at me and says, "Oh yeah, what if I fuck **him**?"

"You want fuck dis grrr, Jossin?" he says to me.

"I'm shitfaced drunk, but I'll try," I say. She's the tall, blonde, Swiss friend of the singer's girlfriend. The other Swiss girl. Blue eyes, and fine as shit. Beestung lips of a goddess and a big, regal, cheese-fed ass. Is this happening?

"Okay, fuck me," she says, stretching her hand out to me. She then shoots a look at Lek to see if he cares, but he's laughing.

"Go. Go fuck," Lek says, smiling at me to the point where it would seem almost rude *not* to fuck her.

"Let's just go try and calm you down. Let's go talk over there." I lead her to the other side of the little kumquat orchard, and soon I have her little sundress pushed up above her waist and her panties down below the bottom of her lusciously cream-colored Matterhorn ass. She's holding onto some kumquat branches and poking her big ass out at me. My dick slides into her instantly. She's more than ready. Soon we're on our way to cum-twatting amongst the kumquats. It *shloops* its way right in and is soon furiously wedging its way in and out with some little *slrrrps.*

After a few minutes of that, I toss her into the grass and twist her legs up and muffle her ears with the insides of her knees. Then, I'm giving it to her good, knocking my dick back into the upper decks of her interior. She's going nuts. One thing about when I get drunk, it has more of a stimulant effect on me. I can drink massive amounts and still converse wittily, even more so, and I'm still agile. My dick stays rock hard, yet it's difficult enough to cum to really have to go after it. Whatever my weaknesses are in life, that's a pretty good ace card: drunken superpowers. I've always had them. And thank the goddesses too. I'd have been killed or permanently imprisoned at this point. The rock-hard cock aspect of my abilities is coming in real handy right now, but I'm having a little trouble getting to the ball tingles and the money shot. It's been ten minutes, and I'm starting to lose my breath a little. I feel like I'm slipping down a hill away from a possible orgasm, so I conjure up one last volley of monumental cock strokes. This chick's lovely cheese hips ripple the mass of kinetic energy straight into the earth, massaging these fruit tree roots and nourishing the kumquats above. She's screaming bloody murder now.

What I don't realize is that now that once we'd dropped down to grass level, the whole party can see us, and now they've wandered over to casually watch, including Lek. This just gets her going more. She makes eye contact with Lek as I mine her for juice. This is getting weird. I throw down my last ten or so pumps I can do in a furious style. Then, finally, the tingle in my balls that signals the rocket launch to come. This allows me to find 20 **more** pumps in there! The audience looks very impressed.

After a prolonged, intense orgasm by the two of us, I finally get to the squirt. I didn't come up with a rubber in all the excitement, so I just pull it out and cover her stomach with the pearly confetti. My stretched-out kabob wags around, squinting its single eye to assess the horizon, back and forth, side to side. Finally, it burbles up some last little globs onto the top of most of her muff hair, approving what it sees. Shit. It's been a while; it looks like the whole month's worth. With all the pain pills I've been on the last few years, I was so out of it I hardly even jacked off. I felt so weak and unsexy I wasn't exactly reeling in the pussay. I'm not surprised getting them working again was like trying to start an ancient lawnmower with a sprained wrist. Look at all that cum. Her belly button looks like an airport cinnamon roll.

The crowd goes wild.

When we get back to the porch for a beverage, the owner of Heaven Beach has woken up and has been watching from the porch in an elegant silk kimono. I bet that maid went and told her about my little fuckfest in the trees. *Shit.*

She's not happy, and me and the Swiss girl have to go light incense on our knees at a Budhha altar at the edge of the driveway, near the tiny ghost house, where Thai people's dead ancestors come to live with them. This keeps them out of the actual house so people can sleep without the chains of the netherworld clanking in the halls. Thai people are superstitious and believe in ghosts—big time. They have things built for them everywhere. It's cute. The dead have almost as much real estate here as the living if you count all the temples as well.

So there me and the Swiss girl are, praying for forgiveness, and it's kind of hot until she gets up and says, "I'm not praying to this little fat man. My god is a woman!"

Maybe I'll fuck her again tomorrow, in the yard at Heaven Beach. There's a huge tree at the edge of the parking lot. I could lean her up against that, maybe get a crowd going? Yard sex is pretty hot for me right now. Is that a kink? Am I such a stage whore that I want a crowd when I fuck too? What is wrong with me?

I guess we're supposed to pray because Buddhism has that thing like the Catholic Church? Where you just ask for forgiveness, and you're in the clear? Good selling point, religion-wise. You need some attention grabbers like that if you're going to sell the rest of that boring-ass package. I'm guessing Buddhism would blend in a reincarnation aspect to forgiveness? I guess the Swiss girl wants to come back as a lizard with a blown-out asshole or something? Fuck that. I want to be an eagle. If you exist, little fat man? Make me an eagle. I bow my head lower to the little fat statue with the incense smoking beside it.

I pretend to be sorry at the time, but I'm like the hero of Heaven Beach to almost everyone else for a week after that. Some of the girls *toosk toosk* me, but they get over it. Mostly it's high fives all around. "Sex Machine," they're calling me. Lek just keeps looking at me and saying, "Amazing." Sometimes I think that's the only English word Lek knows.

All this withholding of sex to myself has been getting tedious, and I'm not so sure anymore that swearing off women was such a good idea.

I resolve to forget that strategy and catch up on lost time. That Swiss girl unlocked the combination on my balls, and they are ready to go into full production mode from here on out. If left unused for too long, they begin to ache at their bottoms. Our body's yearn to be used, don't they? Or they atrophy, right? I'm not trying to allow the entrenchment of nut atrophy, okay? My boys need to play. It's party time.

I start getting pretty drunk in the evenings, hanging out with the Irish and the Australians, in addition to the band Nyok, and their entourage. Excellent little crew, we got going here at Heaven Beach. A break from America is just what I needed.

One morning I wake up with a Thai woman who speaks zero English. No idea where she came from. It's pretty clear we fucked. I start remembering things and try to figure out how to get rid of her. She is sticking to me like wet rice, even when I start getting ready to leave. I think she wants money. *Ooops. What have I done? I guess I'm the exploitative Western Imperialist now, aren't I?! Okay, it's fine, you didn't mean to. Okay, well, give her the money. She probably needs it.* I pull out all I have—about $40 worth of *baht*. "Hey, this isn't for the sex," I say, trying to protect her pride. She looks at me with no understanding. She takes the money instantly and turns, and walks away. I check the floor of my room. Thank god there's a cum-filled rubber down there. At least we were safe. I don't think Thailand needs a bunch of mini Thai versions of me running around.

Thailand has multiple levels of subtlety in its sex industry experiences. You can just buy the girl out of her shift at the titty bar for $10, then pay her $30 or $40 in the morning. Or you can go to where the girl pretends to be your girlfriend for the few weeks you are in the area. She hopes you'll give her money for her life and maybe a few hundred bucks here and there to send out to the country. Then, in the middle of those two levels, there's a level that just happened to me; you bring a girl home from the bar, and she won't go away until you give her some money. These poor girls are often sent away with nothing. It's a tough life out here for a lightweight sex worker.

One day, I'm sitting in the yard of Heaven Beach out on the patio furniture that they never take in at night. I'm showing some kids how to put coins on your raised elbow and swoop down to catch them with your hand. These kids are looking at me like a magician, and when one finally pulls it off, they get pretty excited. I give them the coins, and they scamper off to show their friends the new magic they've learned.

I'm waiting for my buddy, Melbourne Anthony. Last night when we were drunk, we made this plan to do a photoshoot called Old Man Gets a Drink, where we find a hideous, old, English guy with their unfortunate concubine. The plan is for me to ride by on my scooter, stop, and throw a cherry Slurpee on him, and yell, "Naughty naughty, you dirty old fuck!" Then I ride off, and Anthony is supposed to drive by on *his* scooter and snap a picture of the old guy's reaction. We predicted the girls behind them would be smiling in the picture, while the guy would look like a boiled octopus with cranberry sauce dumped on him, all angry and shit. Classic. I've already bought the little cardboard disposable camera that Anthony will have. *So where the fuck is he?*

Anthony never shows up because he fell in love with this Thai girl, and from now on, he's going to pretty much be a dud. That's pretty much the cycle. A guy gets to town, and he's fun for the first week or two until he gets pussy whipped. I can't blame them. Thai women are very charming. I can see why people get swept up in it. They are beautiful and kind, everything the streets of London aren't. It's a play the girls have acted in many times, so they know how to get you skipping down the path the quickest. There's a lot of stages in a relationship to get through in just a few weeks. The trick is to keep the guy in love, even after he leaves. Get him to keep sending you money in exchange for promising to wait for him to come back, which most likely never happens. You don't even have to fuck them then. You just cut and paste the sappy emails from the last sucker, and the money rolls in. A girl could retire with the proper cut and pasted emails. Retire, and never see a naked Englishman again. That's the dream.

Good thing I'm smart, and I've been around for a while. Long enough to see these girls coming from a mile away. My momma didn't half-assedly raise no suckah.

But then, one night, Kiki shows up at Heaven Beach and beats me at pool a few times. She's got a tiny waist that drops down into a big, perfect ass, and a beautiful, kind, *I'd never hurt you* smile. Between that and her long, shiny, black hair and dimpled chin, I'm instantly smitten. The way she shoots a pool shot is pure sex. I told myself I wouldn't fall in love like all these other suckers, but next thing you know, I'm riding on the back of her scooter, telling myself that I'm the *big spoon* to sound tougher, but I'm holding her waist like a lovestruck little bitch, whipped as shit in no time. No better than Melbourne Anthony. We must look pathetic on the sappy double dates we start going on. Oh, well. I got in more than a month before I got caught. I feel like a guy would have to be dead inside to get out of here with his feelings intact. They hypnotize you with the way they move their asses. It's just not fair. I'm stuck like a fly in a web—a web made of *badonkadonk butt.*

Love Struck Little Bitch

Last night I'd traversed through a drunk driving checkpoint with the drummer, Sonny Boy, his snare drum, and Lek, with his guitar, on my scooter. One guy behind me, one in front. It was quite the balancing act, and yes, I was drunk. When you're only going a few blocks at 15 miles per hour? Like I said, in my four to eight drink window? I get *more* agile. It's true; they should do a study on me. I don't even have a driver's license. I've failed the test in America twice, but I bet I would have passed that test a little buzzed. This proves it. It was, as Lek gushed, "Amazing."

We were doing a private party way up on a hotel roof. The Thai bikers sponsoring it loved me. I was doing flips into the pool off the bathroom roof. Nyok was playing extra well, banging out a perfect version of "Raisin in the Sun," as I jumped into the center of the pool, *'Lemme go r-u-u-u-u-n,'* ***Splash!*** What a great last night in town it was. When we told the bikers about how I got us through the DUI checkpoint without flinching, they slapped me on the back, going, "You an outlaw." They made me an honorary member of their Chiang Mai biker gang—gave me a patch and everything. Talk about leaving town on a high note. Fuckin' awesome!

Kiki is a good girl. We have missionary sex where she keeps her shirt on. Half the women in Thailand have super tiny titties and will bashfully keep their shirts on during sex, like, even when they go swimming. Pretty much all Thai people swim fully clothed. I need this—the comfort and safety of regularity that is predictable. I'm slowing down my pace, so I'm not riding life like a rollercoaster all the time. Of course, some slip-ups have to be allowed, like when I had to pray at the Budhha altar with the Swiss girl. But I feel better, more relaxed. Breathing deeper and living in the now, without thoughts of the past or future always interrupting my enjoyment of what's right in front of me. Is this ADHD? It has to be, right? The source of all my adventure and all my pain? The backseat driver in my brain has a fuckin' megaphone if I don't keep way up ahead of him. Sometimes I wonder if I'm naturally hyperactive or if I'm always moving quick just to outrun this piece of shit. I need to learn how to slow down *and* still shut him up. I feel like I could breathe my way out of it. Thailand has been muzzling him a bit, showing me how to live in the now.

Also, having gotten to a more relaxed general baseline, I can identify other things about my constant hyperactive anxiousness that makes some people get frustrated with me. When someone is telling a story about a difficulty, I will often tell a small thing about a similar thing I've been through, about halfway through their story, when I feel like they're taking a breath; to show empathy. I now realize this is seen as offensive to many neurotypicals; regular people who aren't on the spectrum, don't have ADHD, or otherwise aren't different in how they think or behave. Neurotypicals make up the majority of our colonies (cities). They are the worker drones, less imaginative but more bendable to corporate hivelike environments, and so, therefore, have more value as 'meat' to the economy; this explains their abnormal proliferation. They mistakenly think this endorsement from corporate America is not only a net gain for them but that it makes them superior to the minority of the citizenry that is neuro**divergent.**

The interchangeability of the neurotypicals allows them to quickly gang up on a neurodivergent in the workplace, or social setting, if one dares try to challenge the neurotypical superiority order. They need us around to steal creative ideas from, as they are unimaginative for the most part, so at least they can't kill us—sound like the rich kid, poor kid dichotomy? Exploitation shares the same playbook in all its forms. We neurodivergent folks have a harder time unionizing against this abuse because we are all so different from each other, unlike the worker drones, who all arrange their souls under a common flag. I recognize the colonies' need for *some* of these drones—but we're *not* bees. Humans are impressive due to our creative ideas and ability to materialize them, correct? So why do the drones have so much clout? Why do the Nicola Teslas and the Edgar Allen Poes of the world end up rambling to themselves in an alley in shitty underwear? How does someone whose only talents lie in backstabbing their friends, stealing all their ideas, and generally just a horrible piece of shit get so much power? How do they become so worshipped? Thomas Edison was a piece of shit! Tesla forever!

Fuckin' neurotypicals, man. Don't try to interrupt their long, drawn-out stories about themselves, either. Sorry, I thought I was having a conversation with you, maybe you should try writing a blog, so I could ignore you easier. Pardon me while I tune out whatever you say, as our friend Poe would put it, 'ever more.'

Now, in Thailand, I'm trying to compromise on my *drone vs. creative theory.*—maybe my theory is a little harsh and overly defensive—I'm making an effort to let people finish their stories now, trusting myself to still remember what I wanted to add later. Maybe I'm the one enforcing *my* style of conversation. I guess me not wanting to forget, and injecting the part of my own story that reminds me of *their* struggle, is seen as an interruption, or even a highjacking of their story, even though to me it's just an attempt to have a back and forth conversation. (At this time, I'm using the terms 'normals' and 'socially awkward creatives.' These terms: 'neurotypical,' and 'neurodivergent,' come into common usage later, but they fit better, so why don't we go ahead and use them here?)

So I'm learning a lot about myself here in Thailand. I really am. *Listen… wait… don't get so excited all the time.*

I don't tell you about all these inner mind fucks that make me a little socially awkward and difficult to employ in conventional settings to get sympathy from you. I just thought I'd bring you along while I try to untangle it all. Also, you can't have a good story about a comedian without being drawn into some of the inner neurosis of our racing brains. That's like half of it; our thoughts. In them is our exhilaration and our agony, spelled out in terri-beautiful, seemingly infinite, fractal details, or perhaps spinning out from our brain lobes like rainbow sparks tracing off a saw blade, now loose and flying through the cosmos. Whatever. What the fuck was I talking about?

Okay, so being with Kiki is relaxing, so I don't think about stuff like this too much. She shows me how a real Thai person lives. We go to an authentic Thai wedding where I'm the only Westerner. We go to lots of places where Westerners are rare. And of course, we do some tourist shit too, which I like. One day, we go to an all-day cooking class on a farm outside town. We pick all the herbs and mash up a curry with a mortar and pestle—chilis, lime, galanga, lemongrass, ginger, and of course, hot peppers. We eat about six dishes that we make ourselves and leave full and happy.

One night, after playing pool at Heaven Beach, we went to her house on her scooter. On the way, we are the first to come upon a scooter crash. A bloody Thai girl is screaming, cradling her Western boyfriend, bleeding but sprawled on the ground. Things are scattered in the road. I clear some of it out so there's a usable lane. I assess the situation to see if they can avoid an ambulance. It looks like a broken leg to me. He's really suffering, but at least the foot is where it should be. His leg isn't shaped like a thunderbolt or anything. Here comes some cops down the road already. I shake the half-full bottle of Sangsom whiskey that was on the road by them, "Hey buddy, you want to down this real quick, or do you want me to just get rid of it? Cops just turned the corner."

"Just keep it," he says.

We take off, and Kiki lights a special candle for the guy when we get home. We have wholesome sex.

All my ways to extend my stay have run out. I was hoping all the Red and Gold protests would keep the airport shut down so I could stay longer, but no deal. Shutting down the main airport cripples the whole country, so the protestors get what they want pretty quick around here. They just march down the little road to the airport. The king is benevolent here, and everyone reveres him as a god. I'm serious. They fuckin' love this guy. You insult the king in a bar or somewhere? Every Thai person in the place will start jump kicking your head. It's like the only thing that will make them violent. Even the kids will spin kick your nuts. The king would never allow his people to be run down in the streets. So this presents the country with a bit of a problem here: Do we ban the evil, cellphone mogul, former prime minister Thaksin, like the Gold Team (Bangkok residents) want? Or please the farmers, the Red Team, who Thaksin bribed for $100 each? What to do.

Whatever happens, the side that shut down the airport this time has gotten some concessions for now and is willing to let the traffic through again. They have a city people versus country folk dichotomy going on here, much like our American democrats versus republican thing.

I'm broke again anyway, so I guess I'll head on down to Bangkok and get on the plane. I'm fully in love with Kiki, and I promise to come back as soon as the time I have to be out of the country has elapsed.

Like I told you, they make it hard for the average Western guy to have a real-life here in Thailand. Another hurdle to the impossible relationship. Some guys can get their Thai women back to their countries after hopping through a million hoops and paying dozens of fees. Then, after about a year, the Thai girl sees that living in a Western country isn't like they tell you in Thailand. It's garbage. As poor as she is in Thailand, this guy is almost as poor as her; here. What the fuck? *Chai Dam!* A lot of them end up wanting to come back to Thailand pretty quick.

And yet, this is my plan. It looks like I'm just like the rest of the guys who come here broken, looking for exotic love to fix themselves, and sometimes succeeding temporarily. But here's the thing guys, Thailand is just the defi brillator. It can jumpstart your heart, but you gotta go face the music back home and learn to love yourself. After a while of staying true to that, maybe you won't be such a pile of shit, and you can deserve her. Having a hot Thai wife will only bring her down to where you were when you met her. Is that a good place, Nigel Forsythe, of Manchester? Is your life, as it is now, a good thing to bring her into? I mean, Manchester grocery stores barely have *galanga* root, much less *durian.*

But again, this is my plan, to bring Kiki to America. I have to believe in this fantasy right now because I got weak. I came here searching for myself, and a lot of progress was made, but this girl is just a girl. Forget it. I'm blinded by a Thai girl's *badonka* like all the rest of 'em. "I'm going to come back and marry you, Kiki. Don't fuck anybody. I'll be back in a few months once I trim a bunch more weed."

"I know, Joseen," she says, smiling. We will make it work. I'm not a piece of shit like half these guys. She's almost my age, so there's not a generational difference. I never tried to make her subservient to me in any way. I'm fascinated with her culture—we'll focus on that, since Western culture is mostly garbage anyway. We will be Thai together, but in America. Compromise, right? I resolve to get a bootleg copy of Rosetta Stone and learn the Thai language immediately upon returning home. Even though she doesn't understand what I'm saying sometimes, I feel like she gets it. I see in her face that she cares and understands, and even though I don't understand her all the time, I *definitely* get it. I feel like we could sit in silence and still be communicating.

I kiss her one last time before she jumps on a truck to lead a tour through the mountain. She has to keep these idiot college kids from

Europe from getting bitten by poisonous snakes. It's a two-night trek, and I'll be gone by the time she gets back. I watch her disappear before heading on my scooter back to Heaven Beach. They're having a goodbye BBQ for me! I pull into the sandy, T-shaped driveway at Heaven beach bar, and the owner is cooking up shish-kabobs on a fire. She wanted to make it a big celebration for my *bon voyage*. People start wandering in to say goodbye to me. I almost cry a few times. I haven't felt loved in a while. I didn't ***feel*** loveable. This is amazing what G has done for me. I love these people.

Later that evening Nyok stops mid-set, and the singer says, "Our frien' Joseen is going back 'merica. We weel miss him. Good guy, funny guy. We remember you say you comedian Joseen. Come joke us."

"What?" I wasn't expecting that. "Okay, well, sure." I get up and go to the mic, and the entourage crowds a bit closer. The audience is the usual mix of Europeans, Australians, a few Israelis, and Thai people. I see a few of them are already annoyed that the music has stopped. *Shit. Surprising the audience with comedy again? When will I learn? Fuck it. This is just for my friends. Fuck those mean-faced Israelis over there.*

I try a few jokes, and half the audience doesn't speak English. The other half doesn't necessarily warm up when they hear an American accent. I look back, and all the members in Nyok are there, looking a bit nervous. I say, "Just play a song. I'll sing something stupid." They smile, like, *good idea,* and the bass player starts in, *Badoom boom bada.* I'm an okay improviser, but don't expect any miracles here, okay, go—anything, they don't care, just say you love them, *"Looking at the faces of my smiling friends,"* I turn to the band again to include them. They smile at me, *"It makes me cry now that it's come to an end...My care for you guys I don't pretend ..."* Shit, what rhymes with pretend? Like, everything. Shit, these rappers are making easy money. *"If I die too soon, I will have a message sent to you each...with instructions to bury meeeeeeee. At Heeeeeaven Beeeeeach!!!!"*

The next day I crawl on the train back to Bangkok with a mammoth Sangsom hangover and a heart full of joy. Bye, Chiang Mai.

Oh, Kiki

Once back in America, I email Kiki a million times and send her $100 every few weeks. I'm researching ways to maybe get her a visa to visit. I even buy the little long-distance cards to call her on my flip phone. I feel the love is still there through the phone line.

San Francisco is in great mood on New Year's going into 2009 because Obama won the presidency. He's going to fix everything—right after he drone strikes a few villages. I'm in a great mood too. I'm all recovered from my injuries for the most part, and Thailand was medicine for my soul.

But then, we wake up New Year's Day to horrific news. There's a videotape of a cop shooting Oscar Grant in the back as he's being held, facedown on the ground. The racist cops couldn't handle a Black president, and now they had to ruin New Year's. The news shows it again and again. The cop straightens up to get a clear shot and fires into the back of the father of one, a guy just trying to ride the fucking Bart home, after celebrating what looked to him, might be the first great year after eight years of George Bush Jr's bullshit. Instead, he gets snuffed out by a human shit stain named Johannes Mehserle.

Think of how odd it was that someone actually had a video camera back in '91 to tape the Rodney King beating? It was a one in a million chance. Nine hundred ninety-nine thousand nine hundred ninety-nine unfilmed Rodney Kings just had to plead to lower charges instead of having riots named for them. We would have never known about Rodney King, but for that quick-thinking citizen, who magically had a charged video camera handy. Now, we all have video cameras on our phones. The cops have no idea how fucked they are. How fucked the whole country is. With everyone taping the cops now, how many Oscar Grant's will we have each year? How many Rodney Kings? They didn't even kill Rodney.

Look what happened then! This isn't going to be good.

After a few days, I go out to Oakland to join in grief with the people. Unbelievable. *"America the Free"* sounds like a sick fuckin' joke to Black people. Fuck this shit! is the general sentiment in the crowd. Obama was just supposed to be for starters, but all the white supremacist's little dicks shrunk up, so now we have this. So of course, they teargas us. We tell the police to stop brutalizing people, so they brutalize us.

So, 2009 starts off optimistic at midnight and quickly gets fucked up again by morning. Still, we try to focus on the possible new world Obama might offer. He sure does make it sound good. But it's hard. New Year's optimism died on its first day that year. And it was so high just a day ago.

Twitter and Facebook have taken over. No one has heard from Myspace Tom in months. And the I-phones have video cameras now, as that murderous cop is now finding out the hard way.

The double-edged sword of everyone having a video camera in their pockets is that now your traitorous coworkers screenshotting your social media pictures from Mardi Gras will be *passe.* They now have a better form of potential blackmail. Now they can videotape you at happy hour, "Look, boss, he's not sitting at the bar with his head down in misery like a true corporate slave. Look at his drunken revelry. It's almost... joyful."

"You were good to bring me this, Johnson. You can look forward to 50 percent less diarrhea in your gruel this week," says Bezos, the ever benevolent provider.

Holy shit, this second wave of *techie takeover* is real! What happened when I was stuck in my house last year? Google! Yelp! Netflix! Amazon! Paypal! Pornhub! The fuckin' techies want ALL the poker chips, and they brought a lot of neon visors and Redbull this time! IPOs are dropping out of the sky like Elon's dead satellites will be in the coming decades. I draw upon the part of myself that is my all-natural mom to counterbalance to these cyborg designers of the near future. Look at them all. They flood the sidewalks of my neighborhood. This must all be covered in nature and fairness! That's what the Goat Lady would do. This town needs some insane campfire tales and some courage! Someone get rid of all these skyscraper vomiting cranes in South Market!

The techies have bought the whole neighborhood and are just building on top of the ashes of the gay bear's and the raver's nearly extinct cultures.

Tech is everything now. When you win $1,000 scratch-off, you don't get backstage tickets for the Rolling Stones anymore. You get tech! You surround yourself with tech and gadgets. Laptops will soon likely come with a pussy adapter, so you can just get it over with and fuck your computer at night. The porn is free now on Pornhub.com, and instead of paying for it, you just let it study you and advertise to you. Seems innocent enough, right? But wait, it figures out your potential kinks and feeds them—sends you down a darker path. *Oh, you clicked on a cheerleader video? Here's a bunch of videos with pigtails and braces, you sick fuck.*

Snickers candy bars will soon come down from the ceiling in little tech tubes so you can play Call of Duty longer, faster, and harder, while the Pentagon observes the top players from afar. *This kid's droned 1,000 brown people already today, and it's not even lunchtime. He's almost ready for Afghanistan! Write his name down for the recruiters!*

Did your phone hear you say the word 'leaf blower'? Here comes a million ad pop-ups! Is your life boring? Netflix has your back! If you binge-watch The Queen, you can sleep and dream you *are* her for a few hours before returning to your terrible job as an office drone. Is torture porn not enough to get your rocks off anymore? Here's some *narco* beheadings. Jack off to that, you fuckin' weirdo who we made weirder.

The internet should be burned to the fucking ground. What the fuck is this shit? Am I just too much of a flip phone and paper flyer type of dude? Or is this shit disgusting? I have to be the opposite of all this. Offer people an alternative to it. Look at them, people are brainwashed. *Snap out of it!*

We should have been willing to pay a little for content people. Allowing ourselves to be the product was a bad idea. *Unplug! Unplug motherfuckers!* This is all garbage! And it's everywhere! An unstoppable blob is invading our nation and hypnotizing our youth. Soon they won't be doing anything that could reasonably be called playing. I've got to stop this, even if it costs me my life. **Wake up!**

They can't hear me, they're too busy building a fake self on the internet that they need other fake people to believe. *Instagram is still a few years away! I can convince them my body is different! What if I could catfish a guy in Vermont to think my body is better than it is? I can catfish him first before he catfishes me!*

The internet *does* do me one favor, though. After the big migration from Myspace to Facebook, they come up with a thing called *'tagged photos,'* where you can identify your friend and link the photo to their profile. It isn't all AI self-tagging bullshit yet. The goal is to eventually use it to identify and track poor people on smart surveillance cameras the second they walk into a fancy neighborhood. Still, for now, it's just a way for college kids to share photos between profiles. They always present this shit innocuously at first. You have to type your friend's name in a little box to tag them. We've gone from, "Surveillance cameras shouldn't be legally allowed to record my face without posted signs," to, "Look at my tits in Cabo! Thanks for tagging me, Jenny! Lol!" People are creating a public diary through social media. Instead of hiding their diary behind their My Little Pony collection, they're leaving it out for anyone who wants to look at it, only getting sad if people *don't* read it.

So, this Norweigian guy has tagged Kiki in a picture, and it's pretty clear that they are more than just friends. It's a new function, so she hasn't figured out how to untag herself. Tagged photos are a Thai trickster's nightmare! I message him, and he says, "Yeah, I was just living with her for a week." Busted, bitch.

I call her, and she admits it. What the fuck?! I'm so pissed. It's not like I can get any type of revenge on her. Or is there? I create a fake Yahoo email profile pretending to be my mom. I say to her, "What were you and Justin talking about yesterday? He's in the hospital! He's all burned up. He put gas on himself and burned himself up!"

She types back with her tiny little Thai fingers, "Oh, why he do dat? Why he do dat? He so sensitive."

Haha.

Do you think I'm mean? I mean, she did her best to hold up her end of the fantasy I needed. Wasn't I just another Western guy looking for a grand illusion to believe in love? Of course, I was. I hold no ill will towards Kiki now. Although, in my defense, I was significantly weakened by my series of injuries. I wasn't thinking straight. All those pills they had me on. This country has a heroin problem, alright, but the molecules have been slightly rearranged, and now they call it safe-sounding bullshit, like "Oxycodone," "Hydrocodone," "Oxycontin," and "Dilaudid." The dealer isn't a Black teenager; it's the whitest doctor you've ever seen.

Those pills fucked me up as bad as the injury almost, and Thailand,

and yes, Kiki, helped bring me back. I forgive her by the next week after this hard realization has woken me from the trance, but now she won't even talk to me. **I'm** the asshole. And It's not like she could have thought I was dead for that long. We have mutual Facebook friends. It couldn't have been more than a few hours before they see me posting shit, like, "Cheaters are bottom feeders! I got her back, though. Haha."

May as Well Shove a Wine Bottle Up My Ass

I resolve to do what blessed, slut rapper Peaches tells us. And that is to "Fuck the pain away." I get quickly booked in the next Tourettes Without Regrets show. That place is crawling with sluts. That's what I need after the vanilla sex Kiki offered. Nothing but an absolute whore will do to wipe her memory away. I'm going to pressure wash her face out of my brain with anal. So I go and do the show. There are 700 crazy kids in there yelling, and I'm like, *Fuck it, I'm going to try the teepee material.* Now, the *teepee material* is long, and if it doesn't work, it could be a long eight minutes up there. That's why I haven't tried it here. The room is so rowdy you just try to keep it a succession of one-two punches: Set up, punch! Set up, PUNCH! Like that, and not a drawn-out story. But, I just feel like it's time just to risk letting them shit on my most personal piece: the true story of how I came to live in a teepee in Santa Barbara. So there I am, looking out at all of them. I grip the microphone, raise it to my lips, and, "Tourette's?! I know I don't really look like I've suffered enough to even be a comedian; I'm tall, handsome, obviously fuckin' loaded with charm. And I'm hung... like the guy in Ru Paul's screensaver."

Some laughs.

"But I **do**... understand the plight of the suburban whigger! You're looking at one of the world's only whindians!"

Some more laughs. Enough to not ditch the bit. Sweet! The Berkeley kids are sour-lemon facing already because 'Whigger' is a derivative of that other word, and they're trying to get rid of the loophole. Within two years, they will succeed. I purposely make eye contact with an especially sour-faced one. I'll get them; well, not *them*, but the other ones.

Keep needling.

"When I was a teenager, my mom read this article about this stuff called Radon, and in the beginning, everyone thought it came out of the ceiling insulation, so she was like, 'That's it! Houses are poison, pack your shit we're movin' outside!' and that's what we did. So my sister, brother, and mom went out in a field by the apartment, and they watched my mom build out of twine, eucalyptus branches, and palm fronds, a teepee! And we LIVED in that motherfucker!"

A decent laugh and some clapping.

"And this is in the highly image-conscious town of Santa Barbara, folks. We *invented* anorexia. Except we called it something different, what was it? Oh yeah, '*she's* hot.'"

More laughter. Now they're coming along.

"Santa Barbara is so image conscious that if your hoody isn't American Apparel? Babies will reach into their diapers and toss **shit** on you! Like little fashion critic zoo monkeys!"

The laughter is reaching into the high ceilings of the Oakland Metro Opera House now. I basque in a rush like no other. *Why was I scared to do this bit here before? Idiot. It's almost killing now. Okay, focus.*

"So my mom starts buying a bunch of farm animals for my sister in an effort to create the illusion that 'It's not being homeless, it's a permanent unicorn slumber party. Oh, you didn't know a pointy birthday hat can turn a sheep into a unicorn? Well, now ya do!' And my mom would walk up to me in public with a fuckin' sheep on a leash, and one time a guinea pig was riding on the back of the sheep, and my mom had sewed a little wizard hat for the guinea pig, like, 'Hey son, I thought I'd remind everyone your family has a little mini-circus at the edge of town.'"

*Need to trim some of that down. Note that—stop thinking about the lines that get a medium laugh! You're killing! Don't blow it—**shut up!***

"Think of the poor girls that did sleep with me, Tourette's! You're the daughter of an Orange County sheriff, off at college, you flunked your finals, went and drank seven Irish Car Bombs, then woke up in a teepee, ball of sheep's wool sticking to your lip!"

They're beginning to go nuts now.

"You look out the door flap of the teepee, and, 'Is that a rooster wearing a paisley vest?' That's gotta suck, Becky Wilson!"

So I get off the stage happier than shit, ready to slut hunt. There she is, the stripper that sings the *star-spangled banner* on stage as she gets fucked from behind by a furry with a strapon. It's a pretty decent act. A little red head that has been after my dick for over a year. Her boyfriend is in prison, and it's been a while since she's had any dick. She paces around my cock like she's a tiger and my dick is a bloody ribeye. Just pacing up and down the invisible cage of her boyfriend's love. It seems like she would have already sucked it if it weren't for her annoying friend that's always around to bat my dick away from her lips. Could it be? That chick couldn't make it tonight. She has a *different* friend tonight. The friend is looking at me, all cock hungry too. Yes!

Once a guy goes to prison, you're doing the girl a favor by taking her mind off him. He'll come out different. When a significant life change like that comes down the pipes, you really should let the girl go. It makes me mad that you'd keep this sad girl out here waiting by the phone for you, knowing full well you won't be the same person she knew when you went in. I'm all for not sending the guy in the first place if it's just for something stupid, like drugs—which it usually is, if you include the stealing people do to get them, as well as the possession and sales of them.

But what if he kills me? Yes, that can be a prohibitive feature in a piece of ass. But, I'm like most guys in that when a girl wants the dick, and she's super hot, she's probably going to be able to get it. Unless I know the guy or the encounter is attached to my social realm or something. Sorry, Inmate 389365, she will be in relatively the same shape as when you last saw her, just gonna add a tree ring to this pussy here.

Tourette's is such a massive show that little side fucks are negligible. You can easily avoid someone here. And it's such a sexually charged atmosphere that you could see someone getting fucked in the parking lot across the street, near the bathrooms, or backstage. Sex here is like drinking wine in the daytime for South Bay soccer moms—effortless. Even on the stage, you see near acts of penetration all the time. It's a fuckfest around here. It's hard not to get swept up in it. Let's just say Tourette's is keeping the VD clinics of Oakland in business, okay?

So, this new friend looks like she's not only *not* going to bat the cock down, she wants to nibble on some *blood torpedo* too. We all three end up at Cassidy's Bar by my house, and the next thing you know, this little stripper is snorting cocaine off my dick in the bathroom. Kiki's face is getting blurrier by the second! I lift her little ass up near my dick and start working the worm into her moist insides. Damn! This little chick has been awaiting the dick for months and almost starts cumming on the first pump. I blast my load deep up into her little red cunt by the third minute. I hope she's on the pill. If this sounds like risky behavior, I know, I'm like, addicted to insane situations! The fact I haven't died yet might be the biggest lucky streak in American history.

We all three go back to my house, and that's when shit gets insane. I need more dicks in my pants. This one's already getting worn out. The fitted sheet quickly works its way to the floor from all the frantic hole action. These little sluts have more sexual ideas than Asian kids have Pokemon cards. Between nut bustings, I have them jam a wine bottle up my ass to pass the time while my balls refill. I'm looking around the room for interesting things that I could jam into *them*. I'm fucking them one after the other. I fuck them harder than Facebook tries to make you tag someone in a photo.

Soon, because I have a long-ass dick, the cocaine they'd been snorting on it runs out. *Uh oh*. That's a problem. "Can you get some more?" they whine from their cum lined throats. My *prison pussy* is bleeding because we didn't tear the foil off the neck of the wine bottle. "Yeah, we should get some more coke," I say before sending off a flurry of text messages that won't get responded to. Forty minutes later, *years* in "I want cocaine" time, I give up on scoring more blow. "Well, there's one other option," I say, unable to believe what I'm about to do. "My upstairs neighbor is a tweaker. I can probably get us some speed."

They send me up there, and we do the stuff, but not before giving them one last chance to back out, "You guys sure? It's meth. Twenty-four hours of being super up."

"Yeah, let's do it," they say. That's when things get bizarre. I jam whatever I can into these girls for a while as I videotape them 69ing each other. I run around to different sides of the bed to stuff each of their little tiny assholes with my newfound cock blood. One girl eats the pussy like it's a clit kazoo just above the asshole I'm fucking. It's a bit of a Twister game here. The dirtier one even takes my cock from the other girl's asshole into her mouth. *Ewwwww*, I think, looking away, but not before zooming in. The camera is just to make things hotter. Whether or not there is an actual tape in there isn't the point, but there is. There is a tape in there. I am probably taping over some pretty gold comedy sets right now. Worth it, though.

Finally, the depravity ends at about dawn. How much filth can three people invent? My dick is begging me to be left alone. I can hear one of my balls shouting through the bottom of my urethra like it's shouting through a Swiss mountain horn, "There's nothing left down HEEEEEERE!!!"

Even a filthy fuck like me feels regret and depletion the next day. The emptiness of being down from meth is terrible enough. But, when you did everything in the book last night short of fucking a chicken? Can you say, "Deep in a hole?"

The red head calls me the next day, demanding the tape, and telling me her boyfriend knew something was weird over the prison phone and made her tell him everything this morning. She insinuates that she thinks it was all part of a plan to graduate them to meth halfway through the night to turn them into sex freaks. I point out that a lot had already happened before the meth.

Fuck. Now some guy is going to beeline it for my house the second he gets out of prison. Guess I have to obtain a gun now. More importantly, I have to get a decent girlfriend. It seemed important to fuck something hardcore to blur Kiki's image in my soul, but let's get serious, this isn't sustainable. Where do the nice girls hang out? The farmer's market? Crazy bitches lead to ankle stitches. I need to start drinking tea and going to yoga or some shit.

No time for Wound Licking

After I get the wine bottle shoved up my ass, I'm pretty much over Kiki, and it's back to business. I have calmed myself down, and I am ready to see and seize my opportunities. I have honed my craft for five years. I have found my voice: I must give courage to the exploited masses, from average workers to unemployable misfits. Courage to break their psychological chains. I must soothe the abused, if even with only a distraction of temporary absurdity and some laugh dopamine. And finally, I must scold and punish all those people's bullies. I will even identify them in the audience and go after them to the glee of those they oppress. This is San Francisco after all. There are corporate predator types at *all* the big shows. Lastly, I will love the unloved, the ugly, the weird, the awkward, and the smelly. Come here, you little incels, a weirdly large part of my demographic.

I'm looking through clear eyes now. My mission is crystallized. I haven't smoked crack for over a year. I've beefed up the weight I lost from my injuries. For a while, I weighed 150 pounds. It was kind of gross.

I'm fuckable now, and I soon get a chance to try out my regained skills on what is basically a *Viking princess.* Wendy is six-foot-tall, with all chiseled muscle and zero body fat. She cuts through glass ceilings by cutting them with her sharp cheekbones. She's all angles and length. Even her little titties seem to be trying to join the triangle show. Her red hair is straight and short, just past the shoulders. She has a long sharp nose that looks a bit big above her pointy, freckled chin. She is so red headed her eyelashes are like an albino white, giving a crazy, otherworldly effect. She spends 10 or 15 minutes blackening them each morning; the only makeup she wears unless you count high SPF moisturizer.

She's beautiful and a ball breaker. "I dominate alphas" is a quote she drops on me at our first meeting. To which I quickly respond, "Those weren't alphas, babe." I think that's the moment she decides to fuck me, if not to combine our bodies in an athletic *expose* of super sensuality, then as early as possible, to prove her earlier statement true—to smother me in defeat quicker. I'm at a good baseline, but maybe I should take this girl on as a lover/personal trainer. It might be just the extra *oomph* I need to shatter the recovery expectations the doctors at SF General had.

Wait until you hear how we met. Wendy comes up to me at a comedy show with this business card. It's *my* business card, but from like, eight years ago, back from when I was going to be a big movie director, before taking what I thought would be a simpler route to stardom. She was a hot waitress at All You Knead breakfast restaurant up near Haight and Ashbury. I was casting for my movie and thought she had the look for one of the roles. I thought I 'Knead'ed her. So after finishing an order of spinach and bacon Eggs Benedict one morning, I slipped her my card and told her to call me if she was interested. She wasn't until eight years later. So now here she is, in front of me, after tracking me down through Google—kind of spooky. "I was cleaning out an old desk last week, and I found this. It was pretty easy to track you down on the internet since you spam it with your shows so much. You'd be pretty easy to find and kill if someone were so inclined," she says with a serious face.

"Some have tried. So, what did you think of the show?"

"Yeah, you're alright. You don't need me to feed your ego and say it, do you?"

"I guess not. I really did destroy, though," my ego makes me add.

So we go on a few dates to fill the minimum requirement of three to justify a meshing of our taught, long bodies. Bodies devoid of fat and hesitance. Only the grizzle of hard work is here, frantically pumping and grinding at each other. Having sex with Wendy is like being in a wrestling match. A wrestling match she plans on winning. She taunts my balls to the edge, then withholds the pleasure. I never get to a minor nut tingle before she's cartwheeled onto my mouth with her pussy, threatening to suffocate me with her huge labia, the only thing puffy about her. It's kind of crazy. Her pussy lips are so long and inflated that in certain situations, they cradle the whole undercarriage of the cock and balls, like a hot pink, white water raft built for adventure. I consider getting little life jackets for my balls. *Wheeee!* She grabs me by the hair behind my ears and demands, "Eat it! Eat it! My French boyfriend used to eat this shit for hours. You gotta put in work around here, boy! Oh, fuck yeah! Eat that shit!!"

She yells so loud the neighbors probably start putting their ears to the wall. "She's got another one! I can hear her labia slurping into his nostrils. Mix up some margaritas Marge. This one is going to be an Olympic event!"

Did I mention the size of her labia? She says it's from being a masturbation addict. She's not ashamed of it or anything. Not that she should be. I love finding people's oddest features.

She's all, "So, I'm sure you noticed my unusual vaginal feature?" and she laughs. I wonder if I should tell her about Nozomi's valved Nagasaki butthole and decide against it. But then she talks about the different-sized dicks she's encountered, eating up the suffering in my face as she describes one of them as being particularly difficult to ease in. "But we did it," she says proudly as I contemplate leaving her in this restaurant to receive the bill.

For Wendy, the reward is in the work. She considers people who are just joyful for no reason but a view of a sunset, simple-minded. Accomplishment, that's the joy. I imagine the students she teaches English to pick it up pretty quickly. "Pierre! It's been four long weeks, and you **still** don't speak like Shakespeare! Pick it up, Pierre! Or it's back to fuckin' France! That shit better sound like the Mona **Lisa**, or it's no student **visa**! Got me?!"

"But Miss Wendy, the Mona Lisa is presumably Italian?" Pierre might respond.

"Did you just say 'presumably' to me?!"

"Oui. I mean Si. Fuck! I mean yes!"

"Well, 'presumably' is a goddamned decent mid-level word to be using in a sentence, Pierre. Good job, and where the fuck was **that** during your presentation?"

I meet her at lunchtime outside the ESL school, and I can see the students not only respect, but fear her. For some reason, that makes her trying to dominate me a little more acceptable. She does it to everybody.

The doctors suggest I forget about being athletic or working in the restaurants anymore. No one shatters both their feet and just goes back to that stuff. These fuckers don't know who they're dealing with, though. I've returned to a decent baseline—I only limp a little in the mornings at this point—but to come back from that, I'll need a bit of a drill sergeant. I'm just not a sit down in a cubicle sort of guy. I **have** to recover by any means necessary. Ballbreaker girlfriend it is.

Soon, we're at the gym, and I'm not benching enough for her. She comes over from leg pressing 300 pounds, defining her territory with a series of grunts and metal plates smashing back down into place. She sees I've only got a 45 at each end. I've already done a set. It's too late to say I was going to put on some 35s too. *Shit!* "Oh, come on pussy!" she yells. I had to bounce out of there immediately and not go back to the gym with her after that.

I would never have put up with a chick like this, but for some reason, she entrances me. And like I've asserted, I was looking for a trainer. Really, it's because she's hot as shit, and the sex is insane—a workout routine in itself. The amount of sweating I'm doing is working magic, where lazily riding around on a scooter in Thailand did not. Sweating from humidity is not the same as sweating from exertion. It's the most commonly forgotten part of a spiritual rebuilding. You need that workout dopamine. I feel like the missing jewel has been implanted in the magical amulet for it to come alive.

Now, I just need my first big showbiz opportunity. I'm ready for it now. My net is out, and soon, I catch the fat fish. I fuckin' catch one finally.

I'm the Movie Reviewer for Live 105

Al Gonzales comes through! He's got all the inside info for gigs that people always try to make sure I don't get. He's still cool with me even though I kind of nudged him out of Moss Alley when I broke my leg and needed my mom around. He never had to know she left after two weeks. New blood at the pad is good from time to time. Give more people a chance at cheap rent in the city. Maybe they could get me booked at some higher-level shows? That's not why I do it, but it would be nice. Mmmmmkay?

I keep the other rooms in the house so that underserved, marginalized, and minority comedians can have some cheap rent in the middle of all the gigs for a while. I'm not trying to say I'm Bernie Sanders, okay? But I'm not a total salty, angry yeller all the time, either. Wait, maybe I *am* like Bernie.

I rent to other comics and give everyone a year or two to enjoy it. Not one of them ever cleans the house. It seems to be a systemic issue with these comedians. Maybe the filth adds to the suffering they've been convinced they should be immersed in at all times to inspire the best material.

Next, I embark on a stint with Hoogs—who has muscular dystrophy and is one of the best crowd riffers alive—and his derelict brother, Garo, who fancies himself an Armenian-cholo-gangster, but who is really just a toilet clogger and a living room lurker. After their turn is over, I settle on Greg and Julian, who are in there currently; two African American comics who are funny but would see Comet cleanser and think it was garlic salt. They are simply allergic to cleaning.

Al is the only one in the bunch that has done me any good booking-wise. I should have never kicked him out. He gets us the gig info quickly, where before, I'd always show up too late. Without advance information, how can you succeed? This is another talent Al offers, where I lacked before. He's widely accepting and diplomatic. Everybody loves this guy. He's always smiling and lightly complimenting openers and headliners alike, stopping short of ass-kissing. He knows the name of every waitress in every comedy club. A social butterfly, this dude. He looks like Count Chocula's California cousin, always flashing his white teeth and shaking hands with everyone. Fucker should run for mayor of the city. He's got every bit of grease slicking back his hair in an impressive widow's peak that Gavin Newsome, our current Mayor, does. Between the two of them, it's calculated that several hundred pelicans drown in the oil slicks above their collars each year. Gavin and Al seem destined to face each other in a mayoral runoff eventually. My money is on Al.

This time Al has gotten us a gig on the local TV channel for their Creepy KOFY Movie Time show. It's hosted by on-air radio personality No Name, who is made up like a skinheady Beetle Juice, and another guy whose character is called Balrog, a GWAResque demon. The studio is made up to look like a cave of hell or a bondage punishment center, complete with bikinied zombie groupies who roam around in the background, facilitating the hellscape in a sexy way.

They always play B horror movies from the 50s, 60s, and 70s. Our hosts, who are made up to look like shot callers in hell, segway the audiences in and out of commercial breaks with banter, and comedy sets from local comedians. I go up and just do my regular set, adding in riffs about finally getting to hell or some shit. In the end, I jump off the pedestal after grabbing a rubber zombie head off the wall and run at the camera, biting and tearing at the zombie's head, then kicking it in an arc over the camera. The crowd loves it.

I get an email from No Name a week later, asking if I want to come onto Live 105 for a guest spot, the biggest radio station between LA and the North Pole. They play indie rock, grunge, and more rocking selections from the current charts. What I was watching Nyok play in Chiang Mai. Guitar music. Otherwise, I wouldn't consider the offer. "Fuck yeah!" I respond.

Soon, they make me the official movie reviewer. I'm showing up at the movie theatres with my press pass, getting in for free, stoned as hell, and pouring a half pint of Jameson into my giant Coke. I take some notes and come up with five minutes of material to do in the studio.

I get to know the rest of the team, which is Katie; she plays the straight character and does the weather and traffic. Then there's Matty;

he does the sound effects and adds commentary. No Name seems to be the conductor of the symphony. He appears to control the topics, when to move on, and whatnot. I think much of the show's content is what Matty, Katie, and him work out by bouncing things off each other by text messages between yesterday's show and bedtime. It's loose but still organized. I like it, except it's at eight in the morning. I tried to stay up partying the first time, so I'd come in all *party party funtime*? But my body, knowing it's just a trick to get it to do more, peters out by four am, and I sleep a few hours, just enough not to do me any good. I show up hella groggy, but once I'm looking through the studio glass at the big microphones and headphones, I liven up.

Here is a joke I run by the producer, Matty. He is a friendly, positive, hyper dude that seems to be about my age—but steeped in showbiz much longer. Now that I'm on their show, they are going to be getting calls from the public, saying, "Don't book that guy; he's dirty. Have you seen his comedy act? *Whaaaa*." To get ahead of this certainty, I go to Matty and say, "This one might be too edgy for the show. What do you think?" This way, he won't be scared I will get them in trouble with the FCC. Those fines they levy are insane. Five thousand bucks a "Fuck"? That's an expensive call girl. That's the revenue from like five commercials. I can be PG-13 if someone pays me. No problem.

I then tell Matty the joke about the movie 2012. "At one point, our Black president, played by Donald Glover, crawls out of a pile of crumbled drywall, the white, chalky dust covering his face. That's what a brother had to do to become president in this country: whiteface. Do you think Obama would be president if he talked like DMX? Hell no. That guy has to *extra* enunciate his syllables. He has to use words like 'pontificate,' or they'll accuse him of being too "*urban*." You know what *that's* code for."

Matty is holding his hands up and waving me off at this point. "Yeah, hilarious, but no." I knew he'd say that. I just wanted to make him feel comfortable, like, I'm going to play ball; bounce any potentially problematic material off him; not try to cause any ruckus. You know, like Obama.

First is the Movie 2012: "Where were the Mayans? Wasn't the whole 2012 end of the world thing about a Mayan prophecy? So first we steal their land, then we steal their prophecy? Way to go, Weinstein Brothers. We've gone full colonist!"

"It's important to remember that the star of this movie, John Cusack, was in another movie called Better off Dead because that's what he would have been... instead of taking this role. I didn't even pay to get in, and *I* want two dollars. Give me my two dollars, John Cusack!"

I get some good laughs from the people in the studio and keep it a bit short, as it's my first movie review. They thank me, and Matty tells me he'll send me info for Men Who Stare at Goats (This is from notes and memory. I cannot guarantee all these jokes made it onto the air. It should be pretty close. If I ever get access to the archives, I'll transcribe these exactly. That'll have to wait for the second edition. No refunds, assholes.) Here's a paraphrased version of that review:

"I don't know, man. At first, I thought you guys were making fun of how I was raised. I was like, *Who told these guys I lived in a teepee with farm, pet store, and wild animals that my sister collected?* I'm pretty sure I spent an afternoon doing the title of this movie: staring at a goat. The guy wouldn't blink, man. Weird old eye... Now *there's* an idea for a movie!

This movie, Men Who Stare at Goats, was completely different. It seems like the military was so intimidated by hippie culture's new-agey methods that they tried to research them for use themselves? We really do give the Pentagon too much money. It's like they're taunting us with our tax dollars."

No Name gives up a raspy hackle.

"This movie is like if they made Timothy Leary a general and gave him a bunch of money and LSD to make cool vibes into one big, deadly, *uncool vibe*. That's the movie. The title is derived from their attempts to stare at goats and psychically make their hearts stop, like, with their thoughts. Well, I watched how they did it, and I think it's horse crap. I've been staring at Katie's shirt for ten minutes, and not one button has popped off." Katie laughs, heaving her ample breastesses up and down as I try one last time to psychically pop off her already stressed button threads.

They bring me back to review The Lovely Bones: "Uhm. What are you guys sending me to? This movie starts with a little girl narrating the story of her own demise. Uhhh, hey, little girl? Can you say buzzkill?!

Also, spoiler alert! So, it turns out the guy that kills her lives across the street, and he has a giant molester mustache. Gee, where's Sherlock Holmes? This is quite the pickle! I'll take mysteries that insult my intelligence for a thousand, Alex."

Things go on like this for a bit. It's a bit early in the morning, but it's fun and different. Free movies, I've recently begun dating a hot Viking chick, my new material is the best I've ever written. Shit, I'm a radio personality. Many of the comics who used to have to know who was in the room to decide if they should talk to me or not are trying to act like we're buddies now. I don't hold a grudge about it, whatever. What am I going to cry about the establishment had a hard time accepting the anti-establishment comic?

I go to Wendy's house on the Golden Gate Panhandle, and she cooks me dinner several times a week. Her cashmere sweater feels good to hug. We make out at the door for a minute before we go upstairs into the ancient, drafty but beautiful Victorian, where she will cook me something, French.

She's a Francophile (Fanatic of all things French.) In the early days of dating, this would generally be a major flag word. It usually translates to snobby rich girl with a history of bad taste in men that you will endlessly hear about. Additionally, it means expensive cream-based sauces ladled onto overpriced entrees. That's multiple $40 entrees from *your* wallet in restaurants with douchey names like Chateau Le Boeuf, all before the third payoff date. And it's never a guarantee you'll get laid even after all that. There's a lot of professional, free dinner eaters in The City, and that's why I usually refuse to meet for anything but drinks in the beginning.

The real reason Wendy claims to be a Francophile is this boyfriend who used to eat her out for three hours straight. Shit, if some Frenchie slurped on *me* for the length of the extended version of Titanic? I'd go to fuckin' mime college and get a baguette tattooed down the side of my *shtoing-boing*. So, I get it. I'm just not willing to spring for a $100 bottle of *Neuf du Pape* for her to walk down that particular memory lane.

We always share one bottle of French red wine at her house with dinner—just one. I have to show up a little buzzed because that is an annoying amount of alcohol to have.

She seems to be an expert at keeping me in a state *just outside* of bliss.

Sometimes I wonder if she's identified impulse control as one of my problems, and this is part of the training. I'm like an old piece of shit Chevy she rescued from the junkyard, and now she's got me up on the blocks in her garage blasting The Boss. Ever since I got the radio gig, she's been a little less bossy. Good. I'm getting sick of that shit.

"My parents listened to you on the radio today," she says after the first glass of garnet-colored love is poured.

"Oh, really? Are they okay?" I say.

"Haha. No, they said you were funny. They didn't know what a *molester 'stache* is, though."

"Tell them they're lucky they don't."

"You like Veloute?"

"The philosopher?" I ask.

"A sauce," she says.

"Oh yeah, I'm a total sauce whore."

We party on the weekends, but this is how the week goes. She balances out being a health nut during the week by being a raver on the weekends. I dip the Molly just to listen to the music at the clubs she takes me to. We are an odd couple with seemingly little in common, but it somehow works for a bit.

Radius

The radio gig isn't exactly pulling down what you would call 'a salary,' so I decide to hit the restaurants with my resume, which is almost all true at this point. I'm tired of being broke, and I'm as recovered as I'm going to get, so let's get on with it.

I see that something is stirring across the street from The Brainwash, where the old Julie's Supper Club used to be. Sure enough, it's going to be a restaurant.

I waltz on over, turn on the charm, and get the job. When I tell them I used to work for Chef Mina and that I live across the street, the fact that I have all my teeth just seems like a bonus. The Chef shakes my hand and everything!

Chef Kelly is an intense, short, lesbian, Filipina / white lady. The sous chef is her lover, a short, white girl with rosy cheeks. They both have short, straight, brown hair and impressive resumes that were all that much harder to achieve not being men. To have your ass slapped or get feels copped on you in the tight aisled kitchens of New York is probably even more disgusting when you're a lesbian. Not in 2010, though. With the rise of the profitable sexual harassment lawsuit, the guys have to sexually harass each other now—what a hilarious and cruel twist of fate. I'm guessing our chef helped with that little movement.

It's true. There were way too many managers getting blowjobs from hostesses who wanted to be servers. Fuckin' piggy pigs in upper management ruined it for us guys that actually deserve these girls. A little sexual harassment in the workplace keeps things fun, and, if kept regulated to a healthy level, guys quickly learn which girls like it and which ones don't. I thought it was a non-removable feature of the industry, but I guess I was wrong. I mean, come on, let us be people. Even little innuendos raise eyebrows now. Shit, that happened quick.

The bar and restaurant industry went from Jameson's whiskey and cocaine off of dressers to boring adderall addicts who are metal-polishing sidework aggressors.

Chef Kelly is full on chef material. Her eyes pierce you and make you a bit nervous. She doesn't yell, she looks at you with lasers. At the chef's window, you better be quieter than her, which is silent. You have to be sub-silent.

There are two first-time restaurant owners here, Christian, the dreamer, the charm guy that runs to the front door with a big smile anytime anybody walks in. Then there's Orlando Jon, the businessman on his laptop going over the numbers. He's in the back of the room, but still with his eye on the front door. Different types of workers and merchants are coming and going all the time. Christian and Jon are both well-fed but not fat, and also, like Chef and the sous, both have short brown hair.

They look to be about halfway through redoing the place. It seems like they have a while to go. Am I sure I'm going to be working anytime soon? These big-eyed dreamers tend to over promise to anybody who will listen. I mean, the only person who would ever try and open a restaurant and think there's ever going to be a profit is in *la la land,* right? Beautiful and destined to lose. I love them for it. How can you not love someone trying to make something beautiful and unlikely to survive in this dumpster fire of a world, flipping off Satan and building anyway? Especially in this neighborhood. Casual fine dining? Fuck, guys, people come to this neighborhood to dance to music with chainsaws as instruments. Maybe eat a bacon-wrapped hotdog between molly key bumps. What are you doing, and how can I help? You want to bring in a *farm-to-table* restaurant with goat cheese polenta and lamb shanks? Interesting choice, but right on. I love fucking lamb shanks!

There are a few businesses on this block that do okay: Cat Club, Basil Thai, the Brainwash. But the rest of the storefronts appear to be a front, the business owner seems to live in there, or it's a revolving door of different signs that rotate into a graveyard.

It's true, though, the techies have completed their takeover of South Market; sorry, I mean SOMA—once you combine two words of a neighborhood into one word, it's a lock. Gentrification is inevitable, and it's true; most people call it SOMA now. There are actually fluffy dogs being walked through all the junky detritus.

This block is ripe for civilization if you can chase the tweakers and crackheads back to 6th Street. We all saw it happen on Valencia Street. Why not here? I feel like you'd have to nuke the Brainwash across the street. It seems to become a crime swap meet within hours of opening. But look! Now there's a wine bar across the street that specializes in biodynamic European wines called *Terroir.* And Cassidy's closed down after all the bartenders got sclerosis or moved to Antioch. So now it's going to be The Bloodhound, a *hunter's barn-themed* techie bar where elderflower liqueur will flow like venture capital money. The techies will arrive in their protective coworker swarms, going, "Oh, is this how the country folks live? How *geuxsh*. Should we cosplay some Tim McGraw on the jukebox? Oooooh, look, it's a Big Buck hunting video game! Let's shoot stuff! Play Kid Rock! He's a cowboy, right?!"

I'll win a few thousand dollars on their pool table over the next few years, but hanging around the entitled and douchey clients will make it not worth it. The employees of The Bloodhound are lovely, and they deserve every dollar they make for dealing with these prissies. One of the bartender's sisters will do a stint at the Moss House, and I barely pay for drinks—the real reason I'm a regular here. I will get several tooth crowns from drinking thousands of their Recoils. A Recoil is ginger beer, Bulleit bourbon, and that old elderflower liqueur, served up in a frosty jelly glass. As much sugar as a Coca-Cola, at least. I drink about six a night. *Hello dentist*. My demeanor may be street, but my cocktails are New Orleansy sugar bombs. It's a problem.

Spending every night after work in The Bloodhound has immersed me in tech culture. These are literally the people inventing Lyft, Doordash, Candy Crush; you name it. For those who don't know, it's all about apps now, and I'm not talking about *burrata* on *crostinis*. I eavesdrop and talk to these people, trying to figure out how they can afford a stylist at age 23. I gotta tell you, folks. They aren't smarter than us. I guess they learned how to code? That's it. I need a coding intern!

Techies are a bunch of fives and sixes that think their wallets make them tens. As a nine, this is frustrating to be around. Once they realize they can't impress or buy my pants off of me, they hate me for not being able to extract any startup clout from me. They think they're so cool. I love it when I see their money go up in the antlers. There's a chandelier made of deer antlers above the pool table. It's almost fun to stick little $20 bills up there until you're not the one pulling them down again.

One day I win $1,000 off one of these assholes. He thinks he's so smooth. I waggled the hook real good, losing a few $20 games by trying to go for stupidly hard shots. He was so sad when he lost that I think he had to cancel an appointment with his tarot reader. I like the Mad Maxy-Jetsons look they put together for you. Too bad your Wisconsin accent blows the charade. I'm all for people having a chance to start over in the big city, but it's gotta be believable. You're just trying to mash up too many things that don't fit together. It kind of describes your pool game, Chet.

I soon realize I'm smarter than all of these fuckers. After I snookered the guy that invented Travelocity or some shit for $60, he started mumbling some garbage about how he thought we were playing East Coast rules. This guy has more in his checking account than I make in a year, and he's trying to back out of a $60 loss because his butt hurts. It's all about app ideas. 'App' is short for phone application. It's basically a little button on your screen that leads you to a website, like speed dial for consumerism. It's the hottest thing since custom ringtones. I have to get in on this shit.

Soon, I have a bunch of ideas. One is a wine pricing app where you scan the wine list at a fancy restaurant with your phone, and it tells you if they're quadrupling the prices or not. Trust me, they are, especially if the chef has a recognizable name. Shit, they just caught one chef putting cheap wine in expensive bottles, bringing them out to the tables himself, so he could drink in their gullibility, while they drank in his cheap *chianti,* scandalously priced at $400. An app that could destroy wine gouging by assholes in the fine dining industry would be an act of sweet, molten chocolate revenge—this one's for you, Mina.

My next app idea is Soft Beds, a hotel ranking app by the softness of the beds. Side sleepers everywhere will rejoice. That's it. That's the whole app.

And finally, Neighbor 911: if some shit goes down in your neighborhood, everybody on the app within a specific range of you will be alerted to see what's going on. If you live in a rough area, you could all die waiting for the cops to ever show up. A crowd of neighbors poking their head into the alley would seem to discourage murder, am I wrong?

Ooooh, I almost forgot my best app idea! Corporate executive flash mob! If a corporate bigwig who gets his jollies off by raping our mother earth tries to go out to a restaurant, the app alerts everybody in the area, and we go fuck his night up. Can someone do these, please? Unfortunately, my ADHD prevents me from figuring out how to design these apps. I'll split the money with you!

The block of Folsom between 7th and 8th is making a play. The techies have grown less afraid of the crack zombies over the last year or two since they've taken over the neighborhood. They seem to be staking this block to descend upon for food, drink, and dance from their nearby lofts. Sounds good to me. This area was too methy anyway; let's mix it up. Isn't that the best part of this city in certain neighborhoods? The symbiotic variety of people and things? And as a waiter, higher prices, higher tips. In certain problem areas, a little gentrification can help save it. The problem is freezing the gentrification once it's at a moderate level. Not sure it's ever been done before.

So the neighborhood is heading in the right direction. The concept of Radius is impressive: we will source all the beer, wine, and food from a 100-mile **radius** around the restaurant. This net catches a lot of amazing products: Salinas to Mendocino to Sacramento, and out past the Farallon Islands for the seafood. Quite a clever idea. Organic, biodynamic, all that shit. Since the farms and wineries are so close, their representatives come in and talk to us and answer our questions.
I take in every detail to throw into my schtick. I will be part waiter, part farmer, part mystic soil whisperer, "Oh, you'd like to discuss the terroir? Wouldn't you rather taste it? Wouldn't you rather **be** it?"

The cafe side of the restaurant, which we are opening a month early as a test run, will be open for sandwiches, salads, beer, and wine.

I soon meet my other coworkers I'll be working with in the cafe; Sam, a hot Asian girl from Santa Cruz. She's laid back; Acebo, an Asian hipster that you would never question when he talks about your outfit. Fred is great. I feel like he's never told a lie in his whole life, and Jessica, A total Santa Barbara type blonde girl that I recognize and understand instantly. She seems Swedish in ancestry and has the attending *badonkadonk* butt. These guys hire well.

Since I live across the street basically, I always open the cafe, and the techies come streaming in around 8:30 am to use us for cheap office space. I basically provide the caffeine for AirBnB to blow up. Their little start-up wasn't shit in 2010. **I** blew that shit up with dope ass coffee. Do they call? No. Ali Wong is blowing up, too, at this point. Does *she* call? Nope. No one ever calls folks. After you inspire or help them, they want nothing to do with you. You remind them of when they were small. Yeah, I remember AirBnB's Joe and Mike, drawing shit out on napkins and shit drinking cappuccinos **I** made. I'd bring up more coffees to their table and eavesdrop on them. I'd be like, *You want everybody to use their* *house as a hotel? Okay, dudes. That sounds stupid as shit.*

Now, look at me. Ali Wong and AirBnB are laughing at my ass now, aren't they? *Fuck.* When is it *my* turn to blow up? I've been surrounded by people blowing up my whole life to the point where I feel like *I'm* the one helping spark it. **How do I spark myself!?** I gotta make *lattes* and shit? Who knows when the restaurant will ever open, and I can start making ribeye money? I'm a *barista*? What the fuck? Let's just say what I am, "A *barista*," a job so shitty they had to give it a fancy name. The restaurant is shaping up slowly over there. I'm getting worried.

I think the chef was overpromised, and now she's demanding **all** of it. She's using $70 a gallon olive oil, smoking lettuces with almond wood. These poor guys are pulling their hair out, trying to get her all the stuff she requires. The food is good so far. I'll say that. It's just cafe food, but it's the best cafe food I've ever seen: pork belly sandwiches on herb slab, panini grilled until the room is filled with the smell of roasting pork. Blue cheese and flame-graped endive salads, kombucha, sauvignon blanc from a keg. The techies are coming in, and they love this shit. If we could just get the restaurant open. Fifty bucks in tips per shift ain't cuttin' it. I start equating the sound of the milk steamer with poverty. Come on, restaurant. Open.

One day the chef's dad comes to visit, and the chef says, "Hey Justin, this is my dad, Dad, this is Justin, he's a stand-up comedian. Justin, tell my dad a joke."

Now, when you're a comedian, people demand you prove you're funny at the drop of a hat like it's a game of Dance Monkey, Dance. It's best just not to tell people. Tell them you do one-man shows. They never demand anything then. People never want to hear more if you say, 'one-man show.' For some reason, people's eyes light up if they find out you're a stand-up comic. They're like, "Let's see if he can **prove** it."

So, after a few years of that bullshit, I just tell people a regular old street joke when I'm commanded to be funny. "Oh, hello, Chef's dad. Uhm, okay, I got it. So this guy walks into a deli, and he looks at the menu, it says 'roast beef sandwiches, five bucks,' under that it says 'cheese sandwiches, three bucks,' and under that, in little, squiggly, chalk letters, it says 'handjobs, ten dollars.'"

The chef's face looks worried maybe if I commit more.

"The guy goes '*Who the fuck is giving out ten-dollar hand jobs!?*' and he looks over the counter, and there's a hot girl back there, slicing up roast beef on the machine, getting juices on her thin, wife-beater shirt. The guy calls her over, and he's like, 'Are you the one giving out handjobs?'"

I realize this isn't going well. Neither Chef nor her dad look entertained, like, at all. I'm a pro, though, so I can't give up on the bit.

"The girl comes over from the roast beef slicing machine, and she says, 'Yeah, I'm the one,' and the guy goes, 'Well, shit, bitch, go wash your hands, I just want a fuckin' cheese sandwich.'"

I bomb for an audience of two; small-time. I've bombed in front of 500 people before. This ain't shit. At any rate, the chef doesn't ask me to perform on the spot anymore. I thought it was pretty clever to find the correct *sandwich counter* joke that quick since, you know, we were standing in a *sandwich cafe*? Whatevs.

Moss Alley Hits Peak Filth

I don't know if I told you, but Moss Alley is a total pit. Twenty people have revolved through the place since I took it over and not one of them was what you would call a *neat freak*. Even when I got it, it was toxic. I got this place from Dan and Ezzie, kids from the old neighborhood in Santa Barbara. Ezzie had two pit bulls that would be running loose in here, shitting, pissing, and trying to chew their way through the fuckin' walls. The vibe and smell have carried over. When I finally ripped out the carpet, millions of tiny shit flakes came floating down like orc dandruff. It was disgusting.

That was like seven years ago. Now, look at it. It's even worse. Adrianka, the pumpkin-headed, Czechoslovakian waitress from the Purple Onion, takes one look at this house and is all, "You live like junky," which is ironic since *she*'s the one that's about to get HIV. I kid, I kid. But seriously, she was hot but had this giant head. It made Elaine from Seinfeld's loppy melon look dismal, shrunken.

These girls I go after with their slight mutations. What is my deal? There was Nozomi, with the skin flap over her asshole, Wendy with her emergency airbag vulva. Is it because I look so regular? I don't have a decent *comedy body*? Do I think if I drag my steak scepter across their anal anomalies and their Goodyear blimp lips—now, that could be Adrianka *or* Wendy—I think I'll be able to ingest their combined essences? That I'll spontaneously develop a Toucan nose, or something similarly pedigree declaring, comedy-wise. Perhaps some arched, bushy eyebrows. A hunched back accompanied by *skippy bow legs*? Some fuckin' bat ears? Shit, at this point, I'd settle for a slacked *Jimmy jaw*. I just got this Paul Newmany-Vince Vaughn shit goin' on. It's bullshit! My kingdom for some bugged-out eyes and a *scooped-out side shuffle!* Come on, ladies, congeal the essences, crystallize the life forces of your unique and quirky genital features upon my inquisitive, but somewhat regular, *veined-dagjammer.*

So, back to Moss Alley—not sure we're going to get to the bottom of the Nancy Drew mystery, "The Man with the Penchant for Searching out Freakish Labial Traits." This place has turned into a kind of Black militant safe house. Greg and Julian have this caucasian, rubber, barbershop model head. They've given her a punk rock haircut and tattooed her neck, stabbed her in the forehead, and they are currently kicking her back and forth down the hallway, yelling, "Kick that white bitch back down here!" I'm pretty sure they won't protect me when *kill whitey day* comes around.

They're always in the kitchen, talking about, "*Black Lionism* is what threatens them, my brother," and, "They say they own the land, and we got to pay just to sleep here. How do *you* own this land? Where tha Indians go? This Ohlone land, Mr. Landlord." *Shit. Are they talking about me?* They found out I was charging them a hundred bucks more than I pay, and they've been getting all shitty with me. "You're paying $450 to live in the m-i-d-d-l-e of San Francisco, you guys. I moved into this neighborhood when you could still get killed down here. It was just me, ravers, buff lumberjack gays, and crackheads. I deserve a better deal than you for that."

They don't give a fuck. After them living here for two years, I feel like they feel their cycle here ending, and they checked the rent prices for other neighborhoods, realizing their rents will double if they try and stay in The City. They're dropping hints that I seem less cool to them than I used to. I tried to make them clean, and it didn't work out very well. "Can you at least not *add* to the filth?" I feel like that was a no, too.

Recently, Greg was cooking calamari in a frying pan with a few inches of grease bubbling in it, and the freezer burn on the squid is making the grease pop and explode all over the floor. So Greg just adds a layer of cardboard over any part of the floor that collects too much oil. So we'll be sitting in the living room, amongst the trash, and he'll get a call from Molly, the Punchline booker, and look right at me, as he says, "Why yes, I'll be right over to do a set for Dave Chappelle."

One day, I'm eating a burrito from Taqueria Cancun, and Greg starts clipping his toenails next to me, putting his foot on the actual coffee table. Soon, a nail flies out, skimming the orbit of my burrito like a disease-carrying meteor. I consider mashing the burrito all over his foot, but he's pretty big. He played football at his school in Virginia and stays buff without working out. I yell at him and go into my room. I think the real reason these guys are vibing me a little bit is Wendy. She's been over a lot, saying, "We could fix this place up. My friend is a contractor, some Pergo flooring? A layer of paint?" She talks about stuff like this loud enough for them to hear, and they realize she's going to get rid of them. Instead of trying to continue their era, they just sort of accept it, bellyaching a little on their way out. Everyone sees that I've gotten a lot healthier with a ballbreaker girlfriend forcing me along.

Julian will move to New York, and Greg will move to LA, where he will become Mr. Thug Notes, star of a reasonably famous webisode series where Greg pretends to be a thinking man's gangster. He gives kids Cliff's Notes versions of classic books, reviewed in an inner-city dialect they can relate to. I thought it was a great idea. It's well done, and for kids who can't get down with Shakespeare, these webisodes might be just the ticket. It's meant to be just a funny juxtaposition, but I think it could have real teaching applications. Good job, Greg.

Julian in New York? I don't know. He's probably in Ryker's. When he moved out, he left a stack of cum socks in his room; piled high, like a spiraling meat-rotisserie at a falafel stand. Those socks glistened at me from a nasty, dark corner, like a greasy protein stockpile of doom—a purgatorial, soft-serve swirl of baby souls that never had a chance. Full of hope, that baby gravy was when it shot out of Julian's ashamed urethra into those stockings. Their reaction must have been not unlike Joe Pesci when he realized he was about to get shot in Goodfellas, "Ah, no!"

Sorry guys, nothin' but love, but you know I need to clean up my life. I'm 37 now, which is ancient in showbiz years. Good thing I look 27. Like a 27-year-old Paul Walkery-James Franco, now that I think about it. Maybe a little Hilary Swank thrown in? But still, I gotta make moves before I *look* 30 if I'm going to make it into the front of the movie cameras. I want to star in my own movies. Otherwise, Shia LaBeouf is going to end up playing me, and I'm going to be pissed.

Creatively, shit is just spilling out of my brain. Just last night, I wrote out an entire play that just popped into my head. So I'm primed and poised—time to put the next feather in my hat. Soon, I will have so many feathers in my cap it will appear to be *culturally appropriated*—a new term that's been popping up.

And it's confusing which item is prohibited at any time; for instance, I can wear a Tijuana poncho, but not a sombrero this week? Anything Native American is out. Dashiki is out. You can wear collarless Asian shirts, but not if the Asian who made it has dreadlocks. If you decide to try and keep up with this horseshit, just check Twitter every morning. See which hashtags are trending that prohibit what parts of your closet. Good luck. Fuck, this bullshit about my necklace is a little too African-looking. I like ethnic shit precisely because it isn't boring white people shit. Fuck the fuckin' hats, and fuck the fuckin' necklaces!

It's all very confusing. Thank god we have Twitter to tell us what obscure facet of our society to be mad about on any given day. Remember, kids, bullying isn't okay unless it's a douchebag with an English accent on TV. Simon Cowell, Piers Morgan, and Gordon Ramsey get a pass because they are preapproved pop culture bobbleheads. Don't look for logic in any of it. Just follow the Twitter mob!

This PC culture is starting to get stupid. I just got back from Thailand, yo—I *can* still say 'yo,' for now. And this mountain tribe shirt I have? It took this lady three days to make. You don't think I should wear it? Do you know how much *betelnut* she had to chew for that? Gobs, man. Look, I'm with a lot of the wokeness, okay, but there's some bullshit in this package, and I ain't buying the whole thing. Dirty comedians were the original wokesters, after all. But "cultural appropriation." Total bullshit. Traditional garb and necklaces and shit are like half of the tourist dollar that doesn't go to fuckin' Sandals resorts. Are you trying to kill the most vulnerable members of the poorest countries? Do you think the Namibian lady that made the dashiki gives a fuck if a whiteboy wears it? Shit, her daughter is the one giving him cornrows later. They don't give a fuck. It's always some Berkeley University Becky that leaves the protest the second she smells a little tear gas that's talking shit. I never really see Becky at the BBQ. Her coleslaw had raisins in it. Have a thousand seats, Becky,

I'm open to learning, folks. Some of this PC stuff is great. I'm not, like, the white guy fighting to say the N-word here. I took the word 'mulatto' out of my act because it was a mistake. A Black friend explained to me that that term has often referred to a plantation slave who has a lighter complexion because his mother was raped by the plantation owner. I'd never heard it explained that way before. My friend was not mean about it. She just... let me know. I was new to comedy and probably trying to be edgy. I was like a 2-year-old playing with a light socket; I suspected there was something naughty about it but wasn't sure, so I stuck a fork down the hole. It was a humbling experience, but I accepted it and moved on. That was a happy story about PC Culture.

Unfortunately, happy stories are less common than all this other shit.

People are stopping to think about if they should laugh at my jokes, eventually stifling the laughs behind their hands like it's a sneeze or a *Harajuku girl*. I'd rather die than process if a laugh should happen or not. This shit is sick, man.

All these PC directives are getting so numerous and petty the real issues are getting lost in the crowd. And that might very well be the plan. Sometimes, I think it's Carl Rove writing all this politically correct shit on the internet to unfocus any lasers of progressive efforts.

I'm getting more than the customary single person walk out nowadays due to this atmosphere. They're leaving in little pissy groups of three now. Social Justice is upon us, and it wants to know what we think is so funny. All it's doing is plunging me deeper into filth. I hate being told what I can say. I'm trying to fight against all this shit, and I'm not getting much help. People are backing away from me like I just shit myself during the Pledge of Allegiance. Fuck it.

The bookers and other various benefactors who support me during this period should receive acknowledgment for helping in this fight against the vanillafication of stand-up comedy: Jamie DeWolf, Al Gonzales, Matty Staudt, Mike Nelson, Susan Alexander, Kiko Briez, Janelle Boatright, Cafe Macaroni Mario, Tony Sparks, Justin Harrison, Pete Munoz, Kim V, Cody Woods, Julie Anderson, Butch Escobar, Nelson Martini, Elsie's Pete, Molly at the Punchline—I know I kind of blew it with my drinking; those fuckin' $2 drinks, man. Apologies to any that I forgot. Thanks, you guys. You were courageous, and you may have received some bullshit for booking me, but you didn't give a fuck. You are true champions of the unmuzzled artist.

The Purple Onion

"Come on, Mario, I got this regular spot on Live 105. You know? The radio station that's like three blocks that way? They'll let me plug the shows. I'll pack this place out on a Thursday. Keep your weekend stuff the way it is. Just let me have a crack at Thursdays."

I'm trying to get Mario, the chef/owner of Cafe Macaroni, to give me The Purple Onion, the historical, world-famous, cavelike venue, which just so happens to sit underneath this guy's restaurant. I wouldn't say it's fallen into disuse, but it needs a little life pumped back into it. I'm making my big move. I'm officially the movie reviewer for Live 105. Local comics are now proving lightning can strike for you here before you even have to move to LA or New York.

Mario *has* to give me this room. The Purple Onion, a historic, famous, subterranean cave of laughter. Lenny Bruce and Richard Pryor performed here—you can feel Lenny's ghost down there, man. Also, Mort Saul, Phyllis Diller, Zack Galifinakis, and on and on. It's got that unknowable magic that certain venues just have. I must *have* The Purple Onion.

"I don't know, kid. You seem like a good guy. I know you mean what you say, but I had a lotta guys blow sunshine up my ass, ok? And, they don't come through. So, I think I just open for private events on the weekends. You know anybody getting married? We have this for the reception. Good money, weddings. Everybody drinking, eating. Comedy shows? We have to threaten them to buy Pellegrino. Pelligrino is water. The tourists come in free and fuck up the bathroom. I don't know."

I know the weekends are his guaranteed business. That's why I'm trying to chip off the edge with a Thursday show. Plenty of foot traffic in the neighborhood on Thursdays. There's never anything happening at The Purple Onion on Thursdays. That's where the potential lies. I know this from that show when I headlined in the wheelchair. I was trying for months to bang the Czechoslovakian waitress that works here. Remember? Bighead? Well, it turns out she was very informative about things. Things like how much the boss needs to feel like he's going to need to make at the bar for a weekday show in the basement—a few other helpful things.

At that time, I decided I would eventually get a show here. The fact that I got him to say, 'I don't know,' means there's a chance, just like when his waitress asserted the same thing before she eventually *did* pull down her panties. I gotta get this old Sicilian guy to pull down the panties of this comedy stage. Look at that beautiful Purple Onion sign behind those gorgeous red bricks. Keep going. He'll get there.

"They'll drink, Mario. You've seen my comedy style. It practically peels the wrappers off the whiskey bottles itself. I'll be hosting the whole night. I'll **make** them drink; I'll pour it down their gullets, and the waitress can leave whatever bill you want. You get the whole bar, and I'll take the door. That's 80 seats at two to four drinks a seat. That's $2,000 in the register. Serve them the cheap shit; Peroni beer and cheap prosecco mixed with peach puree to hide the taste. Tourist shit. It'll be worth it. All you have to do is turn on the lights and pay the waitress. Adrianka, does she still work here?"

"No, no more, Adrianka." He gets a distant look in his eye, and I lose his gaze to somewhere up behind me.

Shit. She's not pregnant, is she?

"Okay, kid. We try it for one month of Thursdays. If I make close to $2,000 in the register? Ok, we'll keep going."

Awesome! It's all coming together. I'll be in charge of one of the most famous venues in comedy history. I'm having the most fun in my life since my youth in Isla Vista. My girlfriend is a bit of a ballbreaker, but I guess I need it right now. I got cheap rent in the middle of the city, and the restaurant side of Radius is about to open.

The first few shows go pretty well. I've printed up some glossy club flyers small enough to fit in your pocket. We try for the $20 a head, but quickly go down to ten if they seem at all squeamish. Norm, a door guy from The Punchline who loves my comedy, offers to work security for free if I just let him hang out at the shows. "You're hired!" Wendy works the door and collects the money when I have to go and start the show. There's a European girl who works the bar and tables. It's a tight little unit. It works. I'm hitting the sidewalks all day before the show and charming people, giving them the glossy cards, calling them "Half-price tickets!" Very effective. Fuck all this online bullshit. I'm bringing it back to the roots. Between the radio shoutouts and the working of the neighborhood the day of the shows, we're filling a bit more than half the seats. It's what you expect for a weekday. The boss gripes about it, but it's enough to keep it going for the second month.

I am considering selling tickets on Funcheap.com to beef out the other half of the seats. Funcheap seems to be a less evil alternative to other ticket selling sites like Groupon, a full-on predator that requires you to cut your prices in half before giving you only half of that three months later, for a total of 25 percent of the original price. Holy shit. The other comics are having a lot of luck with Funcheap. Stroy Moyd knows the dude, Johnny Funcheap. So I have an in, but I can't do it. I'm sick of the word 'cheap' being connected to all things comedy. Granted, most things in The Bay being billed as 'Comedy Shows' should have to pay the audiences for ear raping them. But, it's right there in the name: Funcheap.

These discount apps and websites promise to save your struggling business, but in the end, after they nickel and dime you and pay you whenever the fuck they please, it turns out to be the final coffin nail in that business. Do they give a fuck? Hell, no. Their cover charge skimping customers just show up and try to wriggle out of the two-drink minimum, and you have no recourse. Anyway, I feel I have to be a counterweight to the apps and the websites anyway. The best way to do business still has to be a handshake, an elevator speech, and a smile. It just has to be. How will people switch over to buying all their shit based on a photograph and a paragraph on a website? I couldn't imagine buying a bike online. I need more than the store itself even wants to offer. I need to launch off a few curbs in the alley before I drop $600. No, this is the right way. I just gotta keep at it.

"Hey, you guys in the neighborhood tonight? I have the best

comedians in San Francisco performing just a few blocks away," I yell at the tourists as they pass me by. Mario told me today that the neighborhood wants me to stop taping Purple Onion flyers to all the pedestrian light poles. That's going to set me back four seats a night. No one said being a hustler would be easy.

I headline myself half the time and get some of my favorite guys to perform. I headline local legends like Brent Weinbach and Louis Katz. We had some brilliant, beautiful moments. The time we had strippers go on in the middle of a show just to mix things up. As the strippers were finishing we had Lynn Ruth Miller, at age 80 I think she was at the time, the oldest comedienne alive, come out and chase them off, saying "I love your act ladies, but how about letting a *mature lady* show you how it's done." Then Lynn Ruth, well, she did a striptease for the ages, getting some cocks in the audience to stand at attention for the first time since the Carter administration. Then there was the time Louis Katz had to finish his set with me holding a flashlight on him because the power went out halfway through. Brendon Walsh, Andy Andrist, both friends of Stanhope, performed. We had Eddie Ifft, a friend of Matty, at Live 105. LA comics you'd recognize from their face, but most likely not what their names are, hit me up for sets. I toss them in the mix before they go to headline their weekday shows at The Punchline, a few blocks away. Good to buy some goodwill with that crowd, I suppose.

Things go on like this for about four or five months before tourist season dies, and the people coming in from my email list and sidewalk hustling just aren't enough without the added, last-minute tourists. The radio shoutouts didn't do shit. Twenty-thousand people heard them, but these people were just trying to get to their jobs across the bridge. The last thing they're going to do is fight their way into the city for dinner and a show on a school night. These poor commuters are going to be asleep before the host even *starts* the show. Poor nine to fivers gotta fight their way into *and* out of the city. By the time they get home at six pm, they're *dunzo*. Do you even know who your kids are at that point? Capitalism is trash. We're getting rid of capitalism.

It was fun. Mario and I make enough to pay for it all and then stash a little in our pockets. We had some fantastic shows. Thank you, Cafe Macaroni Mario, a guy from the old school that still believes in doing business on a handshake and a smile. A slice of the old San Francisco, still hanging on, despite it all. I'd be honored if he considered me a brother in arms. Good flatbread, too, if these stingy tourists would have kicked down the cash to have it brought downstairs. I guess we're just two paper ticket, paper menu guys, living in a Stubhub, Opentable.com world. They might be winning the battle, but I think they've overlooked our tenacity.

Until we can wait out and vanquish these corporate tech predators, I'll just keep making DIY comedy shows *by* broke people, and apparently, *for* broke people. I never wanted to perform in a glitzy theatre anyway. These subterranean comedy caves aren't paying the bills, though, and neither is the radio station. It's almost like us creative people are intended to stay broke unless we miraculously reach Tom Cruise or Pablo Picasso level fame. I've had some people shout out, "Hey Scalesman!" in honor of my stage persona, from a Bart platform, or something like that, but I don't feel like my Stacy Keach level fame—in specific neighborhoods—is skyrocketing anywhere fast.

Fucking Tom Arnold

The morning show is starting to wear on me. I try to think of other ways to get my ideas out there in the broadcasting world. Podcasts are getting big. Maybe I'll try that. Joe Rogan began *his* podcast recently, encouraging thousands of boring white dudes to pair up and try to subject people to their stoned, on the couch musings. This attempt at wonder twin power activating mediocre comedy writing skills usually fails, but at least there aren't many victims—the average podcast will receive 46 listens. Sad. Better than clogging up the open-mics. Keep them from ever even climbing out of mom's basement, that's what I say. Nail them in there like you're trying to get a junky clean. Bang on the door from time to time, like, "You gonna stop signing up on the open-mic lists, Mikey?! No? Ok, see you tomorrow!" Improv troupe colleges are closing down. The podcast is now where the public goes to collect their unfunny stories and skits. I think I'll pass.

Finally, I get to review a movie that has a chance of being positive. I think the idea of having a movie reviewer is maybe to get people interested in going to the movies? And I've been justifiably shitting on half the stuff they've sent me to so far.

Tom Arnold, the guy famous for marrying Roseanne, will be in the studio right after my review. How bad do you need a sponsor for your coke habit to marry Roseanne, right? Fuck. This guy must be snorting down eight balls on the daily, remembering he's married to Roseanne, making him snort faster and faster. "Fuck! She's horny again—*Honnnk!*"

I'm sitting at the table with Matty and No Name. Katey is off in her own little booth. She just did traffic for the people already sitting stuck in it, aware of their situation.

No Name: "So, Scalesman. What did you think of Avatar?"

Me: "Finally, you guys send me to something watchable. This movie was pretty good. I know it's too much to ask Hollywood for fresh, original, quality pictures. They only have all the money in the world. James Cameron, if you're listening, help me. The money Live 105 is paying me barely cover lunch. A non-alcohol lunch. They call me a "Friend of the show" because I'm supposed to do this crap as a favor like I'm just helping them move or something." This is an actual attempt to get more compensation. It will be in vain.

Matty: *nervous laugh*

Me: "So, I've never done the 3-D thing before—holeee macaroni. I usually stumble out of the theatre until my eyes readjust, but this adds a level. You guys almost got me ran over."

Some exaggerated studio laughter.

Me: "Other than that, I'm glad that this was my first 3-D experience—what a delightful visual jamboree. I usually hate computer-generated stuff, but in this case, as an occasional thing? It was great. Stunning to look at, like a girl from Santa Barbara. But also, like a girl from Santa Barbara, some of it relied on cliches for its personality. The Aliens look like reptilian elves, so you got Lord of The Rings mixed with Aliens right off the bat. They're blue, like smurfs, and their lifestyle is **totally** Ewok. It's a mashup of science fiction movies and Saturday morning cartoons. I liked it; I'm just saying."

"There's also our real-world mixed in. The planet the aliens live on is called Pandora. Oh, could that streaming service have paid for that? Like a more obvious Coke can placement? Weren't stadiums enough? We gotta name the planets after companies now, too?"

"Think of Pandora as, like, a Middle Eastern country who is discovered to have valuable stuff under its dirt, and now the American military has to come and 'liberate' them. A story as old as the combustion engine."

"The hero is an army guy in a wheelchair. He has to, through intense concentration, psychically enter another, healthier body, to try and complete a difficult task. Kind of like what Tom Arnold had to do to have sex with Roseanne."

"Ooooof," goes the studio.

Me: "Over all, visually stunning. I recommend it. The budget must have been insane; maybe money better spent buying people in Darfur burritos, but whatever. I predict it will win **all** the awards and will be made into the most lunchboxes. Congratulations, James Cameron. Maybe you can just enjoy being rich now. We get it. Your pictures are gargantuan feats of technology. Let some other guys have a chance. You are to blockbuster movies as Samuel L. Jackson is to old, angry, Black men trying to score a role in Hollywood."

Five minutes after my review is over, Tom Arnold himself walks in. He's the scheduled guest, which I knew. He looks around and deduces who told that joke about how he fucks Rosanne. I meet his eyes to make sure there's no confusion.

I don't hate him for being an unfunny comedian; too tiring. Everywhere I look, there's an unfunny comedian. I wouldn't have enough hate for *other* stuff. I'm just tired of people like him and Pauly Shore, where you watch everyone kiss their ass just because they, somehow, on a slow news week, got famous? Maybe if you're only famous because your mom owns the Comedy Store, or if you did some drug-fueled figure eights on Rosanne's clit? Perhaps that shouldn't be a thing everyone adores you for. Our culture is so fucked up, it might not be able to be saved, but I'm at least going to mock it all the way to hell. Mumble rappers and Skrillex? You're next.

The French Invasion

The restaurant side of Radius is finally opening! We're to show up at a work meeting to discuss the details. Exciting! So, I show up, and there are like six new faces there. What the fuck? Like three French dudes and some chicks with fake tits. They're going to walk in and take all the sweet server shifts after me; Acebo, Samantha, and Jessica did all the work opening the cafe. I swear to god, if they try to keep us in the cafe, I'll burn this place down. It's an old wood building. A little lighter fluid on that cord of almond wood in the shed? It'll go right up. All that dragging around reclaimed barn wood you guys did for six months will be for nothing. I was promised server shifts. I slaved in the cafe for like four months. If these guys try to fuck me, I'm going to go ballistic. I can't even pay attention to the meeting because hearing these French guys jerk their hands up in the air to answer in their little Parisian accents is pissing me off. Acebo doesn't care. He's going to work the bar —it's only employee. We only serve beer and wine, so he's probably not going to be too overwhelmed. He seems unaffected, but these French fuckers are showing up to compete with MY tips.

Christian reassures me I'll be getting server shifts, but I have to be a food runner for a while until the place gets up and running. Besides, "Who knows the food better than you do," says Christian, manipulatively. "You'll be bringing the plates to the table and describing the food."

Ok, fine. For a month, I'll do it. If I'm not a server by then, there's a pile of oily rags in the kitchen that might have an 'accident.'

Robin Williams

Here's the tale about how I was in the San Francisco Sketchfest Comedy Festival that one year. I'm still doing movie reviews for Live 105, a job you might think pays in more than Red Bulls and Death Cab for Cutie key lanyards. You'd be wrong, though.

So it's me, Katie, No Name, and Matty. That particular evening we're all at my home club, the Purple Onion, on a non-school night, to support Matty, who is competing in an impersonation competition of famous comics; a thing called Joke-e-oki.

It works just like karaoke, except you read the jokes of famous comics out of a teleprompter. You try to sound and look like them too. Matty crushes it as Andrew Dice Clay.

Somehow the supposed person doing Richard Pryor didn't show, and I'm suddenly pushed onto the stage with a giant "Richard Pryor" sticker on my fuckin' shirt. This is most likely because I'm the new bitch at the station. They want to see how well I roll with the punches. *I'm supposed to reenact one of the greatest comics of all time... on five minutes' notice?!* Harsh right? Especially because, even though I'm a more than decent comic, my only Achilles tendon? You guessed it, impersonations and characters. I'm like De Niro; I can only play myself. I'm just like De Niro.

So there I am, microphone in my hand, on the stage. Harmon Leon, the inventor of Joke-e-oki, and a fellow Stand-up comic who I'd recently beefed with slightly over a joke premise (even though you can't call premises, just punchlines. That'd be like trying to call dick jokes.) He has a joke about how thrift store clothes are donated because the people that owned them died. This is common knowledge among poor people such as myself. He feels my "Goodwill" joke steps on his joke's toes, even though they're totally different, and most importantly, punchlines that don't resemble each other... at all. I would win in a *court of comedy law*, but he still feels a little bit miffed. Sometimes, senior guys will try to jerk new guys around like that, see if they can make you shelve a bit. He's been in comedy five years longer than me and had a big popular column in the local weekly newspaper, called The Infiltrator. It's pretty good, actually, but that doesn't mean I'm getting my shine box out, okay? Fuck that.

So this little fucker Harmon just looks at me with a cruel smile from the back row working the machines, like the villain in a fucked up stage production of Wizard of Oz. He's refusing to load the goddamn Richard Pryor jokes into the teleprompter! I'm already terrified enough! I don't want to be here in the first place. That's why I tied on three cocktails before we fuckin' **got** here. I'm waiting for the Pryor jokes to load onto the screen, and there's a hundred audience members lookin' at me like I'm a fuckin' idiot. I look to Katie Goodman for support. She just looks at me with a shoulder shrug and some thoughts and prayers, sweetheart that she is. *I freeze.* I certainly know 5 Pryor jokes, but when 100 people are lookin' at you with expectant looks on their faces? I'm fucked, and Harmon knows it. He loves it. I'm not sure whether I should be in respectful awe of him right now or violently charge his control booth.

Out of panic, not remembering even three Pryor jokes now, and because I feel like a skinny kid at a summer camp with his sweats pulled down around his ankles, I just go into my own act. I don't know what else fuckin' do.

I jump up onto the barstool, turn backwards, and pull *up* my pants from my ankles, exposing my emaciated calves, and say, "Look at 'em! Look at my legs! It's like god got tired halfway through makin' me!!! God's all like, 'Well, I spent too much time on those little Claudia Schiffer lips, Oh well, I'll just finish up the bottom half with some leftover pelican beaks!'"

You guys! No one is laughing in the whole Purple Onion, They're thinking *Richard Pryor*, and they're getting, *crazy whiteboy that belongs in a fryer!*

To be fair, there's one guy laughing in the back of the audience. I can't make out who is just laughing at the ridiculosity of it all because the lights are always in your eyes as a performer. It sounds like a familiar laugh. Once my lackluster set is over, I head out. I want to suck up any support I can get as I leave up the stairs, so I take a look at who it was laughing.

It's Robin Williams himself. He must have known what happened the entire time.

Operation Get Wendy the Fuck Out

One day, we're at the mall, and Wendy wants me to hold her big purple purse while she tries something on. I resist, smelling a trick. Guys that hold their woman's purse are considered inferior in America. I usually don't buy into macho bullshit like that, but she's been attacking my masculinity for months, like a personal trainer, but for my whole life. I'm like, *Wait a minute bitch. I'm on the radio, I'm the sole comedy booker of the Purple Onion, I make you cum until the mascara melts off your albino eyelashes,* ***and*** *I have a job. What the fuck do you expect from me? It's like until I have Letterman begging me to come on his show, I'm a little bitch? Nah, fuck that.*

So when she does things like try to get me to hold her purse, I'm naturally resistant. Sure enough, the second I take it in my hands, she backs up a step and points at me in the middle of H&M and yells, "Haha. Look at the little purple purse-carrying bitch!" Everyone looks over.

I told you she's an asshole. I consider tossing her big purple purse out the front door, down into the lower levels of the mall. But instead, I lay it on the floor and leave the store steaming. She *did* say she dominates alphas. So if I stay after this, I'm dominated, right? How long before she's spit-roasting me with a strap on? Nah, fuck this; I'm out.

Instead of breaking up with her, I just start drinking a lot more and revert back to a mess for a while. We just got new floors installed at Moss Alley, painted the whole joint like five colors. We had to live with all our shit piled under plastic for weeks. She's going to be bummed if I throw her out now that Moss is finished. But what if I make her *want* to move out?

I'm as fixed up as I'm going to get. I guess I partly owe her for that. She used me for some stuff too. Fuck it. A bad relationship is a bad relationship. This chick is never happy with any amount of progress. I mean, strangers are yelling my one-liners back at me out of bus windows, okay? I have a Gerard Butler level of fame in North Beach, Downtown SF, the Mission District, and parts of Oakland. So lay off, Wendy!

It's true, I have a decent medium-sized legion of fans now, and most of them are amazing people, but when you tell dirty jokes, some people think that's what you live and breathe for, just degraded, nasty shit. They'll start talking, and I'll be like, "Whoah, but funny. It seems like you're just saying horrific shit just for the sake of it, little buddy. No, no, no. Why would you tell me you fingerbanged a cat?"

You get offered weird gigs too. A fan who works at The Armory, a porn castle in The Mission where a lot of bizarre amputee bondage videos and the like are filmed, offers me a gig for a shaming video, where there's a bunch of people yelling mean shit at a chick while she gets her mouth spit in and a corn cob shoved up her *caboozle*. They want me to come down and humiliate her cum holes while all that is happening. I'm like, "No, I'm a helper of the slut. I empower whores. Can I yell support? Like, 'Your mascara looks great!' or 'Your father's love isn't worth it, seek love from others instead—but not this way!'"

All in all, the fans are great. Of course, I attract some weirdos, but what else is new? I'm basking in a bit of local fame, and it feels great.

I come home disgustingly drunk from The Bloodhound every night for two weeks.

Soon, the never satisfied Wendy breaks up with me. She decides she'll just move down the hall into the guestroom. *What the fuck?* That's not going to work. A roommate is just a girlfriend you don't fuck, right? She's still going to boss me around, just about roommate shit. *Fuck.*

Getting rid of a roommate in San Francisco can be tricky if they know about all the laws protecting them. Why anyone would want to be a landlord in San Francisco is beyond me, you get a lot for each apartment, but if they can come up with it, they can make you their slave. Someone feeling chilly in a section of their hallway can take your life over. If they even thought they smelled gas, you can kiss your vacation goodbye. The batteries in the carbon monoxide detector wore out a year ago? May as well retain a lawyer now. The tenant's union will fuck you up if little Darlene gets chilly again. You might end up in civil court with a jury of senior citizens who are acting as if each case decides the future of rent control itself. As a comic, I've faced some tough crowds, but not *that* tough. Those people take it to the limit on people they see as forcing the poor into the streets; these people are rent-controlled tenants themselves! To win this case, you'd need the guys that got OJ off.

What if I ended up owing Wendy $10,000 or something? This chick will pop out of the bushes on me on the first of the month for the rest of my life, like a vengeful baby mama. This is quite the predicament. I'll have to drive her out the old-fashioned way.

First, I invite my mom, The Goat Lady of Santa Barbara, to come for a stay. A week of that should do it.

Second, I immediately start dating. A talented performer girl from the 16th and Mission crowd gave me the moo moos last week. Dotty. I arrange to meet her at Kilowatt, and we get drunk playing pool. We end up in the alley, and I have her up against a tree, fingerbanging her from behind. I'm ready just to stick it in right there, but she stops me at the last second.

Dotty is an assertive short girl with powerful calves that she likes to talk about. If she sees another woman with grapefruits above her Achilles' she'll just walk up in solidarity and say, "I see you're in the big calves club. Fuckin' awesome, huh?" I don't think she realizes that that lady will probably obsess about her calves for a few months now. She is an outside-the-box thinker that just goes with the flow, approaching any and all creatures we encounter, including them into her spontaneous skits, producing awkward interactions that bear fruit or not. She is kind of a Frances Mc Dormandy, youngish Emma Goldman, with a bit of Judy Garlandy theatricality thrown in? Brown, coarse hair, and no makeup. She doesn't need it. Petite, but powerful and dense. A little hippie-esque, but not so much as to be annoying. Her room is an art studio as well as a sex marathon location. We fuck insanely. The safari noises that emanate from her room the first day I get there must sound like she's adopted a clan of silverback gorillas.

Dotty has just the slightest underbite that juts out a cute chin dimple. Brown eyes and nipples like warped pepperoni. *Ahhh, the subtle mutation.* There it is. Other than weird nips, Dotty is normal and cute. Her vagina pieces are dainty, almost a rebuttal of Wendy's abundant meatiness. She has a tight little body that is exceedingly fun to drive.

She is a bit of a wackadoodle, I think she might have dropped a little too much acid in high school, but whatever, It's fun to date an artistic type again. Some of these girls just don't understand my dreams. They lack imagination. Dotty has so much imagination she operates with no particular plan and just lives her life as if it's one big, improvised theatrical production, whose characters she picks up and discards along the way. She will say whatever pops into her head to absolutely anyone in her path. I think we have that in common. The two of us together must be a bit overwhelming for the regular person just trying to buy their groceries.

One day we were walking in The Mission, and there's a girl in a tight skirt and heels walking just ahead of us, and we see a guy check out the chick's ass, hanging his head into the short lane between her and us to do it. Now, Dotty is what I'd call sex-positive, but with a bit of a feminist streak. His crime wasn't checking the ass out. It was the obviousness. The guy jerked his neck like he thought he just saw his parole officer drive by. So she says to him as we pass, "You know she poops out of that thing? It's kind of smelly back there," then she waves her hand in front of her nose. The dude got served. I don't know if he deserved that hard of a rub, but I laughed.

So, the chick with the sweet ass hears Dotty say that and turns to us with a little head jerk herself. She thinks Dotty was talking to me the whole time. I did laugh, remember? Tight Skirt gives me the *Sicily death curse* look. I shrug my shoulders at her in an *I'm just an unfortunate victim too* sort of way. Now we're stuck walking behind Little Miss Stiletto Heel Clicks. Her sexy walk went from *swishy samba* to, like, a couple of stiff hams stuck to the top of some hockey sticks. I think we might have made her shart before she got to Blondie's Martini Bar.

After meeting Dotty at her house a few times, the obscure location at the end of Cesar Chavez becomes a bit inconvenient for daily travel. So I explain to her my situation with Wendy, and she says, "Sounds like it's time for that bitch to move out."

Great. So we take our gorilla act to Moss Alley, and instead of getting mad the next day, Wendy cries. This is not a strategy I expected. Oh wait, now she's angry. That didn't take long.

My mom finally arrives into town as my second wave attack in "Operation Get Wendy the Fuck Out."

Wendy is yelling at what an asshole I am, and my mom goes charging up to her and says, "Why don't you just leave?!"

And that does it. Wendy moves out. After that, my brother rents a room in the house, thinking he'll hang out in the city more. He's only around for a few days a month. I start to see the benefits of roommate-free living. Life would be great if I could get rid of the construction site outside my bedroom window every morning at 8 am.

I'm mostly recovered from smashing both ankles and both heels, as recovered as I will ever get. My ankle joints are permanently fucked, but still usable. The swagger in my walk is reduced a bit, but I only limp a little in the mornings until my kankles loosen up. My hands are shaking a lot less.

I feel amazing; on the verge. Ready to seize upon my opportunity to launch into the big time. I've got TV show ideas that I have executed and taped, I've made a movie, and I have a pretty decent comedy resume that isn't full of myths like my restaurant one. I just wrote a play that Dotty and Guinevere are going to perform soon. I'm grinding, baby!

I also have a comedy club idea like The Gong Show, but the audience decides by texting the hotline number. A trap door suddenly swallows the comic if the audience decides they suck, maybe a dunking booth full of Faygo for the final round. We could get dogs to chase them off. Here's the thing, it's all terrible comics. The public wants to judge everything now that internet reviewing has offered them a way to shit on everything with no consequences. Well, let's mix that intense, fiery desire in them to write a one-star review and blend that in with their stupid phones that they love so much.

You don't think I'd treat *real* comedians like that, do you? Nah, I'll just use it to toughen up the new open-mikers a little bit. This last concept is the one idea I'm not that into, but I figure that's precisely why it's most likely to work. Sometimes you have to sell out a little to get the real shit going, okay? One of these pots is gonna boil. When it comes to storytelling, my quiver spilleth over. If I have to play a little dirty to get what I need from the showbiz establishment, then that's what I'll do. I'll make them regret it later.

My stories are a little weird, but there's a market for them. Demented intellectuals? Where's my people at?! The audiences are excited. Eventually, the proof has to be in the pudding, right? My fans are fervent too. They'll buy anything I put out. I figure my shit appeals on a high level to about 10 million people just in America. If I could just make them aware of what I do, I could sell each of them a hoodie and a DVD every year. That's $50 times 10 million. That's a half-billion dollars before I even start selling them signed dick pics. That's what I'm aiming for, a half-billion so I can start an organization that cuts the dicks off of child abusers that think they're hidden when they go to the third-world to do their sick shit. Unicef? Meet **Unisnip**. My foundation outlets will dot the earth. I just need that first half-billion—I just need guys like John Waters and Johnny Depp to endorse my shit on their fuckin' stupid Twitters, or whatever.

Hobble the Parisians

I had agreed to be a food runner until they can find someone else. After two months, I start slamming plates around and shooting murderous looks at Christian, who expo's the chef's window, studies the tickets, gives the final inspection, and sends the plates to the correct seat and table. I take over once the plates travel into the restaurant. Me and Christian are constantly interacting as our jobs in the restaurant are directly connected. The busboy can go off and do his own thing a bit more, but most jobs are working with your team so closely that you are exchanging sweat throughout the night. If Ebola ever gets to America, it will kill the restaurant employees the first week. After that, the customers will still boss us around like we're trying to steal from them. I could be on my back, convulsing, eyes exploded, and some rich bitch would be all, "Son, I still need that Dijon!"

I was promised server shifts, and they moved in all these French assholes right before opening day. So now I'm stuck running food for half the money after I slaved in the early days of the cafe. The chef is on top of the world. I *have French assholes opening the wine!* There are not only two French servers and a French manager.

Christian has to feel my anger bubbling over. I wear my emotions on my fuckin' sleeve, and we're close enough to each other to smell melted Old Spice deodorant through our sweaty shirts.

Other than that little hang-up that will soon be solved, things are going great at the restaurant. The vibe is casual fine dining, but the food is every bit as good as at Chef Mina's restaurant. Ribeye steaks from Lucky Dog Farms, Muscovy duck breast with a huckleberry gastrique, sea bass with marble potatoes and piquillo pepper puree, steamed clams with a lemongrassy chorizo broth, the best lemon curd tart in the city. I still bubble with pride seeing it all get laid on the tables, even though I'm getting kind of screwed right now. I'll bide my time, for now, if I have to hobble a few Parisians, then that's what I'll have to do. The reviews on Yelp have been phenomenal, so the mood is pretty good. The tense vibe of fine dining is reduced to half, a manageable level that translates to excitement and not stress. Management understands everyone is doing their best, and if a wine glass breaks, a wine glass breaks. The owners don't run over and act like you just bankrupted them like most places. What these guys lack in experience they make up for in instinct and kindness; you just don't want to let them down, so you don't have to be watched every second like someone who is disgruntled. I'm getting close.

The restaurant came out beautiful too. They kept the famous and beautiful Julie's Supper Club bar intact but completely changed everything else in the restaurant. A lot of dark wood, rustic, farmhousey mystique. We sure did put a lot of work into it, and we're all proud. I'll be patient.

As luck would have it, one of the Frenchies gets caught stealing granola of all things, and I get my promotion. A new guy, Rodrigo, will be the food runner. This fuckin' guy starts disgruntled his first day. Most food runners take a few weeks to realize they're doing just as much work as the server but making half the tips. This guy seemed to know and accepted the job anyway. Fuck it, who cares? I'm serving now! That's all I care about; let them sort that shit out in the management meetings.

I can't beat Frederick at his accent, so I'll have to do it with charm and food knowledge, weaving these elements into stories—my strong suit that never stops giving. I notice these guys have to ask the Chef for half the questions the customers have. That's if they don't just totally bullshit their way through it. This is how new restaurants work; you're just kind of throwing the tracks out in front of the train in whatever direction it starts lurching. Also, with the success of the Food Network channel, Yelp, and just internet reviewing period, everyone is a fuckin' food critic now. They took a few wine classes in Napa, and now they think they know everything. They'll google the flavor notes on the bottle of wine they ordered and quiz the waiter to see if he tries to bullshit it. The customers feel they are our food knowledge equals now; even though they are full of shit half the time, we have to pretend they're right and not embarrass them in front of their corporate, East Coast counterparts. The fucking internet is ruining everything. Can't people just allow themselves to be in wonder at the joys we bring out to them?

No, let's discuss the effects of south-facing slopes on the Pinot Noir grape while the fucking pork chops get cold.

Frederick has started a competition with me, going so far as to try and correct my plate holding techniques in front of the Chef to assert his status as the 'Lead server.' In response, I start memorizing the Food Lover's Guide. I take the wine list and write the flavor profile, depth of body, and what foods it goes with. Next, I study the methods of the farms and their locations that we source from. Finally, I create little jokes about the things I learn that way: "In that herbaceous lettuce mix, you will find 16 different leaves, all trimmed by hand by the farmer who grew them. That farmer's name is Sam, and he plays Bob Marley to the plants. He told me this particular batch on your plates seemed to prefer the Talkin' Blues album. Enjoy."

One thing is the fucking trays. They want us to bring all the drinks out on trays—my kryptonite. I swear they insist on trays in the restaurant industry to keep the poor kids out of the server positions. Our *poverty PTSD* makes us shake too much. It's just beer and wine, though, so I don't have to deal with martini glasses at least. I manage. One side effect of my injury is that my ankle joints collapsed by 20 percent, affecting my balance a bit. The liquid inside your ankle joints communicates with your brain to inform your equilibrium, your balance. So, my tray problem is never going to go away, even if through the relaxation techniques I learned from the Thai people, I can stop stress shaking when I'm in need of a drink, or out of my element, or whatever. I become more at ease quickly, and soon, I'm working my tables like a champ, knowing the exact moment to upsell the second glass of wine, how far to take a joke, instinctively knowing if they want space, or if they want to be entertained. Even Frederick has to admit out loud in front of the chef that I'm pretty good. It's just like being on a stage, right? This shit is easy. As long as I don't feel the boss looking over my shoulder all the time, which I don't, I'll be great. They trust me.

The side of PTSD (Post-Traumatic-Stress-Disorder)—which most people who have spent a few years or more in poverty have—was ladled over my ADHD. This cocktail of workplace mindfuck can cause me to be acutely aware of when I'm being watched all the time. I become highly vigilant, as if I have the eyes of a predator on me in a jungle situation or something. Being micromanaged feels like I'm being hunted, so I usually bounce out of jobs where I feel like that.

Frederick is a great waiter. And having a French accent is a game-changer in this business. People just throw $50 tips at him like it's nothing. Hard to compete with, but my schtick is strong after a few months. We all become like a family, and out of love for Radius, we go outside the limits of what you would typically expect from a regular restaurant employee. We play little tricks on each other like the old *decorate the spent espresso patty like a piece of chocolate cake routine,* where you go up to the new guy and say, "The Chef wants to know what you think of this."

On Halloween, the customers won't tip you well if they are in a costume and you aren't. It's San Francisco, so all the adults wear costumes on Halloween. I usually go with a witch hat and call myself a *grumpy witch.* I then give grumpy service and have an excuse. It's a pretty great costume—all you need is the stupid hat—but not as good as when I'm Salvador Dali Lama. A free-flowing monk robe and a Dali mustache sharpied on. The customers tipped me 30 percent for that one. These costumes are my standby because they're easy and not really in the way, like a minotaur costume or some such bullshit.

So, this particular year, Halloween 2010, I have something very light and moveable inside of—the keyest of aspects for running around a restaurant that will be slammed all night. The chef walks into the dining room to see me polishing wine glasses in nothing but a baby diaper and a blue baby bonnet. My entire abdomen, arms, and back are covered in tattoos: *Hawks, lizards, dragons, butterflies, tigers, bears, oh my!*

Chef Kelly, in a rare show of emotion, drops her jaw, "Uhm, you're not going to be in that when service starts, are you?"

I love how she asked it like it was up to me, "What do you mean? You should see what Jessica is wearing."

Her eyes widen. I have to reassure her that I'm going to throw the Salvador Dali Lama robe over it before service starts.

"Just a little prank, chef."

It gets busy on the weekends. Me and Frederick are sweating our asses off. I start having weekly server dreams about being in the weeds: *I'll finish writing an order for a 10 top in the dream and hear the chef yelling for me, slamming on her hotel desk-style bell over and over again. Then I'll look down at the order pad, and it'll all be mush. Now, the people are looking at me, trying to change their orders. Their faces turn to those of giant rats! They're asking where their cheese plates are! Then, I'm outside the restaurant, going door to door, desperately asking the neighbors if they have any duck breast they could loan us. I try to find my way back to the chef's window because I hear her voice screaming for me. I do not recognize my surroundings. I just hear her voice, screaming at me from an indecipherable direction. Is she inside my head? Ahhhhhhhhh!*

"Did you ever hear the story about the server who had a regular customer who would always order scallops and not eat them? He just got in the habit of eating them himself. He thought it was her way of tipping him extra for what he thinks is superior service, which is just like regular service, except his tongue is up your ass the whole time." I pause and glance over at Frederick.

"There's always that smug little ass kisser server in a restaurant, the one who volunteers to 'keep an eye on things,' when the GM goes up to his office to order a prostitute and play internet poker. 'Remember to request me in your reservation notes,' goes the ass licker."

I scan the small audience of servers for guilt.

"So he's eating these scallops the lady leaves him for months, and then one day people see this skinny, rich lady sucking the juices out of the scallops and putting them back on the plate. She looks side to side to make sure it's clear before each scallop because she's embarrassed about it. She wants the flavor, but not the calories. This ass-kissy server has been eating sucked-on scallops! He doesn't believe it when his coworkers tell him, and next time she comes in, everyone that's clocked in is watching, including the poor guy that's been perfectly grilling these scallops for her. They all watch her, and sure enough, *slurp slurp... thoop,* she pops them surreptitiously into her palm, and quickly back onto the plate."

A look of horror begins to dawn on Jessica and Samantha's faces as I wrap up this week's installment of *restaurant horror stories*.

"Once her favorite server saw that he was broken. Three months later, he was a busboy again. Three months after that? Skid row."

"Eeeeewwwww," Samantha and Jessica go at once. I tell them restaurant tales like this from the lore to horrify them on the slower Wednesday nights when we all gather at the end of the bar and polish the same glasses twice.

After work, we all go to the Bloodhound and play pool; the owners, servers, cooks, and cafe employees. The cooks are all young white males from the culinary academy, as is the custom for mid to high-level fancy restaurants in San Francisco where the customers can see into the kitchen from the dining room. Cooking school, the biggest scam in town. They saddle you with $50,000 in debt with fairy tales about becoming an executive chef, and after three years of making $17 an hour, they will go to trade school. Poor fuckers. They don't know that now, and seem to be okay with the cooking life, despite the horizontal burns up and down their forearms from reaching into the ovens too hastily. Then, of course, there are the Red Bull and cocaine addictions. Ah, the invincibility of youth.

One night we're all drinking in there at The Bloodhound, and Christian is about to take a pool shot, and this chick bumps the back of his pool stick, making him scratch on the eightball. There's $20 in the antlers. I can't take it now! This bitch just cost me $20, is what she did. So, I charge over to her and spit beer foam into her hair through the space in my front teeth. Well, this gets me banned from The Bloodhound for like two months. I was getting sick of their app designer clientele anyways, so a break is fine. Dotty wants me to come over to her house after work all the time anyway, so she is a fan of the ban. Oh well, going to Dotty's house keeps me off the crack. Shit, I've been pretty good about not smoking that trash. I'm almost demonstrating an *arc of character* at this point.

We play poker in the restaurant some nights too. The owners Christian and Jon, generously open up the beer taps for us, and me and Frederick lose our money to the cooks in a poetic redistribution of the wealth. It's a great time in my life, the Radius years.

Viracocha

An amazing thing has happened; one of our street corner mates from the 16th and Mission open-mic is quite the handy lad. He turns the interiors of restaurants into, like, a Japanese whale hunting barn. *Viola!* Valencia Street's hottest new sushi restaurant is born. Using reclaimed wood, estate sale items, thrift store stuff, and whatever else he finds that is cool and looking for a new life.

This is a profitable venture, and he's gotten us a venue! Upstairs at Viracocha is like a typewriter store in a high ceilinged, Nordic barn. You can smell the hay coming off the wood, mixed with the grease from all the typewriters that are for sale. There are poetry chapbooks and nooks for poets to type in, including one that's up in the corner of the window where you have to climb a ladder to get to it. Outside, on Valencia Street, in the heart of The Mission, cyclists ride by and look up at a poet typing away in an upper, fishbowl workshop area. There is a giant Lord of the Rings type door for sale. A wooden swing hangs from the ceiling. There's a huge, burl-clawed bathtub in the bathroom, a library, and bicycles. If you ask for a price, the workers look as if they'd never considered selling that item. It's like a store where they aren't interested in selling anything.

The best part is what the hidden speakeasy leads to. The stairs lead down to a performance venue! There's seats, a raised stage, a bar—the works! And it's beautiful. Somehow unfancy and elegant both. It's hidden down here like a secret world that you have to be *in the know* to know it exists. We don't want the cops to know about it because we have no liquor license or even a permit for live entertainment. It's not that Jonathon can't afford these things necessarily. It's that we refuse to be licensed for what we do. It's fuckin' awesome. We still go to the corner every Thursday, but we start throwing shows here every other night of the week.

At one show, Baby Jesus has someone shave his head while he reads a poem on stage. Within minutes, I have some of the hair shoved down my pants, and I'm prancing around like Loki on an ether binge. At another show, I attempt to tape the world's first stand-up comedy double album. One record will be called *The Goat Lady's Son*; the other, *Love is a Rat Bastard From Hell*. Unfortunately, I abort the idea 15 minutes in due to an un-raucous crowd and me being too drunk to pull it off.

What an amazing place—a magical place! Someone dragged us in from the cold, and now look at us shine!

One night, it's time to premiere my play called: The Broken Tool. Guinevere and Dotty are playing the parts. Guinevere has arranged a roast of yours truly to kill a bit of time. As the play is only like six pages, I suppose that makes sense. There are about forty people in the audience. Decent turnout.

Guinevere has gotten some amazing people for roasters like Will Franken, the mentally insane headliner that the clubs won't touch because he really is quite insane. His characters are brilliant. The Marin Soccer Mom character, based on a lady who once accosted him after one of his performances, is just perfect, "Well, I saw that you had… a SHOW!" He swishes his hair, rolls his eyes, and curls his lip, "Is that what you call that? A SHOW?! Interesting."

Will does an impression of me from when his one-man show was in the main room at the Marsh Theatre, and I was running the comedy room. He'd sit out front chain-smoking Marlboro Reds, going over his act in his head. Then, he'd see me trying to fill the place up with all the foot traffic and decided to do an impression of it, "Hey! Comedy show! You like comedy?! Get the fuck in here!! Get in the train car—I mean comedy show!"

He convinces us he's charging up and down the sidewalk, the very sidewalk upstairs and outside this venue, but a few blocks up. "Hey!? DO YOU LIKE TO LAUGH?! You're gonna get in this show, and you're GOING TO LAUGH MOTHFUCKER!!!!!"

Next, we have Jamie DeWolf, great-grandson of L Ron Hubbard and legendary spoken word performer. He walks up to the mic with intent, "What can be said to roast a career that was stillborn dead? To a self-proclaimed scumbag, asshole, degenerate; the reason why condoms were invented, why babies are born defective, the root cause of yeast infections, and why every mic at The Purple Onion is herpes simplex infected."

The audience is shocked. Roasts are usually horrific, but this is Jamie Dewolf. This guy isn't going to put the mic back in the stand until I'm crying. Why did I agree to this?

"We heard he was moving from Frisco, and we were like, shit, can we help? I wish I had frequent flyer miles just to watch you fail somewhere else. But he's gotta follow his dreams, and sheep go to heaven and goats go south. But I got a question: how you gonna take a bite out of The Big Apple with a jaw full of meth mouth?"

I was teasing the idea of moving out to Brooklyn a while back. It didn't happen.

"He dreams of mermaids cuz he's all washed up… he can fit all his possessions in a garbage truck. The real reason he's moving is 'cuz that stripper you fucked from the strip club is now knocked up. You're hoping her ex-con husband don't get out of jail and you get your body broke. And this guy's funny? When? Just cuz he sounds like the angriest midget alive, or Bobcat Goldthwaite getting choked?"

"Haha," they go. *Did that guy get out of prison?*

"I heard you were great, funny as fuck, before you got hit by the bus. They must have broken every funny bone in your body. Now he's been bombing so long they call him MC Kamikaze. And his taste in women? Sheeeeiiit. Where do I begin?"

I can feel the highly sensitive Dotty tighten with rage in the back of the room.

"You're not a hero just cuz you love heroin. Dancing with Mr. Brownstone, the White Lady, and Mary Jane. No wonder your life is a failure, 'cuz everything you do is *in vein.*"

He taps the microphone head on the inside of his elbow.

Some of the audience is looking at me, like, "You shoot dope?" I look at them and shrug my shoulders, like, *This dude is full of shit, man. Everyone knows I just drink whiskey and tequila, maybe smoke a $20 rock on the weekends.* Jamie doesn't care. He looks like he's having the time of his life up there. His eyes are locked onto me. This is all protected in The Roaster's Bible; rumors, outright lies, it's a-l-l-l legal. Oh look, he's got more,

"Bragging how more women have rode him than a clown's uni-bike, and if they won't fuck him, he brands them a dyke, he's so subversive a real rebel, right? A revolutionary act? Bullshit. He's the only hipster in The Mission without a trucker hat. He turns into a bro asap when he texts, 'Seriously, where's the pussy at?'"

"Haha," I should be waving 'no,' at all this shit in denial, but it's too funny. Does me laughing admit guilt? Fuck it, let them think I shoot heroin, I guess.

"The pussy's not with you, dude. When you use so many needles, your friends call you voodoo. You ain't special just 'cuz you have an extra chromosome, and burying you with a mic in a mass grave is the only way you won't technically die alone. The only man with more mental problems than me, when your whole life has been shit from the beginning, it's only fitting you grew up in a TP."

"Haha," they go. Get it? TP? Toilet Paper? A bit of a stretch lyricality-wise.

"The scourge of the suburbs, the product of marijuana damaged sperm your life's been a joke since your hippie mother's hymen broke. We've all heard your sob story growing up in the hard streets of Santa Cruz, or Ukiah, or was it Santa Barbara?"

Not a lot of fact-checking went on in the writing of this roast. I gotta be honest. Hilarious as shit, though.

"Molested so young you thought a penis was a pacifier, snorting it up with dealers saying someday I'm gonna be funnier than Richard Pryor, ran out of town 'cuz you snitched on so many friends they called you the town cryer, you'll never blow up, 'cuz you have the drive of a car with a slashed tire."

The poor poets in the basement of Viracocha are starting to look sad now. Unfortunately for them, it seems like Jamie is just getting started. Technically, he is a *spoken word* poet just like them, but he is at the more ruthless end of the breed. Hard to believe they're from the same species. The *battle rap* section of Tourettes is like an hour out of the show every month, so he's *from* this culture—a ringleader of it, actually.

"Fuck this ghost of a roast, drag this dog out behind the barn and make him forcibly retire. You'll never succeed 'cuz you live life like abortion's only living survivor. You suck, you talentless, two-bit hack, the ghost of Bill Hicks tumor called, and wants his fucking style back. This ain't a roast; It's an intervention, quit with your sobriety charade and get back on the smack, 'cuz the only time you've been on point is when the syringe is in your tracks."

Brutal. This guy really loves this. There can't be more, can there? Haha, Jeezus fuckin' Christ.

"And I could go on all night about your pedophile mustache, your bloated tick of a belly, and the hymens you've destroyed, but let's cut it short and hunt his hobbled, handicapped ass through The Tenderloin just for sport. Punch this walking punchline, stab him to death with a spork, then tie him to a plummeting airplane aimed at a skyscraper and hit self abort, 'cuz when you move to The Big Apple you'll be the second worst disaster to ever hit New York."

He puts the mic back in the stand, and the audience is just like, *What the fuck?*

"Haha," goes pretty much just me.

Now, it's time for my play to be performed by Guinevere Q, and Dotty, who is telling everyone she's my girlfriend now. I guess I have a girlfriend again already. Whatever keeps me out of The Tenderloin. They pretty much nail it exactly, so I'll just put that here as I originally wrote it. Let's pretend it isn't a bit of an awkward segway from Jamie's roast:

The Broken Tool

by JC Scales

Int. / A living room is occupied by GUINEVERE "He had his dick in my face" Q, A saucy, do it yourself kind of girl, who sits at a small table using an ELECTRIC SCREWDRIVER on a board (The electric screwdriver can bend in the middle, important to remember.)

Her roommate DOTTY comes into the room looking worried and sheepish.

Guinevere stops screwing the driver and attends to her, but still from her seat.

GUINEVERE: What's with the poopy face, Doll Butt? You realize you're hot, don't you? You really should be enjoying that.

DOTTY: I broke another one.

GUINEVERE: You're kidding me? That's three this week! What are you doing?! Last time we had to rummage through Trader Joe's *and* Bed Bath and Beyond for an hour to find a new one!

DOTTY: I know, I know. I came in here so you'd make me feel better.

GUINEVERE: Ok, I will get around to that, but hear this: Einstein stated that the definition of insanity is repeating the same motion expecting a different outcome, and you are like the king of that shit.

DOTTY: I'm just trying to engage the button, Guinevere! But it's just inside the hole, and the tool barely passes the button before it hits the wall surface again. *(all the while Dotty has taken the ELECTRIC SCREWDRIVER, which bends in the middle at the pressing of a button, and demonstrates)* I try to do this flip twist move at the opening to just try to scrape the button... and the tool jams and snaps in the middle.

GUINEVERE: The button is where?

DOTTY: Like less than a half-inch in. I'm just not as handy with tools as you Guinevere, it's supposed to be like that. After all, you *are* the lesbian. Your half of the closet has way more flannel and mud-crusted boots.

GUINEVERE: Don't put me in a box just because I'm in touch with my pussy, okay? So tell me again? The button on that unit is supposed to be farther in.

DOTTY: That's the problem! I've been telling you. I need a tool that bends up more at the end to pop into that button, but I'm afraid the next time that thing snaps, I'm going to have to go to the emergency room and they'll remember I'm the one that gave them the fake name last time.

Dotty does an impression of the future intake worker at S.F General Hospital.
DOTTY: Oh look, it's—looks at paperwork—Chiquita Banana Lady.

GUINEVERE: It is amazing how much of smart asses they are to people who are bleeding. Okay, the tool keeps snapping because the button is too close to the outside of the hole. You're sure it's only a half-inch?

DOTTY: Yes, even less maybe. The guy who made it wasn't paying attention, and he fucked me over forever.

Gwenivere: He **is** supposed to be a man.

Dotty looks upward angrily.

DOTTY: Yes, he is.

GUINEVERE: Ok, so show me what's happening exactly.

Dotty sits for a second in contemplation then goes and straddles the small table.

DOTTY: Okay, so I'm on his cock, and I'm trying to get the curved tip to scrape my G-spot, but as we've discussed, god, or my dad's baby batter had too much pot in it, and now my G-spot is too close to the fuckin' entrance.

GUINEVERE: If lesbians believed in god, I would say, 'He is an angry god.' I guess I could say, 'He is an angry beaver.'

DOTTY: So I have to do a kind of *flick move* by twisting and smearing the head of his cock into my clit first, then popping it up into the hole while jumping down on it with all the force I can. If the tip only flicks and doesn't fold, it all goes perfectly. It's a feeling like no other. But if the tip doesn't flick into the hole and pop the button, if it stays smeared into the clit, it fucking just folds in the middle. Like in half.

GUINEVERE: So this just happened?

DOTTY: Yes.

GUINEVERE: Where is he?

DOTTY: He's in our room.

GUINEVERE: Fuck. What does it look like in there?

DOTTY: Well, the dick snapped off in the middle, and he bled out clutching the broken half, cursing me to hell.

GUINEVERE: So basically the same shit as last week?

DOTTY: Basically… In rosier news, our Jerusalem Artichoke flowers look amazing from all the snapped dicks we've been throwing into the compost.

GUINEVERE: Wait a minute! I've got it. I know a guy that can help you. He's got the shaped cock you need!

DOTTY: Uhm, you're a lesbian. What do you know 'bout dat deeeeock?

GUINEVERE: Well, there's no such thing as a full-time lesbian. Plastic has its limitations. Sometimes we drive around in a van, kidnap a guy, and hate fuck him.

DOTTY: Really?

GUINEVERE: Yeah. You got your cellphone?

DOTTY: Yes.

GUINEVERE: Go on Match.com and look up BananaCockBoyCorkscrew72.

Dotty does it.

DOTTY: Oh my god, that's the cock that I need! A banana corkscrew shaped wang. His status is swinger, so that's good. Oh fuck, he's got pictures of Brazil in his last album update. You don't think he moved to Brazil, do you? How did his penis become graced with the qualities of a banana *and* a corkscrew?

GUINEVERE: He's from a tropical environment, and he's part pig.

DOTTY: His family lives in Brazil? He probably did move there! Fuck! Lets pray just in case there is actually a god.

GUINEVERE: Okay

They get on their knees and face front side by side and pray
IN UNISON: Please god, don't let Banana Corkscrew Cock
Boy have moved to Brazil. Dotty is a special girl with a special problem that only CorkscrewB ananaBoyCock72 can solve.

They exhale and slowly let their heads lower. A short moment elapses and...

GUINEVERE: What if he **is** in Rio?

Dotty raises her head with finality and determination.

DOTTY: Well, then I guess I'm goin' to the Copa-fuckin-Cabana.

Working at Mitchell Brothers Strip Club

I'm supposed to show up for my shift at seven at the Mitchell Brothers strip club on O'Farrell Street. Jamie DeWolf has scored Tourettes Without Regrets a show in there. We will be mixing in with the strippers and making a sexually charged variety show for the ages. I'm forced to drag along Dotty, who is scared I might see some titties, not under her supervision. She keeps insisting she's my girlfriend. She is attached to my hip and mad dogs, any girl who even looks our way. My bosses are here too. Christian leaves the VIP room and can't get back up here. I can hear him yelling, "I'm with Scales!" at the bottom of the stairs. "Should I get him?" I ask Jon, the other owner of Radius. "Nah, let him chill for a few."

We are upstairs in the manager's office. There's a nice pool table, buckets and buckets of beer, and appetizers galore. Some people are doing blow, excitedly going over their act. Everyone is in a great mood.

This is Robert Crumb, the cartoonist's favorite place to be. From the number of his original drawings framed on the walls upstairs, I'm going to guess he didn't have the money to afford to go into the Champagne Room as much as he actually *did* go in there. After coming up short on his tab, I wonder if he had to sit in the manager's office and do these. Also, which of these large-assed women in the drawings were current employees of the Mitchell Brothers at the time? *Hmmm. I think that one.*

I walk into the batter's box next to the stage to get a moment to myself. Sissy, Jamie's girlfriend, is getting off stage, and her naked chest is covered in whip cream. "You want to wipe this off?" She asks me. Before I know what I'm doing, I'm wiping off the whipped cream from her perfect little apple titties. "Shit, won't Jamie get pissed if he sees?"

"Maybe. Doesn't that make it funner?" she responds, wickedly.

I thought I was next, but some chubby, bearded dudes with tassels on their man tits walk by me after they're announced. I'm a little confused as there are multiple stages being simultaneously performed on. Am I in the wrong place? I walk back out into the tight hallway to look for the stage manager so they can call me an idiot. The upstairs hall is lined with performers and feel coppers. I guess I'd be calling the kettle black, considering what just happened. I guess I'll just let my ass get slapped. An Amazonian spoken word performer gives me a good one, and she says, "You gonna helicopter that cock on stage for us today, big boy."

Her boyfriend and co-performer are standing there laughing. You see, he knows we are just playing our roles as hypersexual circus performers for the show's benefit. Dotty, however, isn't as understanding. *Fuck.* Why didn't I just tell her I had a dentist appointment today or something? Her face is so sour she could make lemonade by looking at some water. I get scared she's about to attack the Amazonian chick, which would be interesting to watch because the Amazonian is 6 feet and made of muscle. Dotty would have to climb up on something and jump downwards.

Finally, I get on stage. I step towards the stripper pole and the mic-stand.

"Okay. Let's give it up for Jamie for getting us this show. Jamie is one of the only people to ever get kicked out of a cult for being too hardcore. His great grandfather, L Ron Hubbard, took one look at Jamie after he was born, lit up a cigar, and put it out on Jamie's face. So red and brillowy was his hair, the Church of Scientology mostly used him to get the tough gunk out of the corners of pots and pans."

"This piece of shit is so shady they kicked him out of the Church of fucking Scientology. Let that sink in. He claims to have escaped. Yeah right. He 'escaped,'"—fingers up in the quote position—"with a one-way ticket in business class, paid for by L Ron himself. L Ron warned if Jamie ever tried to come back, he would let Tom Cruise take him camping again."

"Ewwww." You can hear Jamie laughing.

"Do you guys know why Tourettes is an 18 and over show?"

"Why?" goes the crowd.

"Because by the time you're 21, Jamie doesn't want to fuck you anymore. He wasn't going to do shows for a crowd he didn't want to fuck. Barely Legal isn't a magazine to him; it's a requirement."

"Have you ever been to an after party at this guy's house? It's like a casting call for a sequel to *Gummo*."

Okay, I'm not going to get into the whole roast, but I had to get even with him for when he roasted me. It goes on, and it gets progressively worse. I'm sorry, the nature of roasts is like this. You just look at your friend and exaggerate and outright makeup shit about them to get laughs. I'm not sure it's healthy, but it's fun if you're the roaster. It's hard to put a reader into the context of a roast. It's horrific, but it's what you might do if you are from a shattered childhood and you want to express love for your friend. Look how fucked up a comedy roast is on Comedy Central. That's just the mainstream. This is a real-life strip club. What do you think is going to happen in here? A lot of childhood trauma has been displayed on these stages over the years. Why should tonight be any different?

"I'd like to take this time to give it up for the real heroes in this establishment, fuck Jamie DeWolf and his torn-up asshole that he decorates as a Greyhound station to try and fool the wayward youth of America into going into."

"Haha," goes Jamie.

"The strippers!!! Who else could look out at the mangy, happy hour audience of your average strip club, and turn 'Welcome to the Jungle' into high art, while looking out into those desperate faces?! All the while whispering into their ears, 'You have a magical dick.' And people? Every guy alive needs to hear from time to time that he has a magic dick! Gay, straight, or Morrisey. Even ugly guys. **Especially** ugly guys, like Jamie DeWolf."

"Haha."

"All of our mother's reassurances that nobody is better than us, that sharing is caring, and love will always win; once you turn eight, if you're even remotely less than an idiot, you realize that's all bullshit. Now you just need to hear that you have a penis that can cast spells, by a girl that in okay lighting, could be described as a seven. And she needs to seem like she means it! If our penises remain uncomplimented, uncelebrated, and unfeared by hotties, we become convinced that our dicks are benign and ineffective. They become angry, one-eyed, albino mud snakes, squirming in the filth, blind to all but their own misery. So we twist and abuse them with coarse, wool socks... and grainy, hardcore midget porn!"

"Oh fuck," someone recognizes that my bit sees them.

"The uncomplimented dicks become isolated and hateful, potentially twisting into dangerous, horrible, assault mallets. If only Jeffrey Dahmer had been told he had a voodoo dick once or twice, he might have turned out to be a nice guy."

"Haha."

"If someone would have just told Dick Cheney that his lumpy, grey, spotted German helmet was unique and arousing, while still being a source of supernatural potency. If some heroic girl had just jumped on the grenade, bitten the bullet? Dick wouldn't have destroyed 66 percent of the planet WITH grenades and bullets."

I know Obama has been the president for over a year now, but I'm having trouble letting the Bush Administration just walk away unscathed.

"It's the root of all wars, all desperation: fear of a less than regular penis."

A sigh of agreeance and light applause.

"I wish I could trade places with a stripper for a day and go back in time and whisper 'Condoleeza? Your penis while toothed, and unusual on a girl, is sparkly and powerful.'"

Some get up and clap. I bow and put the mic back in the stand. Jamie's brother looks ready to throw flowers onto the stage.

When I get off stage, Dotty has left in a fury. Good, now I can actually have some fun.

Me, Jon, and Christian go and take some seats in the main room, and there is just regular stripping going on. A girl slips on the pole and slides down onto her head from eight feet up and upside down, shortening her performance. *Shit. Is she alright?* We'll never know.

Next, there is a mock boxing match between two strippers. One gets knocked down, the winner pulls down her boxing shorts and reveals a massive strap on, which she then plunges deep into the defeated stripper's pussy, repeatedly. The crowd goes nuts. I'm glad I don't have to follow *that.*

I look over at my two smiling bosses, and I think, *I better get the large parties this weekend, you little perverts.*

Dotty and the Pee Sticks

I'm going to do it—I'm going to break up with Dotty, even though our relationship is mostly in her mind. It's true. We've had regular sex for months because her pussy is so tiny I don't know if I should cum or call 911. Her pussy gets murdered every time. Should I cover it with a miniature sheet? When I fuck her, I feel my dick veering left or right towards whichever ovary is riper. I take more and more risks of spilling the payload into her shallow *baby bunker.* If precum has any inkling of life in it, then I'm going to be in trouble because my dick gets so close to the egg it probably looks like a hollandaised brunch item when I'm finished. After ten years of swearing off condoms and no babies have resulted, I've gotten a little sloppy. *Hey man, I must be sterile. Let me just glaze that egg a little.*

Well, apparently, Dotty's vajay is as fertile as it is shallow. The egg is close to the outside because it knows it's going to go there. At least that's what the little pee stick is telling us right now.

Wow. I just... huh?

I'm almost 40, and I've never gotten a girl pregnant that I know of; I mean, back in the old days, they probably just went and had it done without telling me. What good would it have done to let me in on the decision? I had no money to pay for the abortion, much less the kid.

Well, two sticks later, it looks serious. She can tell from my reaction I'm not into it. I mean, this chick is possessive, neurotic, *and* aggressive. As a baby mama? Fuck no. *How do I convince her to get an abortion?*—this is the only thought on my mind. Between her craziness and mine, this kid would be born with the swastika already carved in its forehead.

"I knew you weren't going to let me have it!" she screams when I break down crying and begging. *Not this, not with her*. I've never been this stressed in my life. So how do I convince her?

Eventually, she relents. We go in, and I hold her hand while a doctor puts a wand in her *carpeted piano* to confirm that, yes, there is a little nugget in there. We schedule the procedure and I have to dote on her in the meantime. She threatens to change her mind a few times, throwing me into a convulsive panic. I understand that this is what her whole biology is telling her that this is what she was created to do—but this **cannot** happen. This chick is crazier than me. This kid's life would be like mine was. I can't have a kid unless I know I can spare them of that. I don't regret my life, but I don't imagine anyone would have the same luck in barely escaping doom so many times.

We get the abortion. I feel terrible. Dotty cries and accuses us of being murderers. She curses me for relying on the *pullout method*. She curses me for not having to get the surgery too. I offer to get a vasectomy so that I receive a blade as well. I really would have if I had health insurance.

I put in a few weeks more and break up with her. Her insanity only gets worse. One night, we're downstairs in the Bart station, and a chubby crust punk girl does a splendid rendition of House of the Rising Sun. The acoustics on the Bart platforms is pretty epic. I give the acoustic guitarist a buck and compliment her singing. When we get on the train, Dotty is like, "Why don't you just go with that girl? She's such a good fucking singer. I bet her pussy is awesome! Go get that awesome pussy, Scales!"

"What the fuck? Ok, look, Dotty. Have you been diagnosed with neurotic tendencies? Because this shit is crazy."

"Oh, look who's projecting! It's mister 'Let me go tell a crowd of strangers about some pussy I recently strangled with my dick!"

"I mean, touche, but just because I'm a little crazy doesn't mean we should be *mixing* our crazies. So I think I'm going to go back to the wallflower types," I say.

"Go! Go get you a wallflower, Scales! Some boring, basic chick with ice in her cunt. Go!" she pushes me out into the aisle where people are staring at this point. Just then, the train pulls up to the Civic Center station, and I get off, into the pissiest station in America.

I thought dating a fellow performer for once would help the creative process. It did but almost killed the rest. It doesn't matter how much you're writing if it's all in feces on the *loony bin* walls. They just wash it away. Bye, Dotty.

The Robots are Coming, and They are Us

It's 2011—0—App designers are taking over the world—0—the internet is to propaganda as vape pens are to tobacco—0—just a shiny new box for an old poison. *R...G....bleat... stewp! &*%@...* ***bzzzzrup!***

Your phone now notices if you stop scrolling to look at a horrific photo of a beaten dog. A message is sent directly to Sarah McLaughlin, alerting her to your vulnerability. As long as the internet exists, you will be permanently filed as a *Reacts strongly to pictures of beaten dogs,* person. Now, you will be horror spammed to tears every fucking day until you've donated to every dog shelter this side of Dayton. Once they know what horrifies you, the "nonprofits" have your soul in a jar. Every tear, a $20 bill to them. Your crumpled body in despair? A plane ticket to Cancun.

They repackage that horror in ten different ways and bondo it into your feed every few hours. How many bloody dogs or *narco* beheadings can we see before we get depressed? Do they give a fuck? Not as long as you send that bloody dog money to Sarah McLaughlin. Horror. Fear. That's what gets clicks. Nothing matters but getting clicks now.

Management has been replaced by Yelp and the online service questionnaire, where if you don't mark every question with a big smiley face, the person who sold you the product is in trouble, not the product. The customers have been told that they are always right and nothing could be further from the truth. Their cognitive dissonance the second they come in contact with a customer service representative is staggering—woe for the poor sap whose job is dealing with the public these days.

Propaganda's ultimate goal is to create a shared psychosis. By 2011 the internet is the greatest tool propaganda has ever had. Millions of cults compete for each brain. There are no breadcrumbs behind you deep in the rabbit hole.

The big-box corps have completed their strangulations of the *mom and pop* stores. Even Trader Joe's, with their medium-sized stores and Hawaiian shirted, helpful managers, throw off a chummy, neighborhood vibe. Don't be confused; Trader Joe attends board meetings. More like Traitor Joe's, am I right?

These stores celebrate their victory by offering croissants made by Chinese child slaves at 40 cents a pop. So orgiastic is the glee of these multi-death corporations such as Target, Walmart, and Costco, their victory celebrations only stop short of hanging the flayed and lifeless bodies of mom and pop themselves outside their own foreclosed storefronts. The Marin soccer moms rejoice at this mass killing as they push around industrial carts full of four-dollar chardonnay. I love you, Costco, but it looks like I might have to burn you down.

Taking advantage of the less fun environment on the eve year of the Mayan prophecy is the politically correct movement, which doesn't want to help anybody. It mostly just wants you to talk how it wants. It wants you to try and sound a little more corporate, and if you can't muster that, at least collegiate—but you'll have to take the corresponding pay cut. This week, Politically Correct Headquarters states that laughing at something means you condone it. What? For me, it's usually the fuckin' reverse. I'm generally laughing at some idiot that I would use as the *opposite* of a role model. Often that's myself. A lot of my words can be used in wise ways, folks, but I wouldn't try to copy or hold my life up as a *how-to guide*.

Laughing at something doesn't have to support or forgive the behavior in the shit show you're laughing at. It can be shaming it; it can be not giving a fuck that much. Sometimes it's okay to laugh at absurd shit without overthinking it because wait for it... life is fucking absurd. If everyone has to morally cosign every chuckle before letting it out, then no one will laugh anymore. And that's what is indeed happening. Even a playground full of children doesn't sound as exuberant as it used to. You're fucking up the kids. ENOUGH!!! Lighten the fuck up, folks. Life is supposed to be fun. It might be our last party here. It might be time to give the lizards another shot.

It would be one thing if those laughs were going somewhere else, but they aren't. We are laughing less as a society because you can't laugh at anything until you've untangled the joke. You have to make sure you're not being tricked into helping the comedian punch down or some bullshit.

By the time you're all, "Okay, that one was okay," the comedian or coworker is halfway through their next joke.

I've decided my comedy will be the enemy of all this. I will do my best to exemplify the disconnected and the disenfranchised who have **found** their power. So gather up, all ye freaks! I shall suckle you at my teat of filth and rage! We will reveal what's behind the mask of the pretty and the safe. We will pick the locks the media puppet-masters have placed on our brains. The enemies are invisible now, and we will need to use the techniques of the shamans to fight them.

Here is another seemingly impossible cultural shift in the generation since I first left my heart in San Francisco: the punkers and the hippies have been overrun and replaced by the techies and the hipsters! Holy shit! The techies and the hipsters have to explain their seizing of these lands in a way that justifies it, so they claim the original occupants are inferior, outdated. Then they ignore them as they starve and shoot up, homeless on the sidewalks in front of the very houses they used to live in.

The hippies and the punks are better than the techies and the hipsters. Just as *all* colonized people are better than their colonizers. What do the hipsters contribute besides $200 Nikes and cappuccinos with designs in the foam? Hipsters are just the cleaned-up version of the punkers and the hippies that the techies prefer to use as their food and beverage slaves. The punks and hippies wouldn't show back up with the sandwiches half the time, so they got replaced with fashion school students posing as SoundCloud rappers.

At least the hippies and the punkers stood for something: "Be kind to mother earth" and "Fuck the cops." So what if they smelled a little? These new San Franciscans are empty, vapid. Get rid of them. I want the smelly ones indoors again and the ones indoors outdoors until they get a little smelly; maybe develop a little more character. Everyone switch places!

Aren't the real firewalls in our hearts?

By 2011 we realize Obama isn't the savior we had hoped he would be. The gig economy, with Air Fee and Fee and (L)Uber at the helm, will soon turn us all into part-time hoteliers and taxi drivers, as we try and get by in the ever constricting decline of capitalism. What the fuck is this shit?

A huge pastime has emerged using photoshop to lay the captions on top of photos in an attempt to entertain each other. Memes are pretty cool, actually, a weird relative of cartoon strips and bumper stickers? When that cat saying "I can haz cheeseburger?" comes out, many people think, *Here is our god! No one else will ever replicate this level of hilarity. Someone find him! Give him all the cheeseburgers he requires!"* Now millions of people are doing it. Life is getting weird really fast, you guys. Is it because I live and exist in the middle of the tech sector of San Francisco? Judging from the amount of Twitter profiles in use, I'd have to say this shit is global. At least Obama tells us about how the Pentagon budget can't be messed with in a cool, silky voice.

Ticketmaster has finalized its merger with Live Nation. Ticketing and venues: corporatized, digitized and finalized. The musicians are really going to feel a squeeze now. If they thought the record company contracts were confusing, wait until they read the licensing agreements to the streaming services. Just kidding, they won't read them. Pandora is popular now. It succeeds where Napster failed. Soon, Spotify will perfect the art of squeezing the artist, and the bass players of the world will have even more things to cry about when they see their four-dollar royalty checks. Four dollar checks for 90,000 streams of their song. The coffee gopher at Capitol Records will now make more than the members of 96 percent of bands, culminating in that coffee gopher's lifelong dream coming true—a truly low bar aiming piece of shit. In the cosmos can be heard a huge groan of collective despair from every decent band on every coast.

In 2011 everyone is a full-blown addict to their phones. People see me on my flip phone, and they don't even want to deal with me. They think if you don't have the latest I-Phone, you might slow them down. "Must run fast, capitalism running me down. Aaaaah."

Click-baitey shit like Buzzfeed's, "Top ten list of horrible apps that are destroying the minds of America's youth. Spoiler alert: Buzzfeed made the list!" So many strong reactions are provoked out of you each day in an attempt to get you to click a link that you are justifiably exhausted, sad, and angry by dinner.

It's like the impulse control parts of our brains have been turned off through pixel hypnosis, so we'll buy more stuff.

People can't even enjoy a fuckin' waterfall without clutching for their I-phone camera.

Technology has dramatically helped put everyone into credit slavery. The ones that squeal from the pain are most likely to turn in any corner cutters they know. Call them into the office—you think the police have been militarized? Wait until you see what they've done with Human Resources.

Art and music are now "content." You don't contemplate it; you scroll by it. You listen to it once with cheap earbuds and forget about it. You barely have to pay for it because it's likely of low quality—but boy, isn't there a shitload **of** it?! American's have been convinced that having, consuming, or being exposed to fewer things of better quality is a stupid way to spend your time. Why do that when you could be bombarded by a million things that vary in quality from pretty good to garbage, all at once? ***More! More! More!*** The Americans demand, "And we want it for pennies on the dollar! Free, if possible."

Even if you're lucky enough to find a halfway decent rabbit hole, the artist probably didn't get paid much. Maybe they got "exposure." This is why the art sucks now. Real artists live in an encampment on the side of a river. Maybe that's what they mean by "exposure," it's to the elements.

The CEO of Spotify is worse than a sleepover at Cosby's house. Drag him behind a motorcycle by his balls! How about looking up local bands and buying their music from them? Leave the parasites out of it. Fuck the record companies! Fuck the advertisers! Fuck the Weinstein brothers, and fuck Zuckerberg. Fuck Twitter, and fuck you if they are as far as you're willing to search for entertainment.

In one generation, we've gone from "Don't come home until dark" to "Never go outside again!" to "I don't want to go outside anyway, just let me play video games." Kidnapping rates haven't changed much; what has? The amount of fear your screens shove into your brain all day long. Nothing sells like fear.

In 2011, if you think companies aren't trying to figure out how to manipulate social justice *Twitter mobs,* and probably are already? Well, have I got a decaf latte for you. Wait until I tell you about five-star internet reviews—half are written by Indian children who wouldn't know an Amazon package from an emu. Okay, I'm hearing they have emus.

And to top it all off: Less. Than. A. Fucking. YEAR. after being convicted of killing Oscar Grant, Johannes Mehserle is getting released EARLY from jail on June 13, 2011. Fuck that! Me and Jon, the owner at Radius, go down to Oakland and get tear-gassed. Whatever I might say about restaurant bosses, this fucker is down enough for the cause to mix it up in the streets of Oakland with the cops. I mean, he didn't throw any bottles or anything, but still. That's a pretty *down for whatever* boss if you ask me.

I'm sorry I have to say this, but I'm not one for pretending. Things are looking dicey. This internet shit is close to checkmating the human species. Right about the time AI perfects consciousness mimicking in their gun-wielding robot dogs, we'll be at the edge of death anyway. Will the dogs get us first, or will we just all starve? Forgetting to eat, thinking the nutrients are in our IOS updates? Wake up, folks!! This is our last chance. I believe in us. Unfortunately, we don't see problems until they become fires. Well, I definitely smell smoke. There's gotta be some flames around here somewhere!

Pride: Facebook

Greed: Amazon

Lust: Youporn

Gluttony: Yelp

Envy: Instagram

Wrath: 4chan

Sloth: Candy Crush

Clown Porn

Some time passes. The first half of 2012 goes by smoothly for me as if it knows that, while it can't offer me an entire year of peace, I at least need a season of non-chaos, or I'll probably die. The abortion, all the injuries, the crack-smoking, the raw dogging of dangerous whores. Even a pedigreed gutter champion like me needs a break. I've been working at Radius five nights a week. I've taken a break from comedy, only going out twice a week or so to perform. Things long ago took a turn for the weird down in Moss Alley, but nothing I can't handle. I've never made it for this long at a house. I'm not sure how to proceed. There's a reason Fear and Loathing is a short book. I've seen some weird, crazy shit in every single part of this building—things you can't just unsee.

The Giants win their second World Series in three years. They swept the poor Detroit Tigers. Tim Lincecum, Brian Wilson, Hunter Pence, and Tony Romo seem like dudes you'd do mushroom shakes with at a *full moon party* in Thailand, not Major League Baseball players. They call them the Band of Misfits. They are also the best baseball players alive. They whisper of an old San Francisco that is past now; brilliant and talented weirdos who know nothing other than betting it all. It's nice to know there are still signs of that, if only in whispers. You only need a spark to light a new bonfire. I'm losing my battle to turn the city into a mass smartphone burning ceremony that ends in storytelling and dancing barefooted at the edge of the flames. I'm just resting before wading back into the hurricane.

Cash comes over one day with his new girlfriend. Apparently, running away while his last girlfriend lay on the ground with a broken hip—and I had to knock out her assailant—didn't bode well for *that* relationship.

I don't really know if that had anything to do with their breakup, just a guess. Cash is a little Kevin Baconey, David Bowie-ish, waifey dude with body modifications—split lizard tongue, and other assorted self butcheries. Hopefully, it helps deal with his childhood trauma. You remember him. He seems downtrodden, a departure from his usual bubbly, helium-voiced self. He has good reason to be sad, though.

This girl, Holly, a short blonde girl, is his fiance. They've decided to get hitched quick because she has terminal cancer. You can see it in her complexion. She's in the second half of the battle. They're running around trying to fill a few bucket list slots. It must be a pretty exciting bucket list since she's the inventor of clown porn. As a comedian, this would be a top candidate for us to marry. Cash is really just doing the predictable thing here.

We talk a little, and I run out of stuff pretty quick. I'm taken aback by the situation. What do you talk about with someone who is about to die? *Do you hope you come back as an eagle? I'd want to be a jaguar or an eagle.* I awkwardly think about saying, unsure how to do this. I value my ability to cheer up the depressed, but I think I fail on this one. It's true; Holly is the pioneer of clown porn. I feel even weirder talking about that. *Which clown accessories do you bring into it? Are there sad clowns jacking off in the background?* I make them something shitty to eat because I didn't think ahead. What beverage do you offer someone in that condition? You might as well drink beer, right? Or does that interfere with the pills they must have her on? Fuck, man. I should have thought this out a little better. I'm just kind of a *wing-it* type of dude. This is a tricky situation. Just smile and be supportive, I guess.

We all just kind of sit there sad, talking a little bit. I feel like you just talk about anything but the elephant in the room, right? So I work my way through it like a rat race victim works his way to Friday.

I feel bad for the girl. She looks barely 30. I hope I just go all at once. The front line of the revolution, even if I'm 50 by the time it ever gets here. If I get fucked up on the battlefield, but it's like a slow bleed? I'll just pull the pin on a grenade when the next Bezos hired rent-a-soldier runs by; take both of us out. Anything but cancer. Who that has seen that shit close up thinks there's a fuckin' god? If he exists, he's an asshole, and I'd like to pour hot lava down his asshole.

It's beautiful what Cash is doing. Comedians are even more tragic than you think. We love the broken things that were thrown away. We take it as a serious part of our job to console them in some way. Some comics have given up on enlightening the masses, now functioning mostly to offer comfort to the most broken of them. In the end, we *are* them.

This girl might have spent the last few weeks of her life by herself. Porn stars usually only have party friends who drift away when you hit bottom. Their family is probably the reason they're even *in* porn, so that's out: lonely shit, man.

Good for you, Cash, you sweet boy. They leave after a while. She'll be dead in two months. Cash will be crushed as hard as if the marriage had lasted 30 years. I have to snooze his Facebook for 30 days because he's making me cry too much.

I have an idea: Let's normalize sex work. Take the rapey, kidnappy, hard drug aspects out of it. There are more than enough lazy, hot people that would rather spread their cheeks than work hard, or go to college. And bless their souls for it. As the world needs sandwich makers, so does it also need lunch break cock suckers. Normalize it—along with sex generally—and mass shootings will go down starting immediately in this fucked up country. There is no need to trick 18-year-old kids into whoring at the Hollywood Greyhound, using Machiavellian mental manipulation techniques and meth. If it were respected and regulated, these boys and girls would be happier and safer.

Incels could have their hands held down the path of healthy sexuality until they get the hang of it—for an affordable fee—and we could all be way better off. This fuckin' country needs to wise up before it's too late. Call your fuckin' senator and tell them that! Make pussy as easy and cheap to get as a gun around here.

The girlfriend experience is $30 a day in Thailand. In America, it's $3000 a day. So let's meet in the middle somewhere. How about "I'll fuck you and talk to you nicely for 15 minutes afterward for $150?" If the incels can't afford that, we'll have to send out a pussy stimulus. Or, the other choice is just to keep raising a bunch of sexually repressed mass murderers. That makes sense.

Relationships are rough. Wendy was a major ball breaker that was never happy with any amount of progress. Then, with Dotty, I had my first abortion that I knew of. What a year that was. I tossed and turned over the Dotty debacle for a week or so, but, being hardened by life in many ways, I recover quicker from stuff that's outside of me. Dotty, because the little pre-baby was *inside* her, took it rougher. Also, women's whole biology is about having babies. They'll have a baby inside a volcano if they have to. So the time remaining that I spent with her was just to not leave her like that. Purely obligation. It didn't take too long into the relationship to realize that she had what you'd call a *high anxiety baseline.* Remember, I was trying to figure out how to ditch this crazy chick when she showed me that pee stick. Imagine how fucked up *that* day was. Shit. My stomach hurt just saying that. Maybe I'll get my wires snipped. The money has been good at Radius. I could probably afford it now. Then I could just spray my jizz willy-nilly. That's worth a few grand. I'll fill up an ice cube tray in case I change my mind later. Cover my little jizz cubes with saran wrap to keep it fresher.

I had a few girlfriends back in 2010. They cleaned me up. I even have a dentist now. It's a new year, time to get back to old ways. A year of drinking less and cutting out the crack entirely has improved my sense of general well-being. I should probably ruin that. I guess I could dabble with some crack.

I hit the reliable corner, the one the Tenderloin Post Office is on. It's covered with Hondurans. But where's *my* Honduran? His little brother, who I always used to snub, runs up to me and says, "Victor got caught."

"Oh well, okay, give me a $20 rock then."

I pedal my bike back through Zombieland to Moss Alley. *Fuck.* I don't know if the crack quality is low now or if this new generation of crack dealers just doesn't have any integrity. I go out like four times over the next few weeks, and it's the same deal. Maybe the corner with the real crack moved?

So, after my comedy nights, I sometimes end up upstairs at Steve's now, smoking meth. Not a bad guy. He only asks to suck my dick once and takes a firm "No." Refreshing. Meth is terrible in the way that acid is terrible. I could smoke a $20 rock, work on a new joke, jack off, and be asleep by 4 am. This shit keeps you going into the next day. Not safe for work. I can't be doing that shit on a regular basis. Whenever I strike out on crack runs twice in a row, I'm up at Steve's. We go to the casino across the Bay Bridge, and I play Texas Hold 'Em. Poorly. I get so excited from all the lights and blinking slot machines I bet on every hand. Then I have to wait for Steve to go broke on the slots.

We take big meth hits out of a pipe in his truck before we go in. Casinos are like if meth was an amusement park. No wonder tweakers are drawn to places like this, toothlessly grinding their jaws and chain-smoking, feeding the nickel slots from a Slurpee cup full of coins, and letting their long cigarette ashes fall where they may. Not anymore, though, at least the smoking part. California with all its crazy laws, "Interferin' with our fReeDuhmbs." So keep feeding them slots while your kid's grandma has to feed your kids. The poor people in this country never had a chance; grandmas can only do so much.

On nights we don't go to the casino, I'll just interview Steve. What a life. A gay prostitute tweaker with a tiny show dog. "So, Steve, What's the last thing you want to see when the hotel door opens when you go on an outcall?"

"Japanese businessmen in diapers," he replies without hesitation.

Bambi Lake in her Stained Satin

I show up one night after touring the part of Valencia Street where I got run over by a cop car and where I once talked to KRS-One in front of the Elbow Room. I suddenly arrive at the 16th and Mission open-mic, as one does: you just kind of pop up from an escalator or turn a sharp corner, and *boom*, there it is, you either get murdered or tell a poem.

The usual suspects are there; Frank Chu is in the background wandering back and forth with his protest sign of potentially-sensical gibberish. He's a screensaver for the news at many events around San Francisco, just there in the background, with his ever-changing sign. Tonight it says, "12 Galaxies of Clinton dysmorphia, and yes, probably yo mama tam be in." There's an Airbnb ad on the side that's exposed when he walks towards Pancho Villa's Taqueria. I see an opportunity to jump on stage, but a beautiful man-lady gets to the edge of the chalk circle at the same time as me, and instead of roshambo-ing me to see who goes first, not that I wouldn't acquiesce to a delicate ladyboy like this—even though she's past 50 now and has soot marks on her satin dress from gripping dumpster ledges for drug money. There's still something elegant and proud about her. She says, with a ragged yet feminine voice, "Hold up honey, I'll get to suckin' you, but let a diva get her rocks off first for once. You caucasian males are like bulls in a china shop when the slippery sockeye comes out. Stay awhile. Let me come up with some ideas."

She puts her long finger out and tickles underneath my chin. I'm intrigued, and stay close to the edge of the chalk circle, to see what divine inspiration this performance looks promising to be. Then, she launches into her hit song, The Golden Age of Hustlers:

"In San Francisco, long ago, I made my living hooking. On Polk Street, at the Old Black Rose, I was always lookin', for some dumb man to pay my rent,

and some young man to love me, and so many were heaven-sent, I thanked the stars… above me. "

A pause for reflection.

"Sticks and stones may break my bones, but words will ever hurt me. The queens and hustlers of the red-light zones, they never did desert meeeee. The scent of nuggets and prospectors, they drifted up from The Grubstake, where I shared so many cheeseburgers with my husband, huuusband."

The crowd is entranced now—and growing!

"The golden days, the golden age… of hustlerrrrrs!" she croons, up into the moon above us.

She takes a moment, where a piano jolt would go, and then, *"I saw the best bodies of my generation… sold, parted, and destroyed by drugs and prostitution. Pretty queens on the corner, the midnight cowboys in the doorways, if you want it, Daddy!"*

She shoots me a look, and narrows her eyes until you can't see them through the thickly-caked mascara, then looks to the sky again and says, *"Get it here, it's a candy store in more ways than ooooone."*

She gets off stage as if she's walking a catwalk. She can go from that to dock worker in ten seconds. I've seen her around and talked to her a bit at the Brainwash. I think she's spectacular. If I were gay, I would end up tragic like this, still never dying because I'm indestructible, just like Bambi. She's way past her prime but still has that raunchy diva air in her step. I think that's where I saw her last, smoking crack in the alley and then walking into The Brainwash like the Princess of Monaco. A tragic figure to be sure. But, if talent and moxie couldn't keep *her* off the streets, then what chance do *we* have? Don't do drugs, kiddos. It's such a fleeting feeling of flying that runs out quickly just when you're at the highest point. That's what happened with that angel who flew too close to the sun, and their wings burned. That angel sounds like a dope fiend to me. That angel is Bambi Lake, a filthy-mouthed little angel.

So I get up, unchallenged. After all, I patiently deferred to the tattered Queen of Polk Street, as of course the gallant Prince of Filth would being outranked. I launch into my bit:

"I can't match Bambi's elegance, so I'll go the other way with weirdness. **Kenyan** marathon runners, 16th and Mission, are the fastest in the world! They prefer to run barefooted. Now I want you to picture the look on the face of Nike's top corporate executive, the day he saw a Kenyan break the New York Marathon's all-time record... barefooted. I'm guessing he shit his pants and then went, 'You get those fucking Kenyans in this office right now!'"

Half the audience has a look on their face, like, *long set up for this bit, huh?* Yeah, I do what I want. I learned classical, and now I just play, babies. Just like uncle Miles laid it down. Or was it Monk?

"Kenyans! Name's Bill! I'm in the shoe business, and you just showed the whole world that the fastest people in it don't even fuckin' like shoes!"

Ok, maybe this is more monologuey than stand-upy. That's why I love this corner, I can scream anything I want, and it's an acceptable medium here. One guy came in an Andy Warhol wig and read the ingredients off some soup can labels. It killed.

"Kenyans! Name's Bill! It's almost like you're trying to attack me. I know your rocket ships runs on lentils and songs of the Savannah, but mine runs on Cash! Money! Duckets! Let me tell you a little something! I don't know how you guys do shit in wherever goat milk farm you guys ran here from... but in America, sports isn't necessarily about sports... it's about thugging out! And more importantly, it's about selling high-priced accessories to people who *wish* they were thugs. Thugcessories, if you will. You think when a girl sees you in fresh Nike workout gear, she sees a guy who can run fast and make jump shots? No! She sees gunshots! Bam! Bam! Bam! Livin' in the city motherfuckers! Bling-Bling-Double-Bling! Hot mamas on your dingaling!"

"Haha," they finally start giving in.

"That's how we roll, in Niketown! Now, the night before the race, we want you guys in the strip clubs! So we've arranged for Steve-O to drive you around in a hummer limousine to show you what New York's about. We want you smoking cigars, smashing bottles of Hennessy on the wall, and teabagging cocaine **into** stripper's noses."

"Haha," still not as big of laughs as they should be. Should I reiterate that I'm playing a character of an evil Nike executive in this bit? *Stop analyzing the bit when you're on stage, dipshit! Watch the tape later.*

"So, Kenyans! As you're teabagging the cocaine into the stripper's nostrils... pause for our photographers. That's going to be our new billboard. 'NIKE! Get your **gangster balls**!' Now I got some champagne and pussy in back if you're ready to play ball. Start wearin' some f-u-h-k-i-n' shoes and shit. Otherwise, I swear to god I will build a factory in all of your villages! You think I'm kidding with you, Kenyan?! What's wrong with this guy? You speaky English? Anyone know how to tongue-click around here?!" I say this part to someone in the audience with a case of the wrinkly, judgment nose. It's best to just make the front row the Kenyans for this routine anyway. *Toot-toot-tot-tot* my tongue goes.

"I'm glad you think this is funny! I will have your grandmother dragging around cowhides in the hot, Kenyan sun, two cents an hour! The day of the race, Kenyans, all we want you to do is get two miles ahead of the German guy, go back to the strip club, pass out some more teabag-sniffies."

I act out the situation. As if the words I'm saying aren't disturbing enough to some of our more delicate guests. The other half is laughing now, canceling out those lemon-sucking, judgy, A-hole's distaste.

"And then catch back up to the German guy in the final quarter-mile of the race, blowing cigar smoke in his face. That's how Nike goes 'Yeah, Adidas, go ahead and smoke it.' Then you get up to the finish line, stop, turn around, then tackle his little East Berlin ass, put out your cigar on his ass cheeks in Nike swoosh dots, and then pick him up, throw him on the third place Norweigian guy, then run up to them, kicking them in the head and fucking chest, yelling, "Nike Power! Nike Power, motherfuckers!!"

I pause, out of breath. Yeah, this must be a monologue.

"That's how you get the big endorsements, Kenyans! Stop fuckin' around, and just be like Mike… Tyson." I finally bow and leave the stage. Charlie Getter claps because he loves that bit. The bit I've refused to shitcan for getting medium laughs at best, because fuck it, brilliance is brilliance.

Don't they see that it's a juxtaposition of the CIA dropping off crack in the ghetto and Nike, seeing the success of *that* program, just wanted to clothe the combatants in the crack wars to follow, making those wars worse? Because you had to kill more guys to afford the Nike "Air Force 1s"? I never heard of anyone getting shot over Chuck Taylor's. That's all I'm saying.

A Chance to Punch a Supreme Court Judge I Hate

Tonight is an easy, high-paying, private party with a two-choice menu for each course: 'soup, or salad?', 'beef, or chicken?' , 'panna cotta, or cake?' Easy as pie, except pie isn't a choice. The California Bar Association is having a big dinner celebrating the stifling of progress with even more red tape than last year. NIMBYs rejoice, there won't be any poor people housing anywhere near you for years to come—your checks all cleared, you uptight bumper sticker liberals. So the lawyers are ecstatic. The bar association has chosen Radius to spend some of the money! This is excellent news. Even the Chef seems a bit less grumpy. We've also recently been featured on Check Please, Bay Area, the local foodie show where three yuppies go on and pretend they know about food and wine. They all pretentiously sit at a wine and cheese-laden table with our host Leslie Sibrocco, an effervescent blond that hints with her demeanor that the wine in their glasses has been bottomless for at least an hour.

I wouldn't say Radius is the toast of the town yet—more like an undiscovered gem—but things are looking up. Once every month or two, one of these come-ups will appear and keep us feeling positive. It's a tough business, restaurants, and any outside encouragement is welcome because it's not going to come from the chef. What happened to these people, the chefs? You'd think 24-hour access to *foie gras* would cheer them up a little. This is what the Cordon Bleu grads are aiming for? It's like in comedy. The headliners are the most miserable ones half the time. Why the fuck do we do this?

I'm at the end of the bar, polishing glasses with Samantha and Frederick and telling a story about last week. Fred was there, but Sam wasn't, so I get to tell it again in all its gloriousness. "So, I'm over there at table 12 and taking the order, right? And I look across the street at the Brainwash, and there's a guy obviously presenting a stolen bike.

Normal Tuesday, right? But remember my bike got stolen last week? It was fuckin' my bike the guy was trying to sell! I just felt it. There was no reason for me to look across Folsom mid-order like that. I just felt it. So I say, 'Pardon me a minute,' and I fold my apron, put it by the door, walk across the street and say to the dude, 'Are you selling that? Let me check it out.' Now, it's been spray painted, but you know when you get on your bike and pedal it a few times. So I took off."

"Really?" says Samantha, the hot Asian girl who should hate Frederick and me for always getting better sections—sorry, I opened the cafe for fuckin' months, and he's got that French accent going for him. But, thankfully, she is a hateless creature.

"Yes. I could not believe it myzelf. He was back to zee tables in time to deliver ze mussels to zem. Zey wayah... in dizbelief," attests Parisian Frederick.

"Got my bike back and 35 percent tips from the three tables that watched it go down. What a neighborhood, huh? Livin' in the city!—can't beat it. We hate it, and we love it."

Just then, some Secret Service dudes come in to search the place and give us the *up and down*. Tonight's guest of honor for the bar association dinner is Supreme Court Justice Anthony Kennedy, the piece of shit that gave Florida to GW Jr. instead of Al Gore, costing Gore the election. The *inconvenient truth* was that old Al was just too much of a wimp to run this country like the fossil fuel industry and the Pentagon wanted. The fix was in, and this is the guy that did it. The so-called *swing judge* swung the presidency right to the piece of shit republicans. What the fuck?

So these Secret Service bootlickers bring in their bomb dogs and whatever else and decide that we all look okay. The judge will be here soon. *Fuck*. Should I slap the fuck out of him? And say, "That's for Florida, you piece of shit!" I mean, I have a rare opportunity here. When's the next time I'll get a chance to slap the fuck out of a Supreme Court judge?

They get here, the lawyers, and they all stand around drinking wine as we pass salmon mousse-filled endive leaves and shit. They talk excitedly about all the money they've made and about future money they're going to make for creating absolutely nothing. Nothing but complicated words the general public will have to just pay them to untangle back again—what a hustle. These are people who might be in prison if they hadn't happened into the law—and boy are they drinking. Lawyers make the Oil Can Henry's crew from last month look like rookies.

We finally get them all to sit down, and the Secret Service dudes do another sweep before sitting down to their dinners on the cafe side of the restaurant.

The lawyers have an *open bar,* so we scramble to get them all the drinks they want for the first 30 minutes. Jessica is bartending and wouldn't know a sense of urgency if her water broke, so I hop back there and start helping out, signaling to *her* brain to move even slower. The glass washing machine is moving slower than usual too, and I'm not sure we are going to have enough Bordeaux glasses to pull this off. I send Fred for some generics in the cafe.

The judge is in my section. He's ordered the beef, so I go to lay down the steak knife. I subconsciously grip it tighter as it passes its closest to his jugular. Just that I could've, is enough. I can still slap him if I want to after dessert. They'd say I had a knife and charge me with attempted murder, might as well just do it for real, right? I mean, eight years of GW. He subjected us to eight years of GW. I mean, if he hadn't, they'd have still figured out how to fuck Gore in the ass. He just had too much of a Jimmy Cartery vibe, talking about the environment and shit? That don't play down at the oilfield convention. They weren't just going to let an unwarlike president who likes trees happen. Not in America. Not after Carter. That was a *one-and-done.*

Thank god I was so comedy-obsessed those eight years. It didn't penetrate me as much as it might've. I got some good jokes out of the GW administration. Some comics lamented their leaving because the material was so easy and flowed like a waterfall. All I have to say about that is *if you need to live in the middle of that... to come up with jokes. You don't belong on the stage.*

Man, these lawyers and judges are confident. Every meal they eat, we could poison, but for some reason, we don't, and as a result, all these pieces of shit end up living long lives. It's mind-boggling. But they didn't account for the fact that I was at my gay, prostitute neighbor's house smoking meth last night. I feel squirrelly. Maybe I should just slap him. A compromise?

I look at Jon, at the Chef's window, doing the final plate wipes, and checking for quality, and he seems to know what I'm thinking. He's from Orlando. He knows when there's a strong *thinking about Florida* vibe near him—hanging *Chad? How about slapping Anthony?* He looks over at me. I decide I can't slap the judge. The restaurant would be totally fucked over as a result, and as with most restaurants, it doesn't take a lot of bad news to close your doors for you. I love this place. More than I hate Anthony Kennedy, I guess. Maybe I'll just ask him as he leaves if he regrets Florida. He'd probably just convey with his eyes that he was following orders before having me tazed. *Following orders,* that's what the guards at Auschwitz said, Anthony. At least I didn't call him, 'Your honor.'

The Mustache Eating Contest

Okay, so I had some girlfriends, and it cut my vices down long enough to get strong again—with all the injuries it took two girlfriends in a row this time—I feel like I'm finally back to peak performance. I'm going to perform at Tourettes for like the 30th time. I'm out of material for these people. It's mostly the same audience every month, and they start booing if you tell jokes they've heard before. I am a prolific joke writer, but after 30 performances here, I'm feeling the pressure to come up with new shit all the time, and for like a year after the wheelchair, my output wasn't exactly *riverlike, more* like rivulets. I had comedy rivulets. I relied on old stuff for most of it. Tourettes don't play that. I tried to recycle a set from five years ago last time, and they fuckin' remembered. Fuckin' horseshit.

My Brooklyn accent isn't that terrible, so I invent a character called Crack Baby from Brooklyn. It's time to face my fear of playing characters. I had some leftover diapers from Folsom Street Fair and from when I freaked out the Chef at Radius. I don't have a diaper fetish. I just like to freak people out. That's my fetish. Even in San Francisco, a grown man wearing a diaper gets a reaction. So I'm up there, in front of 700 people in a diaper, yelling, "What?! Yous muthuhs fuckahs nevah seen a 40-year-old crack baby from Brooklyn befoowah?! Yeah, I know, I know. Nobody evah wants duh white crack baby at dee awfanage. 'I want an exotic one! Do yous got any Costa Rican crack babies?' Angelina Jolie announced last week, while I stood deyah, looking my cutest! She ended up leavin' wit' duh Burmese orphan wit' DMT fetal syndruhm! This is fuckin' bullshit!"

"Hahahaha," some of them go, while half cross their arms in disapproval. Crack babies are off-limits for them, which is exactly why I'm doing it. I'm telling you, these Berkeley college kids are policing me.

At a show called Tourettes Without Regrets, no less. I find the one with the most hateful look on their face.

"Look at dis guy! His face is moowah sowah dan my diapah. Awwwwwww. Look at 'im. *Waaaaahhhhhhhh.* Dis is what 'is face looks like, *Waaaahhhhhhhhhhhh.*" I go on much longer than necessary with the "*Waaaaahhhhhh,*"-ing, until *Mr. Crossarmed Cultural Anthropology of the Renaissance Major* wilts down into his chair where he fucking belongs. I add one more, "*Waaaaaaaaaaaaaaahhhhhh!*"

"Okay, okay, let's have a contest. I need two volunteeyahs."

A bunch of people raise their hands. I pick two girls, one pretty and one that looks like a dock worker.

"Bring yuhs chayahs, ladies."

I get them up, sitting on the stage, one on either side of me. "Okay, heeyahs duh contest. I will fuck duh shit outta duh one dat eats dis mustache off my face. I'll fuck you mightily wit' my crack baby dick," I then reach into my diaper and wipe two big slashes of what appears to be baby shit above my lips. A Yosemite Sam-sized mustache of excrement. It's actually chocolate pudding that I had a snack pack of stashed in the crotch area of my diaper, but I'm such a dirty piece of shit that they think it might be real.

A collective groan of disgust rises into the rafters of the Oakland Metro Opera House, "EEEEWWWWWWWW!" they all go at once. The dock worker-looking girl squeals and jumps off the stage. But the other girl, the cute one, just starts eating this pudding off my face, and we end up making out right there. I had no idea this skit would go so well. Our tongues are swirling around each other, and I think, *Should I just bend this girl over this chair right now and plow her? That would even beat the time at the Thai house party.*

I decide to stop while this is all still somewhat legal, and I raise my arms in victory, put the mic back in the stand, and look at the defeated, sour-faced guy. I suck in his defeated look. Jamie Dewolf is doubled over laughing and can barely control the room. The Crack Baby from Brooklyn character might have a future.

I end up getting a ride from the girl that ate the mustache, and I have to pay her the promised crack baby dick that she won fair and square. *Maybe life as a white crack baby is salvageable*, I think, as I plow her from behind, diaper around my ankles. Am I sick? I feel fine. This is not normal, though, right?

The New Server

Well, things had been going too well. The double-edged sword of ambition has sliced one of our owners—Christian's—mental health in half. He won't be coming back. He was acting sketchy, and now he's gone. The problem with shooting for the moon is the fall back to earth if you miss. These guys have built a beautiful restaurant. The press and reviews have been excellent, but this neighborhood just isn't ready for anything that is this high quality. When it comes to low quality thrills, you can't beat South Market. You can do meth; techno music; you can be a crazy who screams into the void in tortured anguish; you can have anal sex with a guy who was just screwdrivering dirt out of the sidewalk cracks; shoot up krocodyl; whatever. This area just isn't ready to be civilized.

If these guys had put this restaurant in the Mission District? They would be in the Bahamas getting the profits wired to them on Paypal. It's beautiful what they are attempting. Everyone that works here believes in the place and does way more than they would at another job. Half the chairs in the cafe came from my house after me and Wendy broke up. She made me buy a 12 person dinner table, and we were going to have dinner parties every two weeks. Haha. That dinner table is a shelf for papers I'll never look at now.

So Christian is gone, and it's just Jon now. He hired a new server that looks like the female version of him. She has three shifts, just enough not to be able to work anywhere else, but not enough to do anything fancy on her day off. Jon is corralling her right towards his cock, and it looks like she's into it. I'm fucked. I've lost a shift already to make room for this chick. Any misstep, and I feel like I could lose more. The old chef has been gone—we had another few—and now the original line cook from day one, one of the Cordon Bleu kids, Peter Cham, has been promoted to head chef. It **can** happen, kids. You can make your way up to chef. It's rare, but it happens. Ten years as a restaurant employee, and I saw it happen once.

We suddenly find ourselves on a stormy ship at the SS Radius. I wouldn't say sinking, but those glory days of plenty are behind us, and it's time to tighten our belts and start focusing on efficiency and cost-cutting. The ribeye steaks me and Frederick are eating at the end of our shifts sure aren't 8oz anymore, but at least we're eating ribeyes. Why ribeyes over a *filet mignon*? Because half the reason *filet mignon* is forty bucks is that the name is fancy-sounding. It's actually one of the less flavorful cuts. Granted, it's amazingly tender, which is the only real quality that would make it almost as valuable as, say, a tri-tip or a *carne asada*, but not in the same category as, say, a ribeye. Why does it cost so much, then? Mainly because the rich *old money* pieces of shit can actually get their dentures through it. That's the real reason it costs more; you're offering an old, rich guy a chance to eat blood again. Make sure to serve it to him rare because he's a piece of shit vampire.

We aren't coming back to party at Radius after The Bloodhound closes anymore. Every Thursday, Friday, and Saturday, we'd come back here until 4 am, and Jon and Christian would open the beer taps; wine if that's what the girls wanted. This was how Jon would get pussy from owning a restaurant. That was getting too expensive, opening up the taps late-night half the week, especially if one of the girls wouldn't go see the Patty Hearst cage in the basement with Jon. It's true, there's a little cage you could store a human down there. Rumor has it, there was a tunnel between here and the Brainwash that the Symbionese Liberation Army would ferry Patty back and forth underneath the street when the neighborhood got invaded by the pigs. When I think I have big tippers that would be into that, I take them down there to see it.

So now Jon is going back to an old restaurant boss stand by, fucking the staff. He's pissed I fucked the new blasian cafe girl that he liked, and that's probably why I lost a shift to Caitlin. It was worth it. Blasian pussy is some of the best you can get. You could take the ugliest, most snaggle-toothed brother alive, mix it with the most hideous, Mrs. Potato Head, Asian lady, and somehow that baby will grow up to be the hottest thing on the planet. Why are people just mixing with their own race? The rewards for cross-race impregnation should be pretty obvious to everybody at this point. Let's destroy racism with interracial sex! Someone organize an orgy in the park!

At any rate, things aren't quite as cool at the restaurant as they used to be, but it's still Radius. I'll always love this place. One night we're in the cafe late-night, drinking. We still do it, but just on Saturdays, not half the week. And this new Cordon Bleu kid that we just hired is in the cafe, swirling red wine in a glass and sniffing it. I'm like, "What the fuck are you doing? are you drunk, or did you just swirl that?"

"It releases the aromatics. I'm pretty sure I have a *supertaster* palate. So I'm going to be a *sommelier,*" he says.

"Well, well, well. What do we have here? A *supertaster,* is it? How's about supertasting deze nuts? *Haha,*" I say, hammered, having drank six Recoils and some other shit. The bartenders at The Bloodhound are way too nice to us. It's becoming a problem. You have to at least *try* to roast the new guy, though. Radius is pretty easy, but a restaurant is a restaurant. You gotta be hazed. Hazing is so endemic in restaurants that if you don't roast a guy constantly his first few weeks, he gets nervous he's getting fired. The lack of abuse makes him feel like an afterthought, and he tosses and turns all night, feeling uncared for. I'm just trying to help him feel loved, "Hey, we got a future *sommelier* here. Ok, I'm going to bring a cab and a pinot, and let's see if you can even tell the difference."

I go and get two glasses of red wine from the dining room that I've poured an ounce of purple joy into each of. He tastes both, looks at the rafters in contemplation, swishes, swallows, and, "That's the pinot noir, and that's the cab," he says, pointing at the two empty glasses in their turns.

"They're both the same wine, dipshit," I say, like a twisted knife.

The new guy in his Boston Redsocks hat and bulging forearms looks at the ground in shame. I feel bad, but it's roast or be roasted around here. That's the real reason these nice little girls don't have as many shifts as me. You gotta be half gangster, half charmer to survive in the front of the house in a restaurant. A hard dichotomy few can navigate well. So when it does come time to kiss ass, I just autopilot the character I use for that. I don't kiss all the table's asses, not even close, but it's the ones that require it and don't receive their gluteal smooches? They're the ones that will make your life hell. Not getting handed a printed-out internet review by your boss at the start of tomorrow's shift is enough reason to pucker up. Fuck it. I know who I am. Someday, I'll show them all.

Motormouth shows up all high on meth, or crack, or something and me being drunk, I try to, like, grab him around his head lightly, like an affectionate *noogie,* we used to call them? Motormouth, however, takes it a whole different way in his methed-out, hellscape brain and thinks I'm trying to headlock him. So he pulls me backwards onto the ground and puts his feet into my chest, then flips me into the wall. I'd gotten these sturdy leather boots to help me with the last injury. Motormouth himself had shown me the specialty store by his house where orthopedic specialists are there to help you. The irony of one of these fuckers sticking into the drywall. When my body falls to the ground, the boot just stays stuck there, snapping my tibia and fi bula like a pretzel stick in hardened hummus.

"Aaaaaahhhhhhhhhh!!!!" For months, the people that were in that room will have nightmares about that blood-curdling scream. Well, I'm off to San Francisco General Hospital again. Does anyone need anything? Plasma? Dilaudid?

So rather than bore you with the details of yet another hospital trip, let's fast forward 12 weeks into the future, after some more metal implants and pain pills. This accident is far less intense than the shattering of both my heel bones, and I'm able to work again soon. The doctors that fixed me would tell you that that is impossible, but here I am. Motormouth feels terrible and brings me like a thousand dollars to help with bills.

I can get around on crutches, so I'm not dependent on people for anything this time. Not that they stop by after the first few weeks anyway. It's like the fourth time it's happened since I started comedy—is it comedy that's killing me? Never get hurt really bad, folks. You start getting frustrated with people you would have previously stabbed for. They don't even make sure you have sandwiches after the first two weeks. Someone concluded that's where the marker is for when humans became civilized. When they dug up a prehistoric femur that had been bound and healed, that means someone had taken care of them for several months. I thought that was an interesting theory.

The time I shattered both feet, I wasted away to 150 pounds, not because the meds killed my appetite—which they do somewhat—but because I couldn't even get out of the house to get food. The buzzer was broken, so I couldn't even get delivery. People are long gone after the 30-day point. That's not entirely fair since my neighborhood is a nightmare, and your car is likely to be stolen when you visit me. Also, I'm kind of a suffer-in-silence type of dude? Maybe I'm so fierce that people figure I'll be fine no matter what? Also, I'm kind of an asshole. Okay, so perhaps I'm not the best case study for the *broken femur theory*.

So, I finally get back to Radius. Jon promised he'd save my shifts for me. This all *did* happen due to his irresponsible after parties. At least that'll be my angle if he tries to fuck me in the end. The chairs we knocked over wrestling were from **my** house. This place owes me. I was there the day the doors opened. I cling to these ideas out of desperation because I'm about out of money. I sensed my shifts were now being claimed by Caitlin, Jon's long-butted, chick-version doppelganger.

Jon stayed true to his word, and I have shifts waiting for me, two of them. Caitlin has five. She's his girlfriend now. She started with two shifts when I had five. This little bitch flipped me like Motormouth did, just with finances. Oh well, the glory days of Radius were over anyway. I love Jon, but a lot of the dreamy heart and soul left when Christian left. Now, we are an efficient machine with less fun, much more by the book. We haven't had a poker night in a year, much less many after-parties. And look what happened at the last one.

These cement floors are killing my feet, and I have to take four Advils to get through a shift now. Pretty sure that's not good for the old kidneys. I think I'll trim weed for the rest of the season, perfect my best one hour of stand-up that will finally catapult me to medium stardom. All I want is a Shelly Long level of fame.

One night, drunk, I say to Jon, "What's up with Caitlin sucking my shifts out your dick?" and that's that. I'm not really a breaker-upper; I'm a fucker upper. That was an instant, "You're fired!" Getting fired with a bang is kind of my thing. I do get hired and fired again at Radius once or twice after that, but we are near the end. The writing is as on the wall as the spackled hole where my ankle snapped. The place will close next year, but Radius will always be my favorite restaurant I have ever worked at—what a time we had. Thank you, Jon and Christian. I wish I met more people with your vision and courage.

Headlining The Punchline!

Dayum. Just as my first decade in comedy is coming to a close, I'm headlining The Punchline! A promo is made commemorating it: March 13th, 2013.

It's around the time when Christopher Dorner, an LA cop, went nuts and killed some other cops in a highly planned out, multi-location murder spree. It turns out they fired him because he tried to report excessive force by police in his department. During the search, they impulsively shoot into several grey trucks, which resemble the one Dorner is driving, hitting a guy, and not exactly debunking Dorner's excessive force accusations. Imagine another grey truck on the road. That's weird.

He almost got a captain but only found the captain's daughter, and so he killed her instead. That's some cold-blooded shit. I almost sympathized with the guy, but I guess when a guy snaps, he can get evil.

If you can't beat 'em, join 'em is for suckers and losers. Rich assholes have known for eons that a better strategy is that if you can't beat 'em, drive them insane, then take advantage of the chaos. That's what happened to Christopher Dorner and Ludwig Van Beethoven. Mass shooters cause convenient chaos. If you're a rich asshole, you don't want a calm, reasonable populace. They'll organize against you. The rich pieces of shit that meet in Davos know you gotta keep the public a little scared, a little crazy, and a lot broke, so they're always scrambling.

The proliferation of mass shootings serves those elitist's purposes, and that's why it's quite possible the CIA identifies angry white men in comment threads on Tucker Carlson's Twitter and puts them to work. Why wouldn't the evilest organization in the history of the world turn its sickness within the borders of its own country? Wouldn't that be the ultimate thrill for those sick puppies? The purpose, to keep everybody on edge, trying to just survive the *week*, so they don't start planning for *years*; which might include getting rid of the ruling class.

Guys like George Bush and Donald Trump see a mass shooting in the paper and smile. Why would *they* worry? They never go in a crowded public space unless there's security up the ass. These types of events just ensure the future security of their continued plunder.

Does it all sound like the plot for Lethal Weapon 5? It isn't. The shit happened for real right here in Cali. This guy went after and killed some dirty cops, had several rifles, a pistol, smoke grenades, the whole bit. His manifesto talks about waging asymmetrical warfare against the whole police system. He had a detailed hit list. To be honest, he was so organized I thought it was weird he didn't get more of them. You don't hear about him as much because he doesn't fit the narrative of Muslim attacker or isolated, every day redneck that had finally had enough.

I guess when it's cops being attacked, they actually get off their asses and catch the guy real quick. If you stick to killing sex workers and hitchhiking skateboarders, you can have a long career and just retire in Florida. You just open your scrapbook of newspaper articles about yourself out on the porch; maybe give a wave across the street at the other retired mass killers. "Hey, it's Summer Camp Sam, the psycho that's kept 'em squealin' in '77! Hey Sam, remember the 80s? Didn't blood look amazing splattered across neon parachute pants!?"

Most serial killers retire in North Florida, it's true; they never get caught because the cops would have to hang out in trailer parks, questioning people all day in the heat. It's just hookers anyway, so they don't give a fuck.

But you kill a cop? or a rich guy? They'll catch you **that** day. The only reason it took two weeks to find Versaci's killer was that Florida's cops are even more inept than average. Also, the victim was gay, so they didn't care as much. They finally had to care, though, because, after all, rich is rich.

This proves two things about the police: cops *could* solve crimes, but they just usually just don't give a rat's nut. If you're not some rich piece of shit or a cop? They ain't gonna find your chainsaw, Dave. Second? They're actually the safest motherfuckers out there. Who is going to risk a statewide manhunt and a dozen helicopters in the air within seconds?

Hey, cops? Do you want to get shot less? Stop kicking your way into people's homes and lying to get your warrants. Fuckin' wrong address half the time too. These motherfuckers, always going, *"Oh, it's so dangerous."* Bullshit, I looked at the stats. Cops are like ten spots below *pizza delivery guy*. Even termite inspectors get rat bites on their noses from climbing under houses—you never see *them* getting jumpy to the point of killing an unarmed marsupial. If a balloon pops near a cop he empties the clip into the party clown, twisting the balloon animals; now he's bleeding from his liver because a kid wanted the rhino horn pointier.

We should drug test cops to make sure they're *not* shooting roids and that they ***are*** smoking weed. Stoned cops would shoot fewer people and come up with more abstract scenarios to catch the killers. I say we keep them stoned and *off* roids. Call me a nutcase.

We should do that and change the laws so that cops can personally be charged *and* or sued for anything from filing bullshit charges on up. *Boom!* Problem solved. The problem would go away overnight. Why are the taxpayers paying off the lawsuits for their own dead kids that the cops killed? What in the motherfucking bullshit is that?! This bootlicking of uniforms and guns in this country is disgusting and frankly unAmerican. Whatever happened to "I fought the law, and I won"? Now everybody is all, "StEp on mY nEk harDehr oFficer, caN I poLish yer gUhn?"

Anyways, this guy Christopher Dorner was trying to turn in dirty cops for brutalizing the people they're supposed to be protecting. Now, five people are dead, which includes Dorner himself. Fucked up situation, but if we're going to have *lone wolf shooters* all the time now, can they at least be less random, more vigilante? I do condemn Chris Dorner. He killed family members of bad people without knowing if those family members were bad themselves. That's Narco shit, but I am less sad about this story than the other ones. It sounds to me like the other victims were trying to puppeteer Oscar Grant games and became Oscar Grant contestants.

It was a remarkable thing that just flashed through the news in a week, and I thought about it leading up to my headlining The Punchline. In your performance, you want to briefly discuss the biggest story of the week if there's something remarkable. This certainly fits the bill. When I think about this week, years from now, this story will always be weirdly attached to it. I can't find a way to really make it funny, and so it isn't in the performance itself. Too fresh to make anything of it. It was so crazy I needed it to soak in. Crazy fuckin' world.

Anyways, so yeah, I'm headlining The Punchline after a decade in comedy. It's early 2013, the techie takeover of the city is almost complete. They're about to break ground on the Salesforce building, which, when completed, will dwarf everything around it. Some think it will look like a giant dildo; others, a humongous, hideous middle finger that points at the old part of the city.

At this point, apps and websites run every part of most of these sorry assholes' lives. If you don't have a smartphone, you may as well go lie down in the gutter and die. The big takeover came quick. They'd learned from their mistakes after the last tech bubble burst, and they came back ready, bulldozing, redesigning, and repurposing everything within the 7X7 miles that is San Francisco. Some neighborhoods have somehow retained their old San Francisco character; North Beach, Haight Street, Mission Street, but NOT Valencia. Hayes Valley has gone from a place where white people go to die, to where history goes to cry. It's like a Google campus over there. Where did the hood go? Do these fucking techies fear nothing? They took on the Western Addition... hood? And won? The arrogance is shocking. And impressively, they fucking won? I guess money really does beat everything—even the Page Street Mafia. Now, if you can find an iced coffee for less than five dollars over there, I'd be surprised. I hear they roast the beans on the crying cheeks of hipsters on rent day.

I'm still alive, motherfuckers! Until I'm dead, you haven't won. All of San Francisco's history, its eclectic creativity, pioneer spirit, rambunctious nature, and its empathy for the downtrodden and the weird? Its ability to see the beauty in the insane and the broken? It beats in my heart! I won't let you kill that. You still have some Emperor Nortons to defeat, Twitter! And we all have swords and our own currency! It's called honor, heard of it? My sword is my mouth, and I'm not going to suck your dick with it! I'm going to *scream* your dick **off** with it! Do you hear me, Zuckerburg?! I'm going to run up huge bills in the San Francisco emergency room they named after you and **not** pay! And then I'm going to scream your dick off!

And the fact that you try to seal up your victory as I headline The Punchline? Methinks you are being a bit hasty in your victory celebrations. I was here before you, and I'll fuckin' be here when you leave. I'm a fuckin' cockroach! I'll embed myself in your cupboards and shit into your soylent green until you puke. I will be here to laugh when you pack up to go destroy Texas and Florida. Spoiler alert: they're already destroyed. And if you come back to California, I'll be here waiting. I'd advise you to stay away from this beautiful bitch this time. San Francisco is mine!

I walk in feeling confident and wanted at The Punchline for the first time ever, and after what seems like forever, I'm brought up by the host. I'm perfectly in my four drink window and bring up a full beer to make sure I stay in it. I set the beer down with my cheat sheet posing as a cocktail napkin, just in case I lose the order of the jokes in my head and have to sneak some peeks. I'm sure I'll be fine. I'm up there on the stage, and they're all smiling. This should be fine,—*whoooooo*—okay, take the mic… and:

"Punchline! I don't **like** chicken omelettes! It's like making a mother wear a jacket made out of her own babies!"

Medium laugh. Did I start too weird? I'm an odd guy. Must I pretend at first that I'm normal in order to gain their trust? It feels like lying, but I suppose it's been a strategy that has worked. Well, going back to normal now would seem awkward, right? *Shut up! You're on stage now. Do the next weird-ass joke, fucker!*

"The Bushmen of Africa, when they kill an animal, they apologize to it and explain to him that his family needed the nourishment! I was very impressed when I saw that on the Nature Channel, Punchline! So much so that now, when I'm at In-N-Out Burger, I say 'Burger!'"

I hold a fictional burger up to my face with my free hand, "Burger! I'm sorry shit had to go down like this, man! But bein' that you only cost two bucks and some change, you're the only gazelle my people could catch today! Furthermore, I apologize I was unable to afford any proper burial garments, such as bacon or **cheeeeese**!!"

A medium laugh. It's okay. I'll get them.

"Tiger blood! Tiger blood, motherfuckers!!" This is during the time when all I have to do is yell "Tiger blood!" to get them laughing because I do have some Sheenesque qualities. Sheen's on-camera meltdowns were still fairly fresh in the public's mind. Cheap but effective. *Okay, think of something.*

"I didn't want to admit I was addicted to Facebook until I tried to finger scroll a clit."

I feel guilty about these laughs because I have a flip phone. Okay, pull the nose up.

"Hey, did you guys know that there's such a thing as eyeball herpes?"

They *gasp* and *ewww*.

"Yeah, you can get herpes in your fuckin' eyes, man. I was like, 'What?! I'm already spending $20 a month on condoms?! And now I gotta buy GOGGLES?!'"

They all laugh, except one guy in the second row. He's looking at his phone. "What the fuck are you doing, bro!" I say.

"I'm googling if there's really eyeball herpes, like in that joke you told."

I scream at him, "How about you jam that cellphone up your ass, so the vibrations finally have some meaning!?"

"Haha," they laugh at the foolish yuppy. His girlfriend looks like she's trying to look like she doesn't know him. I'd never clown a girl for being with a dummy. She's already gotta date him.

"I'm about to update your anus! You think I read half the fucking county jail library so you could just pull out your fuckin' little phone and be like, 'Oh really? We'll see about that.'? What the fuck? How about you look that shit up later, and when you see it's true, you can text me my fuckin' laughs, bro! Maybe me and your phone should just gangbang you. It can shit in your brain while I jack off on your fuckin' soul. Corporate executives pay a grand for that!"

They punish him by laughing until the room shakes. "Leave your phones in your pockets, people. I want to see your beautiful faces, not a row of Apple and Samsung logos. Fuckin' Jesus, people! Throw your smartphones in the trash! They're brain cancer! We're going back to beepers and payphones babies! When you had 40 minutes on the bus, you had to either talk to a stranger or daydream. Now, we don't do any of that with phones, just a row of imaginationless dumbfucks with their mouths wide open, their faces lit up by their phone screens. Phones killed daydreaming, man. Perhaps its greatest crime."

Ok, I'm losing them. Never tell addicts they're addicted. Let's go into the crowd. I remember the previous comic complimenting a guy in the first row's sideburns. I know Josh Keppel is here, and his sideburns are far more impressive than this guy's could ever be. So I call them both up on stage and have a "chop off," of sorts. The only hair Josh has on his head **are** the sideburns. And they rise, like mighty checkmarks, nestling his ear and taking off straight up, past his temple, all the way to the ***top*** of his head. The audience agrees that Josh is the champion of the sideburn championships. The other guy accepts his loss and leaves the stage, most likely to go buy rogaine and inject it directly into his mutton chops so he can try to be the champion next year.

Ok, let's keep it moving with the jokes. One of the comics brought all his friends from Hayward, aka "The Stack," a tough little town. They're starting to get rowdy.

"Hey! How come they call roommates 'roommates?' They should call it, 'Hey, want to be enemies next year?' or, 'Oh, was that your Ben and Jerry's,' or, 'Hey, wanna clean my beard hair off the sink for fucking' ever?"

"Haha," they go.

"Fuckin' roommates, man. On Craigslist, they're all, '420 friendly,' then they show up, and not only did this lady look like she had a lawyer, she looks like she *is* a lawyer. Fuck Craiglist. They're like, 'Does this house have multiple bathtubs? My Pitbulls like to relax after attacking children all day!"

"Haha," from most of them, but "Boo," go the dog lovers. I'm telling you, you can make fun of almost anything, but don't fuck with those dog people, man. They'll stab you in the parking lot. The hair-lipped orphan crowd might *flash* a blade, but the dog people will *use* it.

"Fuck roommates! Be more careful when choosing a roommate, even than a lover. What can a lover do to you? Run you over? Give you Aids? Big deal, a roommate has keys to your fuckin' house! They can come into your room at 2 am and tell you stories about Tijuana!"

"Hahaha."

"It's better to live in a cardboard box by the airport than to live with a selfish piece of shit that uses potato chip grease to jack off to porn in the living room. Remember when you found him passed out like that, underwear around his ankles, sitting in *your* lazy boy. How horrified were you when you went in for a late-night snack and found that shit? But you didn't **have** any snacks anymore because they were *your* fuckin' potato chips! Fuck you, Jared! That's his real name, too."

Now, they're going nuts. Many of them are like Jared or have roommates just like him. This would not work on an old crowd, who were able to buy their houses at age 22. Know your audience, folks. These impoverished 20 somethings that have to cram four people into a two-bedroom at Bay Area rates are eating this shit up. I've riled them up a little too much, and the mezzanine to my immediate right has, I believe, accidentally spilled a drink on their table, and some of it has splashed down onto this hipster couple that is three feet down over a little wood rail. The hipster girl seems to have gotten the worst of it. The hipster guy, not realizing he's surrounded by a bunch of kids from The Stack, stands up to protest, perhaps thinking this girl will fuck him on the first date if he acts like a tough guy for her.

"Whoah, bro. Sit down. She's not going to fuck you on the first date," I say, attempting to control the situation. "Where'd you two meet, Okcupid.com? How about saving the big throwdown for old date number three, Huh?" The girl looks impressed. Now I feel like it's the second date. Maybe he *could* close the deal. But, on the other hand, his mustache has too much wax in it. I'll leave it at a coin flip.

"And you guys up there! I know you all fuckin' came together, don't be trying to take over the whole place, turning it into a Haystack house party and shit. This is *my* fuckin' night. I waited a goddamned decade." The waitress is there with a washcloth now. They laugh because they think I just guessed where they were from, like how comics are supposed to be psychic about shit like that. I probably could have, but it's not hard to find out from the club employees and the other comics if there's a segment of the audience that all have something in common. So now, everybody is kind of chilled out for a second. And I tell the waitress, "Can you buy this lovely couple a round? And the one that spilled from up there a new one too. It was an accident. I'll pay for it." *I won't.* Let's take her into the home stretch before this devolves again.

"They say that if you put a frog in a pot of warm water and slowly boil it, Punchline, it will die without ever knowing anything was wrong. I'd like to compare that to moving into your girlfriend's house."

"Haha."

"Think about it. You get there, and at first, it's really nice; you've escaped Potato Chip Grease Jared? Sure, you went to Home Depot last Sunday and looked at color swatches with names like "salmon" and "avocado," but at least she does nice little things like lick your B-hole through Saranwrap on your birthday."

"Haha," they go.

"It's like a fuckin' jacuzzi at first: 110 degrees, baby. But then, after a few months, around Christmas time, you find yourself at her parent's house wearing a pink LeTigre shirt with the fuckin' collar flipped up. You're puking up eggnog because her grandma called you a 'pink shirt wearing pussy,' and challenged you to a *nog-test*."

"Haha." Ok, let's land this baby.

"It's gettin' warmer, Frog Boy! Bubbles are gettin' bigger! 140 degrees! The months wear on, and now blowjobs are only given out if you do something amazing, like show up to a job interview sober."

"Guffaw, snoooot!"

"It's even hotter! Full boil! That's about the time your little fucken' frog nuts pop like popcorn kernels! But don't worry, here come your millions of froglets you got from thinking you were just gonna move in here and save on rent. So now you got **froglets,** bro! You're fucked frog boy!

"Hahaha."

"Here they all come, to rip... and to tear... at your shredded, ribbony, fluttering on the subtle currents... practically exploded... daddy nuts! Your frog nuts are just calories to your ungrateful froglets! Which you gave your freedom for!!! And now your balls are just a fucking juice box for them!!"

They are stunned into silence. This is going to be like stabbing a semi-truck tire with a buck knife. 3...2...1

"And that... is why you should never... move into your girlfriend's house."

"Hahahahahahahaha!!"

All these showing up to interviews stoned motherfuckers are laughing enough to call it. I look back and forth at them all, huff it in like silver spray paint in a paper bag, and walk off stage with one of the greatest feelings a man could ever have: killing at The Punchline.

The next day I feel euphoric—The Punchline, I killed it! I've not only dominated the haters and validated the superfans who always believed, but I've also created a temporary dopamine well that is deeper than the Mariana Trench. My belief that that trench is endless allows me to not think about its depletion, and I attain perfect contentment. I turn over every big laugh I'd gotten last night, and I'm there again. I feel my hair shaking from their laughter. Their love flows into me like lightning bolts. The surge is so powerful my body threatens to tear my flesh apart.

Do you know what killing feels like? Like your father hugging you, apologizing, and saying he'll be a better dad, and he means it this time; it feels like getting a Diamond Back bmx bike on Xmas instead of a banana seat Huffy; It feels like when you ask to ride the gorilla at the zoo, your mom says 'yes,' instead of 'no,' and now you're ripping around the zoo on a fuckin' silverback, jumping off hippos and shit; It feels like all the people that laughed at you when you weren't trying to be funny, to humiliate you, just woke up to a stocking full of poop; It feels like curving the cue ball around three other balls to nail in the eightball to win a $100 bet, just as the bartender sets down your beer and shot, clapping when you sink it, waving off your money; it feels like giving your mom a picture you drew of you and her and she cries with joy, and hugs you sooooo tight your eyes pop out a little; it feels like a bad roommate moving out; it feels like getting your asshole licked by Eva Mendez, alternately blowing cocaine up there with a slurpee straw, while Rosario Dawson herself is in front cramming the whole kielbasa down her throat and moaning, creating a vibration that rides from her struggling diaphragm to the edge of your grundle, all the way to the end and back! Rosario and Eva then lift you onto their shoulders as you have your midway point 5th orgasm and carry you down a parade route where everybody from your hometown is cheering and throwing flowers at you. All your old bosses and the guards at the juvenile hall have to run out and grab the flowers and bring them to your house later! "We're getting tired; we need more *bro broth*," begs Eva, as she kicks the old vice-principal, who paddled you in 8th grade, out of the way onto his face into a pile of dog shit.

Do you feel that? Times it by ten. That's killing on stage at The Punchline when the room is full. Your asshole hums like a fighter jet engine and your eyeballs float on a minty wind! You can almost lean into the laughs, like Leo and Kate at the tip of the Titanic.

It carries me through the entire next day. In the evening I hit a big wall. The whole week leading up to the show, I was pumping more dopamine than vice president Biden at a cheerleader camp. Now, I'm dizzy with fatigue. I have a mini anxiety attack trying to think of ways to get the happy levels up again—and now we are in a thought spiral. I steady myself after some coffee. I think about whether or not I've achieved closure with finally headlining The Punchline. It seemed like the most important thing in the world in the years leading up to it actually happening. Does that allow for a type of relaxation, or does now the even bigger job of being the 'best headliner' loom? Where does it end? The carrot is always up ahead, it seems. Did America do this to me? With its rollercoasters and its slam pits? It's buffalo wings; it's deep-fried mac and cheese balls? It's ass eating, and it's roller derbies? Is the American mindset not just caught in a never-ending pursuit of adrenaline and conquest?

I go back to Thailand in my brain, where I'd achieved at least *some* moments of zen. I slow it all down. I've achieved a lot. What's the urgency? Take it easy, bro. What is it? What is it **you** want from this? This is for you as much as it is for the audience—let's face it, it's probably closer to a 60/40 split; if we're all being honest with ourselves, am I right performers?—what do **I** want? I let myself drift, trancelike, and ponder the question, like Mr. Miyagi on vacation. *What is it all for?*

After a while, it comes to me. I know what I want. It's evening now, and I go for a walk. I come out from under the freeway bridges by 14th Street. I see Virginia, the Tamale Lady, and buy a tamale from her cooler she drags all over the neighborhood. I chew the masa and the pork slowly, letting its divinity drip down into my flavor bud pockets. That's **one** of the things I wanted.

I wander on. Soon, I see it. I see what I'm *really* searching for. I approach a place I know well, and I see the warm, loving face of Baby Jesus. His name is Jason, but that's what I call him. I see Loberg's old, sad, or maybe just stoned eyes, but with a big bright smile beneath them. I see Guinevere Q with her guitar strapped to her and Miguel with his poem-filled moleskin. Duo, Jonathon, Julie, Charlie's mad smile, and all the others.

It seems I've arrived at the bricks in the plaza above the 16th and Mission Bart in the middle of a calm moment. Maybe they've all gone once, and it's unclear who should do their second one. They look at me as if I've arrived at a serendipitous moment. Charlie sweeps his arm, creating a current that swooshes me to the center of the chalk circle without me realizing I'm stepping there.

I step into it, ready to ride a bull while playing chess, and almost tear up at all those faces which love me, knowing full well about my flaws and irregularities but loving me anyway. How can a man fail when his friends love him?

I start my set: "So, my buddy was telling me about how he infiltrated this group of hot chicks by saying he was gay, and I was all, 'That's stupid,' but then I saw he was like, showering with them and shit, so I was like 'hmmmm,' and I went up to the same group of hot chicks, and I was like, 'Hey ladies, my name is Justin, and I don't even *have* a penis!'" I pull down my pants to reveal what appears to be a penisless pube pelt. I've tucked my shlong behind me and crossed my legs a bit, quickly as I unzipped, like a magician. The dope fiends behind me just see a guy poking some brain out the back, but in front, the illusion is impeccable. They don't know what the fuck to think. *Is that why Scales is so weird? He's like a Ken doll down there?*

"*Huuuhhhh?*" They gasp—some laugh. But they don't turn away. These people have never turned away from me.

Love, acceptance, and understanding. A place I don't feel like an alien in a capitalist slave costume trying to decipher the worker's handbook, but I'm from mars, so I don't understand the fuckin' language in the handbook!

It was **here** the whole time, on the corner of 16th and Mission. Who has ever found salvation here?

If you can die knowing ten people truly, truly love you; and you loved them back? Even one person—let's be honest, for me, I need at least enough people for a comedy show—you did it. All the likes on Facebook, all the chocolate ice cream, all the cocaine? It's all an attempt to fill that hole where the love should be, man.

Look at that. My hands aren't shaking at all right now.

The End

Epilogue

Well, thank you for reading this book. Honestly, you guys didn't look like what I'd call *"readers."* I wrote this bullshit inside my locked bathroom with my kid banging on the door, telling me, "No one poops that long, Daddy!" *Bang! Bang! Tadang! Bang!* So if it sucked, jokes on you, your money is already being spent on candy and remote control helicopters at Walgreens by my little rat's nest-headed kid. But wait, before we part ways, I'd like to say a few things in defense of the foulmouthed in general, not just me. We are a dying race of people. Hear us out:

Why *do* some people seem to have such a problem with the things that I say these days? I haven't changed much. I'm talking about my own life. Can't I talk about my own life? Too messy? Am I causing a scene? Does my trauma make you feel weird? The door is right there. Why the fierce opposition from an ever-growing amount of people? From their critiques, it's like they're hearing something that I'm not even saying. I'm trying to *help* you motherfucker. Are you even listening to the words I'm saying? Or was there a flag word in there that the internet told you to be triggered by this week? It's like people are too stupid to analyze context anymore.

Why *are* people so easily triggered now? Could it be that our fucked up capitalist culture is creating shell-shocked people that jump at the slightest commotion now? That's it. I'm pretty sure that's it. I love these broken people because they were the ones who dared to care. When the rest turned it all off and started backstabbing for the slightest of favors from corporate management, the good ones dared to care. But, unfortunately, it didn't pay off. The repeated abuse has crushed them, and now they jump at a bottle clanking in the trash can. *I'm* on your side, little buddy.

Whatever happened to sticks and stones will break my bones, but words will never hurt me? So instead of a snappy comeback, people try to dox you and get you fired now? What is this pussy ass shit? Where I'm from, we teased a little bit out of love. They got us halfway to robots between that and a gentle hand on the shoulder being eliminated from our society. This is bullshit.

Remember quoting movies at work for laughs? Better not quote a film from a decade where people laughed at fucked up shit—which is all of them except this one.

And it's all because people are being trained by our modern culture to listen to jokes wrong. The TV, your phone, and even our schools are taking all the humor out of everything. They're making the mischievous nature of stand-up comedy seem like a felony. Who knew it was actually jokes causing all societies problems all this time? (That last sentence was sarcasm, another dead art)

Seriously society, where did the fun go? Remember the 90s? That shit was a blast! Remember Too Short? Now, look at us.

Some things about being politically correct are great. Racial stereotypes are tired, and you don't hear them being used as much these days. It's not so much that some of them are so offensive but just as bad; they're **worn out**. Tired shit like, "Asians can't drive." Have you ever seen a million scooters take off at a green light in Bangkok, motherfucker? It's like watching blood cells travel through an artery. Chaotic, but somehow seamless. What's another one, "Black people are loud in movie theaters." Okay, okay, but that's only because they heard us talking shit.

White people? We white people don't really smell like wet dogs. The shit is tired. Our race is one of the least revealing things about us. I'm a white male. With that as your only clue, you would likely guess almost nothing accurately about me. My shoes reveal more about me than that detail. What town someone is from, their job, or even if they have a sibling is usually more informative. A Chinese dude from Ohio and a Chinese dude from Hong Kong have zero in common. There may be a time for someone's race to be known in a story, but that's usually not what's happening when I hear people start dropping the stereotypes. Also, are you presenting cultural differences as a racial characteristic? That's a common mistake I see at the open-mics.

I'll take a hilarious stereotype that's not true over a dry fact about your childhood any day. I'm the dirty comedian, though. I can't really help you with the Twitter mobs. Should we prohibit these types of jokes?

No. Let the guy wonder why only six people showed up to his show.

Also, sorority girls wearing an Indian war bonnet *is* inappropriate. Who gives a shit? Do you know what else is inappropriate? Pretty much every joke you've ever heard. Don't we have bigger fish to fry in our society? While you're busy with that, the cops are still shooting people with zero accountability. The planet is literally dying, and Art History Major Kim is making a full-time job out of telling white people they can't have dreadlocks. Get your fuckin' priorities straight. Cultural appropriation is a negligible issue considering what we're up against. I'd end by saying "for realz tho," but... you know.

Also, noting a cultural difference is not only not racist, but it's showing an interest in people that aren't like you. It's the fucking opposite of racist, you syphilitic tiddlywink! It's actually what we need more of, not less. All this disallowing of certain talk is liberal elitist garbage. If the right-wingers want to imprison your body, these pieces of shit want to imprison your mouth. Forbidding words just imbues them with the power of taboo anyway.

It's all about keeping the poor from finding their strength, and I'm not hearing it. Don't accept chains on your body OR your mouth. You don't like what I have to say? Rebut me. People are trying to make other people jobless and homeless by ratting them out to the Gestapo out here? Fuck you. I'm starting to see which one of you folks would have rated out Anne Frank's family.

How will I survive? In a time when simple words are hand grenades that only kill the pin puller? My brain is already like a motorcycle with no neutral. At life's intersections, I have to put my feet down and hold it still while the wheels spin and smoke until the light turns green again. Full throttle synapses. I must have made my brain this way because I like it, but boy, does my mouth get me in trouble these days.

Do I care? Sure, but not so much because of any personal consequences I might suffer as a comedian. I'm used to a few people in every crowd being butthurt by my honest but crude style of expression. It's lost me some fans, but it's gotten me more. It's even gotten me fired but from shitty jobs. I mostly care because it's just bad for society to be upset with anything that isn't a 99 percent match, as Netflix might say about the serial killer documentary Aunty Nelly is obsessed with. This requirement for things we can accept leaves us divided into 99 camps, just like the ruling class wants.

When I was a kid, we had two types of heavy metal: good metal and shitty metal. Now look, we have Death Metal, Black Metal, Doom Metal, Folk Metal, Glam Metal, Gothic Metal, Grindcore, Industrial, Power Metal, Speed Metal, Nu-Metal, Thrash Metal, and on and on. Nowadays, if you like Power Metal, you have to hate all the other metals and make anybody who likes Death Metal feel bad because only the little specific things **you** like have merit, and everybody else needs to be shamed for their choices. Fuck that shit. When did everybody get so closed-minded? And have you ever thought that maybe all these hyper-categorizations are what makes us so easy to surgically target by social media? Just be a fuckin' person that likes random stuff.

There are some benefits to being a dirty comedian, none of them financial. One is being open-minded. I have seen and enjoyed a lot of different crazy shit in my life. I can listen to most of those types of metal without having to make someone feel bad in a chat room. Live and let live.

So, back to Flag words and everyone being perpetually offended now. Let's say my social media post about how 'Obama liked drones too much, did his dad never get him a remote control plane, or what?' any number of things I've said, what if I get fired for that? I speak out for the first amendment for you and *your* job. I don't really give a *fuck* about mine. Fire me. When I get fired from a job, I usually end up bumming around SE Asia for six months before coming back refreshed, to tolerate a different but just as shitty job; until it's *Bangkok time* again. Do your worst. After Covid is over, I'm going to want to use my passport. Maybe I should say something inflammatory now to make sure I know which days to pack.

Look, PC Culture is like cocaine. It should be enjoyed in moderation. The right amount can be healthy, But some of these people are the same people as the fuckin' grammar nazis. You don't talk how their college professor talked. It's elite, classist bullshit. We grew up less than upper-middle class, so our ideas aren't valid, and we should probably just let THEM drive the planet, is what... the real vibe that is being driven home here. They claim to be the victims, but usually, THEY are the ones being aggressive. Also, I notice most of them are Caucasian and aren't regularly seen commingling in real life with the marginalized people they so fiercely claim to represent. But watch when they clock in as a *social justice warrior* on the internet. Savior complex, anyone? Add colonial bullshit to elitist bullshit. I got tear-gassed twice last year, and I didn't see Women's Studies Savannah or Berkeley Bigelow anywhere.

It was a bunch of poor kids, the ones who always do the "actual" fighting, whether it's Vietnam or Oakland. Take a thousand seats, Becky; your great-grandpa already stole all the land beneath them.

As any stand-up comic worth his salt, I'm 50/50 on *woke culture*. Look, you guys, I'm glad people are starting to see through the patriarchy and the capitalism, but I reserve the right to talk about crack pussy that I've scored. Do you not tell stories where you use non-period blood as lube? Then don't come to my shows. Easy fix.

What are some pluses and minuses to the rise of PC culture? Plus: Guys like Woody Allen don't get a free pass to just marry their daughter, and no one says anything. Guys like Epstein and Weinstein die in jail—*allegedly*. I don't know about legal procedures against Woody's thing. Still, I think it's a good thing if people don't give this guy millions and millions of dollars to make movies about his exploitative, sexually fucked up brain. So that's good. We're holding people accountable regardless of their social status now; that's as big of a plus as you can get. History hardly ever does that. So let's push to keep **that** aspect of *woke culture*.

Minus: We risk living in a humorless world because the nature of most jokes—at least the side-splitting ones—is that there is a victim, and we can't laugh if there's ever a victim in something now, we have to go "Awwwwww," instead. The *wokesters* have no trouble with their swelling membership right now, so as a dirty comedian, I'm going to play the other side, so everything is fair and balanced, even if I have to be one of the few voices defending smut these days. Wasn't that the thing about the Bloods and the Crips? There were way more Crips, so you had to have a bigger heart to be a blood? Well, I guess I'm the blood gangster of free expression and pussy jokes. **What's up Cuzzins! Bang! Bang! I'm doing my dick and pussy thang!**

I agree that you have to ratchet up the quality of the overall joke as you ratchet up the filth. Comedians relying on the shock of the premise for laughs because their mind isn't poetic enough to write good punchlines? They get tedious by the fifth minute.

People are trying not to laugh at your filth because we were all brainwashed into thinking that Jesus's ghost hangs out in the rafters of comedy clubs, writing down names like Santa. Your dirt has to be *so* funny that they just *have* to laugh.

And you know? I've *tried* to keep my dirty thoughts in my mouth—thank Boognish I didn't let society do that to me—and I know I need to learn how to *slow down* my thoughts so that I have fewer *of* them.

There are so many individual thoughts elbowing their way through my brain at any given time—some of them even good—that they squirt out of my mouth, like a reverse money shot. The intensity feels like I'm trying to shoot a laser out of my forehead; the thoughts have to be let out somewhere. They just won't shut up. I was one of the kids in school they labeled 'hyperactive,' and they threw us into the *fuckup trailer* in the back of the school, and they forgot us.

Unfortunately—for the easily disturbed—it's just my brain biology for my mouth to operate on spontaneity. I'm an impulsive wanderer of my mind; I don't just slowly drift off into a daydream. I'm quickly taken to it. My subconscious brain will walk up and look through my eyeballs, and almost every time, it will say, "Ok, this is bullshit, let's go!" Next thing you know, I'm sitting on a magic carpet floating in my brain, wondering if platypuses have gangbangs. When people try to talk to me, I'm like the person wearing headphones, "Uhm, wait a minute, were you trying to talk to me? Why? Did you want to discuss 'bill play' in Australian marsupial mating habits?" Bosses aren't a fan of these types of conversations when you're clocked in, weirdly.

Here's the thing, I don't want to change. This is how my creative mind flourishes. My mouth just says what it says, and sometimes **I'm** even surprised by what comes out of it. Some of it is stupid, but a lot of it is pretty great. I've never allowed that spontaneity to be stifled—the uninterrupted flow of creative thinking since I read Lord of the Rings as a child. So, do I try to adapt techniques for things like working and socializing? Since being in what is basically a permanent daydream seems to hinder that? Do I even bother developing a system where I won't be getting in trouble all the time at jobs that poison my soul anyway? Or does the world just have to figure out that this is how I am? Should I put in decoy headphones?—to get a little peace? Boss is going to hate that—fuck bosses though, am I right?

I feel like the world just doesn't value people like me anymore. We struggle in the workplace. Some of us figure out how to turn our abstract differences into a sort of superpower at work. Those of us who don't? We have trouble keeping a job. Then comes the anxiety, then the depression, and PTSD.

"That should give you some good material," people say to the performer. They think suffering is awesome for us. Fuck off with that shit. My best works have been created with the rent paid and hot coffee steaming near my egg-filled stomach. Assholes. It's so they don't have to give a fuck. *HoMeLesS tEEnaGers bEgging in tHe StreETs hAve a LeXUs pArked neArBy*, they tell themselves.

Bosses don't like a guy who is always telling the truth, either. They want that shit in all *corporatese*, which absolves them of all responsibility if harm is done but praises *only* them if it all goes well. Fuck that. I tried to talk in *corporatese* for a job, and the words just got stuck in my mouth, which was a bummer because they tasted like warm dogshit.

I've found that people *want* the truth. This bullshit being force-fed to us from mainstream culture and our jobs isn't what the customers and the workers are trying to order. So many play along because they're afraid to be ostracized, then possibly made homeless by this tag-teaming of our souls by corporate and PC culture.

I would have learned *corporatese*, if I could—when I was weaker. Sure I would've, but I just couldn't learn to control my compulsion for poetic chaos and talking too much about whatever pops into my head. These abilities look pretty terrible on your Linkedin profile. Just the words: **Linked. In.** Gross. But in a capitalistic society, the paycheck decides your destiny. If you aren't linked **in,** you're linked **out**. In our constant and desperate pursuit of money to pay off all the premiums, we eventually forget how to be a human. I think I would rather be homeless than suffer that, and it looks like I may just get that chance. For my dirty mouth that I can't control—tell every competent, dirty-mouthed person you know about this book!

It would be better to allow all words than for people to put all their feelings through a filter before expressing themselves. In our society, we've devolved to a point where the words people say no longer resemble the original thought. It must be wrung out of anything potentially offensive, and it almost has to be changed, diluted, or told in a way as to be deniable later; an alternative to "I'm kidding if you are" *wink wink*. You find yourself keeping it vague so it can't be tied down to a specific thing. The result is no one is ever saying anything of substance because *that* might remotely offend someone or mark the speaker as a shit-stirrer. We now have a nation full of Tony Soprano-type restaurant managers who cryptically insinuate things to the hostess. Or perhaps a roommate who doesn't know how to put someone in check for eating all their food, so they just drop a bunch of *ignore it if you want*, chickenshit hints. We suddenly all speak in passive-aggressive or corporate-repressive. No wonder so many are now manic-depressive.

Only one solution, folks! Say it loud, and say what you mean—

Jesus fuckin' Christ, people. Drop the corporate-speak and let yourself be a freak. You're going to get cancer in your ass from keeping it all tight like that.

In many ways, *wokeness* is the correction of thousands of years of living under the patriarchy. In that way, it's a good thing because its heart is in the right place. However, I'd prefer to pick and choose what I like from all the PC mandates like I did with Buddhism in Thailand. Unfortunately, you have to be as politically correct as the most sensitive person at your workplace now. Bosses are scared of getting sucked into lawsuits. So if someone wants to bring their emotional support dog to work and have everybody refer to it as "Princess Most High," well then, you better fuckin' do it, or you're going to find yourself in the HR office, being *asked* if you're high. And don't say the 'Most High,' part sarcastically. Princess will know.

On the other side of the coin from corporate culture following us home and even into our beds, making sure we always restrain ourselves, is the rise of the PC movement. A lot of these stricter ways of policing behavior are a result of people coming awake to just how deep the rapiness of the patriarchy is installed in American culture, from "Boys will be boys" to judges in rape trials being rapists themselves. People are sick of it. So, in this way, the new behavior policing is good, but it can get taken too far. Rape culture and letting the privileged get away with almost anything has gone on for too long. It must be eradicated. Yes, the Dirty Comedian is pro-feminism and a friend of the gays. No refunds if you came here looking for me to hate and shit on everything. I did do plenty of that in this book, but it's more nuanced than that. So, if you're a misogynist or some shit, fuck off.

So, what does punishing rapists have to do with my little dick and pussy jokes? Why are people trying to lump me in with that shit just because I'm sexually explicit? The participants in my sexual scenarios are willing. Are we to swear off sex entirely as a country? Corporate America would love that. Sometimes I wonder if they are behind the worst parts of the PC movement, detracting from its good parts. They both agree on eliminating sexual discussions that go beyond innuendo—what the fuck is innuendo? So you admit you need the filth, but you're just a pussy about it? Comedians who bow to this strategy lose my respect—we'd definitely have more time to work with eliminated sexualities.

That's why they're really pushing the *no-flag word* workplace to lessen distractions; to eliminate basic human needs because it interferes with maximizing their profits. They want us to hold in our emotions like a bellyful of piss until our scheduled 30-minute lunch break, where we have to choose between running for the food truck or the bathroom. Amazon factory workers are wearing fucking diapers, so the bosses won't see them taking time off the floor. Burn this shit down! They can piss in their diaper while they package up your body pillow, but they can't *say* piss? What has happened to our country?

It's not necessary to become intolerant puritans with no senses of humor to address and remove rape culture, folks. Eliminating the topic doesn't remove the problem, and maybe that's the point. Disallowing talk of certain things is to sweep it under the rug and most likely allow their continuance in real life. When **talk** of something gets you punished more than the **doing** of it, then the patriarchy is at work. If you can lose your job, get blacklisted in your industry, become homeless, then die, for merely saying something at work, when "actual" rape just gets you a wink from the judge and a dismissal of the case, or maybe probation? It's time to burn it down. It's time to burn all this down.

Yeah, I tell some jokes where I sexually degrade myself, but that's my choice of how I like to spend my Tuesdays. Who told you comedy shows were G-rated? I think some of you motherfuckers doth protest too much, too, with your recently cleared browser histories and your badges, robes, and managerial name tags, which attempt to insinuate you are an authority on everything from how I spend my personal time to morality. Your robes, badges, and name tags actually tell on you. I don't fuckin' buy it. I've never cleared my browser history once, and you are all free to scan it for every clip of "Bangkok Anal," "Midget Gangbangs," and "Bukaki Marathons," that I've *tortured the porpoise* to. I'm unstifled and sexually healthy! I'm the fuckin' *opposite* of rapey. A champion of free, unrestrained, unchained speech AND pussy.

Beware the uniformed or robed man who pretends to have answers or always tells people how they should be. When no one is looking, they are the most devious pieces of shit in the bunch. It's as if they get extra rocks off playing in a theatre of opposites. Trust the man with a dirty mouth! He is far more likely, to be honest and fair with you.

The patriarchy will try to convince you that the foulmouthed are guilty of what *they* actually are because that's one of their tactics: projection. In reality, because we are free, healthy explorers of sex, we are their opposition. They are very aware of this and will seek to smear the foulmouthed whenever they can. They're like republicans in that way. We foulmouthed generally don't bottle up our sexual instincts to come out as rape later as we see with all these priests, Hollywood producers, and politicians these days. Don't confuse *rapey* sex with *sketchy* sex, okay? One is despicable and should be punished by public castration, and the other is the greatest thing there ever was. Also, in certain situations, rape jokes *can* be funny. It's hard, but it's possible. It helps if you're a white male and *you're* the one that gets raped in the joke. People love that.

A mind stifled by self-censorship will eventually stop bothering to imagine anything good.

People with dirty mouths are nonconformists. This is their real crime. The ruling class doesn't like boat-rockers.

Sometimes I'll just see someone's sour face in the audience, silently complaining in advance. How do you **not** shout inflammatory shit at them? I don't know. Maybe you guys are just better than me.

Just because I yell doesn't mean I'm wrong.

The foulmouthed are your most imaginative neighbors and the most likely to help you move a couch up some stairs. An imaginative citizen will create inventive loopholes to get by in a capitalist society without it squeezing her dry. The ruling class really doesn't like that. You could teach the others little ways to sidestep the requirements of capitalism. This is the real reason they want to punish the foulmouthed; our creativity and our demands to remain free. You know what else those old, white, male dinosaurs from long lines of evil hate? Youthful fun. That's why you see less and less of it these days. They're making their play, the big psyop into debt slavery. Are you going to let it get you? To a point, you have to choose to get into their candy van. Getting hooked takes a little effort, folks. Put the capitalism crack pipe down, grandma. Your little wrinkly lips are blistering up.

How did we go from "Let's do it!" to "I'm just gettin' through it" between our 20s and 30s? I'll tell you. It's from trying to fit our soft fleshy human bodies into the cold, steel hole of capitalism. Fuck that shit, cousin!

Just don't do it. Let's go on a mass strike! Let's go cause a ruckus in some affluent neighborhoods instead of burning down our own.

My persona in comedy has always been to just be so far over the top people just can't fuckin' believe it. You can get away with it that way. Ninety percent over the top doesn't cut it. You gotta commit in full. Don't be *scrrrd* folks. That's how people were in the neighborhood I grew up in. I am partly a product of my environment. I just grew up thinking it was normal to light couches on fire in the street and bunny hop them on beach cruisers. That was a Wednesday.

The stand-up comedy stage is one of the only places left in America you can hear an intelligent conversation about sex. Bullet riddled bodies you can get everywhere, but sexual pursuits? **Immoral!** Look at those sexually degraded Frenchies over there, fucking anything that moves, losing wars, and holding their politicians accountable. "It's un-American to be hypersexual like them!" Which must be bad, right? Since we're supposed to be fuckin' number one? So anything that is *un-us* must be evil, right? Sex is something we should hide. We should whack it with the door locked and start feeling guilty already mid-spurt. Fuck all that.

There are some dirty things still allowed in our society for now. The fact that Ali Wong, South Park, and Family Guy can say whatever they want, and the same people who would morality shame a non-famous talent for similar statements, lap that other stuff up? Why is a white kid with saggy pants and cornrows ridiculed for cultural appropriation, but Gwen Stefani can wear actual people in the form of *Harajuku* girls? The general public has been brainwashed, that's why. They'll support the other stuff because it's sanctioned by pop culture. They are unsure unless they are told it's okay by their little fuckin' phone screens, which they worship. Billions of dollars are spent each year to **keep** them brainwashed. The hierarchy of capitalism is no accident, fame is manufactured, and it's charged for by the bag. Its corners are protected not by guns but by the mental manipulation of the masses. How about telling that shit to 'fuck off!' by supporting your local garage band? Or better yet, your local foulmouthed comedian?

P.S. I could give a shit about the Harajuku girl thing. I was simply using it as a comparison. Let's face it, Gwen could do some shuckin' and jivin', wearing an SS uniform and an oversized sombrero, and I'd still eat a mile of her shit just to get to her butthole. Don't worry. I'll eat it real mean to punish her.

Remember when De Niro took Cybil Shepard to the porn theatre on their first date? And she was all, "What the fuck?" Well, that's the story of me and show business.

So, *punching down*, that's a term being used to some good and some bad. Let's talk about that. Comedian Katt Williams is a big fan all of a sudden of comics getting canceled for punching down. I wonder why, Katt? Is it because you'd be the only motherfucker allowed to tell jokes anymore if this concept were taken to its extremes? I mean, as a 3-foot tall comedian, Black, bald, crackhead that got knocked out on a viral video by a 13-year-old kid, it would be pretty impossible for you ever to punch down. You might have tried harder punching up, though; that little kid fucked you up.

So let's look at this: I'm punching down? How so? I'm a fucking comedian, the lowest economic or social strata possible; I grew up in a teepee and was in a group home; I have skid marks in my boxers as we speak, and I once went a decade without seeing a dentist. I struggled with undiagnosed learning disabilities my whole life, making me virtually unemployable in almost all industries. I've been beaten by the police six or seven times. Also, I had a bald crackhead phase as well—just like you Katt! I'm a lot closer to Katt Williams than Mark Cuban, so why am I being held to Mark Cuban standards? That of the white colonizer and exploiter. It seems like you decided to go cherry-picking for what I represent as a person?

So, what criteria are you using to say I'm punching down in my joke about a fat, Black lesbian? Oh, that I'm a white male? All that other criteria that describes me far better than that isn't what we're using? Because it didn't suit your little censorship agenda? It's better if I'm just a "*white male*" right now? Even though that describes two percent of who I am in totality?—sounds hella racist to me. To judge someone in a bad light solely because of their race? Without accounting for any of their other qualities or actual actions? Hmmm. It sounds like I deserve a jaywalking ticket, and you're committing the felony here. Why can't I make a joke about a fat, Black lesbian? Fuck Oprah! Fuck Katt Williams, and fuck Pauly Shore. Again.

Let's even play your little game for a minute, Katt. You **can** tell a funny joke about people in wheelchairs, marooned harelips, or why do old, naked dudes with blown-out assholes and their balls dragging behind them seem to be the most comfortable people on the beach?

That's what you mean by punching down, right? You just gotta follow the rule of *dick and pussy* jokes: the more fucked up the premise is, the more the punchline has to ratchet up in funniness and absurdity. A lot of dipshits ruin it by forgetting that last part. Maybe they don't forget; they're just incapable.

"What about *cancel culture*, Dirty Comedian?"

Well, it depends. If it means to get someone fired for what a sensitive person in the office misperceived as harassment, or mindlessly joining a Twitter mob to destroy a small business based on iffy evidence, all because you needed that thrill of doling out cowardly, anonymous, punishment, from a position of fake moral superiority? Then no. But when *cancel culture* means to remove someone from pop culture for being an unscrupulous, rapey, elitist, "The rules don't apply to me," douchebag? Well, then go ahead and cancel the fuck out of **all** of them because mainstream media is poison, and they are pretty much all complicit. Anybody who gets canceled from that shit should be happy they're not being brought to prison. Life in solitary for creating Here Comes Honey Boo-Boo. Whoever greenlit The Apprentice should be publicly hung. Cancel all these motherfuckers! When are we going to reckon with the fact that most modern pop culture *should* be "canceled" just because it sucks? Do you think I give a fuck about being canceled? I want nothing to do with these showbiz pieces of shit. I cancel **you** motherfuckers!

I've ***been*** canceled. I might have fewer fans than Dane Cook, but do you think I want those pieces of shit at *my* shows? They've been canceling me for years. They claimed I'm a sexist and a racist, but I save women from violent men by beating the shit out of them. I kept half-priced rooms open in my house for minority and disabled comics for the whole decade I *did* comedy; rooms in a prime, middle-of-the-city spot, where I could have easily rented to the techies for double. So ask my accusers where their proof is. Of all the hours of shitty, fan-recorded comedy performances of me on Youtube where I'm shithoused drunk, you'd think there'd be one N-word that Nato Green claims I regularly used in my act. Ask him about when he made some bullshit claim like that, and I offered him ten grand in front of like a thousand people if he could pass a lie detector test while making those same claims. He backed out like a little bitch. Only a fucking liar would back out of an easy ten grand and a chance to humiliate his enemy. I can prove all of this, by the way.

When I eat the tear gas, they all seem to be off eating ass: Bay Area *bumper sticker liberal* comics. They attack me because I remind them of their fraudulence. If you need me, I'll be in the trenches fighting for their children's futures while they nitpick about microaggressions.

And finally, people think because I'm a little angry that I must be unhappy. On the contrary, my triumphant hatred of certain things in this world; my poetic condemnations, outright vanquishing them, has brought me so much serotonin and dopamine you wouldn't even fuckin' believe it. Sometimes I'll crank it to the memory of their faces, captured in freeze-frame in my *wack folder*, of the exact moment they realized I'd beaten them; every manager, roommate, or lover. Their sour, horrified face is right there waiting in my *spank bank*. And that is what I offer you: secrets of how to do the same. It's not a cult—I probably won't have sex with you, and I refuse to wear anything flowy. Just heed my stories. Use them as a blueprint for your own Haterade-supplied happiness.

Join the movement! Join the foulmouthed motherfuckers of the world! We refuse to muzzle ourselves, and if you try to put muzzles on us? Prepare to get fuckin' bit!

Ok, now it's really the end—no wait, one more little thing:

Handbook for Foulmouthed Motherfuckers

(Copy this page at a mom-and-pop print shop that won't report you for printing subversive material. Leave copies around, give them to trusted friends who cuss like a city bus driver whose teenager's period is late.)

Eat apples, exert yourself until your shirt is soaked five days a week, roast the fuck out of the backseat driver in your brain first thing after breakfast, so he knows who the boss fuckin' is going out into the day. Breathe deep as far as you can, as slow as you can, and as deep as you can. Take the tracking device / brain shitter into-er—your I-phone—and throw it into the trash. It has no place in the Foul Mouth Revolution. Less alcohol, more weed, mushrooms, and swimming in rivers and streams. If assholes are colonizing a specific area, go 20 feet away. Don't get so wrapped up in people that are sending out bad vibes; maybe they're just miserable. Turn away from them, take those 20 steps, a whole new scene. The world is in an ambulance. Are we going to apply a tourniquet? Let her rest? Or are we going to twiddle our thumbs and leave the morphine drawer closed?

Never say "fudge" when you mean "fuck." Power yields nothing unless it's forced; therefore, negotiations with those in control are always a lie, intended to stall you forever. Never have publicly known members or leaders. They'll just kill them. There's only this handbook; check to make sure the copy you have is the original. Demonstrate assured destruction of their precious economy, the only thing they care about and deliver anonymous ultimatums from the people. Did you ever notice how they never try to rehabilitate the head zombie in a movie? That's because once you reach a certain level of evil, the only solution is decapitation, which brings us to this point: devise a test to catch rich people who try to blend in after the revolution. Hand them a bag of Top Ramen and ask them what it is, ask them how much a six-pack of beer costs, say, "Damn, that was crazy when the Nasdaq tanked," and see if their lip quivers.

Destroy all rich people's shit, study guerrilla warfare, call out capitalist bootlicker bullshit wherever you find it. Learn how to breed bed bugs and termites, then get a job in fancy homes, hotels, golf courses, and the like, spread them like Pauly Shore spreads herpes in Cancun. Break into unused buildings and homes, rip out the motion sensors and security, then come back a few days later and live there. Teach the homeless how to rappel up to buildings' upper windows.

White people born before 1960 and their shoes cost more than $200? They've done all of this. Get them. Don't get caught, and never surrender. They only care about their precious economy—destroy it! Go where rich people hang out and light fireworks at them, harass them, chase them. Make them regret they tried to grind up the entire planet so they could snort it in a weekend at Vail, at the cost of even their own children's future. You can't negotiate with that. Realize this has always been a class war, and things like racism, baseball team fanaticism, or *over-wokism* is only meant to divide us.

There are 10,000 assholes doing all of this. Stop them however you can. Flush lit M 80s down the toilets of all government buildings, glue bricks into their driveways, light the M 80s (quarter sticks of dynamite available in Tijuana) in wealthy neighborhoods when they try to sleep, put sugar in their gas tanks. Remember that a gallon of splashed red paint can ruin their fancy establishments' entrances and remind them of the murdered Indians that used to live there. Smash Teslas to pieces and take the batteries so we can go off-grid. Drone them, track them on their phones, gum up the works on all their shit. Destroy fossil fuel industry infrastructure. Stop buying their shit, grow gardens, organize strikes, put raw shrimp in the curtain rods of their homes, superglue their locks, pop all their tires, infiltrate their luxury play areas by getting catering jobs and put acid in their soups. Fuck up their golf courses! Get them and their stuff! Slingshot broken spark plugs into all the rich people's upper windows! Especially the stained glass ones. Get the Catholic churches! Only fuck up shit rich people own. Leave the little people alone. Get them! The rich fuckers and their bootlickers! Good luck! I'll see you out there.

–The Dirty You-Know-Who

The memoir you are holding is the third in a trilogy by JC Scales. The first two stellar tomes of preposterous havoc are *The Goat Lady's Son and the Child Gladiators of Isla Vista*, and *Coconut Fisticuffs*. You don't have to read them in order, but you should definitely read them. What are his qualifications to demand you buy two more books than you already have, you ask? Well, first of all, he's writing this author page blurb in the third person, which, they say is a sign of insanity. If that's not an indicator of rapid, page-turning pandemonium, then I don't know what is. Also, I—I mean he!—has headlined over 200 comedy shows; he was the first resident comedian in the long-running mega-show Tourettes Without Regrets; he was the movie reviewer for Live 105; he grew up in a teepee; he hates Pauly Shore; he was the sole comedy booker for the world-famous Purple Onion comedy club; he is a three-time Dirty Haiku Champion of Oakland, and he fucks like a methed-up honey badger.

JC Scales lives happily in San Francisco with his beautiful, tolerant, pretty wife, and his handsome, equally hilarious son. Buckle up kids, this is going to be even wilder than you already think.

Made in the USA
Monee, IL
16 January 2023

25369335R00233